H. Krzystak

S0-BTC-098

301.361
W69u

132869

DATE DUE			

WITHDRAWN

URBAN SOCIOLOGY

Robert A. Wilson

David A. Schulz

College of Urban Affairs and Public Policy
University of Delaware

CARL A. RUDISILL LIBRARY
LENOIR RHYNE COLLEGE

Prentice-Hall, Inc., *Englewood Cliffs, New Jersey 07632*

Library of Congress Cataloging in Publication Data

WILSON, ROBERT A (date)
   Urban sociology.

   Includes bibliographical references and index.
   1. Sociology, Urban. 2. City and town life—
United States. I. Schulz, David A., (date)
joint author. II. Title.
HT111.W54   301.36′1   77-20936
ISBN 0-13-939520-2

**Prentice-Hall Series in Sociology,
Neil J. Smelser, Editor**

301.361
W69u
132869
July 1985

© 1978 by Prentice-Hall, Inc., Englewood Cliffs, N.J. 07632
All rights reserved. No part of this book
may be reproduced in any form or
by any means without permission in writing
from the publisher.

Printed in the United States of America

10 9 8 7 6 5 4 3 2 1

PRENTICE-HALL INTERNATIONAL, INC., *London*
PRENTICE-HALL OF AUSTRALIA PTY. LIMITED, *Sydney*
PRENTICE-HALL OF CANADA, LTD., *Toronto*
PRENTICE-HALL OF INDIA PRIVATE LIMITED, *New Delhi*
PRENTICE-HALL OF JAPAN, INC., *Tokyo*
PRENTICE-HALL OF SOUTHEAST ASIA PTE. LTD., *Singapore*
WHITEHALL BOOKS LIMITED, *Wellington, New Zealand*

To Lynn, Helena, Andrew,
Alison, and Lisa

Contents

v

11
Urban Crime: Issues of Social Deviance and Social Control　234

12
Minority Groups　261

4
URBAN POLICY AND PLANNING *291*

13
Social Science and Public Policy,   293

14
Urban Political Process and Social Planning 313

15
World Urbanization 334

Preface

Teachers of urban sociology have long recognized the need for a book which integrates a sociological frame of reference with the analysis of the problems of cities. From our experiences, both in teaching and consulting in urban communities, we have attempted to write a book which allows the reader to employ this orientation as he ponders the issues which arise in a rapidly urbanizing world.

Besides covering the traditional elements of urban sociology, we have included chapters on the neighborhood, crime, housing, community, and world urbanization. These are intended to examine the issues from the viewpoint of the sociologist, as well as to draw from other disciplines and perspectives whenever necessary. In a sense, this approach signifies our feeling that sociology has come of age—to the point where the sociologist can play a more direct role in making public policy.

This book reflects our conviction that the practice of urban sociology should be an interesting, even vibrant undertaking. Although we cannot find much to say about cities that is funny, we find a great deal that is ironical. In lieu of a direct attempt to entertain, we have sprinkled the book lightly with *New Yorker* cartoons, signifying that we are willing to laugh (at the right time, of course) in spite of the ominous nature of urban problems. In short, the book is written from the perspective of the teacher who wants to cover the field, but still relate it to today's world, and who wants to be interesting and urbane, yet pragmatic, and above all to stimulate the student to learn more on his own. A large order to fill, but these are our goals. We thank Ed Stanford, of Prentice-Hall, for nudging us in that direction.

R. A. W.
R. A. S.

part 1

Elements of Urban Sociology

part I

chapter 1

The Study
of Urban Sociology

The chief function of the city is to convert power into form, energy into culture, dead matter into the living symbols of art, biological reproduction into social creativity. The positive functions of the city cannot be performed without creating new instrumental arrangements, capable of coping with the vast energies modern man now commands: arrangements just as bold as those that originally transformed the overgrown village and its stronghold into the nucleated, highly organized city.

Lewis Mumford[1]

The city has become the natural habitat of Western man. It is an almost totally man-made environment. The hand of its creator is seen everywhere, from the graffiti-covered subway trains to the aluminum and glass-skinned skyscrapers. As a habitat man adapts to it, fills its ecological niches, responds to its pressures, is shaped by its demands. As a product of human restlessness, the city expresses modern man in all of his dimensions—manifesting here rational, planned improvement; there the carnage, chaos and violence of neglect; and everywhere the restlessness of human striving and change.

The American dream of the good life for all was born in our small towns and, some of us would say, has come to its fullest expression there—or so we would fancy in our homespun nostalgia, forgetting the revolutionary roles of Boston and Philadelphia. But in the last half of the twentieth century, the city has offered the greatest hope for most of us. For good or for ill, we are committed to its future development. We are urbanites all, insofar as the culture of the city pervades the farms and small towns of our nations. Through newspapers, radio and television the cosmopolitan life is decimated. The news of the nation is made predominantly in

[1]Lewis Mumford, *The City in History* (New York: Harcourt Brace and World, 1961), p. 571.

our cities. The problems we face are defined largely in the way urbanites would define them—poverty seems so much more visible in New York than in Appalachia if only because so many more people are looking for it there.

In our time the reality of city life may still seem harsh and unmanageable to many, suburban greenery more restful than urban shades of gray, but the American dream has become wedded to the future of our cities and the vitality of our nation fastened to their growth and development. Barring some unforeseen catastrophe, the nation can eat well off the efforts of the less than six percent of its population who will continue to till the soil and harvest the crops. What then is the promise of the city which so many of us have recently come to call home?

In the hundred years following the Civil War, the large cities of the United States experienced their greatest growth. At the same time, American sociology slowly began to emerge as an academic discipline. At first, sociologists focused on

"The Connecticut Turnpike's connected to the New York Thruway,
The Thruway's connected to the Garden State Parkway,
The Garden State's connected to the New Jersey Turnpike,
The Jersey Turnpike's connected to the Pennsylvania Turnpike . . . "

Drawing by Whitney Darrow, Jr.,; © 1966 The New Yorker Magazine, Inc.

the social problems of large cities. This early sociology, with its emphasis on "meliorism," the treatment of social pathologies, produced a heritage of applied urban sociology. Most of the studies conducted by the University of Chicago during the 1920's and 1930's stressed a direct interest in solving problems like crime, delinquency, prostitution, and mental illness.

As the field of urban sociology developed in the United States, the problem focus diminished and was replaced with a concern for developing general theories of urban structure and process. Later works like the Lynds' *Middletown* (1929) and Hollingshead's *Elmtown's Youth* (1949) attempted to analyze an entire community structure, rather than focusing on the solutions of problems.[2]

The end of World War II saw an increase in the number of academic sociologists and greater specialization. The study of social deviance and crime became a field in its own right, while urban sociology became increasingly concerned with the study of social class and ethnic subcommunities. Today, urban sociology is characterized by its emphasis on comparative urban structure. The concern with social problems emerges as a by-product, rather than a direct focus of either research or writing.

The Promise of the City: A Life of Abundance

Since World War II, the American economy has been characterized as one of abundance—not scarcity. Real personal income has steadily improved for most of us. The Gross National Product has become ever grosser. While inflation may yet totally undermine whatever gains the average American has been able to make, most Americans have been able to realize a higher standard of living for themselves and their families than at any other time in our history. By any material measure of economic prosperity. Americans are well off indeed. Our cities have come to symbolize this promise of abundance. Relative to the poorer rural hinterland, cities hold this promise throughout the world.

More and More of Everything.   The fantastic display of products in the typical supermarket presents a common component of this promise. In many ways it seems the shallowest, in others the most basic. Without the ability to overcome deprivations such as poverty and illiteracy, life must be conducted at a very minimal level indeed. The city promises more and more of everything: more jobs, more chances for getting married, finding a home, getting a good book to read or a place to stay for the night. Apparently every need can be met.

Real Choices, Greater Opportunity.   Some would argue that this apparent variety is not an accurate measure of abundance because it really reflects a diminishing of alternatives, not an increase in them. Under the influence of selling to mass markets, the taste of the individual is reduced to the taste of the average, some

---

[2]Robert S. Lynd and Helen M. Lynd, *Middletown* (New York: Harcourt Brace, and World, 1929); A. B. Hollingshend, *Elmtown's Youth* (New York: John Wiley and Sons, 1949).

would argue. For those with unique taste in food, clothing, books, movies, television and so forth, it is necessary to leave the supermarket and the national networks, develop one's own library and grow one's own herbs. Be as it may, in the city it is possible to find people who do just this—and have access to those who cater to the taste of the average man as well.

Whether or not you can take advantage of them, the city offers in its many and diverse locations a variety of life styles—from bohemian to bop, from genteel to vulgar, reflecting the colors and hues of the world's diverse peoples and persuasions. They are found in the cities of America often in greater number than in the cities of their native countries. Thus, 18.2 percent of the population of New York is foreign-born. This includes 214,014 Italians, 142,652 Germans, and 117,363 Russians. Another 811,843 Puerto Ricans, although not born in a foreign country, speak Spanish, not English, as their mother tongue.[3] At one time it was widely believed that all of these diverse peoples quickly gave up their essential differences and became Americans all. The idea of the "melting pot" is being resisted by more and more Americans as they strive to preserve their own unique heritage. When new experimental life-styles are added to the traditional differences, it seems likely that urban diversity will increase, not diminish.

A Mirror for Man.   And so the image of the city as the stage upon which the whole human drama can be enacted seems appropriate as a promise, if not as a reality. It is evident that our cities present us with the occasion for the realization not only of the American dream, but also for an enrichment of it in a wide variety of different styles of life. In the city it is possible to experience the clash of ideas, values, life-styles, competing products and slogans in such a way as to be able to make conscious, intentional, compassionate, personal choices about one's own life with some idea of the likely consequences for having done so. However one might wish to live, it is likely that in the city someone else has lived in a similar way. It is possible to go and see what this means, to feel something of the flavor and taste of a different way of life, to experience something of its heart. It is possible to do this, that is to say, if it is possible to remain open and to affirm with Terrance, "I am human and nothing human offends me."

The promise of a creative personal life-style is enriched by a cultural civility that permits such pluralism, but it is difficult indeed to be open. It is difficult indeed to work collectively for a way of life that will allow others who have benefited from such collective efforts to live their lives in a manner that seems to undermine the very principles upon which we have based our own commitments. It is difficult for a nation that has been at war for the better part of its recent history to offer even conditional amnesty to those who would not go to war. It is no less difficult to affirm the rights of citizenship for others who do not seem to value what we hold dear. It is difficult but possible.

[3]United States Bureau of the Census, *Census of the Population, 1970, Volume 1, Characteristics of the Population, Part 34: New York—Section 1,* (Washington, D.C.: [United States Government Printing Office], 1973), Table 81. These figures are for the City of New York, whose population in 1970 was 7,894,798. The New York Consolidated Area has a population of 16,178,750.

Problems of Perspective in an Abundant World

If there are difficulties in permitting the personal vision of the good life to survive, so also there are difficulties in defining the common goals and collective values. What, for example, is the "good" *city* like? Some of us would say that the good city is beautiful, while many of us hold that our cities are, in reality, ugly. Ugliness, of course, is a matter of culturally conditioned perception. Long after the era of the *Saturday Evening Post* and the mass migration from American farms, the anti-urban bias lingers. From this perspective, urban ugliness might best be reflected in a series of adjectives that mean essentially non-rural: crowded, dirty, treeless, non-green, frantic, chaotic, etc.

Many Americans think a great city needs something to take their minds off its urbanity. San Francisco has its hills, its bay, cable cars and Golden Gate Bridge; Athens, its Acropolis; Rome, its Colliseum; Copenhagen, its Tivoli; Paris, its Eiffel Tower and Louvre; New Orleans, its French Quarter. Contrast this with Chicago and its stockyards, Baltimore and its congested slums, and Los Angeles with its maddening freeways, and we have the city without its window dressing, the city in its basic functional form—minus the window dressing for tourists. Thus we come to the point of how some people differentiate a "good" city from a "bad" one. The good ones, like San Francisco, may be perceived as good from several perspectives, but, mainly from that of the tourist. If a city's physical scale, vistas, eating and entertainment are enjoyable, then the city may be seen as a good one from a tourist perspective. Living there permanently, however, may be something else. From the resident's perspective, the good city is more likely to be seen in terms of the services and atmosphere it provides—its parks and recreation, municipal transportation and schools, or even its tax structure. What living is like from day to day depends much more upon how these services are administered than upon how the city looks to tourists, and yet a good portion of the money spent to renew our cities seems to be spent in order to increase their tourist attractiveness.

The tendency shared by many Americans to see the city in negative terms is fostered to a considerable extent by professional visionaries. Sociologists like Simmel, Weber and Wirth, all of whom came from German villages, saw urbanization as a necessary but unfortunate process. Anthropologists such as Robert Redfield extolled the virtues of the little community and remained largely skeptical of the values of the large metropolis.[4] At least since Louis Wirth, the city's heterogeneity, large size, high density, secular cosmopolitan atmosphere has tended to be seen as contributing to man's alienation rather than affording an opportunity for the richer life.[5] Simmel's *Metropolis and Mental Health* portrayed the city as leveling all human values to the common denominator of a moneyed economy.[6] The noise,

---

[4]Robert Redfield, *The Folk Culture of Yucatan* (Chicago: University of Chicago Press, 1941).
[5]Louis Wirth, "Urbanism as a Way of Life," *American Journal of Sociology,* (1938):1–24.
[6]Georg Simmel, "The Metropolis and Mental Health," in Paul K. Hold and Albert J. Riess, Jr., eds., *Cities and Society: The Revised Reader in Urban Sociology* (New York: The Free Press, 1957), pp. 635–46.

confusion, multi–faceted stimulation of metropolitan life is primarily a flayer of nerves. In Simmel's view, the human organism must recoil before the onslaught of such a bombardment or lose control. E. Franklin Frazier's *The Negro in the United States* described the urban environment as a "city of destruction" because of the damage inflicted upon the family.[7] Frazier blamed the city for breaking up the large extended family and leaving the often "broken" mother and child dyad open to the uncertainties of the urban economy and the enticements of street life.

There are, however, some visions of what the city should be like that provide hope while describing the reality of city life as harsh and destructive. Foremost among these is found in Lewis Mumford's *The City in History*. Mumford stresses balance—work and leisure, city and country, a mixture of public life and privacy. This life-style glorifies the potential of the city as the only adequate stage upon which the full human drama can be enacted. It stresses the value of alternatives for as many persons as possible. That is to say, if one lives and works in an urbanized area, one needs a respite. For the rich this balance may take the form of maintaining a country home and a city home, taking lots of vacations, or interacting in many situations that are different from one another. Mumford's philosophy implies that the optimum is reached when most of the people have access to as many life–style options as possible. In a "freeenterprise" economy the rich have always had the most options, the middle–class somewhat fewer, and the lower–class the fewest. The fundamental issue of the quality urban life, when framed in this way, does not deal with urban design, but rather relates to how we can provide the most options for residents and users of the urban environment. Such a philosophy does have implications for design, as we shall later see. Mumford, of course, has been a leading advocate of the Garden City, which features parks on green belts that serve to blend the city more fully into its natural environment.

Assuming that a fundamental element of urban policy of the good city is to provide as many life–style options to as many people as possible, it does not automatically follow that all who have the opportunity will take advantage. Banfield's *The Unheavenly City Revisited* suggests that most of the serious problems of the city concern the 10–20 percent of the urban population that is lower–class.[9] Lower–class persons, according to Banfield, are "present oriented" and unable to defer gratification. The life of immediate gratification of whatever needs one can gratify has a certain attractiveness for some persons. Those social scientists, such as Banfield, who believe that the poor are entrapped in a culture of poverty argue that many, if not most, cannot choose alternatives voluntarily unless their impoverishment is eliminated first.[10] Others—Rodman, Valentine, and Rainwater—contend that the poor can work their way out of economic despair, but it may take time.[11]

[7]E. Franklin Frazier, *The Negro in the United States,* rev. ed. (New York: Macmillan, 1957).
[8]Lewis Mumford, *op. cit.*
[9]Edward Banfield, *The Unheavenly City Revisited* (Boston: Little Brown, 1974), p. 11.
[10]The classic position was given by Oscar Lewis in his *The Children of Sanchez* (New York: Random House, 1961), p. xxx.
[11]Hyman Rodman, *Lower-Class Families: The Culture of Poverty in Negro Trinidad* (New York: Oxford University Press, 1971), p. 196. Charles A. Valentine, *Culture and Poverty* (Chicago: University

Almost everyone agrees that the major problem of the poor is a lack of adequate income.

The perspective of the impoverished is one that must be taken into account in describing the good city. Planners and other professionals who shape the future of our cities often are unable to do this. This is indeed ironic, because in many ways it was the agony and struggle of the poor of our cities that brought the urban crises to our attention in the 1960's.

Urban Crises: Merely Unheavenly?

In the calm of the 1970's it is easy to forget the turmoil of the late 1960's. Then, the problems of our cities seemed endless and hopeless. Riots, vandalism, high crime rates, and the suddenly visible poverty of urban ghettos were subjects of national interest. Poor transportation, battles over neighborhood control of the schools, political scandals on the local level, and health hazards of air and water pollution made the news then and continue to do so. Our center cities still show the scars of the violence that broke out in the streets and flared up on the college campuses. Whatever the reasons for the tranquility of the 1970's, it is surely not because we have solved the problems of the 1960's.

Books like *The Unheavenly City Revisited* tend to take our minds off this fact, however, by suggesting that much of what we thought to be a problem is not really so. Banfield's intent appears to have been somewhat different. He wants to make the problems of the city appear to be manageable by distinguishing between problems which are important, but need not be dealt with immediately, and those which are serious and demand immediate attention. The latter problems are largely confined to the lower class.

Middle–class myopia confounds the analysis in seeking a heavenly city in terms of its own definition of heavenly. Thus the amount of air and water pollution that is found in our typical city is irritating and uncomfortable, but certainly should not be seen as a serious problem. They are a small price to pay for progress. And much of what middle–class persons might consider to be substandard housing can also be seen as affordable housing from the perspective of the poor. It may be that poverty that is defined as relative to a standard consumer package supposedly available to all average Americans is the wrong way to define poverty. It is surely less damaging to the bodies of poor Americans than the poverty of a Calcutta slum or a Latin American favella. Banfield's argument may be correct, but somehow to respond in this fashion seems to be giving way to pessimistic views about what is possible and settling for much less than most of us would deem as desirable.

Recent patterns of urbanization.   The problems of perspective are made even more intense by the recent growth trends of our metropolitan areas. Those tending to

---

of Chicago Press, 1968). Lee Rainwater, "The Problem of Lower-Class Culture and Poverty-War Strategy," in Daniel P. Moynihan, ed., *On Understanding Poverty: Perspectives from the Social Sciences* (New York: Basic Books, 1968).

Pittsburgh (Triangle Park). A city once known for over-crowding and air pollution has now cleaned up its air and created a park in a once-congested area. (*Photograph by George D. Hetrick.*)

share similar perspectives on our problems have tended to flock together—despite the myth of the melting pot. In particular, the central cities have become increasingly poor and black, the suburbs increasingly affluent and white.

Almost 69 percent of our entire population lives in what the census calls Standard Metropolitan Statistical Areas.[12] Seventy-five percent of black Americans live in these SMSA's and over 58 percent live in the central city of such an area. In contrast, while about 68 percent of the white population lives in the SMSA's, only about 28 percent live in the central cities.

The recent growth of American cities, particularly those of the North, has been characterized by a very slow rate of growth in the central cities, surrounded by a very rapid rate of growth in the suburbs. The central cities have become increasingly black as rural blacks continue to emigrate from rural areas and more affluent whites immigrate to the suburbs. Thus the cities are left with the problem of trying to meet the needs of an increasingly poor population while suffering a decline in tax base.

Although the central city's residential population is declining, it remains a major employer in most SMSA's. Municipal governments have tried to regain some of their lost tax revenues by increasing wage taxes. This source of income, coupled with recent federal funds, has undoubtedly helped, but some unintended consequences are beginning to appear. For example, in Wilmington, Delaware, New

[12]United States Bureau of the Census, *Statistical Abstracts of the United States: 1974*, 95th ed., (Washington, D.C.: United States Government Printing Office, 1974), p. 17.

Castle County suburbanites are petitioning the state government to permit them to vote in city elections on the premise that, since they pay the wage tax, they should have the right to vote. If such a precedent is established, the suburbs would immediately dominate the politics of the central city. If, on the other hand, the present course continues, it is evident that the central cities will not be able to provide the needed services without outside aid.

The urban-suburban split is not the same as the rich-poor division, however. The rich, whether they live in the suburbs or the central cities, own their property, control the job markets, manage the economy, in their own interests as best they can, and exercise political power in great disproportion to their number. Many Americans feel that it is only just that they do so because they have earned it. The poor, on the other hand, have accumulated a heritage of disadvantages that make it difficult, if not impossible, for them to realize the American dream. The inequities of the American class structure are nowhere better seen than in our cities, where it is often the case that the rich and the poor live close together. This is particularly true of southern cities, where they lived together because the wealthy needed domestic help and the poor needed jobs, but it is also true in the North. For example, in Boston aristocratic Beacon Hill has survived for generations in the midst of a deteriorating city. Cutting across any ecological division in urban life–styles is the impact of social status. Class culture affects the way people vote, discipline their children, worship, look for a job and trust in the future. The growth and development of the city and its governmental crises cannot be understood without an examination of the differences in life–style that stem from status and income differences.

The problem of governance.   Many observers feel that large cities such as New York are ungovernable. The New Yorker has become legendary for his capacity to endure the constant turmoil, threatened strikes, continuing destruction and rebuilding of his city, as well as the ever present uncertainties of his services.

And yet with or without governance, planning, political action or anyone's consent, our cities are changing. We can describe the changing population, witness the transformation in land use, observe the changing fads in architecture, and marvel at the ever changing contributions of technology to our life–styles. We can note with mixed emotions indeed the effects of the cybernetic revolution on our labor force and family life. We can stand idly by or intervene with urban renewal programs and Model Cities. We can foster a war on poverty, vow increased dedication to the procurement of civil rights for every citizen and speak with feeling about the ideals of justice and equality for all before the law. We can invent machines for living, rapid transportation, improved communication, and space flight. We can develop computer simulations of urban populations and their problems, so that we can play at alternative solutions to the plight of our cities. We can witness and participate in all of this change and still wonder at our ability to control it.

While some of us might still entertain the notion that someone is in charge of the government in Washington, few of us would argue that anyone is in charge of

Seen from the Observation Deck of Rockefeller Center, The Big Apple's skyline is punctuated by some of the most distinguished architecture in the world. At the center is the one and only Empire State Building. Off in the distance—in lower Manhattan—are the twin towers of the World Trade Center. (*N.Y. Convention & Visitors Bureau*)

the change that is taking place in our cities. Daley might have been the political boss of Chicago, but most of what happened in Chicago went on without his knowledge or intervention.

We sometimes act as though big business or big government were in charge when we call upon them to redress our grievances. We tend to think that a corporation is really running things when it changes a building code in its favor, or decides how a tax rate shall be fixed, or procures utility rates that are highly favorable to it. But upon closer inspection, it often seems that the unintended consequences of these acts bring greater cost than the intended benefits. Thus the corporation gets a good buy on the land or service, but the character of the city and the services that it is able to provide change. Supporting businesses move out, the readily available supply of labor dries up, the quality of potable water deteriorates. Thus big government fails when the housing that was intended for the poor is not built as a result of housing authority efforts. Typically, more buildings are torn down than are put up. The remaining space goes to expressways, small businesses, universities and other vested interests.

In the last analysis, the problem of governance in the city of abundance is a problem of managing conflicting and competing interests. Politics is the art of the possible. The possible arises out of the compromises and limited contributions of diverse elements involved in the political process. The more abundant the city, the richer the conflict of interests. Not all interests can be met at one time. Confidence in the system as a whole stems from the conviction that if one's own needs are not catered to at this moment, there will be a "next time." The poor are those persons for whom waiting till next time has become totally unrealistic. In many ways, incorporation of their interests into the legal and political process is the basis of the true reform of government that has not yet been achieved.

The problem of governance is reflected in yet another issue—the role of the expert. As a democratic people we are rightly suspicious of experts. We do not readily take to the idea of planned change. At the same time, we are reluctant to say no to technology. Historically speaking, we have granted almost unlimited right to the innovator in the areas of technology, physical resources and business. Our environmental crisis is a result of not forcing these innovators to adequately calculate the cost of their enterprises. Had they done so, and the information made public, they may not have been permitted to go ahead with their innovation. This is what happened to the SST. It was simply too costly a venture. At the same time, we are almost unwilling to talk about experiments in social innovation that seriously disturb the status quo. We have made more progress, perhaps, in the area of intimate relationships than in any other in this regard. It is evident that we must begin to more boldly experiment in changing social institutions if we are to harness the power that we have generated by our technology and stem its destructive side effects at the same time.

Ironically, reform government has given more credence to the expert and rational planning of the long range variety, but it is doubtful if it has, in and of itself, produced better government. Reform governments are staffed by professionals who understand the problems of the affluent, but tend to misperceive the problems of the poor. Reform government thus tends to institutionalize a rather standard set of middle–class values and expectations about the goals of good government. It rarely transforms the bureaucracy radically. Studies have indicated that the poor often benefit more from the political boss and the party system.[13] In this system, they at least have the greater opportunity to influence the politicians in those areas of most personal needs—favors and political plums. Neither style of government favors everyone equally.

We must accept the conflicting interests that are an inevitable part of the political process of a democracy and include the planner in such a way that his plans emerge from the process rather than impose narrow goals and visions upon it. We must also recognize the inherent limitations of intentional change in situations in which the unintended consequences of public policy are often more costly than the intended benefits. Sociologists, with the help of social indicators, computer simulation, survey research and a host of other techniques, can assist in the process of governance. However, they should never be allowed to become the exclusive governing group. Our founding fathers realize that no man is good enough to govern

[13]Robert K. Merton, *Social Theory and Social Structure,* rev. ed., (New York: Free Press, 1963), pp. 72–76.

another without his consent and were generally optimistic about the human capacity to adapt to changing situations and to change them for the best. Social science tends to be skeptical on both counts.

The Field of Urban Sociology

Urban sociology has enjoyed great status as a speciality within the sociological enterprise in the past. Max Weber, Georg Simmel, Ferdinand Tonnies (among others) contributed to its development on the continent. Their works belong to the classics of the discipline. In America, Louis Wirth and the Chicago School have been most influential in shaping the discipline's understanding of urban life.[14] Urban sociology began to decline in popularity when more and more sociologists tried to distinguish the speciality of urban sociology from other specialities. The interests of urban sociologists were diverse and seemed to range over the entire field of sociology. What made their studies urban?

"What is a city?" Ask anyone if they can recognize a city when they see one and it is unlikely that anyone would say no. But Sociologists have had great difficulty in defining the city for their purposes. No small part of the problem, Martindale suggests, derives from the fact that the cities have lost their integrity in the West.[15] From the Greek city-state, in which the city was the principle form of government and a relatively autonomous economic unit, to the present day, the city as a separate entity has suffered decline. The traits once associated with cities have become widely dispersed throughout the culture, and the city as a metropolitan area has become quite dependent upon state and federal forms of government. The rise of urban societies has spelled the demise of the city as a distinctive autonomous unit.

Urban sociologists have given a number of answers to the question of the city's nature as a unit of analysis. Gutman and Popenoe suggest three basic types: the city as a small community, the city as a population aggregate, and the city as an urbanized local community.[16] The central feature of Wirth's classic article is that urbanism as a way of life can be derived from an analysis of the impact of several key population characteristics: size, density, and heterogeneity.[17] The work of Park, Burgess and McKenzie attempted to relate ethnographic characteristics of urban life to the spatial distribution of urban population in the well known concentric zone model of urban development.[18] Others, such as Zimmerman and Sorokin, were

[14]Examples of other "Chicago" urbanologists are Harvey W. Zorbaugh, *The Gold Coast and the Slum* (Chicago: University of Chicago Press, 1929); Nels Andersen, *The Hobo* (Chicago: University of Chicago Press, 1923), and Louis Wirth, *The Ghetto* (Chicago: University of Chicago Press, 1928).

[15]Don Martindale, "Introduction" to Max Weber, *The City* (New York: The Free Press, 1958), p. 62.

[16]Robert Guttman and David Poponoe, eds., *Neighborhood, City and Metropolis: An Integrated Reader in Urban Sociology* (New York: Random House, 1970). p. 9.

[17]Louis Wirth, "Urbanism as a Way of Life," *op. cit.*

[18]Robert E. Park, Ernest W. Burgess and Robert D. McKenzie, *The City* (Chicago: University of Chicago Press, 1967).

more concerned with the characteristics of urban populations that distinguished them from peasant population.[19] Redfield and Sjoberg continued in this tradition though with notable modifications.[20] Gibbs and Hawley concentrated on describing the urban environment as an ecological niche with distinctive impact upon population characteristics, derived primarily through such variables as density and spatial interaction.[21] Finally the Shevky-Bell method of area analysis assumes that significant aspects of urban life can be explained in terms of the variation between census tracts of certain gross indicators such as racial composition, age, income, etc.[22]

A second major approach to the problem of definition attempts to describe the city as a particular kind of community. A leading exponent of this approach is Roland Warren.[23] Warren contends that a community is a group of people responsible for the integration of societal functions that have ''locality relevance''. In this context, the city is to be distinguished not so much because of its size, density, and heterogeneity, but because of the distinctive social structures necessary to integrate these functions for large numbers of people. Among the most salient of the structural features are: (1) the complex division of labor, (2) differentiated interests and association among urbanites, (3) increasingly systematic relationships to the larger society, (4) increasing bureaucratization and impersonalization, and (5) distinctive transfer of functions to profit enterprise and government from voluntary association and personal initiative.[24]

Gideon Sjoberg identifies eight schools of urban sociology defined in terms of the single factor they feel is most important for urban growth and development: (1) urbanization, (2) subsocial, (3) sustenance, (4) economic, (5) environmental, (6) technological, (7) value, and (8) power.[25] Redfield and Wirth are leading advocates of the urbanization school because their primary interest is differentiating urban from rural populations. In contrast to the small town, the city is a focus of fluidity and change. It is seen as disorganized in large part because the researchers valued the organizational principles more commonly found in small towns or peasant societies. Studies such as Gans and Rainwater's qualify this perspective by pointing out the basis of organization within subpopulations of metropolitan areas.[26]

For the subsocial school (Park, Burgess), the fundamental explanatory principle has been impersonal competition, reflected in the convergence within the

[19]Pitrim Sorokin and Carl Zimmerman, *Principles of Rural-Urban Sociology* (New York: Holt Rinehart and Winston, 1929).

[20]Robert Redfield, *Peasant Society and Culture* (Chicago: University of Chicago Press, 1956).

[21]J. P. Gibbs, ed., *Urban Research Methods* (Princeton, N.J.: Van Nostrand, 1961). Amos Hawley, *Human Ecology* (New York: Ronald Press, 1950).

[22]Eshref Shevky and Wendell Bell, *Social Area Analysis: Illustrative Applications and Computational Procedures* (Stanford: Stanford University Press, 1955).

[23]Roland Warren, *The Community in America* (Chicago: Rand McNally, 1963).

[24]Warren, *op. cit.*, p. 77.

[25]Gideon Sjoberg, ''Theory and Research in Urban Sociology'' in Guttman and Poponoe, eds., *op. cit.*, pp. 86–108.

[26]Herbert J. Gans, *The Levittowners* (New York: Pantheon, 1967). Lee Rainwater, *Behind Ghetto Walls* (Chicago: Aldine, 1970).

Chicago School of two lines of thought—social Darwinism and classical economics. Firey and others have shown the limitations of the view that urban spatial patterns can be explained in terms of this competition by noting the importance of different value configurations.[27]

In the ecological (or sustenance) school, represented by Duncan and Schnore, four basic elements are interrelated: environment, population, social organization, and technology.[28] Expanding upon the effect of technology, the industrial profile developed by Duncan classifies fifty of America's largest cities according to their technical capabilities. As representatives of the economic school, Shevky and Bell argue that "it is not the city which is an underlying 'prime mover' in the recent transformation of Western society, but the necessities of economic expansion itself."[29] This transformation is primarily a transformation in scale, which is indicated by (1) changes in the distribution of skills, (2) changes in the structure of productive activity and (3) changes in the composition of population.

Lewis Mumford is typical of what Sjoberg calls the environmental school because he argues that the problems of the city result primarily from the fact that urban life has become increasingly divorced from its human scale and its natural environment.[30] To correct this, Mumford advocates the construction of belts and garden cities in which high-rise buildings are kept to a minimum and structures blend organically with their landscape.

The technological school represented by Ogburn stresses the impact of technology, especially the development of transportation and communication networks upon the developing cities.[31] Hawley once contended that the spatial distribution of population throughout a metropolitan area was "a direct response to the increased ease of movement."

Although it is exceedingly difficult to relate values to precise aspects of urban development, there is no doubt that cities are shaped to some degree by images of what men feel is desirable in them. Washington, D.C. reflects the values of American federalism in its radial design emanating from the capital, for example. As city planners are given more power, their ideology becomes increasingly important as a variable of urban change.

Finally, the power school contends that what has been called planning in the past reflects power more than value orientation, because it is the values of a few that are imposed upon the many. This is clearly a function of their relative power.[32]

---

[27]Walter Firey, *Land Use in Central Boston* (Cambridge: Harvard University Press, 1947).

[28]Otis Dudley Duncan and Leo F. Schnore, "Cultural, Behavioral and Ecological Perspectives in the Study of Social Organization," *American Journal of Sociology,* 65 (1959), 132–146.

[29]Shevky and Bell, *op. cit.,* p. 94.

[30]Lewis Mumford, *op. cit.*

[31]William F. Ogburn, "Invention of Local Transportation and the Patterns of Cities," in Holt and Reiss, *op. cit.,* pp. 274–282; Fred Cottrell, *Energy and Society* (New York: McGraw Hill, 1955).

[32]See, for example, Martin Meyerson and Edward C. Banfield, *Politics, Planning and the Public Interest* (New York: Free Press, 1955); Edward Banfield, *Political Influence* (New York: Free Press, 1961).

St. Louis, one of America's largest cities, originally developed as a river port.
(*St. Louis Convention and Visitor's Bureau.*)

From this overview, it becomes apparent that many of these variables interrelate in the works of the various urbanologists and in the processes of urbanization. The categories are only analytically separable and even then are not very distinct. Thus, technology is a major means of achieving power, and power is the ability to impose one's own conception of what is valuable or desirable on someone else. It is logically as well as empirically difficult to discern which one is the prime mover.

The issue, then, becomes that of measuring the impact of many variables under varying conditions in order to determine their scientific (or generalizable) validity. At the same time, we must remember that their historical or policy relevance may be quite different. The implications of policy research and its relationship to urban sociology will be discussed in a later chapter.

A Brief Overview of This Text

This book seeks to do two things: (1) provide a review of the body of knowledge about urban society, particularly as that knowledge is drawn from the discipline of sociology, and (2) assess the usefulness of urban sociology in the analysis of urban life and urban problems. This second point is most important. We shall dissect the theory and method of urban research and concentrate on those aspects that are most useful in understanding and coping with the problems of the city. Urban studies may not be able to solve our urban problems. They should, however, help us cope more rationally with them.

Part 1 (The City in History) describes the origin and development of ancient cities. This will provide a broad overview of how urban settlements came into being and serve as a basis for understanding the development of contemporary urban trends. The chapter on urban ecology reveals the relationship between the geographic city and its social counterpart, uncovering the rich heritage which underlies the most recent theories. Chapters on social stratification and social participation provide an analysis of the social structure and process of urban areas and complete our treatment of the elements of urban sociology.

Part 2 offers an examination of the typical sociological units used in analyzing urban areas. We begin at the household level with a chapter on the urban family. Next is a portrayal of the urban neighborhood, followed by a chapter on the community. Part 2 ends with a discussion of the suburbs, which now contain the majority of America's urban population.

Part 3 presents three chapters on urban social issues. A chapter on crime offers a diagnosis of the problem as it relates to cities. This is followed by chapters on housing, minority groups and segregation.

Part 4 presents a broad discussion of urban policy issues. Beginning with a chapter on social science and urban policy, we ponder the future role of the urban sociologist. Some of these issues are discussed further in the offering on world urbanization and the chapter on social planning and political process.

chapter 2

The City in History:
The Preindustrial City

If a modern city were somehow to be buried intact and unearthed thousands of years later by anthropologists, what would they know about life as it existed thousands of years before? Undoubtedly, by examining the physical aspects of our culture—our streets, buildings, tools, books, recordings, and video tapes—our successors could tell a great deal about us. Because of the development of communications over the past several centuries, especially the computer, which is capable of storing and retrieving massive amounts of information, future scholars would probably know more about our culture than we know about the great cities of the ancient world.

Much of what we do know about ancient cities is the result of work by archaeologists. While some of the cultural history of the ancient cities has been culled from writings on stone tablets or hieroglyphics on temple walls, most knowledge about these ancient settlements has been discovered by examining other kinds of artifacts.

This chapter considers the historical and archaeological evidence of the development of ancient cities. In reviewing this information, the student should begin with several questions which relate to the modern cities (1) What common sociological features do ancient and modern cities share? (2) What factors associated with urbanization are related to technology? (3) What social and economic factors precede urbanization?

The social scientist is concerned with the total culture of an ancient city. Culture, as used here, refers to a total style of life transmitted from generation to generation. Culture usually evolves over a period of centuries. Culture consists of three components. *Institutions* are social organizational forms which enable a society to function in a systematic manner. Examples of institutions are the family, the political system, the church, the educational system, and the economy. Institutions are mutually agreed-upon ways of doing things, which become the building blocks of social organization. *Ideas* are also transmitted from generation to generation, sometimes in a form of values, but frequently, particularly in preliterate cultures, in the form of an oral tradition of myths and proverbs. *Artifacts,* or man-made objects, are the third element of culture. By examining the physical ruins of an ancient culture, the archaeologist gains clues about its non-material aspects.

When ancient cities are excavated, almost every man-made object furnishes information about the style of life. The remaining structural outlines of the city tell whether it was fortified; where the poor, the rich, and the leaders lived; what kind of a sewer system existed; what kind of a water-supply system was used; where grain and valuable goods were stored; and where the temple was located. Religious artifacts and symbols usually reveal what kind of gods were worshipped. Usually, the nature of the gods explains the dominant concerns of a society: *i.e.,* rain, sun, war, disease, or money. Tools and the metal from which they were forged give indications of the level of technology. The different kinds of specialists found in the community—priests, carpenters, masons, warriors—tell whether the economy could maintain a large number of persons not concerned solely with growing and gathering food. Similarly, the market-place, if one existed, indicates what kind of goods were distributed and traded. The size and number of rooms in living quarters provide rough ways of estimating the population. Finally, the residential pattern of the city—where people lived, worked, and played—tells a great deal about the social stratification of the city.

In most ancient cities, the wealthy and upper classes lived in the middle of the city, surrounded by slaves and poorer people on the fringes. This perimeter formed a barrier against invaders from the outside. This ecological pattern is in distinct contrast to the modern American city, where the upper classes more often live in the suburbs or the urban fringe. The location of the city within the surrounding region also tells a great deal about the way in which it evolved. Ancient cities in the Middle East were generally located on the sea or along rivers, where the rich alluvial soil provided an excellent foundation for growing maize or corn. Because of access to nearby navigable rivers, many ancient cities served as a hub for trade with outlying areas, resulting in the exchange of both goods and knowledge from one culture to another.

In these early stages, urban civilizations thrived in temperate climates. Man had not yet learned to cope with a short growing season and with the difficulties of storing food and fuel for the long winter. Residents of the colder regions were typically migratory hunters and gatherers. Thus, from the work of archaeologists and anthropologists, we have pieced together what we believe to be the technology and social structure of many ancient cities. During this same agricultural era, writing was invented. For the two or three thousand years prior to the time of Christ, we can rely on some written records as well as other artifacts found in archaeological "digs."

A Roman outpost in Syria, Dura Europos was founded on the Euphrates about 300 B.C. by the Seleucid successor to Alexander the Great. At first a center of Hellenism in the East, it was later a Roman stronghold until Valerian lost it in A.D. 257. Yale University archaeologists have studied the site since 1922; finger-like ramps are their excavation dumps. (*Courtesy Yale University*)

The Four Periods of Urbanization

There are four major historical epochs which describe the evolution of urban life. These are characterized by Sjoberg in terms of "level of organization."[1] Each of these eras is typified by its own form of technology, economy, social organization, and political institutions. These periods are: (1) the folk society, (2) pre-industrial or feudal settlement, (3) the industrial city, and (4) metropolitan complex. This chapter is concerned mainly with the pre-industrial settlement.

The Folk Society

Prior to the first urban settlements, which are dated approximately 3500 B.C., most of the world's human population was organized into folk societies. These were essentially small, self-sufficient groups of people who depended primarily on hunting and gathering. Although they sometimes raised food crops and domestic animals, folk societies were unable to develop permanent settlements. As a result, they roamed through large areas, dependent for food upon the wild animals and plant foods of the region.

 Environment. Nomadic groups often ranged over thousands of square miles, following herds of wild animals and seeking temperate climates during severe weather. Like the twentieth century Eskimos, folk societies often had a home base,

[1]Gideon Sjoberg, "The Origin and Evolution of Cities," *Scientific American,* Vol. 213, No. 3 (1965), pp. 55–56.

where they laid over for the long winter, departing for hunting or gathering trips during warm weather. These home bases were developed mainly for protection from the elements and did not comprise permanent settlements, since no one lived there year-round.

Economy.   Since there was rarely a surplus of any sort (either crops or animal products), the folk society was made up of a number of small, self-sufficient bands or tribes. Division of labor, if any existed, was based mainly upon age and sex. Men hunted and fished. Women, children and elders tended the camp, making clothing and preparing food.

Government and law.   The folk society maintained its social order through custom and tradition. Since the dominant sociological unit was the clan or tribe, most social relationships were based upon kinship. The folkways, mores, and roles passed from generation to generation provided a basis for leadership, continuity, and social control within the community.

Family.   The family was the unit of procreation, socialization, and work. The extended family was both the unit of production and the unit of consumption. Relationships with other extended families or tribes were strained, or even danger-ous. This resulted, not surprisingly, in distrust of strangers. Persons who were not related to the family unit were defined as enemies and were often abused or even killed.

Religion.   In the most primitive folk societies, religion was characterized by emphasis upon magic and reliance on totems or sacrifice. Magic was used for protection against the outside world—which included lightning, floods, wild ani-mals, and other tribes. The dominant religious concern was providing hope in the face of uncertainty in a threatening world. No emphasis whatsoever was placed upon long-term social goals or ethics.

Education.   Skills like shelter making, hunting, fishing, child rearing prac-tices, and folk medicine were passed along orally. There was no written tradition and no numerical system. The level of knowledge remained almost constant from generation to generation.

Social stratification.   Folk societies did not have elaborate social stratifica-tion, although they did possess a leadership structure vested in the physically strong, the best hunters, or the eldest members of the tribe. Men usually had higher prestige and social standing than women, probably due to their greater size and strength.

Culture and personality.   Survival skills like physical prowess, hunting, and gathering were essential components of anyone who was to exist within a folk culture. Anthropological studies suggest that the most respected personal quality among preliterate groups is an authoritarian (or at least an authoritative) personal-ity.[2]

Ecology.   Since there were no permanent settlements, no traditional urban

---

[2]Everett E. Hagen, *On the Theory of Social Change: How Economic Growth Begins* (Homewood, Illinois: The Dorsey Press, 1962), pp. 311–312.

ecology existed within folk societies. There were, however, migratory patterns, and relationships of dominance and submissiveness between various groups within the larger regions.

This brief description of the folk society provides a basis for comparison with other, more urbanized societies.

Preindustrial or Feudal Settlement

People began to live in cities about 5,500 years ago.[3] These early settlements were cities of substantial size and density. They contained a variety of occupational groups not directly involved with agriculture.

By this time literacy had emerged as an important and necessary element in urban life. Literacy made possible a more complex social order. Written traditions replaced oral ones, spurring the development of complex government and production modes and the regulatory techniques which bureaucracies need in order to survive.

Literacy is also a prerequisite to the development of mathematics, physics, and astronomy. Literacy provides the medium for an ever increasing variety of technical specializations within a society. V. Gordon Childe describes the impact of literacy and other factors on the social structure of the pre-industrial city.[4]

Childe's criteria of the pre-industrial city.   From an analysis of anthropological evidence of ancient cities. Childe identified ten characteristics of pre-industrial urban centers. (1) Full-time specialists, including transport workers, officials, draftsmen, and priests were found in pre-industrial cities. These specialists were able to exchange their services for part of the small agricultural surplus. (2) Pre-industrial cities had more people crowded closely together than the Neolithic villages which preceded them. Most settlements contained between 7,000 and 20,000 people, although one middle-eastern city, Uruk, is estimated to have contained 50,000 people.[5] (3) Pre-industrial cities often generated great art forms, including architecture, sculpture, and painting, produced by full-time artists. (4) Writing and numerical notation were evident. Initially these skills were used for bookkeeping and documentary purposes—*i.e.,* to keep inventories of grain, tallies of the tributes paid to the local priests, and records of landholdings. (5) Measurement and predictive sciences (such as arithmetic, geometry, and astronomy) were developed by the literate elite. These calculations helped in developing a calendar, which in turn resulted in efficient agricultural planning and harvesting. Mathematical notation also provided a common measure for design of buildings and temples. (6) Tribute

[3]Gideon Sjoberg, *The Pre-industrial City: Past and Present* (New York: The Free Press, 1960), pp. 25–51.

[4]See V. Gordon Childe, "The Urban Revolution," *Town Planning Review,* XXI, April (1950), pp. 3–17. For additional discussion of the criteria for describing a city see Sjoberg, *op. cit.,* 1960, pp. 33–35, and Kingsley Davis, "The Origin and Growth of Urbanization in the World," *American Journal of Sociology,* LX, March (1955), p. 430.

[5]Robert M. Adams, "The Origins of Cities," *Scientific American, 203,* September (1960), p. 154.

and taxes were collected from the farmers by the local political and religious elites. Initially these tributes were collected in the form of grain. (7) Citizenship in the pre-industrial city was based on residence in a geographical area, rather than membership in a family or tribe. Membership in the state, in turn, was paid for by taxes, which the state itself used in part to provide certain services, most notably protection from marauders. (8) Monuments and public buildings were a prominent feature of the pre-industrial city, symbolizing the power—both political and economic—derived from the accumulation of agricultural surplus product. (9) The surplus product also facilitated trade with foreign countries and made cities dependent upon resources beyond their local boundaries. In the ancient cities of Sumeria, both stone and wood were prized commodities, for which grain was traded. (10) The accumulation of surplus grain by the local elite resulted in a more differentiated social structure than was evident in folk societies. The local elite, which had more access to these resources, generally assumed religious, political and military leadership. Upper-class people were able to accumulate status symbols—clothing, jewelry, household objects, and even musical instruments, which symbolized the vast social gap between the elite and the peasantry.

Childe contends that all ten of these characteristics or traits are found in almost all early cities. Collectively, Childe's facts summarize the difference between the social order of urban areas, as compared to the earlier folk settlements.[6]

The first cities which met all of Childe's criteria appeared approximately 3,500 B.C. in that area of the Middle East now called Iraq. Cities also emerged in central Mexico around 3,000 B.C. While the two eras are close in time, cities appear to have been invented independently in the two hemispheres.

Environment.   It is generally acknowledged that cities first developed around 3,500 B.C. in "the Fertile Crescent," the eastern portion of an area commonly referred to as Mesopotamia. The soil was excellent, and the water supply was adequate. Moreover, the region served as a trade center where voyagers and travelers of different cultures met for thousands of years. This exchange of ideas and cultures probably resulted in the development of innovative concepts and inventions which stimulated the evolution of the villages of Mesopotamia into larger cities.[7]

Although Mesopotamia was the first area where cities developed, cities also developed in the Nile Valley around 3,000 B.C. During the same period, the cities of Mohenjo-Daro and Harappa were established in the valley of the Indus River in what is now Pakistan. By 1500 B.C., cities were flourishing in Greece, Italy and the larger area of the Roman Empire. In China, during this period, the Yellow River region also produced urban settlements.

About 2,000 years later, during the first century B.C., cities developed in the New World. It is known that the Mayas, Zapotecs, Mixtecs and Aztecs built urban settlements on a large scale, although the culture and technology of these cities are

---

[6]For a summarization of the overall characteristics of the pre-industrial city, see Sjoberg, *op. cit.,* 1960, p. 321–343.

[7]Sjoberg, *op. cit.,* 1965, p. 20.

still being investigated. Incan cities are large, in contrast to those of the Middle East. (One Incan city has revealed more than 8,500 structures and a population numbering over 100,000). However, the Incas lacked a writing system beyond symbols for representing speech patterns. Their primitive number system was mainly based on certain wide classifications of elements. These New World cities also existed without animal husbandry, the wheel, or the rich soil of alluvial river beds. The factor that made the New World cities possible was the development of maize, a hybrid grain crop, which was highly productive but required relatively little effort. This surplus crop appeared to compensate for the limited technology and overcame many of the obstacles to urbanization which were not encountered in the Fertile Crescent.

Economy.   The technology of the pre-industrial city was restricted to power generated by humans and animals. Tools consisted of simple hand implements—hammers, plows, saws, axes, knives, and stone-cutting equipment. The social stratification system consisted of three classes. The cities were governed by priest-leaders, who did little manual labor and tried to avoid all social contact with those who did. Second, craftsmen, organized into guilds, merchants, and others offered a variety of professional services. Recruitment into these occupations was gained on the basis of kinship or marriage. The training was very specialized and secretive, preventing outsiders from entering. Finally, the most numerous class consisted of serfs, who were involved primarily in planting and harvesting of grain, and a large number of servants and slaves. Slaves made up about a third of the population of some cities.

Little standardization of prices or product quantities existed. Systems of weights and measures were also primitive or non-existent. For the most part, transactions were based on haggling between buyers and merchants. Intermixture of currencies and measures made the trading process still more cumbersome. Because of the distrust and absence of standards, buyers had to be extremely wary in every transction. Although there was some accumulation of capital through a surplus of grain, the surplus was small. Thus, large capital investments in buildings or streets was very difficult. Finally, credit was non-existent or poorly developed, precluding the transfer of any surplus into investment capital.

Government and law.   Members of the elite families dominated the local political structure. In the earlier cities, the same group managed to combine political, economic and religious power, reigning as priest-rulers for many centuries. Lesser political positions were held by members of the same ruling family, who administered both the larger province and the city. Usually, the power of these priest-kings was based upon religious sanctions and appeals to tradition. Decisions were made on a particularistic basis, depending upon the individuals involved rather than upon general principles or rules. The government offered services on the same basis; the elite made policy primarily for its own good rather than the community's. These inequities, combined with other factors like the lack of a fixed salary system, resulted in general inefficiency and corruption.

Family.   Most individuals lived within the confines of the same family all of their lives. Marriages were arranged by parents. The typical family was large and extended, with many relatives residing in the same household. The men of the family totally controlled the women. Upper-class women were confined largely within the home. Lower-class women, by necessity, played a more active role in the community and were given more freedom and responsibility. The older men typically held the greatest power position within the family and dominated the younger members. The family, rather than the school or the church, was the primary socializing agent for the entire community. It was the focal point for both leisure and work, since jobs and community position were based totally upon ascriptive criteria, or lineage. Family ties were crucial in determining a person's social placement within the community. Since little opportunity was present to leave the community, a person's social position and career opportunities were virtually fixed at birth.

Religion.   Upper-class members occupied the top positions in the religious hierarchy. Because this group was the only one which was literate, only its members were permitted to translate the sacred religious writings, which were inevitably interpreted to the advantage of the upper class. Almost all areas of life were regulated by religious sanctions—family, politics, economics, education, even leisure time. Periodically, both masses and elite participated in religious festivals and rituals, which provided a symbolic means of strengthening and re-uniting the total community. Strong reliance was placed upon magic, which was used to protect persons from evil spirits, restore people to health, and predict the future.

Education.   The only members of the community to receive a formal education were members of the upper class. Members of the lower classes, in contrast, were socialized and educated principally in the home. The curriculum in the schools was devoted to religious and philosophical writings, all of which reinforced the values of the elite. Practically no science curriculum was contained in the formal educational system of the pre-industrial city. The primary goals were to maintain the current social order and style of life.

Social stratification.   In contrast to the modern industrial city, the pre-industrial city revealed three basic layers of stratification: (1) the political religious leaders; (2) the merchants and tradesmen; and (3) the serfs and slaves. The system could be considered a caste hierarchy rather than an open class-system. It was almost impossible to attain social mobility by moving from one class to another. Occasionally, merchants who had accumulated an enormous surplus product managed to move into the upper classes.

Culture and personality.   Although it is almost impossible to determine the relationship of personality and culture through archeological evidence, research on pre-industrial cities of the present era indicated that a rigid social structure is associated with what is commonly called an *authoritarian personality*. A person with an authoritarian personality responds principally to power. If he is in a position of control over others, he uses his power in a most dictatorial and autocratic manner. If he is in a position where he must submit to the control of another, he is servile and docile in his acceptance of dominance by others. Because of rigid adherence to the ongoing social order and the emphasis upon stability, there are few incentives for leadership or innovation. Hence, the innovative personality which has frequently been identified in the development of industrial societies seems largely absent during this pre-industrial era. One is prompted to ask: who made the innovations which resulted in a transition from the folk society to the preindustrial community? The evidence examined here suggests that it was the artisans and merchants who were responsible for many of the economic and technical developments.[8] Their contact with traders from the outside world and their capacity to make use of the surplus product made possible the innovations which lead to development of more advanced societies.

Ecology.   Located in the center of the pre-industrial city was the nexus of governmental and religious power. The members of the upper class also resided here, while the lower classes and serfs were scattered outward toward the perimeter of the city. Tradesmen usually lived in one particular area or quarter which bore the name of their trade—carpenters, weavers, etc. Often one site served several purposes. The city center was usually devoted to religious, educational, and governmental activities. The centers of the large pre-industrial cities were typically dominated by a large religious edifice, a temple or a religious palace, which often towered high above the other buildings in the city. This area was most defensible against penetration by intruders.

The Prehistoric Settlement of the Middle East

What were the sociological characteristics of the first urban settlements? The Fertile Crescent, in which these cities developed, is located in the countries now known as Syria, Iraq, and Jordan. Outposts of this civilization have recently been discovered within the present-day boundaries of Iran. Most of the earlier cities of the area were along the Tigris and Euphrates Rivers. These settlements possessed a system of numerical notation, which was used primarily for keeping inventories and sales of agricultural products and other valuable commodities which were produced. These cities had a writing system used to record agreements on tablets made of a very soft soapstone.[9]

Not all of the ancient cities in the Middle East, however, were located on the Fertile Crescent. Around 3,400 B.C., the Ealamite culture began to flourish in southeastern Iran, about sixty miles from the Arabian Sea. Unlike other urban settlements which relied on grain trading for an economic base, the city of Tepe Yaahya based its economy on trading soapstone tablets mined in the nearby mountains. This community had an administrative structure whose sole function

---

[8]Sjoberg, *op. cit.*, 1960, pp. 327–328.
[9]C. C. and Martha Lamberg-Karlovsky, ''An Early City in Iran,'' *Cities: Their Origin, Growth and Human Impact.* (San Francisco: W. H. Freeman and Co., 1973) pp. 28–37.

Iran. Vertical view of a town ruin on the south bank of the Gurgan River. This map view shows the entire plan of the city quarter photographed. A citadel formation is visible on the north bank (lower right-hand corner). (*Courtesy of the Oriental Institute, University of Chicago.*)

was distribution of soapstone.[10] The tools of this period included implements of both bone and flint. The culture also developed a form of hybrid agriculture and animal husbandry. Excavations have identified animal bones of domesticated gazelles, cattle, sheep, and goats. Early agricultural efforts yielded a variety of hybrid cereal grains. Metal workers of this era were thus able to generate the high temperatures needed to smelt copper into molten ore. The inhabitants of Tepe Yaahya produced bronze by a primitive form of smelting.

Analysis of the writing of Tepe Yaahya reveals records (found in the excavation) dealing mainly with receipts for goods. A fundamental question regarding the culture of Tepe Yaahya is whether it was self-generated or whether it was a by-product of the fusion of different cultures. The archaeological evidence indicates that a form of bartering existed, which allowed the acquisition of artifacts from foreign cultures, but that a highly developed trading economy did not exist during this era. In general, the evidence indicates that the culture of this city was largely a local phenomenon. It was after the fourth millennium B.C. that a substantial trade flourished with distant parts of Persia, allowing the development of a much more extensive urbanized settlement.

[10]*Ibid.*, p. 28.

Preindustrial Cities in the Western Hemisphere

Around 3000 B.C., the Mayan culture flourished in the Yucatan Peninsula, in what is now the country of Mexico. The Mayans employed a form of hieroglyphics and developed a very accurate calendar. The Mayans were also adept in astronomy and mathematics. While they never discovered the wheel or developed the use of metals, they invented agricultural, weaving, and pottery-making skills independent of any other culture. The Mayans based their religion on nature worship and built elaborate temples and ceremonial structures in the centers of their cities. Anthropologists doubt whether the Mayan cities included any specialists other than priests and their functionaries, raising the question of whether Mayan cities actually meet Childe's criteria.[11] Both the size and density of Mayan settlements (approximating 100,000 population) suggests that they possessed an urban culture.

A derivative civilization of the Mayans' in the area of Mexico was formed by the Aztecs who are well known for practicing a religion based upon human sacrifice. The Aztec's civilization was conquered by the Spanish under Cortez in 1519. It was based in Tenochtitlan, the area of the present Mexico City.

Other pre-industrial cities developed in Egypt, India and ancient China. Archaeological work in China continues and suggests that in this area, too, urban culture was invented independently of that of other regions.

The Industrial City and Beyond

Technology is the key to the development of the modern city. Technology is made practicable by massive production, distribution and consumption of goods. Almost 5,000 years passed between the development of pre-industrial cities (3500 B.C.) and the evolution of industrial cities of Europe (approximately 1500 A.D.). Prior to that time, most of the world's population lived in rural areas. Even in those European and Asian countries where cities existed, the urban population comprised less than five percent of the entire region's people. It was extremely rare, prior to 1500 A.D., for any city to have a population over 10,000 persons.

In order for cities to become something more than religious and administrative centers (which were the focal points for outlying agricultural areas), both a new technology and a new social order had to evolve. Whether the social order precedes technology or technology precedes social order is a point which is still being argued by historians and social scientists. It is generally acknowledged, however, that the development of the factory system and large scale industry is usually accompanied by a series of social and economic changes which almost inevitably occur during a

[11]Robert Braidwood and G. Willy, eds., "The Central Andes," *Courses Toward Urban Life* (Chicago: Aldine, 1962). Bruce Trigger, "Determinants of Urban Growth in Pre-Industrial Societies," in Peter Ucko, Ruth Tringham, and G. W. Dimbleby, eds., *Man, Settlement, and Urbanism* (Cambridge, Mass.: Schenkman, 1972). Noel P. Gist and Sylvia F. Fava, *Urban Society* (New York: Thomas Y. Crowell Company, 1964) pp. 16–17.

period of rapid urbanization and industrialization. These changes may be measured in output per capita, literacy, political participation, or development of an elaborate series of laws regulating contracts between persons and firms. Technological shifts are always accompanied by major changes in the social structure of a developing area. For example, changes in the economic institutions usually bring about re-organization of the family structure and function. Rapid industrial growth also generates a need for new educational systems, which in turn, produce a large number of literate and skilled persons. This trend usually results in a demand for political and economic adjustments which reflect new collective definitions of comfort and productivity. Neil Smelser described the effect of economic development on social mobility in this way:

> We cannot escape the fact that persons must be shuttled through the social structure during the periods of rapid development. Often they have to move to an urban setting. They must fill new occupational roles and new positions of leadership. They must learn to respond to new rewards and deprivations and to accept new standards of effective performance. Development often requires more movement of persons than during pre-development periods; certainly it requires different forms of movement. The ease with which movement is affected, furthermore, depends largely upon the social structure, the characteristics of the developing social structure and the emerging tensions between the two.[12]

This social mobility, inherent in a period of rapid urbanization and industrialization, is traditionally conceptualized by economists as a function of supply and demand. Lebergott, an economist, attributes the capacity for economic growth of the United States first to its abundant natural resources, and second to its flexible adaptation of economic and social institutions which foster economic development. (Lebergott, 1964)[13]

Although an area may have the natural resources required for urbanization and industrialization, it may not possess the other economic and social prerequisites. Underdeveloped areas are frequently caught in a trap of low per capita output. One part of this trap is the *supply* factor of production, and the other part is the *demand* for products.

On the supply side, capital is unavailable because of the low capacity of people in underdeveloped areas to save. Low capacity to save is an indicator of a low level of income. The low income level, in turn, is a reflection of low productivity in the economy, which is primarily due to the lack of capital. The lack of capital can be traced to the small capacity to save, thus completing the cycle. The net result is an economic system with a set of mutually related values, which are all relatively small-scale in comparison to more urbanized and industrialized areas.

In sum, there appears to be a series of economic and social factors which are

---

[12]Neil J. Smelser, "Social Structure, Mobility, and Development," in Nei Smelser and Seymour L. Tipset, eds., *Social Structure, Mobility and Economic Development* (Chicago: Aldine Publishing Co., 1965), p. 2.

[13]Stanley Lebergott, *Manpower in Economic Growth* (New York: McGraw-Hill, Inc., 1964).

prerequisites for industrialization and urbanization. Although these factors are necessary for urbanization, they are not sufficient to cause urbanization and the subsequent rapid social mobility which generally accompanies it.

Economists generally attribute rapid industrial growth to three situations: (1) The factors of production—land, labor, and, capital—are available in sufficient quantity and are exchangeable; (2) the social organization facilitates the systematic movement of labor and capital in order to optimize land utilization; (3) the value system of the society encourages and rewards behavior which increases the productivity of the system.

Once the industrialization process began in the United States, the demands within the labor market brought large numbers of immigrants from Europe, most of whom started at the bottom of the occupational ladder. In spite of this, immigration generally marked an improvement in life-style and entry into an occupational system in which status was based upon achievement rather than ascription. Thus, the American dream of upward mobility was realistically based, in the beginning, upon the manpower requirements of developing urban areas.

Conclusion

People began to live in cities about 5,500 years ago. The first urbanized societies evolved in an area of the Middle East known as "the Fertile Crescent," a region with rich alluvial soil and a plentiful water supply. Because the area was a major crossroads for traders, it brought together people from divergent cultures for thousands of years. Based on the work of archeologists we have derived a definition of a city: "It is a community of substantial size and population density that shelters a variety of non-agricultural specialists, including a literate elite."[14] Prior to the era of the pre-industrial city, people sometimes lived together in large numbers, but these communities were usually temporary or seasonal bases where migratory groups laid over for the winter.

The history of the city may be classified into four periods: (1) The Folk Society (prior to 3,500 B.C.), during which no permanent settlements fitting our definition of the city existed; (2) The Pre-industrial or Feudal Settlement (3,500 B.C. to approximately 1,750 A.D.); (3) The Industrial City (1,750 A.D. to approximately 1,900 A.D.), (4) The Metropolitan Complex (1,900 to the present). In this chapter, we have mainly discussed the second period, the era of the Pre-industrial City.

By identifying the social structure and function of ancient cities, we have been able to establish a baseline or bench mark from which to gauge the development of modern industrial cities. In considering the sociological characteristics of the first cities, we should be able to assess whether contemporary urbanization reflects an extension of the historic trend, or a fundamental shift in the mode of urbanization.

[14]Sjoberg "The Origin and Evolution of Cities," p. 55.

Probably the most comprehensive abstraction of the social organization of the ancient city is provided by Childe's criteria. The reader should consider each characteristic, asking himself whether twentieth-century cities exhibit these same trends. According to Childe, the prehistoric cities had ten attributes which set them apart from the previous temporary settlements:

1. *Full-time specialists,* such as priests and artisans, were evident.
2. *Population density* was greater than in previous epochs.
3. *Great art* developed independently in individual cities, in the form of architecture, sculpture, and painting.
4. *Writing and numerical notation* were evident.
5. *Measurement and predictive sciences* (as well as writing) were developed and practiced by a literate elite.
6. *Tribute* was paid to the priest-rulers in the form of taxes.
7. Inclusion in the community was based on *geographical residence,* rather than membership in a tribe or extended family.
8. *Monuments and public buildings* were made possible by the surplus grain product, which was converted into capital for public works.
9. *Trading* developed with other cities, some within the same region and others far away.
10. A more *differentiated social structure,* including more social strata, evolved.

Many of these same processes are evident in the developing countries of today. Urbanization brings about a radical restructuring of the social class structure, causing a shifting of roles and statuses which existed for thousands of years. The needs of an urbanizing society dictate that massive upward social mobility must occur. Many developing nations are hindered by the same economic problem that blocked the development of ancient cities—the lack of a surplus or profit which would permit an investment in transportation systems, factories, warehouses, and educational systems which are necessary in an industrialized society. Even areas which are rich in natural resources (such as oil) frequently are unable to develop a social organization which has the capacity to exploit these resources. Leaders and innovators must emerge who are able to provide an impetus for new values which support a work ethic and changes in other values which support the new social order. When societies urbanize and industrialize they seem to pass through a period during which the new values (which invariably differ fundamentally from the old) are rationalized and incorporated into the culture. This aspect of urbanization, sometimes called modernization, is discussed in the chapter on social participation, work, and leisure.

chapter 3

Urban Ecology

Ecology has become the watchword of a social movement which seeks the good way of life. In its most classical usage, however, ecology refers to a science which studies the inter-relationships between organisms and their environment. The current ecological movement seeks to establish an optimal balance between living things and their environment. Emergent social movements (like the ecology movement) are inevitably rooted in a conflict between those who seek change and those who prefer a traditional philosophy or way of life. The present controversy involves such a value conflict over the meaning of the phrase, *ecological balance*. People not only differ vastly in the kind of life-styles which they prefer, but also disagree as to the social philosophies and policies which will best serve future generations.

There are a number of contemporary issues which encompass many other dimensions of the ecological debate. First is the age-old question of the optimal population, the "best" number of people, which focuses on whether worldwide fertility should be limited through the implementation of governmental policies on birth control, abortions, and euthanasia (mercy killings), and whether population should be dispersed in underdeveloped areas. Sociologists are certainly not strangers to this debate. Over the years they have continuously analyzed the doctrine of Malthus, which holds that the earth's human population grows at a much faster rate than its food supply, with the disasterous consequences of famine, death, plague, disease, and social deviance (referred to by Malthus as "vice").[1] It has been demonstrated beyond doubt that even during the affluent twentieth century, the Malthusian doctrine manifests itself in the incapacity of the world to produce food and other resources for its burgeoning population (particularly in the developing

[1]See V. D. Glass, ed., *Introduction to Malthus* (London: Watts and Company, 1953).

33

Newest and tallest exclamation point on the San Francisco skyline is the 853-foot Trans-America pyramid. In the background is Telegraph Hill with its fluted column, Cost Tower. (*San Francisco Convention & Visitors Bureau.*)

nations). The population problems of modern industrial cities appear to be related principally to planning for metropolitan services and developing policies for orderly growth. Since Western nations have the human capacity and economic resources to choose from a large number of future alternatives, which involves satisfying not only sheer economic necessities but also esthetic preferences for different life-styles, the ecological debate typically ranges over a wider territory. Often, the distinction between human needs and tastes becomes blurred or lost. For some, ecology signifies a preference for forests over farms, for country over city, for natural foods over supermarket fare, even for breast-feeding over bottle-feeding. While the classical concept of ecology suggests a delicate balance in nature—that the overall conditions of organic life (plants, animals, and people) are bound inexorably with their environment in a total system—the future of the entire ecosystem will not be determined by some mysterious balance which occurs naturally within the system itself. Man, the inventor and manipulator, has always modified the system by his very presence and probably will continue to do so even more conspicuously in the future. The current ecological stir appears to have been brought on because man is finally able to visualize some of the consequences. Hopefully, he will make wise decisions for the generations which follow.

This chapter is about the human ecology of urban areas—the way in which people relate to their environments. It deals principally with the classical studies of urban populations which attempt to relate social structures and processes to the urban environment. In reading this chapter, the student should ask himself these questions:

(1) What is urban ecology? (2) What are the historical trends in the development of urban ecology? (3) What are the specific theories and methods of urban ecology which are most useful for examining (a) the social structure of the city, and (b) areas outside of the city? (4) Which methods are most useful in analyzing social problems? (5) What are the limitations of ecological theories and what other analytical frameworks might be used to supplement or to replace them? We begin by examining Louis Wirth's classical theory of urbanism.

The Ecological Theory of Louis Wirth

Sociologists have struggled with the meaning of the word "urban" throughout the history of the discipline. While it is relatively easy to identify large population concentrations, commonly referred to as urbanized areas, it is more difficult to characterize the style of life and social interaction patterns within these locales. It is even more difficult to develop a theory which relates the degree of urbanization to social interaction patterns of the smaller neighborhoods of a city. In American sociology, a theoretical base for urban sociology evolved through a series of studies conducted at the University of Chicago during the 1920's and 1930's. In a summary statement, "Urbanism as a Way of Life" (1938), Louis Wirth spelled out the seminal theoretical concepts which were to occupy urban sociology for the next quarter-century.[2] Wirth's theory, simply stated, suggests that there are three principal elements of urbanization—population size, population density, and population heterogeneity. Another way of stating the theory is that the larger, the more dense, and the more heterogenous the population of an area, the more urbanized is the style of life.

Size of Population

People living in a large city are limited in the number of persons they can know well. In contrast, social relations in the small town or village are usually characterized as deep, extensive, and total, in that they involve many different situations and roles played by the same people. In a rural community, one constantly socializes with the same people at work, at church, at school, at leisure time, even at the doctor's or dentist's office. Relationships in this setting manifest many of the characteristics of the primary group, in that they are similar to those found in the family, tribe, or folk society. Contrast this to Wirth's composite of *urban* social relationships.

> Characteristically, urbanities meet one another in highly segmental roles. They are, to be sure, dependent upon more people for satisfactions of their life-needs than are rural people and thus are associated with a greater number of organized groups, but they

[2]Louis Wirth, "Urbanism as a Way of Life," *American Journal of Sociology,* 44, July (1938).

are less dependent upon particular persons, and their dependence upon others is confined to a highly fractionalized aspect of each other's round of activity. This is essentially what is meant by saying that the city is characterized by secondary rather than primary contacts. The contacts of the city may indeed by face-to-face, but they are nevertheless impersonal, superficial, transitory, and segmental. The reserve, the indifference, and the blasé outlook which urbanites manifest in their relationships may thus be regarded as devices for immunizing themselves against the personal claims and expectations of others.[3]

Translating Wirth's ideas into ecological terms, the implication is that the social organization of a large human settlement makes a life-style which is based principally on primary relationships very difficult. Encounters tend frequently to be limited to situations which involve specialized, limited aspects of a person's total spectrum of roles. It is both this role fragmentation and limited integration among different roles which causes a kind of alienation, known as *anomie* (which in French means normlessness). *Anomie,* in turn, is associated with a larger number of social pathologies, such as crime, suicide, and mental illness, which are brought about by a poorly integrated social structure.

Population Density

People tend to live closely together in urban areas. This proximity is found not only in housing, but also in the workplace, in the leisure setting, and of course, in the crowded mass-transit systems and highways of urban areas. This crowded physical space also effects both the frequency and quality of human interaction. In sheer physical terms, because there are many people living within a small space, the probability of encounter is much greater than in a less densely populated area. Stated another way, it is likely that there will be more social acts, of both a deviant and nondeviant nature, in a city than in a rural area.

Urban populations are dense because historically, it has been necessary for people to crowd together in order to realize the benefits of their functional interdependence, as for example, those that exist between corporations and banks. In the past, problems of communication and transportation have made it necessary for these two interests to work side by side. This makes the available space in the business district scarce, which means that it costs more to buy land there. Because of the cost of land, there is a rational tendency to use every inch of space as efficiently as possible. Land costs in modern cities are usually highest in the most desirable commerical locations, resulting the construction of high-rise buildings and skyscrapers. Residential space is also sold at a premium; as a result, the most poverty-stricken population is crowded into slums and ghettos, while the more affluent live insulated lives in condominiums or in middle-class suburbs, free from the congestion and pollution of the center city. Thus, a number of factors determine the differential land use patterns of urban areas. Among these are prestige, access to

---

[3]*Ibid.,* p. 53.

Drawing by Weber; © 1971 The
New Yorker Magazine, Inc

"Excuse me, sir. I am prepared to make you a rather
attractive offer for your square."

transportation and communication, healthfulness, physical attractiveness, and of course the predominant land use concentration which already exists in various areas. All of these factors translate into an economic utility, which determines the supply and demand, and, therefore, the cost of land. The supply of usable land is limited also by topological features, such as high mountains and bays, as well as the transportation and communication system of an urban area.

Population size and population density are complementary concepts. It is impossible to have a densely populated settlement without a sufficient population base. On the other hand, it is quite possible to have a large number of people living in an area without being packed closely together. It is also possible to have quite dense areas that do not seem to be so because of good planning. Usually, older cities which developed before the era of rapid transit and expressways are more densely populated (at least in their core areas) than newer areas which evolved during the era of the automobile and the modern mass transit system.

The sociologist is concerned with differences in overall social interaction patterns as these relate to urban density. Although people may live in close physical proximity, there may be not only little contact, in terms of the total amount of information communicated, but the nature and depth of the interaction also may vary substantially. That is, social space may be quite different from physical space.[4] Although it is common to attribute many of the problems of the slums to overpopulation (among other things), there is sparse evidence to indicate that it is density alone which causes the problem.[5] Different cultures have varying norms and practices regarding physical and social space. In highly crowded Asian and Japanese cities, for example, persons have lived close together for centuries with little visable discomfort, because they have been able to create privacy, even in the midst of densities which would evoke great discomfort among Americans. In contrast, studies of American lower-class neighborhoods suggest that conflicts between groups regarding the distinction between public and private space, such as juvenile gangs' battles over turf, are often a focal point for urban grievances.[6]

When approaching the concept of human density, then, it is not only important to focus explicitly on the precise characteristic which is dense, but it is always necessary to raise the issue—density ganged by what standard? Housing density is usually measured in terms of the number of persons per room. Land density is measured by the number of people per square mile. While both land density and housing density have a strong impact on life-styles, there are many more factors which regulate density in terms of total social space. Even in a neighborhood where residential space is crowded by both criteria (housing density and land density), the other places where people interact frequently may offset the effect of a crowded neighborhood. The school, the church, the workplace, and the city parks and recreation areas, may provide a respite, even in the United States, which places such a premium on space.

Generally, however, Wirth's observation that density is one of the principal components of urbanization still holds. Modern techniques of communication and transportation have made it possible for the sprawling modern city to vastly reduce the physical density of its neighborhoods. But in terms of social density, this technological evolution may have done little to alter the frequency and intensity of human interaction. Scott Greer has referred to this transformation in social space as an increase in "scale."[7]

[4]Arnold S. Feldman and Charles Tilley, "The Interaction of Social and Physical Space," *American Sociological Review,* 25, No. 6 (1960).

[5]Irving Roscow, "The Social Effects of the Physical Environment," *Journal of American Institute of Planners,* 27, No. 2 (1961).

[6]Gerald D. Suttles, *The Social Order of the Slum* (Chicago: University of Chicago Press, 1968).

[7]Scott Greer, *The Emerging City* (New York: The Free Press, 1962), pp. 33–54.

Population Heterogeneity

Historically, because major cities throughout the earth have been trade centers, they have attracted people from cultures outside the area and different subcultures within. We deal with the development of ancient cities in another chapter in more depth. It is sufficient at this point for the reader to keep in mind that because major urban areas have been historically cultural and trade centers, they have attracted and maintained a highly diverse population—one which varies substantially in values, skills, ethnic composition, educational and occupational levels, and even in age and sex composition.

From the standpoint of regional economics, the labor force of an urban-industrial area is more differentiated than that of a rural area. The staffing of such a work force requires many kinds of specialists, production workers, and service workers. The result is that the occupational structure of an urban area is complex, offering many kinds of jobs and requiring many kinds of skills. This differential in occupational and educational level, in turn, produces an urban social class structure which encompasses a larger number of social classes than is found in rural areas.[8] Because of the occupational opportunities presented by urbanized areas, they have attracted migrants which bring many cultural patterns. Most large cities have enclaves of recent arrivals who have not yet been fully assimilated into the overall cultural life of the city. In London, migrants from former British colonies have recently increased the racial and cultural heterogeneity of that city. In the United States, the urban "melting pot" has been fueled by various streams of migration from Europe and, more recently, by Southern blacks and Puerto Ricans. Similarly, in Latin America and in Africa, urban centers have been the destination of a stream of culturally diverse immigrants from rural areas who have been displaced as a result of agricultural mechanization and political upheavals. Overall, throughout the history of mankind, the city has been more diverse in many ways than rural areas—in terms of ethnicity, culture, social structure, and general life-style.[9]

Wirth believed that it is primarily this heterogeneity which accounts for the anomic quality of urban life. In addition to the city's cultural diversity, the fragmentation of social relationships is compounded by the seeming unconnectedness of various facets of urban life. Where one resides, where one works and the kind of job one has, one's income, one's interests and allegiances are not well related, either spatially or culturally. This heterogeneity, Wirth said, also resulted in people's clustering into various ecologically segregated areas—ethnic ghettos, poverty areas, and middle-class neighborhoods. Whether the adverse effects of heterogeneity

[8]Peter M. Blau and Otis D. Duncan, *The American Occupational Structure* (New York: Wiley, 1967), pp. 277–294.

[9]Gideon Sjoberg, *The Pre-industrial City: Past and Present* (New York: The Free Press, 1960), pp. 27–28.

(*anomie* and social disorganization) were as pronounced within these clusters is an issue which Wirth does not address in much detail.

Since Wirth's publication of "Urbanism as a Way of Life" in 1938, there have been many criticisms and modifications of the theory. His pronouncements on the importance of size, density, and heterogeniety, however, are the keystones of urban ecology. In the discussions which follow, we trace the evolution of urban ecological methods. In large part these methods reflect challenges, refutations, and subsequent modifications of Wirth's theory of urbanism.

Natural Areas

While Wirth's theory of urbanism provides a theoretical underpinning for the University of Chicago studies, the actual studies which resulted in the methodological building blocks were the product of other sociologists. Employing an organic analogy, the city was conceptualized as a series of interdependent, functional units which were labeled *natural areas*. Zorbaugh, who originated the concept, suggested that a city may be broken into many smaller areas ". . . which we may call natural areas, in that they are the unplanned, natural product of the city's growth."[10] These locales are the result of transportation routes and industrialized areas, with parks and geographical features acting as boundaries to concentrations of different populations. Because of their proximity to industry or transportation, natural areas reflect a physical identity which is also differentiated through the cost of land. Administrative units of a city, such as wards and service districts, may be coterminous with natural areas. However, administrative areas are usually different from natural areas. Since natural areas are actually sociological units, differences in crime rates and rates of family disorganization can be meaningfully related to the social context of each area. Some of the later Chicago studies examine different kinds of natural areas in rich detail, from a participant observer's perspective which is still rare in sociology. Studies like Shaw and McKay's *Delinquency Areas* and Zorbaugh's *The Gold Coast and the Slum* are landmarks in the development of ecological methods.[11]

Ecological Process and Ecological Methods

Before examining several ecological theories and methods employed by the sociologists, it is well to consider the issues of fundamental interest to students of the city and to consider the usefulness and limitations of ecological models. Urban

---

[10]Harvey M. Zorbaugh, *The Gold Coast and The Slum* (Chicago: University of Chicago Press, 1928), pp. 188–199.

[11]Zorbaugh, *op. cit.* Also Clifford R. Shaw and Henry D. McKay, *Juvenile Delinquency and Urban Areas* (Chicago: University of Chicago Press, 1942), pp. 60–68.

ecology is based upon identifying and mapping geographical sectors of larger land area, then analyzing the social phenomena which are peculiar to the various smaller areas. The maxim, "A picture is better than words," conveys the dominant methodology of the early ecology studies. By visually identifying certain population concentrations on maps, a great deal of knowledge can be gained about the social life of various geographic sectors. Although it is possible, through the use of maps, to identify concentrations of rich and poor, or young and old, this information alone does not identify the various subcultures or social interaction patterns of different locales. Mapping provides clues about norms, values, and sentiments, but an understanding of the social life of an area requires participant observation, surveys, and an exploration of the history of social trends.

In the ecological models which follow, urban areas are compared by showing some kind of a central tendency for each locale. Census areas may be compared in terms of median income, median years of education, or other kinds of averages, such as infant mortality or crime rates.[12] The fact that a person resides in an area which has a high crime rate, however, does not necessarily indicate that he is more likely to commit a crime (or be a victim of a crime) than a person residing in another area. Ecological studies provide no information about individuals—only for aggregates. They do not tell us what kind of a person living in a high crime area is likely to become a criminal. Stating the problem in another way, suppose that a person lives in an area where 30 of every 100 persons are arrested during the average year. While this is an exceedingly high crime rate, the average adult (70 of every hundred persons) does not commit a crime. Moreover, while the area has a low median income and a high employment rate, this does not allow us to infer that the area residents commiting crimes are either poor or uneducated. The criminals may be drawn from the part of the area population which is not reflective of its central tendency. From this example, we can see the danger in making predictions about a particular individual residing in an ecological area. To do so constitutes the "ecological fallacy"—making inferences about the characteristics of individuals based upon the characteristics of a group.[13] Fortunately, however, sociologists are often more interested in focusing on the group than on its individual members. When describing an ecological area, one first seeks group tendencies which produce a composite overview. Later, if there is some significant social feature which requires further exploration, the researcher may attempt to differentiate the particular subgroup in which the action is taking place. Rarely does the urban researcher need to examine the behavior of individuals as individuals.

---

[12]A median is that point in a distribution between which an equal number of cases fall. For example, if an area has five families with annual incomes of $4,000, $5,000, $7,000, $10,000 and $11,000, the median is $7,000.

[13]W. S. Robinson, "Ecological Correlations and the Behavior of Individuals," *American Sociological Review,* 15, June (1950).

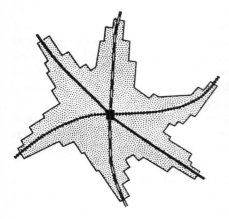

Figure 3.1 The Star Theory. *Ralph Thomilson, Urban Structure (New York: Random House, 1949), p. 143.)*

Major Ecological Models

The ecological models discussed here fall into four major categories: spatial, natural, social, and economic.[14] All four methods usually employ area typologies, which may be shown on maps. Each method also employs a different theoretical orientation, resulting not only in different explanations of the social process of different locales, but also in a set of area boundaries which vary substantially, depending upon the method employed.

Hurd's Star Theory

Probably the first theory of ecological process in the United States is attributed to R. M. Hurd (1903).[15] Known as the *star theory,* it suggests that a city grows from its center along its major transportation arteries, resulting in a star-shaped configuration (Figure 3.1). This form was most common to cities with streetcar, subway, or rail commuter lines, and seems to reflect the large city before the advent of freeways and other highways designed primarily for high speed communication by automobile. The population was concentrated within walking distance of the transportation routes, a pattern which is still manifest in cities with well-developed mass-transit systems. When cars became the predominant mode of travel, the spaces between the points of the star began to fill in, marking decreased reliance on public transportation.

---

[14]This typology is suggested in Ralph Thomlinson, *Urban Structure* (New York: Random House, 1969), p. 142.

[15]Richard M. Hurd, *Principles of City Land Values* (New York: Record and Guide, 1903).

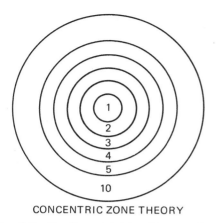

THREE GENERALIZATIONS OF THE
INTERNAL STRUCTURE OF CITIES

DISTRICT

1. Central business district
2. Wholesale light manufacturing
3. Low-class residential
4. Medium-class residential
5. High-class residential
6. Heavy manufacturing
7. Outlying business district
8. Residential suburb
9. Industrial suburb
10. Commuters' zone

CONCENTRIC ZONE THEORY

Figure 3.2   The Concentric-Zone Theory. *Chauncy D. Harris and Edward L. Ullman, "The Nature of Cities,"* Annals of the American Academy of Political and Social Science, *242 (November, 1945), p. 12.*

The Park Burgess Concentric Zone Theory

Best known in sociology is the *concentric zone hypothesis,* developed at the University of Chicago by Ernest Burgess and Robert Park during the 1920's.[16] Various ecologically-based social groups within the city were seen in terms of competition, conflict, assimilation, and accommodation with each other. This social process, according to Park and Burgess, could be located within five distinctive zones of land use, which take the form of concentric circles or ovals (Figure 3.2). Proceeding outward from the city's core, these zones are commonly named: (1) the central business district, (2) the zone-in-transition, (3) the zone of workingmens' homes, (4) the middle-class zone, and (5) the commuters' zone. Occasionally, two other zones are shown: (6) agricultural areas which are still within commuting distance, and (7) the hinterland.

The central business district (C.B.D.).   This innermost zone is the typical location of central banks, large department stores, specialty stores, restaurants, motion-picture theaters, and live theaters. Most of the employees of these enterprises live in outer areas, as do their patrons, who are largely visitors or commuters. This central zone is devoted principally to retail trade, business, recreation, and some light manufacturing. Very few people actually reside here. Those who do are predominently older persons without children.

The zone in transition.   Sometimes designated as a *wholesale and light-manufacturing zone,* the next outlying ring is most commonly referred to as the *zone*

---

[16]Ernest W. Burgess, "The Growth of the City," in Robert E. Park, Ernest W. Burgess, and Roderick D. McKenzie, *The City* (Chicago: University of Chicago Press, 1925).

in transition. Because the central business district is usually expanding outward, this area is constantly in a state of flux, pushing outward into the surrounding lower-class residential neighborhoods. The predominant land use pattern here is shifting from residential to commercial. Speculators and slumlords often deal in large blocks of land; holding them temporarily, providing a minimum of maintenance. Within a relatively short period, most of the buildings in this zone will be sold and bulldozed to make room for the expanding business district. Historically, the zone in transition has been a port of entry for lower-class minorities who have migrated to the cities. For example, areas which were populated originally by large concentrations of German immigrants experienced successive waves of Irish, Poles, Italians, blacks, and Puerto Ricans, as each group made its way outward into middle-class residential areas. This area is also the habitat of prostitutes, pimps, muggers, hustlers, and others involved in petty theft and robbery. Usually, in larger cities, the zone of transition also contains massage parlors and skidrows, some of which, like Manhattan's Bowery, are infamous throughout the world. Ironically, this zone often contains contrasting pockets of wealth and poverty. The most luxurious apartment complexes often co-exist with the most poverty-stricken slums and ghettos. Sociologists have found this area to be a good laboratory for research on social problems and social deviancy and alternative life-styles.[17]

The zone of workingmens' homes. Unlike the two innermost zones, which reveal a somewhat mixed land use pattern, the third is used almost exclusively for family housing. The quality of the housing, while still consisting mainly of detached homes, is better here than in the zone of transition, reflecting the blue-collar occupations of the owners. This area, too, contains ethnic ghettos. But in contrast to their counterparts in the innermost zones, these areas manifest far less turnover. It is not unusual for families to remain permanently in these ethnic neighborhoods, even after they have secured an income base which would easily permit a move to outlying middle-class zones.

The middle class zone. The fourth zone is populated mainly by white-collar workers—owners of small businesses, middle-management personnel, and some lower-paid professionals, such as teachers and policemen. The housing here is of the single-family detached variety. There are some hotels and apartment complexes, but these, too, are occupied by middle-class persons.

The commuters' zone. While still part of the functional urban area, the boundary of commuters' zone may be beyond the corporate limits of the older city's administrative and political boundaries. In Park and Burgess' time, the commuter zone was the exclusive province of the upper-middle and upper classes. Besides some of the older incorporated communities, the commuter zone now includes *suburbia,* which is made up of a mixture of unincorporated housing developments, ranging widely in original purchase price. The style of life here is based on the ownership of two or more cars. One is used to commute to the work place; the other

---

[17]The chapter on "The Neighborhood" lists additional studies conducted in the zone in transition.

is most typically a station-wagon used to transport children almost everywhere, because there is usually no public transportation, no walkable streets, and no bikepaths to take the mother–homemaker on numerous shopping trips and errands.

Ecological models like the concentric zone hypothesis are known as *gradient theories,* because they rest principally on plotting social phenomena according to the distance from a central point in an urban area. Park and Burgess showed that home ownership increased in each succeeding outlying zone, signifying a gradual increase in social class. They found also that there was a gradual decline in foreign-born population in each of the successive outlying zones. The zonal hypothesis provided the theoretical underpinning for many other studies which sought to explain social interaction as a by-product of distance from the urban center. Several of these studies which relate to social deviance, crime, and mental illness are discussed later in this chapter.

The Hoyt Sector Theory

A third spatial theory is known as the *sector theory.* Unlike the two preceding spatial theories (Hurd's star theory and the concentric zone hypothesis), the original study attempted to capture ecological change over a period of time.[18] Hoyt, a geographer, mapped data describing the high-rent areas of 142 American cities for three points in time—1900, 1915, and 1936. From these data, he visualized the typical American city as divisible into pie-shaped areas (Figure 3.3).

Hoyt's theory focuses on the growth and expansion of high-rent areas which, rather than forming a concentric zone, are found in the outer areas of one or more quadrants of a city (see Figure 3.3). A number of hypotheses about high-rent areas have been derived from observing the growth patterns of the 142 cities. First, these areas tend to expand or develop along well established transportation routes, toward other trade or building centers. Second, high-rent residential districts expand in a direction with no topographical or man-made barriers to growth, toward high ground or along waterfronts free of industrial development. Third, high-rent areas tend to expand in the direction of the homes of the community elite. Fourth, high-cost apartments usually appear near established business areas which are close to older residential areas. And fifth, high-rent areas are located adjacent to medium-rent areas. The growth of these neighborhoods continues in the same general direction for a period of thirty years or more.

Hoyt used the term *high-rent* synonomously with high mortgage value or assessed value of the housing unit. The sector hypotheses are not actually a theory, but rather comprise a series of principles abstracted from the data on the 142 cities. They do help to clarify the pattern of city growth and give valuable insights on emergence of one type of ecological patterns.

[18]Homer Hoyt, *The Structure and Growth of Urban Areas* (Washington, D.C.: Federal Housing Authority, 1939), pp. 112–122.

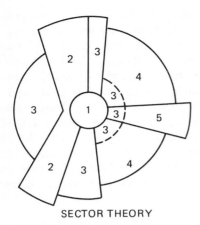

DISTRICT

1. Central business district
2. Wholesale light manufacturing
3. Low-class residential
4. Medium-class residential
5. High-class residential
6. Heavy manufacturing
7. Outlying business district
8. Residential suburb
9. Industrial suburb
10. Commuters' zone

SECTOR THEORY

Figure 3.3 The Sector Theory. *Chauncy D. Harris and Edward L. Ullman, "The Nature of Cities,"* The Annals of the American Academy, *242 (November, 1945).*

Harris and Ullman's Multiple-Nuclei Theory

All of the ecological theories previously discussed were gradient-oriented, in that they were based on the distance of various areas from a central location. Harris and Ullman's approach (1945), however, is based upon the fact that modern industrial cities usually develop several business centers, industrial centers, and residential centers (Figure 3.4).[19] Cities of previous eras did not have access to the transportation technology which makes the urban sprawl both possible and profitable. Harris and Ullman state four principles which form the crux of their theory. First, certain activities require special resources and are concentrated in areas where such resources are located. Heavy industry of a production-line variety requires large one-floor buildings and easy access to interstate highways and railroads. Such industries tend to cluster where these conditions are found. Second, similar activities benefit from close proximity to each other. Automobile dealers may profit from a location on an auto-row which draws customers from a wide area to compare and shop for cars. Third, some types of land use patterns are incompatible. High-class residential areas and industrial areas have needs which clash. Industrial areas require high-intensity transportation and are usually noisy and smoky. Residential areas, in contrast, should be as free of traffic, noise, and pollution as possible. Fourth, the high cost of land (or land rent) precludes some uses of high-cost locations. Land near the commercial center of a city is so expensive that only certain utilizations are economically feasible, usually high-rise office buildings, certain kinds of stores, and restaurants.

[19]Chauncy D. Harris and Edward L. Ullman, "The Nature of Cities," *The Annals of the American Academy of Political and Social Science,* 242, (November, 1945), pp. 7–17.

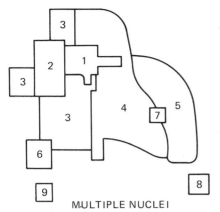

DISTRICT
1. Central business district
2. Wholesale light manufacturing
3. Low-class residential
4. Medium-class residential
5. High-class residential
6. Heavy manufacturing
7. Outlying business district
8. Residential suburb
9. Industrial suburb
10. Commuters' zone

MULTIPLE NUCLEI

Figure 3.4 The Harris and Ullman Multiple Nuclei Pattern. *Chauncy D. Harris and Edward L. Ullman, "The Nature of Cities,"* The Annals of the American Academy, *242, (November, 1945).*

All four of the theories discussed so far have resulted in generalizations concerning the growth of urban areas and the accompanying changes in land use patterns. The four theories are useful to the sociologist in explaining the social milieu of residential areas in particular. All four also lead to the conclusion that the primary determination of the differences in residential neighborhoods is the cost of land, which in turn reflects a dominant mode of transportation. Beyond these generalizations, the theories, by themselves, allow little more than speculation regarding the social fabric and life-styles which are unique to a particular zone or sector. Probably, these approaches are most useful for the sociologist in establishing a framework through which the social life of an area (or areas) may be compared, as a shift in the predominant pattern of land use occurs.

McKenzie's Ecological Processes

A sociological theory of changing land use was developed by McKenzie (1926).[20] Instead of focusing on configurations and shape of areas, McKenzie developed a typology of the various ecological processes, which in turn, manifest a significant impact on the social life of an area where a change occurs. Changes in a human population may all be traced to the demographic factors of births, deaths, and migration. While births and deaths have some effect on patterns of stability and change, in most cities, intra-city migration has historically had a far greater impact on the ecology of residential areas. McKenzie identified seven ecological processes which incorporate both notions of population shifts and changes in the dominant

[20]Roderick D. McKenzie, "The Scope of Human Ecology," in Ernest W. Burgess, ed., *The Urban Community* (Chicago: University of Chicago Press, 1926).

land use pattern. First is *concentration,* a trend toward greater human density in an area, for more people to congregate in the same space over time. This is a *centripetal* process. Second *deconcentration,* or a dispersal of a population over time, a *centrifugal* process. *Centralization* is the third process. This is the clustering of people around a central point, such as a business district or recreation area. This process differs from concentration in that people may be concentrated with no reference to a central point. Fourth, *decentralization* occurs when the same functions are fulfilled by several centralized locations rather than one. When goods like groceries and clothing become mass production items, it is no longer necessary to journey to a central location to be assured of quality. The development of outlying shopping areas usually marks a general decentralization process with respect to goods and services. Fifth is *segregation,* an increasing homogeniety of one type of people or land use within an area. Segregation, in this sense, may include an increase in the proportion of people of a single social strata, ethnic group, or occupational type. The concept of segregation also includes a lessening of mixed land usage (commercial and residential), *i.e.,* along a super highway—to the point where it is almost entirely devoted to fast-food restaurants and gas stations.

Invasion is the movement of one group or function into an area which had been dominated by a different group or function. Most planning and zoning conflicts revolve around a proposed change in the basic character of an area through the development of a new land use. Inner-city tensions are often exacerbated by the invasion of an ethnic group which is perceived by the original residents as threatening an established life-style. Finally, *succession* is the total change in the established group or land use in an area. In most urban communities, invasion and succession may be characterized as an ongoing cycle, with most zones or areas undergoing a gradual change as the larger urbanized area expands in size and population.

Although McKenzie's ecological processes are mainly intended to provide a comprehensive typology of the kinds of changes which may occur, this scheme interfaces well with each of the spatial theories presented previously. Park and Burgess' zone in transition captures the dynamism of invasion and succession, and the notion of expanding concentric zones.

The invasion process is evident in the expansion of Hoyt's high-rent sectors. McKenzie's decentralization notion is also implicit in the development of the multiple nuclei, each serving different populations (as hypothesized by Harris and Ullman). The evidence suggests that there are different methods of conceptualizing and bounding ecological areas, but irrespective of which techniques and assumptions are employed, the processes which produce change are essentially those enumerated by McKenzie.

Shevky, Bell, and Williams—Social Area Analysis

Since World War II, there has been only one major advance in ecological theory and methods, *social area analysis*. This is a social process theory, which is based on a set of assumptions concerning changes in life-styles and institutions which reflect changes in the degree of urbanization.

Shevky, Bell and Williams (1949, 1955) developed a comprehensive scheme for classifying urban areas in three dimensions: social rank, urbanization, and segregation.[21] The three dimensions were derived by a study of data from the 1940 Los Angeles federal census. The researchers analyzed a large number of characteristics tabulated for the city's several hundred census tracts (enumeration areas averaging 2,000 to 3,000 population). They employed an inductive statistical procedure known as *factor analysis,* a correlational technique which reduces a large number of variables to a smaller set of factors, each of which contains a number of the original variables.

Starting with several hundred variables ranging from average income per tract to the average age of the population per tract, Shevky *et al.* found three distinct sets of variables, from which they developed both a theory and a typology of urban areas. The *social rank* index is comprised of (a) an occupational ratio, based on the proportion of blue-collar workers in an area, and (b) an educational ratio, which indicates the proportion of adults who have completed less than seven years of schooling. The *segregation index* consists of the proportion of persons in an area who are foreign-born, black and non-white. The *urbanization index* is made up of (a) the fertility ratio of an area (number of children under 5 years per 1,000 females aged 15 through 44), (b) the ''women-in-the-labor-force ratio'' (the number of females in the areas labor force per 1,000 females 14 years and older), and (c) the ''single-family detached dwelling units ratio'' (the number of single-family houses per 1,000 dwelling units of all types.) The result of this procedure is that each area is assigned three indices which indicate its rank with respect to the overall area's socio-economic structure, its degree of segregation, and its level of urbanization.

The theoretical argument made by Shevky and Bell focuses on the changes in *scale* which take place during the development of an urban-industrial society. The steps in the formation of the social area index construction are shown in Figure 3.5.[22] Simply stated, during periods of urbanization, there are changes in the range and intensity of the functions performed by the labor force, which are gradually reflected in a declining proportion of manual laborers and an increased level of formal education (social rank). Secondly, there are changes in the function which the family and household perform as an economic production unit. These changes are monitored by the increased proportion of women in the labor force, a declining emphasis upon large families, and a tendency for an increasing proportion of adults to reside in apartments or living arrangements other than the traditional family home (urbanization). Finally, there is increasing complexity of social organization and

[21]Eshref Shevky and Marilyn Williams, *The Social Areas of Los Angeles* (Los Angeles: University of California Press, 1947). Also see Eshref Shevky and Wendell Bell, *Social Area Analysis* (Palo Alto, California: Stanford University Press, 1955).

[22]Shevky and Bell, *op. cit.,* p. 4.

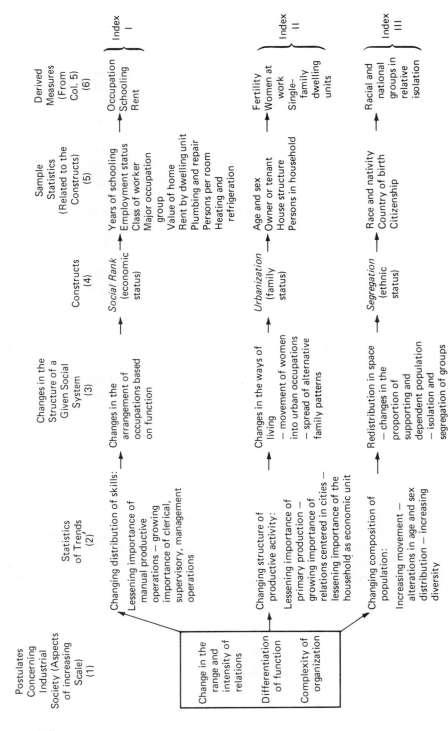

Figure 3.5 Social area analysis. *Eshref Shevky and Wendell Bell, Social Area Analysis (Palo Alto, California: Stanford University Press, 1955), p. 4.*

increasing heterogeniety, which produces residential clusters of persons of diverse origins (segregation).

The social area indices were conceptualized as monitoring signals that increases in *scale* are occurring. Scale, as used here, refers to changes in economic and social organization which are brought about by industrialization and which effect the ecology of urban areas. Whether social area analysis is comprehensive enough to be considered a general ecological method has been the subject of intensive debate for over two decades. The method is generally recognized, however, as the latest major contribution to established ecological theory.

Explorations in Social Area Analysis

Like most ecological techniques, social area analysis does not provide, by itself, an understanding of the social organization and life-styles of an ecological area. It is a valuable framework for testing hypotheses concerning the manner in which urbanization, segregation, or social rank relate to attitudes or social interaction patterns. Bell employed a social area analysis of four census tracts in San Francisco, chosen because each represented an extreme social area typology.[23] One area was low in both social rank and urbanization indices, an area populated by men who resided in inexpensive rooming houses. The second area was high in social rank, but high in urbanization, a high-cost apartment area, populated by small families and working women. The third area was relatively low in urbanization and below average in social rank, a neighborhood populated by families living in single houses and having lower-than-average incomes. The fourth tract was low in urbanization but high in social rank, made up of upper-middle-class families residing in large, single-family homes. Bell surveyed a large sample of male respondents, delving into frequency of contacts with neighbors and level of participation in clubs and organizations. Men in the two high social rank neighborhoods belonged to far more organizations and were more active participants than their counterparts in the two neighborhoods which were lower in social rank. In contrast, the neighborhoods low in urbanization (and high in family status) revealed far more informal contacts and friendly neighboring than the two higher-class areas.

A second study conducted by Scott Greer (1956) was carried out in neighborhoods which varied only in the degree of urbanization (but similar in social rank and integration indices.)[24] Greer found that the lower the degree of urbanization in an area, the higher was the degree of neighboring and social life centered around the locality. Areas highest in urbanization showed more of pessimism and negativism toward life in general. This study gives some evidence to the idea that urbanization, as defined in social area analysis, encompasses some of the attitudes and ways of life which Wirth alluded to in his seminal ideas in "Urbanism as a Way of Life."

Social area analysis, as its originators suggested, has proved to be a versatile typology upon which to build a body of theory and knowledge concerning ecological processes. Some of its specific applications and extensions may be found later in this chapter.

Beyond Social Area Analysis—Factorial Methods

Social area analysis was the by-product of what many sociologists would term *abstracted empiricism,* in that the theory appears to emerge from configurations of data rather than a test of an elaborate set of hypotheses conceived before collecting and analyzing the data.[25] The methodological technique which is often used to generate new theoretical notions is *factor analysis,* which identifies mathematicaly independent variable clusters within a large set of variables. A hundred or more variables may be reduced to three or more factors, each comprised of three or four variables. In ecological studies, this technique allows the researcher to analyze a lot of information about many areas at the same time and to identify several distinctive types of areas, without having to test all of the possible combinations of variables.[26] Once a researcher has identified a set of factors, a great ·deal of ingenuity and creativity is required to interpret the social process which the factors reflect.[27] Moreover, after a set of hypotheses has been produced by inspection of a data-set, they must be confirmed through an extensive test-retest process, whereby the theory is validated, shown to be reliable, and articulated in more detail.

Since American sociology is little more than half a century of age, most data on urbanization are limited to relatively young cities. The time span is very narrow when one considers the fact that cities first appeared on the earth more than 5,000 years ago. Generalizations about urbanism and theories of urbanization developed through the analysis of American cities are limited in validity until they can be compared with international data. A number of recently completed factorial studies of European and Asian cities permit us to make some ecological comparisons.

Berry and Rees conducted an extensive analysis of six cities across the world, including Calcutta and Chicago (1969).[28] Employing factorial techniques, they identified three ecological dimensions: socio-economic status, family-cycle stage, and minority group status. According to the degree of industrialization of the country or area, the three factors tended to be associated differently. In southern cities of the United States, ethnicity and socio-economic status were highly associated. Ecological areas populated by blacks were also typically at the low end of the socio-economic scale. Northern cities, in contrast, revealed a high degree of minority segregation, but the segregated areas were far more dispersed through the socio-

---

[23]Wendell Bell and Maryanne Force, "Urban Neighborhood Types and Participation in Formal Organizations," *American Sociological Review,* 21, (February, 1956). Also see Wendell Bell, "Anomie, Social Isolation and Class Structure," *Sociometry,* 20, (June, 1957).

[24]Scott Greer, "Urbanism Reconsidered, a Comparative Study of Local Areas in a Metropolis," *American Sociological Review,* 21, (February, 1956).

[25]C. Wright Mills, *The Sociological Imagination* (New York: Grove Press, 1959), pp. 50–75.

[26]For a discussion of factor analysis as used in sociology, see Hubert M. Blalock, *Social Statistics* (New York: McGraw-Hill, 1960), pp. 383–391.

[27]It is not obvious that the three ratios making up the urbanization index in social area analysis (fertility, women in the labor force, and single family detached dwelling units) are related directly to a theory of urbanization.

[28]Brian J. L. Berry and Phillip H. Rees, "The Factorial Ecology of Calcutta," *American Journal of Sociology,* 74, (March, 1969).

economic strata. One of the most important contributions of Berry and Rees is the identification of family life-cycle stage as a determinant of urban ecology. Families with children tend to congregate in certain areas, as do childless households and elderly people. Life-cycle state, viewed in this sense, is at least as important as socio-economic status in the explanation of residential areas.

Cairo is the subject of an extensive factorial study completed by Abu-Lughod (1971).[29] This study provides a particularly important comparison with American work, since Cairo is an ancient, pre-industrial city now passing through a period of modernization. Abu-Lughod found three principal factors which statistically differentiated the areas of this city—life-style, settlements of unattached, migrant males, and social pathology. Life-styles, according to Abu-Lughod, incorporates both socio-economic status and the degree of familism. (These two factors, in the Cairo study, are not statistically separable). Those who reside in high-status areas have a kind of Westernized culture and life-style, stressing delayed marriage, low birth rate and emphasis on higher education for women. In contrast, low-status areas manifest a more traditional family style characterized by overcrowded housing, illiteracy, and a female role which stresses early marriage, high fertility, and child-rearing, to the exclusion of higher education and entry into the labor force.

In terms of life-style, Cairo revealed thirteen sub-cities, each of which had vastly different population distributions, housing types, business enterprises, dress patterns, and probably different belief systems. Surrounding the city was a band of migrants, whose life-style differs little from that of the primitive industrial villages of the Middle East. There was also a traditional urban slum population in Cairo, whose precarious subsistence and subculture resembled the stereotypic Cairo of a century ago.

The latest ecological technique to emerge from factor analysis has been developed by the National Institute of Mental Health.[30] This new procedure has resulted in over 100 social area indices based on readily available census data. The National Institute of Mental Health has calculated these indices for every census tract in the United States, employing data collected in the 1970 population census. Although efforts to employ these indices in basic research is in a relatively early stage, the availability of this data-base should spur increasing utilization of social area analysis in policy research and program evaluation.

Economic Theories of Ecology

Economists are not usually concerned with ecology per se; they are more concerned with geographical location and cost. For the economist, ecological area may be

---

[29]Janet Abu-Lughod, *Cario: 1001 Yers of the City Victorious* (Princeton, N.J.: Princeton University Press, 1971).
[30]Harold F. Goldsmith, Elizabeth L. Unger, Beatrice M. Rosen, J. Phillip Shambaugh, and Charles D. Windle, "A Typological Approach to Doing Social Area Analysis," D.H.E.W. Publication, No. (ADM) 76-262 (Washington, D.C.: United States Government Printing Office, 1975).

translated into "market area," but the resulting generalizations may be similar to sociological models, in that they focus on land use patterns. Most economic models assume that locational decisions are made through an optimization process, whereby many factors are brought into play. Considering the development of a local ecology, business or residential site selection may be conceptualized in terms of certain postulates developed by the German economist Von Thunen over a century ago.[31]

Von Thunen asked the reader to imagine the existence of a single city in the center of a fertile, flat plain. The plain is surrounded by a wilderness and contains no navigable rivers. Under these controlled conditions, he showed that products having high transportation costs (fruits, vegetables, and milk) tend to be produced nearest the city. Products are produced in concentric zones, with the products having the cheapest transportation cost being produced in the outermost rings. Land nearest to the city was shown to have a relatively high cost, a function of lower production and transport costs.

Von Thunen's approach can readily be extended to explain ecological form and density.[32] The central business district or ecological center of a city replaces the city in the plain; the surrounding areas are used for residential and other non-agricultural purposes. Since the central point is the point of maximum accessibility to all parts of the city, producers located here can benefit most from low transportation costs. The competition for land in the central zone results in a concentration of land users who have both small space requirements and high transportation costs. The central area is also important for households, in that it is a place of high employment density and an area where many goods and services are sold. From most outlying areas, the cost of transporting people or goods to the center is extremely low. Thus, households with large transportation costs (relative to total budget) or small space needs tend to locate near the center. In Von Thunen's model, then, two locations which have the same use will differ in land cost, primarily because of differences in the transportation costs.

Recent Economic Models—Alonso, Muth, and Siegel

Three economists (Alonso, Muth, and Siegel) view location selection as a "utility maximization procedure constrained by income."[33] According to the Alonso model, when the costs of goods other than housing is constant, the housing decision is a kind of trade-off between the amount of land and the distance from the central location, since commuting costs increase with distance. As family income increases, more of everything is consumed, *e.g.,* both land and transportation services. But people who desire larger lots will move further out anyway, since land cost is lower in the outer areas.[34]

---

[31]Johann H. von Thunen, *Der Isolirte Staat in Beziehung auf National o Konomie und Landwirtschaft,* (Stuttgart: Gustav Fischer, 1966).

[32]Werner Z. Hirsch, *Urban Economic Analysis* (New York: McGraw-Hill, 1972), pp. 52–53.

[33]For a discussion of these theories see Hirsch, *op. cit.,* pp. 54–57.

[34]William Alonso, *Location and Land Use* (Cambridge, Mass: Harvard University Press, 1964).

The Muth model (1969) incorporates the same variables of distance and cost, but suggests that income differences raise the amount saved on land in the periphery to a proportionally higher rate than the increased commuting costs.[35] The inference is that those with higher incomes are in a position to buy more desirable outlying property, because the cost of commuting increases at a slow rate, while the price of land decreases relatively fast in successive outlying areas.

The Siegel (1970) approach involves the Von Thunen notions of time and distance, but includes other factors including accessibility, environmental quality (including the social stratification of the area), the nature and quality of public services available, and aesthetic qualities. A "rational" person chooses housing which maximizes the utility of not only land and transportation costs, but of these additional social and environmental factors as well.[36]

Like many of the ecological theories developed by sociologists, the locational theories offered by economists are based on a limited number of factors which explain and predict the manner in which land-use patterns are shaped. Although major ecological theories from both disciplines perform this function reasonably well, neither incorporates a sufficient number of variables to give specific explanations of life-style and social interaction at the local neighborhood level.

Ecology in Action—The Analysis of Social Problems

The University of Chicago studies emerged from a concern about the social problems of the city.[37] One of the obvious by-products of mapping the social problems of urban neighborhoods was the capability of resource management, of being able to direct and concentrate services where the problems are most intense. Social pathologies, like crime and suicide, are invariably concentrated in certain ecological areas. The basic ecological theories, reviewed earlier, provide a base for the development of more specialized theories of deviance and control. Sociologists have been involved in analyzing the ecology of social problems in most cities. Much of this work, however, is "journeyman" in style and does not find its way into the mainstream of sociological literature, but many of the major advances in theory have evolved from studies which initially had a simple fact-finding thrust.

The Ecology of Social Deviance

Building on the Park-Burgess concentric zone theory, Walter Reckless conducted an ecological analysis of commercialized vice in Chicago (1926, 1933). Using a *natural area* approach, Reckless found "... that both crime and vice depend upon

[35]Richard F. Muth, *Cities and Housing* (Chicago: University of Chicago Press, 1967).

[36]Jay Siegel, "Intrametropolitan Migration of Minority and White Households," (Stanford, California: Stanford University Press, 1970), as discussed in Hirsch, *op. cit.*, pp. 54–57.

[37]See the chapter on neighborhoods for a complete bibliography of the Chicago studies.

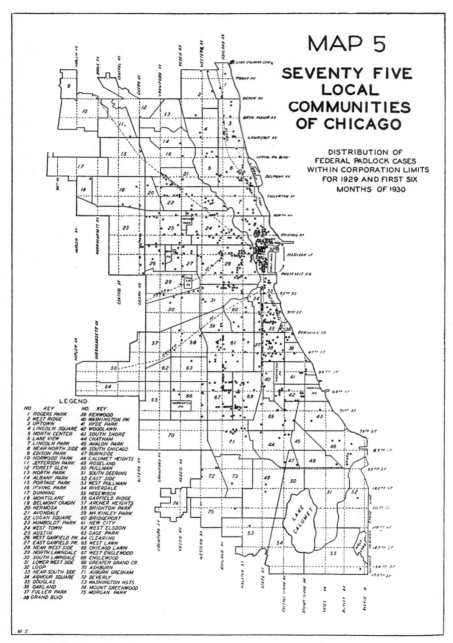

Figure 3.6 *Walter Reckless,* Vice in Chicago *(University of Chicago Press, 1933).*

mobility and collections of people; both forms of activity are legally and morally isolated and must hide in disorganized neighborhoods in order to thrive."[38] Also concentrated in the same natural areas was a high incidence of poverty, divorce, dissertion, suicide, abandoned infants, and suicide. Ecologically, these neighborhoods evidenced a high degree of social disorganization, which Reckless believed was the main cause of these social pathologies. This disorganization was attributed to high level of residential turn-over, preventing the development of an organized social structure. Thus, Reckless' vice areas corresponded with the *zone of transition* in the concentric zone theory. One measure of this disorganization was the ecological distribution of "federal padlock cases," which represented business establishments which were shut down because of violations of the federal alcoholic beverage prohibition (Figure 3.6). Crime and vice were seen as resulting primarily from the urbanization of Chicago including:

> The decline of the old form of community life, the decay of neighborhoods, the problems of adjustment of incoming peoples without families, Negroes and immigrants from abroad, the development of transportation facilities, including the automobile, the changes in the status of women, the development of mechanized living conditions in apartments, the growth of leisure and the declining influence of neighborhood.[39]

Crime and vice were not viewed as a direct result of poverty; rather, they were related to the social disorganization brought about as a result of "urbanization as a way of life."

Earlier theories of criminal ecology, like Reckless' analysis of vice, were mainly variants of the gradient hypotheses, grounded in plotting crimes in terms of distance from a central point in the city. Shaw and McKay (1942) continued in the Park-Burgess tradition, focusing on the innermost zones of the city (Figure 3.7).[40] Basing their analysis on juvenile court referrals, Shaw and McKay showed that the same areas retained the highest delinquency rates for three successive decades (1900–1933). Delinquency was attributed to *cultural transmission,* to learning a set of divisive values, a point of view which persisted in the same ecological areas despite the departure or death of the original residents. This cultural conflict was attributed to the economic marginality of the people who resided in the zone of transition.

Factorial ecology has also been applied in the study of delinquency. A well known study of delinquency in Baltimore (Lander, 1954) provided a fundamental challenge to studies employing a gradient hypothesis.[41] Lander concluded that delinquency was related to a pattern of ecological disorganization and anomie. More-

---

[38]Walter C. Reckless, "The Distribution of Commercialized Vice in the City," *Publications of the American Sociological Society,* XX, 1926, pp. 164–176. Also see Walter C. Reckless, *Vice in Chicago* (Chicago: University of Chicago Press, 1933).

[39] Reckless, *op. cit.,* p. 271.

[40]Clifford R. Shaw and Henry D. McKay, *Juvenile Delinquency and Urban Areas* (Chicago: University of Chicago Press, 1942).

[41]Bernard Lander, *Towards an Understanding of Juvenile Delinquency* (New York: Columbia University Press, 1954).

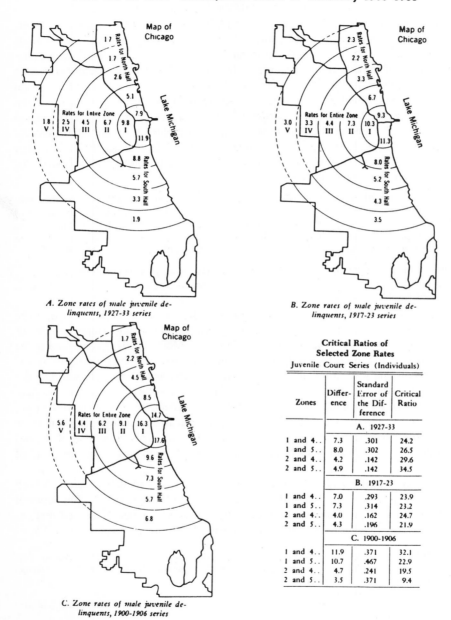

A. Zone rates of male juvenile delinquents, 1927-33 series

B. Zone rates of male juvenile delinquents, 1917-23 series

C. Zone rates of male juvenile delinquents, 1900-1906 series

Critical Ratios of Selected Zone Rates

Juvenile Court Series (Individuals)

Zones	Differ- ence	Standard Error of the Dif- ference	Critical Ratio
	A. 1927-33		
1 and 4..	7.3	.301	24.2
1 and 5..	8.0	.302	26.5
2 and 4..	4.2	.142	29.6
2 and 5..	4.9	.142	34.5
	B. 1917-23		
1 and 4..	7.0	.293	23.9
1 and 5..	7.3	.314	23.2
2 and 4..	4.0	.162	24.7
2 and 5..	4.3	.196	21.9
	C. 1900-1906		
1 and 4..	11.9	.371	32.1
1 and 5..	10.7	.467	22.9
2 and 4..	4.7	.241	19.5
2 and 5..	3.5	.371	9.4

Figure 3.7 Delinquency zones of Chicago. *Clifford Shaw and Henry McKay,* Juvenile Delinquency in Urban Areas *(Chicago: University of Chicago Press, 1942.)*

over, he asserted that juvenile crime was not strongly associated with either a gradient pattern or with poverty concentrations. Rather, the areas with the highest incidence of delinquency were those characterized by racial heterogeniety and a low proportion of home ownership. As an area approached a racial mixture of fifty percent whites and fifty percent blacks, the social structure of the area apparently was subjected to disorganization and anomie, (which was also reflected in the low level of home ownership and the high rate of delinquency.) Areas revealing these characteristics were not necessarily in a zone in transition or close to heavy industry, but were scattered throughout the inner city. Several critiques of the Lander study (Gordon, 1967; Bordua, 1959; Chilton, 1964) dispute Lander's findings, contending that factors such as poverty, overcrowded and substandard housing are more highly associated with delinquency than social disorganization.[42] In sum, studies of the ecology of delinquency tend to indicate that the most accurate theories take both social deprivation and social disorganization into account.

Mental illness also manifests an ecological pattern which suggests a clear linkage with the neighborhood environment. It is difficult to estimate the true prevalence of pathologies, such as crime and mental illness, which remain partially hidden from view. In the case of mental illness, estimates of frequency are usually made from admissions to mental health programs. In the case of crime, estimates of the actual crime rate are based on the number of crimes known to the police. Dunham (1937) was one of the first American sociologists to study the ecology of mental illness.[43] Basing his study in Chicago, Dunham compared the hospital admissions for schizophrenia with those for manic-depressive psychosis during the years 1922–1934 (Figure 3.8). The highest rates of schizophrenia were concentrated in the central zones of Chicago (the same areas which exhibited the highest prevalence of vice in the Reckless study and delinquency in the Shaw and McKay study.) In contrast, the highest concentrations of manic-depressive psychosis were found scattered throughout the community, revealing no relationship to a central point. While the Dunham study did not provide an explanation for this distribution, later researchers (*e.g.*, Hollingshead and Redlich, 1958) attributed this pattern to the fact that schizophrenia is more predominant in the lower social strata, while manic-depressive psychosis is more common among members of the middle and upper classes.[44] These differences, according to Hollingshead and Redlich, are attributable to the differential stresses in different parts of the social strata, differing attitudes about acting out symptoms of mental illness, as well as different attitudes toward mental illness as a treatable disease, and differing diagnoses by the medical profes-

[42]Robert A. Gordon, "Issues in the Ecological Study of Delinquency," *American Sociological Review*, 32, No. 6, (December, 1967), pp. 927–944. Also see David J. Bordua, "Juvenile Delinquency and Anomie," *Social Problems*, 6, (1958–59) pp. 230–38; and Roland J. Chilton, "Discontinuity in Delinquency Area Research," *American Sociological Review*, 29, (February, 1964), pp. 71–83.

[43]H. Warren Dunham, "The Ecology of Functional Psychoses in Chicago," *American Sociological Review*, II, (August, 1937), pp. 467–79.

[44]August B. Hollingshead and Frederick C. Redlich, *Social Class and Mental Illness* (New York: John Wiley and Sons, 1958).

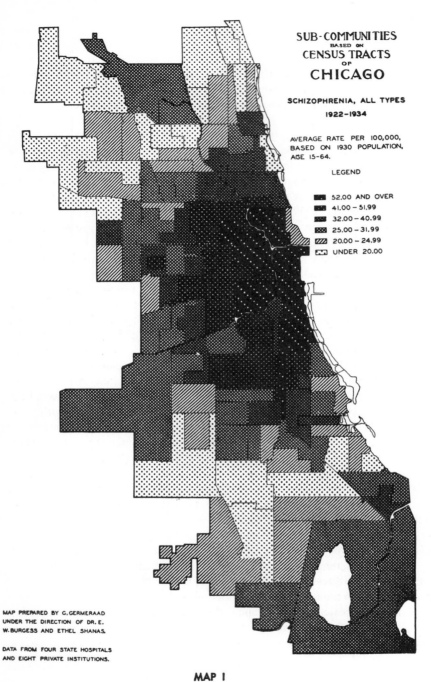

SUB-COMMUNITIES
BASED ON
CENSUS TRACTS
OF
CHICAGO

SCHIZOPHRENIA, ALL TYPES
1922-1934

AVERAGE RATE PER 100,000,
BASED ON 1930 POPULATION,
AGE 15-64.

LEGEND

52.00 AND OVER
41.00 – 51.99
32.00 – 40.99
25.00 – 31.99
20.00 – 24.99
UNDER 20.00

MAP PREPARED BY G. GERMERAAD
UNDER THE DIRECTION OF DR. E.
W. BURGESS AND ETHEL SHANAS.

DATA FROM FOUR STATE HOSPITALS
AND EIGHT PRIVATE INSTITUTIONS.

MAP I

Figure 3.8

60

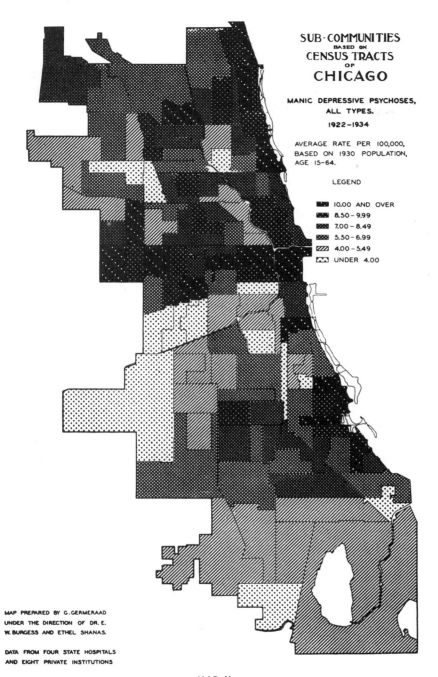

SUB-COMMUNITIES
BASED ON
CENSUS TRACTS
OF
CHICAGO

MANIC DEPRESSIVE PSYCHOSES,
ALL TYPES.
1922-1934

AVERAGE RATE PER 100,000,
BASED ON 1930 POPULATION,
AGE 15-64.

LEGEND

10.00 AND OVER
8.50 - 9.99
7.00 - 8.49
5.50 - 6.99
4.00 - 5.49
UNDER 4.00

MAP PREPARED BY G. GERMERAAD
UNDER THE DIRECTION OF DR. E.
W. BURGESS AND ETHEL SHANAS.

DATA FROM FOUR STATE HOSPITALS
AND EIGHT PRIVATE INSTITUTIONS

MAP II

Figure 3.8 *Warren H. Dunham, "The Ecology of Functional Psychoses in Chicago,"* American Sociological Review, *August, 1934.*

sion, according to the social class of the patient.[45] In other words, the differences in the distribution of the two kinds of mental illness may be primarily the result of attitudes and subcultures of both the patient community and the medical community.

Critiques of Classical Urban Ecology

Most urban ecological theory is still based on Wirth's factors of urbanization: size, density, and heterogeneity. Criticisms of urban ecology generally attack this conceptualization in two ways. According to some, changes in size, density, and heterogeneity of population do not lead to the fragmentation and disorganization of social life which Wirth described. Others argue that the theory does not go far enough. It explains the obvious, but does not account for the subcultures and lifestyles of various neighborhoods and subgroups within the urban areas.[46]

In a reaction to the "economic ecology" of the Chicago school (which emphasized the cost of land in locational decisions), Firey (1945) maintained that "sentiment and symbolism" should be construed as ecological variables.[47] In a classical study of land use in central Boston, he showed that certain areas maintained a certain character, despite invasions and successions which had long since altered the character of the other areas within the same radius of the city's center. The three areas which Firey studied were: Beacon Hill, which has for over two centuries persisted as an upper-class neighborhood; the Boston Common, which has remained a historic shrine and city park since the founding of Boston; and a lower class area known as the North End.

Firey wrote, "Beacon Hill has for fully a century and a half maintained its character as a preferred upper-class residential district, despite its contiguity to a low-rent tenement area, the West End. During its long history, Beacon Hill has become the symbol for a number of sentimental associations which constitute a genuine attractive force to certain old families of Boston."[48] The Boston Common, to Firey, also represents another example of spatial symbolism. The Common has become a "sacred" object, articulating and symbolizing genuine historical sentiments of a certain portion of the community. Like all such objects, its sacredness derives, not from any intrinsic spatial attributes, but rather from its representation in peoples' minds as symbolic of collective sentiments." The third area, the North End, is an Italian ghetto which retained its high proportion of "native-born" Italians over the years. Residence within a ghetto, Firey contended, ". . . is more than a matter of spatial placement; it generally signifies acceptance of immigrant values and participation in social institutions."[49]

[45]*Ibid.*, pp. 300–303.

[46]See, for example, Scott Greer and Ella Kube, "Urbanism and Social Structure," in Marvin B. Sussman, ed., *Community of Structure and Analysis* (New York: Thomas Y. Crowell Co., 1969), pp. 93–112.

[47]Walter Firey, "Sentiment and Symbolism as Ecological Variables," *American Sociological Review*, X, (April, 1945), pp. 140–148.

[48]*Ibid.*, pp. 140–143.

[49]*Ibid.*, p. 144.

Louisburg Square in Beacon Hill area, Boston, Massachusetts. One of Boston's loveliest and most historic streets. It is noted for its interesting red brick bow front homes, its cobblestone streets and gas lights. Many prominent Bostonians are residents of the area and maintain it as a private park. (*Massachusetts Department of Commerce and Development.*)

Wirth's theory of urbanization was also criticized by Gans (1962).[50] Noting that a number of changes had taken place since Wirth's time, most notably the great exodus of middle-class whites from the city to the suburbs, and the decentralization of industry, a number of specific criticisms were raised: First, Wirth failed to distinguish the ways of city life from those of other areas in the mass society. The city, in many instances, no longer receives the brunt of disruptions brought about by technological and social shifts. Second, Wirth's characterization of the "impersonal, segmental, superficial, transitory and often predatory" way of life applies principally for certain areas of the inner city, not the city as a whole. Third, there is insufficient evidence to prove that size, density, and heterogeneity result in the adverse social consequences which Wirth suggested. Wirth's formulation ignores the fact that (the inner city) population consists mainly of relatively homogeneous groups, with social and cultural moorings that shield it fairly effectively from the suggested consequences of number, density and heterogeneity.[51] Instead, Gans suggests that the inner city is typically comprised of five types which exhibit different "social and cultural moorings." The first type is *cosmopolites,* including students, artists, writers, musicians, entertainers, and others who need to be near

[50]Herbert J. Gans, "Urbanism and Suburbanism as Ways of Life," in Arnold Rose, ed., *Human Behavior and Social Process* (Boston: Houghton Mifflin, 1962), pp. 625–48.

[51]*Ibid.,* pp. 625–628.

certain cultural facilities. The second group is the temporarily *unmarried* or *childless,* who will reside in the inner city for a relatively short time. *Ethnic villagers,* who still follow a life-style similar to that of the small European village comprise the third group. The *deprived* population, which is poverty-stricken or handicapped by illness or lack of skills is fourth, and the *trapped,* who remain behind after an area changes because they cannot afford to move out or are otherwise trapped, are the fifth group.[52] Thus, Gans's interpretation of the ecological configuration of the inner city is based mainly on life-cycle stage, persisting ethnic subcultures, and economic mechanisms which cause people to be trapped or downwardly mobile. This typology also has the capacity of expansion into other areas of the city and into the suburbs. Gans's work on a suburb (1967) and in an Italian neighborhood (1962) are two excellent examples of the socio-cultural approach to the ecology of the urban area.[53]

Conclusion

We began this chapter by discussing four ecological approaches: spatial, natural, social, and economic. To these should probably be added the *symbolic* (Firey) and the *socio-cultural* (Gans). All of these theories have developed gradually, in response to the inadequacies of previous approaches. Each method still finds application, depending upon the problem investigated. However, when we aspire to a complete explanation, both spatial ecology and socio-cultural factors are important in gaining understanding. The sociologist of the second half of the twentieth century, whether studying the ecology of crime, or mental illness, or the general dynamics of an urban community, may be tempted to rely on statistical reasoning alone. But to explain the meaning of social process and social structure in an ecological context, he, like his predecessors, must gain a command of local history and an understanding of the socio-cultural tradition of the neighborhood.

[52]*Ibid.,* pp. 626–630.
[53]Herbert J. Gans, *The Levittowners* (New York: Random House, 1969), also Gans, *The Urban Villagers* (New York: The Free Press, 1962).

chapter 4

Urban Social Stratification

Any city dweller can tell you something about a person if you tell him where this person lives in the city. What he tells you may not be entirely accurate or in much detail, but if he has lived in his city for any length of time, he has probably formed an impression about different parts of the city, maybe only to the extent of wondering whether or not he would like to live there. Neighborhoods have their reputations and people have aspirations about their social standing. The sensitive real estate salesman, therefore, must determine early in his negotiations with prospective clients if the customer is looking for a "status move" or a "good buy." If the customer is looking for a status move, the agent can reasonably conclude that he is buying into a particular neighborhood. He might well be willing to pay more for a house in that neighborhood than for the same kind of house in another less prestigious neighborhood. If the customer is looking for a "good buy," however, he is apt to want the most house for his money with residential considerations of considerably less importance.[1]

The residential patterns of a city reflect imperfectly, but often dramatically its class structure. The urban mosaic of richly varying life-styles is not simply randomly laid out. It is patterned roughly according to the economic resources available to particular groups of people. In this chapter, we are interested in the way the social structure of a city is organized around various systems of social ranking, the most common of which is based on an assessment of economic resources.

A social class can be defined as a large group of people who share similar

[1]Richard P. Coleman and Bernice Neugarten, *Social Studies in the City* (San Francisco: Josey-Bass, 1971).

life-styles because they enjoy similar life changes in the economy of a society.[2] Indeed, in our large cities where most people are strangers to one another, economic cues (such as the neighborhood that they can afford to live in) assume much greater importance than in small towns or close-knit neighborhoods, where persons know one another well.

In this chapter, we will look at the city as a stratified or layered aggregate of people in which social ranking is a pervasive aspect of everyday life. What can we say about how such ranking takes place in our cities? What are some of the practical consequences of such ranking for the life-styles of persons in different classes? Are our cities helping us become more or less of a nation of average persons.

Social Class and Urban Neighborhoods

We can describe cities in terms of spatial configurations of life-styles that reflect economic resources, because certain locations in urban areas are more desirable than others. People try to live in the neighborhood they can afford. Why they are more or less desirable is a function of a whole host of factors such as ethnic preferences, home size, accessibility, and proximity to desirable physical features of the landscape. Brian Berry makes the following generalizations about the association of life-styles with particular urban areas:

> . . . High-status neighborhoods seek out zones of superior residential amenity near water, trees, and higher ground, free from the risk of floods and away from smoke and factories, and increasingly in the furthest accessible peripheries. Middle-status neighborhoods press as close to the high-status as feasible. To the low-status resident, least able to afford costs of commuting, are relinquished the least desirable areas adjacent to industrial zones, radiating from the center of the city along railroads and rivers, zones of highest pollutions, and the oldest, most deteriorated homes. From these areas the poor, too, aspire to depart, and are now doing so in increasing numbers, leaving behind widening zones of housing abandonment in the hearts of the central cities.[3]

Clearly we can find exceptions to such generalizations. Boston's Beacon Hill straddles the oldest part of the city and is surrounded by otherwise undesirable housing. It exists because of the Boston "Brahmin's" strong identification with the historic past and his sense of roots in the colonial buildings. Philadelphia also has succeeded in restoring portions of its colonial heritage in Center City and Society Hill. Other things besides simple spatial location account for the desirability of a

---

[2]The terms *social class* and *social status* are often used interchangeably or in conjunction as in *status-class*. It is useful, however, to distinguish, after Weber, between class ranking based on economic resources and status ranking based on prestige. Individuals may be ranked differently along each dimension in complex urban societies leading to what Gehard Lenski has called the problem of *status crystallization*, discussed later in this chapter.

[3]Brian J. L. Berry, *The Human Consequences of Urbanization* (New York: St. Martin's Press, 1973), p. 51.

neighborhood. Yet we cannot, thereby, discount spatial location as meaningless. It may enhance the desirability of a neighborhood or diminish it. It is rarely neutral. Neighborhoods tend to retain their distinctive reputation as desirable or undesirable.

Ranking in Locations and Locales

The typical urbanite not only ranks neighborhoods in terms of their desirability, he tends to infer the rank of people from the neighborhoods they live in. When he does not know the neighborhood, he uses other cues to assign people to a place. Anslem Strauss distinguishes between two types of urban areas: *locations* and *locales*.[4] In urban locations, people know each other by name, and have some recollection of each other's family history. Here, social ranking can take on fine shades of meaning. Locales are places in the city such as Fifth Avenue in New York or Rush Street in Chicago where people encounter each other as strangers. Indeed, people congregate in these areas in order to enjoy the scene and wonder at the different kinds of people that can be seen there. In such impersonal presentations of self, the signs of affluence or lack thereof, are much more important cues for social interaction than they are in locations. Locations tend to be made up of people with similar economic backgrounds in the first place.

New suburbs provide yet another kind of environment in which ranking occurs because here people do not know each other well, and yet they have reason to believe that they have similar economic resources because they can afford to live in the same neighborhood. Here too, economic cues are very important because they are visible and impersonal. Dress, house, car, and the kind of care given to a front lawn suggest much about a person's resources and economic rank.

The extent to which ranking varies with the extent of knowledge about the person being ranked is well illustrated in the case of Young and Willmott's study of the transition from the London neighborhood called Bethnal Green to the new town of Greenleigh.[5] In Bethnal Green, neighbors knew a great deal about each other. The history of families faded back into antiquity. The kinship networks were extensive and supportive. Neighboring was commonplace. After World War II, many persons moved from Bethnal Green to the new town of Greenleigh, giving the common explanation of, "It's good for the kiddies." The move to Greenleigh disrupted the neighboring patterns, and families who had become accustomed to being surrounded by friends found themselves surrounded by strangers.

In this new situation, the daily pattern of neighboring broke down and people kept to themselves. Importance in the community could not be assumed any longer; it was constantly being negotiated. The basis of this negotiation, at least in the early years of Greenleigh, was an evaluation of the home and property owned by families,

[4]Anselm Strauss, *Images of the American City* (New York: The Free Press, 1961), p. 66.
[5]Michael Young and Peter Willmott, *Family and Kinship in East London* (Baltimore: Penguin Books, 1957).

rather than upon the personal characteristics of family members. Comparing those who stayed behind in Bethnal Green with the persons who moved to Greenleigh, the authors observe:

> ... Bethnal Greeners are not, as we see it, concerned to any marked extent with what is usually thought of as "status." It is true, of course, that people have different incomes, different kinds of jobs, different kinds of houses—in this respect there is much less uniformity than at Greenleigh—even in different standards of education. But these attributes are not so important in evaluating others. It is personal characteristics which matter. The first thing they think of about Bert is not that he has a "fridge" and a car. They see him as bad-tempered, or a real good sport, or the man with a way with women, or one of the best boxers of the Repton Club, or the person who got married to Ada last year. In a community of long standing, status, in so far as it is determined by job and income and education, is more or less irrelevant to a person's worth. He is judged instead, if he is jduged at all, more in the round, as a person.[6]

Without these personal assessments, people in Greenleigh become highly anxious about whether or not they fit in.

> People are not very friendly here. It's the same on all the estates. They've nothing else to do when they've finished work except watch you. It's all jealousy. They're afraid you'll get a penny more than they have. In London, people have other things to occupy their minds. Here, when they've done their work, they've nothing to do. They're at the window and notice everything. They say, "Mrs. Brown's got a new hat on." They don't miss anything. I think the trouble is they've never been used to a nice house. When they come from London they think they're high and mighty. If you've got something, they'll go into debt to get it themselves.[7]

Possessions as a means of putting people in their place in Greenleigh were reflected in the habit of watching people move in. All eyes assessed the value of the furniture as the movers paraded from the van to the new house.

It is evident that you cannot deal with strangers in the same manner as you deal with intimates. Few people have the ability to let their hair down in public. In large cities, most people must deal with each other as strangers. Many of the exchanges they make with others, therefore, are impersonal, calculated, and rational in a narrow sense of the term. Simmel saw the cause of this impersonality of the cities somewhat differently, but he describes the city in terms similar to the description of Greenleigh. The deepest problems of modern life derive from the claim of the individual to preserve the autonomy and the individuality of his existence in the face of overwhelming social forces, of historical heritage, of external culture, and of the technique of life.

> ... The metropolis has always been the seat of the money economy. Here, the multiplicity and concentration of economic exchange gives an importance to the means of economic exchange which the scantiness of rural commerce would not have allowed. Money economy and the dominance of the intellect are intrinsically connected. ... The intellectually sophisticated person is indifferent to all genuine individuality because

[6]*Ibid.*, p. 161.
[7]*Ibid.*, p. 160.

relationships and reactions result from it which cannot be exhausted with logical operations. In the same manner, the individuality of phenomena is not commensurate with the pecuniary principle.

Money is concerned only with what is common to all; it asks for the exchange value, it reduces all quality and individuality to the question: How much? All intimate emotional relations between persons are founded in their individuality, whereas in rational relations a man is reckoned with like a number, like an element which is in itself indifferent. Only the objective measurable achievement is of interest.[8]

Ranking others into social classes, whatever the origin of the motivation, serves as a means of reducing uncertainty in the interpersonal environment.[9] A quick assessment of the social rank of another person who approaches you on the street enables the exchange, however brief, to proceed with less stress than if the other were totally unknown. In historic communities within large metropolises, such as Bethnal Green in London, such information is not needed, but when the Bethnal Greener leaves his borough and moves about in greater London, his ability to discern status and class cues is a means of putting him at some ease in a relatively unfamiliar environment.

Form and Stone conducted an interesting study of social ranking in Lansing, Michigan, a city of 100,000 persons and concluded that . . .

The bestowal of status in the city is often an inference from symbolism to social position; in the small town the bestowal of status proceeds from the evaluation of rights and duties appropriate to social position, and the relevant symbolism is basically symptomatic.[10]

Respondents in Lansing were asked how they would recognize members of four social categories ("high society," "middle-class," "working-class," and "down-and-outers") in the anonymity of the central business district, either on the street or in a department store. Informants from the lower stratum tended to use class symbolism to distinguish strata; middle-stratum persons tended to use status symbolism; those from the higher strata even more consistently employed status symbolism to describe other strata. Informants from all categories used class symbolism to describe "down-and-outers." "Lower-stratum informants were able to identify 'high society' with greatest facility; middle-stratum informants, the 'working-class'; and upper-stratum respondents, the 'middle-class.' "[11]

---

[8]Georg Simmel, "The Metropolis and Mental Life," in Robert Guttman and David Popenoe, eds., *Neighborhood, City and Metropolis: An Integrated Reader in Urban Sociology* (New York: Random House, 1970).

[9]For a more detailed discussion see Reinhard Bendix and Seymour Martin Lipset, *Class, Status and Power,* 2nd ed., (New York: The Free Press, 1966), pp. 47–97.

[10]William H. Form and Gregory P. Stone, "Urbanism, Anonymity and Status Symbolism," in Guttman and Popenoe, eds., *op. cit.,* pp. 333–346.

[11]*Ibid.,* p. 337. In this context, *class symbolism* refers to the inference of social position from an assessment of family assignment based on long term interaction. *Status symbolism* is more common in the city because of the segmented anonymous life of the urbanite. In the city, status may be temporarily appropriated by the "correct" display and manipulation of symbols, rather than the direct enactment of rights and duties.

The authors further classified the responses according to the content of the symbolism as follows: 1) style symbolism, which emphasized the strategy, not the content, of appearance; 2) displays of possessions such as clothes, jewelry, etc.; 3) social identities such as occupation, education, etc.; 4) social appearance of individuals; and 5) attitudes. Form and Stone found that "matters of taste and style may be crucial in setting the temporary status arrangements formed in the anonymous situations of city life."[12]

As we have suggested in the case of the new town, the city is not simply divided into intimate location and anonymous locales. Further refining Strauss' conception of location and locale, Gerald Suttles distinguishes the following life-styles in the urban setting as they are related to class. First is working-class communities, ghettos and ethnic centers, where interaction occurs in informal meeting places, street corner gangs, and church groups. The collective life is dominated by precinct politics. Second, in middle-income, familistic areas, the management of children shapes the informal relationships, and formal organizational ties are stronger than in lower income areas. Third are the affluent apartment complex and exclusive suburb, generally sequestered and centered around private clubs and businessesmen's associations. The fourth life-style is found in a variety of life-styles, including home-grown talent and misfits who not only are able to tolerate one another, but rejoice in the cultivation of their differences.[13]

A Characterization of the Urban Class Structure

Still more subtle clues for social ranking can be derived from an analysis of the class structure in our cities. The urban class structure in the United States can be characterized in terms of five different classes. Persons of different classes tend to live in different locations, work at quite different tasks, think in different ways about their families and the world in which they live, an draw upon quite different resources that the city might provide. Their life-styles are reflected in their mannerisms and suggest their class. The class, in some degree, determines their destiny in our economy.

The Upper Class

The upper class constitutes about 1–2 percent of most metropolitan areas population. In the east, it seems appropriate to distinguish between the old aristocracy and the newly rich. In the former case, the size of its wealth is not as important as the

---

[12]*Loc. cit.*; see also the distinctions made by Bernard Barber, "Family Status, Local Community Status and Social Stratification: Three Types of Social Ranking," *The Pacific Sociological Review* (1961), pp. 3–10.

[13]Gerald Suttles, *The Social Construction of Community* (Chicago: The University of Chicago Press, 1972), p. 72.

When the upper class shops, cost is of relatively little concern. The process of selecting a dress is quite different for this woman compared to the middle-class woman buying clothes off the rack. *(Harvey Bara/Monkmeyer Press Photo Service.)*

length of time families have retained the wealth. The old aristocracy, because of wealth inherited over many generations, is seen as more cultured. refined and important than the family of a young oil company executive. In the far west, however, the distinction is less tenable. Persons are able to achieve the equivalent of old aristocracy status in a generation.[14]

One notable distinction between the old aristocracy and the newly rich is the extent to which the former tends to live in patrilineally extended families while the latter is much more cut off from kinship ties. The upward mobility as well as moves in pursuit of the job sever the ties with relatives, in the case of the newly rich. In contrast, the preservation of the family fortune tends to preserve a patrilineage, dominated by the oldest males in the old aristocracy. The threat of disinheritance is a significant force in shaping the behavior of family members, and sequestered neighborhoods and private schools and clubs prevent children of this class from too much exposure to the wrong kind of person. Hodges' study in San Francisco found that the upper class in the Bay Area were to be found "doing things in the city" and listed their diversions as "partying, gin rummy, watching baseball, and foreign films."[15]

[14]Ruth Shonle Cavan, *The American Family*, 4th ed., (New York: Thomas Y. Crowell, 1969), pp. 86–87.
[15]Harold M. Hodges, "Peninsula People: Social Stratification in a Metropolitan Complex," in Gutman and Popenoe, eds., *op. cit.*, pp. 309–333.

One old aristocratic location in Philadelphia is called The Main Line.[16] Here, inconspicuous consumption and the style of life is important. Family heirlooms, geneologies and history are preserved from generation to generation. One thing that a child born into a family of the Main Line knows for certain is that he is somebody. Regardless of what he makes of his life, he comes from a good family and this gives him enormous social credit as well as economic resources in competition with others of less standing.

The Upper-Middle Class

About 10–15 percent of our urban population are professional persons with college diplomas and careers to fulfill. Feldman considers this class better named the "organizational class" because its true social function is to fill the posts of corporate organizations and manage them in the interests of the upper class.[17] The organizational class does the dirty work for the upper class while providing an institutional, and often residential, buffer between the upper class and the lower classes. One thing children of this class know is that their parents can't assure them they will enjoy the same standard of living they enjoyed as a child when they grow up, hence children of this class become high achievers or drop-outs, depending upon how they interpret the pressures placed upon them by their uncertain social position.

Hodges characterized the personality of this group as gregarious, hyperactive, socially at ease, and concerned with career and school. Upper-middle-class families are child-centered and easy going with children. Religion is taken as a social activity rather than a way of life. Hodges found that the native habitat of this class in San Francisco was service clubs, such as Kiwanis and Lions, and its favorite diversions were do-it-yourself projects, *Time* and *Harper's* magazines, bridge, and golf.[18] Families of professionals are next to those of the newly rich in being separated from the daily interaction with kin. The pursuit of the job has meant for them also that it has been necessary to move when new opportunities opened up.

Form and Stone argue that "middle class" is not a status symbol at all, but should rather be understood in Goffman's terms as a collective symbol. Almost all Americans consider themselves to be middle class.[19] Feldman contends that most organization-class Americans assume that members of "lower" classes want to share in, or envy, the achievements of their organization class and their hopes for geographic, economic, and social mobility. We are only recently discovering that at least some persons from lower classes are quite content with the way in which they live.[20]

[16]Baltzell, E. D., *Philadelphia Gentlemen: The Making of a National Upper Class* (Glencoe, Ill.: Free Press, 1958).
[17]Gordon Feldman, *The Deceived Majority* (New York: Transaction Books, 1973.)
[18]Hodges, *op. cit.,* p. 319.
[19]Farm and Stone, *op. cit.,* p. 338.
[20]Fellman, *op. cit.*

The professional career affects how children are raised. Upper class parents are more inclined to focus their attention on the child's attitude, while lower class parents are more inclined to concern themselves with the child's behavior. Kohn contends that these differences in child-rearing derive from the patterns of behavior created on the job. Upper class professionals are engaged in careers which demand that they improvise on the spot and generalize often without guidelines, whereas working class persons are confronted with jobs that generally require that they follow standard operating procedures and adhere to job descriptions. Both types of parents are realistically training their children for what they perceive to be their most likely future—the upper middle class being careful to train for independence, the working class for conformity.[21]

The parental bond also has striking variations by class. A number of observers have noted that parents discipline their children differently in different classes, for example. Upper-class parents tend to use withdrawal of love as a means of discipline (''go to your room'' or its equivalent), whereas lower-class parents are more prone to use physical punishment.[22]

The size of the conjugal family is also correlated with class. The higher the class, the smaller the family. Community studies such as Elmtown found an even greater association between average family size and class (upper, 1.5; lower-lower, 5.6).[23] Rainwater discovered that there were also notable differences in preferred family size. Upper middle class Protestants preferred three children or less (80 percent), whereas lower lower class Catholics preferred four or more (60 percent).

> . . . neither religion or race seem to make much difference in desired family size at the lower-lower class level. At high status levels, Protestants want fewer children than Catholics, and within religious groups there are only minor differences among social classes.[24]

Lower-Middle Class

The lower middle class constitutes about 35 percent of the urban population, and is made up primarily of clerks, neighborhood businessmen, foremen, and skilled craftsmen. The classic distinction between ''white'' and ''blue-collar'' worker is blurred. People in this group stress togetherness, church-going. They see themselves as the ''typical American.'' They say they save for rainy days, but are more likely than anybody else to own a Cadillac, Lincoln, or Buick. They are most commonly found at church, lodge meetings or the PTA, when not at home. Common diversions includes Bible-reading, gardening and magazines like *Life, Reader's*

[21]Melvin Kohn, *Class and Conformity* (Homewood, Ill.: The Dorsey Press, 1969). A partial replication of Kohn's findings was carried out by J. D. Wright and S. R. Wright, ''Social Class and Parental Values for Children,'' *American Sociological Review,* 41 (June, 1976), pp. 527–537.
[22]Kohn, *op. cit.*
[23]August Hollingshead, *Elmtown's Youth* (New York: Wiley, 1949).
[24]Lee Rainwater, *Family Design* (Chicago: Aldine Publishing Company, 1965), p. 122.

Digest, and *Saturday Evening Post.* TV fare includes detective stories; this group also likes canasta and watching football.[25]

The lower middle class thus described has been recently lumped together with the working-class, made up largely of blue-collar workers, into a category called "middle America." This was the "silent majority" of the Nixon years.

Feldman describes the way of life of the middle American of Boston's Brookline-Elm district. He wears white starched shirts, suits with baggy pants, work shirts with his name in red on the breast pocket, white ankle-high cotton socks, uses a tooth pick after he eats, carries his lunch in a paper sack, and off duty drinks bourbon and 7-Up. She wears wire-stiff bouffants, girdles, and at-the-knee print dresses. She saves Green Stamps, and is active in the Girl Scouts and PTA. A Bible adorns her coffee table and there is an American flag decal on the family car. She lives for the kids. They live in a box-like suburban tract house or just ahead of the urban-renewal wreckers in a gritty, decayed inner-city neighborhood. Vacation is visiting with relatives, or staying home and painting the house. A treat is dinner at Burger King or a movie. Family fun is a drive, a backyard hamburger barbecue, or watching TV.[26]

> In general, the part of middle America represented by Brookline-Elm is characterized by a way of life centered around a geographically stable, closely knit family, including relatives beyond the immediate family, nearby friends, and sometimes also around an ethnic group or a local church.[27]

Time magazine declares . . .

> Above all, middle America is a state of mind, a morality, a construct of values and prejudices and a complex of fears—fears of crime in the street, the breakdown of law and order, confusion and anger at black militants, peace marchers and student protestors; at rising prices, rising taxes, shrinking incomes, drugs, and ever more visible sex. . . . The American dream they were living is no longer the dream as advertised. . . . This, middle Americans will say, with an air of embarrassment that such a truth need be stated at all, is the greatest country in the world. Why are people trying to tear it down?[28]

Upper-Lower Class

This class is also commonly called the "working class." It makes up about 35–40 percent of our urban population. The typical markings of this class are union membership and a skilled or semi-skilled occupation. The typical working class person is a high school drop out with 11 years of schooling. The male of this class is closest to the ideal of the two fisted, tatooed, he-man. He is typically ill at ease with strangers and wants to improve his social position. Although he dislikes masculine

[25]Hodges, *op. cit.,* p. 316 ff.
[26]Feldman, *op. cit.*
[27]*Ibid.,* p. 34.
[28]*Ibid.,* p. 21.

women and feminine men, he typically helps with dishes and diapers. He also typically experiences migrane headaches and insomnia.[29] Hodges listed the habitats of this class as the great out-of-doors, Sears, Wards and Penney's. The installment plan was made for this class. On television, the favorite programs are soap operas and westerns. Poker is the favorite game.[30]

Form and Stone discovered that working class males are identified not only by styles, but also by object-symbolism such as the typical hats, shoes, and occupational uniforms. They were also thought of by others as visiting certain stores such as Wards and Sears.[31] Their hands were thought of as dirty and their nails and hair rough. The above description of middle America as a state of mind seems most aptly applicable to persons in this class who have also been characterized as "rednecks" or "hard hats."

The Lower-Lower Class

At the bottom of the social ladder is the lower-lower class, comprising about a fifth of the urban population. In the United States, this class is a very heterogeneous class. It contains people who are respectable but impoverished, who hold steady jobs, work hard, attend church, and still do not make it. It contains the chronically unemployed, those who are cyclically out of work—such as unskilled construction workers—or those who have been unable to find work for long periods of time. It contains persons on welfare, the disabled, the discouraged and the down-and-outers.

Hodges found that the personality characteristics of this group could be summarized in their generally pessimistic view of life, their wariness of strangers, apathy toward politics, and fearfulness of being thought of as odd-balls. Persons of this class tend to be loyal to their families, although their families cannot help them as much as families in other classes might. Children, it is felt, should be seen and not heard. Television constitutes a major component of the recreational activity of this class. Pool and bowling are also enjoyed extensively when possible. The wife is a major buyer of romantic magazines.[32]

In Form and Stone's study of Lansing, Michigan, the down-and-outers were most visible to all groups.

> Their style of life is distinguished by excessive drinking, shabby dress, obscene language, and slovenliness. In the imagery of the observer, shuffling gait, stooped posture, and the expression of indifferent attitudes (such as laziness and indolence) are characteristic of the category.[33]

---

[29]Richard Sennet and Jonathan Cobb, *The Hidden Injuries of Class* (New York: Random House, 1973).
[30]Hodges, *op. cit.,* 315 ff.
[31]Form and Stone, *op. cit.,* p. 338.
[32]Hodges, *op. cit.,* p. 311 ff.
[33]Form and Stone, *loc. cit.*

Rainwater's explanation for the inverse relationship between socio-economic class and family size notes that lower class persons both prefer large families and are ineffective contraceptive users. Consequently, lower-class parents generally have larger families than they want. Lower lower class persons are less effective contraceptive users, Rainwater argues, because they live in highly segregated conjugal roles in which husband and wife share relatively few activities. They do not share the responsibility of effective contraceptive use. He also discovered that effective contraceptive use was related to the wife's enjoyment of sexual intercourse and that lower-lower class women were least likely to experience strong satisfaction in their sexual relations.[34]

Finally, one of the issues in the War on Poverty of the last decade was the effort to increase the participation of the poor through the community action programs. It might seem reasonable to suppose that those who were most abused by the status quo would be the ones to protest the loudest, but historically this has not been the case. An explanation for this lack of participation is offered by Maslow, who contends that it is necessary to satisfy basic human needs for safety and security, before it is possible to move on to meeting the needs of belonging and self-esteem which are necessary for active participation in politics. According to this view, the poor do not participate because they are too much caught up in meeting their more basic needs for safety and security. This assumption has been supported by numerous studies of low-income families and by analysts of the political participation of the poor. Community action programs, it would be assumed, might be able to enlist the short range participation of the poor through various rewards that could be offered, but the long term participation can not be assured unless the conditions of poverty are drastically reduced.

In spite of all the hardships of living at the bottom of the heap, lower-lower class families exhibit considerable stability. The distinction between the stable, settled, respectable families and the unstable, unrespectable ones is very pervasive in lower-class life. In the Clay Street neighborhood of Washington, D.C., studied by Joseph Howell, "hard living" was a way of coping with urban life chosen by persons from Appalachia who recently moved to the city.[35] It generally earned them a disreputable reputation amongst persons from similar backgrounds who settled down. And yet, "hard living" does not seem to be simply a matter of choice. Circumstances often beyond the control of those living hard make it very difficult for them to settle down. Though they may wish to settle down, some cannot.

Howell claims the following characteristics describe this life-style: 1) heavy drinking; 2) marital instability; 3) toughness which involves an abundance of profanity, and acting tough as well; 4) political alienation—the feeling that there is nothing personally at stake in the politics of the city; 5) rootlessness, involving a sense of not belonging anywhere and a high rate of mobility; 6) present-time

---

[34]Rainwater, *op. cit.,* p. 276 ff.

[35]Joseph Howell, *Hard Living on Clay Street: Portraits of Blue Collar Families* (Garden City, N.Y.: Doubleday and Company, 1973).

orientation in living from hand to mouth without much thought for the future; and 7) a strong sense of being loners.[36]

In contrast to "hard living," with its emphasis upon violence, toughness and solitary drinking, there also exists at the bottom locations called "skid rows." We are told that the term originated in the Puget Sound region, where many itinerant workers built makeshift shacks near the road along the skid used to transport logs from the surrounding hills into the Sound. This area was known as "skid road," and because the people who lived there were likened unto the driftwood of society the term has carried over to similar populations elsewhere. Skid rows are locations in our urban areas in which those defeated in the rat-race come to nurse their wounds and eke out their existence. Like the logs, they too have had the skids put under them.

Skid Row

Elmer Bendiner contends that the search for what binds Bowery men together usually begins with an examination of their drinking behavior, since the bottle is an important feature of Bowery life.

> The Bowery Man is a social drinker with a sense of group responsibility. He panhandles for liquor money to hold up his end of the bargain so that he may contribute his mite to the collective fund. Then when the bottle goes round he takes only one gulp at a time, and that one is nicely proportioned to his investment in the bottle.
>
> If his particular drinking group stakes him to a drink, he repays it with scrupulous correctness. There is an elaborate courtesy in these circles that only a gauche newcomer from uptown would violate. For example, when a man is pitching a line to someone who might give him the price of a drink, he is not to be interrupted or distracted. If he fails, another can try, but there is no uncouth struggling over a "live one" as the prospect is respectfully dubbed.[37]

But drinking is an asset, not the basis of the life of the community. On the sunny plateau of a high, a Bowery Man has the camaraderie that is more precious to him than love or friendship. He does not want friends, with their incessant demands upon him, but he craves the illusion of friendship. As the Bowery Man flees from real friendships, so also he flees from sexual encounters. "There is in part, the atmosphere of a monastery—a silent withdrawal from all the joys of the world save the passport to Nirvana contained in a little alcohol."[37a] Yet it is evident that not all social or heavy drinkers end up on the Bowery. The contrast between drinking on the Bowery and elsewhere can be caught in the study by Alcoholics Anonymous that 92 percent of the moneyed and family-bound class of chronic drinkers are solitary drinkers, whereas only about 10 percent of Bowery men habitually drink alone.[38]

The basis of social solidarity in Bowery life, many observers agree, is the need

---

[36]*Ibid.*, p. 368.

[37]Elmer Bendiner, "Bowery Man on the Couch" in *Eric & Mary Josephson, eds., Man Alone: Alienation in Modern Society* (New York: Dell, 1975), pp. 401–410.

[38]*Ibid.*, p. 401.

to have a place where "an effortless going to hell is the accepted way of life."[39] Men on skid row need support in their conviction that, contrary to what they might be told by friends they may have outside, they cannot do any better. While other men assert their worth, Bowery men find solace in denying it. The world persecutes failures, though it creates systems of competition in which failure is inevitable. Skid row welcomes them.

> Those who no longer aspire, who do not wish to rise on anybody's shoulders, who do not wish to sell more, make more, show more, even give more than others—these are among the "inadequately socialized" who have built the modern Bowery. There they need struggle no longer against the critics, the status-seekers and the status-markers who pigeonhole people.[40]

Bowery community is thus created by the society that casts the derelicts out. It exists as a necessary component of a success-oriented, achievement-conscious society. Its community is made up of what is left over from the struggle and a firm persuasion that such a struggle is personally not worth it.

> The parents who send their children joyfully off to life-adjustment courses do so with the notion that they will have fewer conflicts, fewer tensions. Life will be smoother.
> But if life isn't smoother and the ideal is still tranquility, if the tranquilizers are too expensive or in the end fail to secure the all-important inner peace, then it may be a consolation to us all to know that there is a Bowery, a place where life is thoroughly anaesthetized.
> It is our brothers who have pioneered there.[41]

Notice, however, that in the careful ranking of the drinking-circle and in the need for at least the appearance of friendship, the ghost of the established hierarchy haunts even those who have officially dropped out.

Class and Ethnicity

Early studies of American communities concluded that ethnic minorities were gradually assimilated into the mainstream. As families became upwardly mobile, class distinctions replaced ethnic differences. Thus, Irish, Italian, and other ethnic minorities followed the traditions of the old country in ethnic urban enclaves while they remained in the lower class. But as they became middle class, usually in a generation or two, they lost their ethnic distinctiveness. Lloyd Warner, in his *Yankee City* series, viewed ethnic difference as something to be overcome in the "melting pot" tradition.[42]

[39]*Ibid.*, p. 408.
[40]*Ibid.*, p. 409.
[41]*Ibid.*, p. 410.
[42]W. Lloyd Warner *et al.*, *Social Class in America* (Chicago: Science Research Associates, 1949).

The Melting Pot

But it soon became apparent that Warner's generalization was not adequate. The United States is not a melting pot in which ethnic differences disappear. In *Beyond the Melting Pot,* Glaser and Moynihan were among the first to point out this persistence.[43] Will Herberg concluded from his investigations that, while the second generation might reject the ways of the old country in their move away from the old neighborhood, the third generation returned to its ethnic heritage, albeit in a distinctively Americanized way.[44] Many observers pointed out that the melting pot clearly did not apply to black Americans who, because of skin color, are highly conspicuous and frequently denied access to the larger society because of prejudice. Caste distinctions, they argue, prevented blacks from intermarrying, moving up the economic ladder, and participating in the mainstream. In the ethnic ghetto, ethnic differences functioned virtually as caste differences, making intermarriage with other groups, for example, difficult if not impossible. But assimilation into an industrial society necessitates the abolition of such distinctive life-styles as patterns of everyday life. Even the rigid caste structure of India must yield to the necessities of the factory and assembly line.[45] The third or fourth generation Irishman or Scotsman can return to his cultural heritage as a source of pride and a basis of voluntary association, without being bound by peasant culture the way his poorer ancestors were.

Each spring, persons of Scottish ancestry assemble for the annual Scottish games in Fair Hill, Maryland. Most of the persons who attend these games are middle and upper class, proud of their heritage, and skilled in the sports and dances of Scotland. It is, unlikely that their daily lives are much influenced by Scottish life-styles. For the upper classes, the heritage of the old country does not guide the daily behavior so much as provide them with voluntary association and festive celebrations. For the first generation, lower class immigrant, the old way of life is the only way, even if it must be lived in a foreign country.

The Black Experience

An examination of the black experience suggests how race, ethnicity, and class are intimately intertwined. Many observers contend that the effects of caste discrimination on blacks has been so pronounced that it is wiser to speak of a black stratification system that parallels the white system, than to speak about a single stratification system in America.

---

[43]Nathan Glazer and Daniel Patrick Moynihan, *Beyond the Melting Pot* (Cambridge: The M.I.T. Press, 1963).

[44]Will Herberg, *Protestant, Catholic, Jew* (Garden City, N.Y.: Doubleday, 1956).

[45]See the discussion in Gehard Lenski, *Power and Privilege* (New York: McGraw Hill, 1966), pp. 77 ff.

79

In 1890, after the industrial revolution was well under way, 80 percent of the black population lived in rural areas of the United States. The demand for unskilled labor being generated by the factory system was then being met through emigration of other ethnic groups from overseas. Two world wars brought the black population into the cities in large numbers, particularly in the north and west. By 1960, 73 percent of the black population lived in urban areas; 58 percent in the south; and 95 percent in the north and west.[46] By 1974, 74 percent of the black population lived in Standard Metropolitan Statistical Areas; 58 percent in the central city portion, and 16 percent outside the central city. Thus, while blacks were tied firmly to the agricultural economy of the southeast prior to the Civil War, by 1974, they were well established in the central cities. They came to the city under quite different working conditions than other ethnic groups, however. The nature of the labor market required fewer and fewer unskilled laborers. Jobs that were dependable and that paid adequately to support a family were hard to find. But there were more jobs in the city than in the country, where the need for field hands was also diminishing as a result of increasing mechanization of agriculture and the encroachment on the small farm by large agri-businesses. Consequently, blacks constituted only about 11 percent of our population, but they made up 28 percent of the impoverished population in 1958, and 33 percent of the poor in 1972.[47] About 56 percent of the black population was poor in 1958 and about 32 percent in 1972. Therefore, although the conditions of urban blacks have improved over the two decades, blacks constituted a greater percentage of the poor population in 1972 than they did in 1958, an indication that the conditions for improvement of status favored whites more than blacks during the same period.

In the central cities, black ghettos persist, in spite of the War on Poverty and the urban riots of the 1960's. Indeed, the extent of residential segregation in the cities is increasing.[48] During the early 1960's, it seemed as though middle class blacks might remain within the central cities, thus providing much needed income and leadership resources. However, by the 1970's, it has become evident that middle class blacks will follow the pattern established by middle class whites and establish enclaves in the suburbs or extend the black ghetto beyond the city limits. Thus, the central cities of our nation are becoming increasingly impoverished and increasingly black. To add to the burden of the central cities, there is now good reason to believe that tax rates and federal support programs in effect establish a subsidy for the suburban commuter. The commuter generally pays lower taxes and receives a greater proportion of federal revenue-sharing because of the more rapid growth of the suburban fringe.[49]

[46]Reynolds Farley, *The Growth of the Black Population* (Chicago: Markham, 1970,) p. 50.

[47]U.S. Bureau of the Census, *Statistical Abstract of the United States: 1974,* 95th edition, Washington, D.C.: United States Government Printing Office, 1974, p. 389.

[48]Report of the Social Science Panel on the Significance of Community in the Metropolitan Environment, *Toward an Understanding of Metropolitan America* (San Francisco, Canfield Press, 1974), p. 18.

[49]*Ibid.,* p. 153.

The conditions of lower-class blacks were dramatically brought before the American public in 1965, when Daniel Patrick Moynihan's working paper intended for use by top administration officials was somehow made available to 2,000,000 persons by the Department of Labor. It was entitled "The Lower-Class Negro Family—The Case for National Action."[50] In this brief description, designed to stir up the administration, Moynihan chose to interpret the conditions of the poor, black family headed by a female.[51] Much of the thinking about what do do with poor blacks tended to focus on how to overcome problems thought to have been engendered by this family structure. Upon reflection, it clearly looks very much like blaming the victim. A more reasonable interpretation of the problems of these families is to see their condition as a function of deprivation and exclusion from the mainstream of American life, due to prejudice. Discriminated against on the job, still being last hired and first fired, black males have a difficult time fulfilling the provider role expected in the husband-wife family typical of the middle class. Consequently, about one-third of all poor black families are headed by females and a little over half of all black children spend at least some of their lives in female-headed families. Most poor black families are complete; further, there is ample evidence of the strength that is provided by the female-headed families, in spite of the heavier responsibilities placed upon the single parent.[52] It is also very evident that low-income black males do indeed provide support for unmarried black women and their children, and often spend considerable time caring for the children.[53] Poverty and prejudice are more plausible causes of the problems experienced by low-income black families than family structures, however much the latter may differ from middle-class norms.

The riots of the late 1960's have been interpreted as expressions of black urban unrest. The typical rioters were

> . . . young Negroes, natives of the ghetto (not of the south) hostile to the white society surrounding and repressing them and equally hostile to the middle-class Negroes who accommodated themselves to white dominance. The rioters were mistrustful of white politics, they hated the police, they were proud of their race and acutely conscious of the discrimination they suffered. They were and they are a time-bomb ticking in the heart of the richest nation in the history of the world.[54]

There is little evidence that the nation has done much to disengage this time-bomb. The conditions of the ghetto are the same or worse; unemployment among blacks is

[50]Daniel Patrick Moynihan, *The Negro Family: The Case for National Action* (Washington, D.C.: United States Government Printing Office, 1965). For a detailed discussion of the report and the reaction to it, see Lee Rainwater and William L. Yancey, *The Moynihan Report and the Politics of Controversy* (Cambridge: The M.I.T. Press, 1967).

[51]Charles Valentine, *Culture and Poverty: Critique and Counter Proposals* (Chicago: University of Chicago Press, 1968).

[52]Robert Coles, *Children of Crises* (Boston: Little Brown, 1964).

[53]David A. Schulz, *Coming Up Black: Patterns of Ghetto Socialization* (Englewood Cliffs, N.J.: Prentice-Hall, Inc., 1968).

[54]*Report of the National Advisory Commission on Civil Disorders* (New York: Bantam Books, 1968).

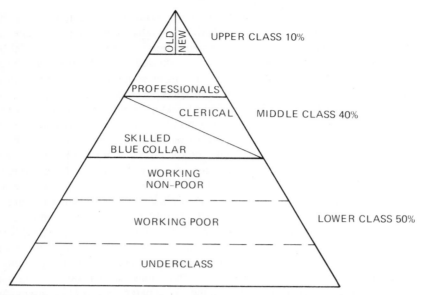

Figure 4.1 Social classes in the Negro community. *Andrew Billingsly,* Black Families in White America, *(Englewood Cliffs, N.J.: Prentice-Hall, Inc., 1968), p. 123.*

almost twice as great as amongst whites in 1974.[55] In some areas the rates are higher, with regional unemployment rates for minorities ranging from 6.1 to 12.2 percent of the labor force.[56]

The black stratification system, therefore, differs considerably from the white, as suggested by Andrew Billingsley.[57]

Upper classes.   Upper class blacks tend to associate primarily with other upper-class blacks. Families in this class have the greatest separation from the masses, both geographically and economically. However, the parallel nature of the black system can nowhere be better portrayed than by an examination of the relative insecurity of this upper class, in marked contrast to the relative security of the white upper class. The old upper class is composed of families headed by men and women whose parents were upper- or middle-class: judges, physicians, dentists, high government officials, educated ministers of large congregations, college presidents, and wealthy businessmen.[58] Although there are blacks who are millionaires, most of these upper-class black families, if ranked by the criteria of the white community,

[55]Statistical Abstract, *op. cit.,* p. 342.
[56]*Ibid.,* p. 343.
[57]Andrew Billingsley, *Black Families in White America* (Englewood Cliffs, N.J.: Prentice Hall, Inc., 1968.)
[58]*Ibid.,* p. 124.

would be middle-class. The vulnerability of the upper-class black is further reflected in the fact that he earns considerably less in his lifetime than upper-middle class whites, and frequently must rely on the income of his wife in order to maintain his status. Significantly, the status of a black family is as much a reflection of the education and occupation of the mother as it is of the father. According to Billingsley, Senator Edward Brooke of Massachusetts, Roger Weaver, former Secretary of Housing and Urban Development, and Thurgood Marshall, Justice of the Supreme Court, are good examples of men in the old upper class. The success of these men reflects their opportunity in the wider society (having had a measure of economic security denied to the vast majority of black Americans), as well as the personal effort they exerted in their careers. They are by no means self-made men, if any of us are.

The new black upper class has risen to its status in one generation. Typically, these are the families of entertainers and athletes, although they now include public officials like Mayor Stokes of Cleveland and Mayor Hacker of Gary, Indiana. Although some of these new upper-class families come from the middle class, the majority have risen from the lower class. This is true in the case of both mayors, at least. The class orientation of athletes in America can be seen in the fact that upper-class black athletes in football, basketball, and tennis tend to come from middle-class families because these sports have recruited players from colleges and universities. Those in baseball and boxing, on the other hand, tend to come from lower-class families.

Families of the black upper class are smaller than those of comparably educated whites. The number of female-headed families is comparable to the number in the white community when family incomes exceeds $7,000.[59] The family structure of the black upper class is nuclear, with considerably less emphasis on the extended family than is found in the white upper-upper class, but more than would be characteristic of the white middle class.

Another group must be classified in the new upper class, the "shadies, those gamblers, racketeers, pimps and other hustlers who often manage to become wealthy, to wield a considerable amount of influence, and to garner a great deal of prestige in the Negro community."[60] The inclusion of this group in the black system should make us consider that the ordinary study of the white community simply omits any discussion of the class status of Mafia members and other hoodlums. These types manage to become wealthy and do, in fact, wield a great deal of influence by both legitimate and illegitimate means. The dismissal of this segment of the white community as simply a part of the underworld does not adequately reflect their position, power, and influence in our society.

The middle classes.   Life-styles, rather than occupation or income, sets the black middle class off from the other classes:

[59]Alfonso Pinkney, *Black Americans* (Englewood Cliffs, N.J.: Prentice-Hall, Inc., 1969), p. 71.
[60]Billingsley, *op. cit.,* p. 125.

Blacks in the 1970's are moving to middle-class neighborhoods. Twenty years ago these boys might have been playing in a congested street. *(Blair Seitz/Seitz Photographers.)*

The middle class is marked off from the lower class by a pattern of behavior expressed in stable family and associational relationships, in great concern with "front" and respectability and in a drive for "getting ahead." All of this finds an objective measure in standard of living—the way people spend their money—and in public behavior.[61]

Middle class occupations include teaching, social work, accounting, law, and entertainment, as well as independent businessmen, clerical workers, service workers, and even some laborers. Middle-class blacks are frequently Methodists and Baptists, and unlike the lower class, who professes church membership but rarely attend as adults, middle class blacks are faithful church-goers and are quite civic-minded.

Billingsley describes the family life of these blacks as precarious, even though in most cases, their incomes are above the nation's median. It is striking that, in order for blacks to earn between $9,000 and $13,000[62] a year, it is necessary for both parents to work, even though in several instances, one or the other parent is a college graduate. The husband-wife relationship is described as egalitarian or

[61]St. Clair Drake and Horace Cayton, *Black Metropolis: A Study of Negro Life in a Northern City* (New York: Harper & Row Publishers, 1962), pp. 661–662.
[62]Billingsley, *op. cit.,* p. 122 ff.

slightly patriarchal. There is no indication of a matriarchy in these families. Since Billingsley, a number of books have presented a more balanced picture of black America by focusing on the wide variety of family life-styles to be found in the black community.[63]

The Lower Classes.   Billingsley places half the black community in the lower class. Within this class, he distinguishes between the working non-poor, the working poor, and the underclass. In 1968, about 60 percent of all black children lived in poverty. Poor black families are large, usually complete, and commonly linked through the mother to a matrilineal kinship structure. Poor blacks have attracted much recent attention, but a distorted picture of the lower class emerges from this concentration on the poor. Taking the characteristics of 173 families living in a black ghetto of Hartford, Connecticut, Charlotte Dunmore describes the "average" family

> The family is Negro and Protestant. The mother was born and reared in the rural or semi-rural southern United States. She came to live in Hartford sometime after her eighteenth birthday. The family has two legally married parents and contains 4.7 members. Father is the chief breadwinner, earning $4,800 per year from his employment as a skilled craftsman, steward or machinist. Mother, who stays home to take care of the children, perceives them as growing, developing human beings amenable to her control, if only a limited degree. The parents want their children to have at least some college education. They hope that their children will become skilled technicians, specialized clerical workers, or go into one of the minor professions—library science, teaching, the arts. The children are involved in at least two organized community activities (Scouts, the "Y," settlement house, etc.).
>
> Mother has achieved a rather high degree of integration into her neighborhood and is involved in a meaningful (to her) give-and-take relationship with her neighbors. At the present time, she is participating in at least two community activities. She is a registered voter and voted in the last election. She listens to the radio, watches television, and reads one of two Hartford newspapers every day.
>
> The family is geared to obtaining a better life for its children, including more education and more materially rewarding, status-giving employment. Hartford is perceived as a racially prejudiced community, and education appears to be considered the primary method for circumventing this prejudice.[64]

What does it mean to be poor and black? Billingsley describes seven bases for describing the life-style of these families. First is location. The conditions of life for low-income black families are most abject in the rural south, less so in the urban south, and still less so in the urban north and west. Achievement is highly associated with this geographic patterning. Second is socio-economic status. It makes a great difference in both family structure and achievement if the family is in the underclass, the working poor, or the working non-poor. Third, the life-style of the family

---

[63]John Scanzoni, *The Black Family in Modern Society* (Boston: Allyn and Bacon, 1971). Robert Staples, *The Black Family* (Belmont, California: Wadsworth Publishing Co., 1971). Charles V. Willie, ed., *The Family Life of Black People* (Columbus, Ohio: Charles E. Merrill Publishing Company, 1970).

[64]Charlotte Dunmore, "Social-Psychological Factors Affecting the Use of an Educational Opportunity Program by Families Living in a Poverty Area, Doctoral Dissertation, Brandeis University, quoted in Billingsley, *op. cit.*, pp. 137–38.

Table 4.1 *Money Income of Families—Race and Region by Income Level: 1972 (As of March 1973. Based on Current Population Survey)*

Race and Region	Total (1,000)	Under $1,000	$1,000-$1,999	$2,000-$2,999	$3,000-$3,999	$4,000-$4,999	$5,000-$6,999	$7,000-$9,999	$10,000-$14,999	$15,000-$24,999	$25,000 and over	Median[1] Income
					Percent Distribution, by Income Level							
All families[2]	54,373	1.3	2.2	3.7	4.5	4.9	10.2	16.8	26.1	23.0	7.3	$11,116
White	48,477	1.1	1.7	3.1	4.1	4.5	9.7	16.7	27.0	24.2	8.0	11,549
Northeast	11,599	0.7	0.8	2.8	3.7	3.8	8.5	16.3	27.6	26.6	9.2	12,307
North Central	13,708	0.9	1.5	2.6	3.6	4.1	9.0	16.2	28.6	26.1	7.4	11,947
South	14,508	1.4	2.8	3.9	4.9	4.9	11.6	18.1	25.8	19.8	7.1	10,465
West	8,661	1.4	1.3	3.2	3.9	5.2	9.7	15.7	26.2	25.2	8.3	11,724
Negro	5,265	2.8	6.7	9.3	9.4	8.7	14.1	17.4	17.5	12.2	2.1	6,864
Northeast	1,007	1.5	4.1	7.2	9.6	8.1	14.1	17.5	21.7	13.9	2.3	7,816
North Central	1,077	2.4	4.2	8.1	8.2	7.0	12.3	16.4	22.8	16.4	2.4	8,318
South	2,676	3.6	9.2	10.6	10.4	9.9	14.6	18.0	12.9	9.1	1.8	5,763
West	505	2.3	3.8	8.5	5.8	7.4	15.6	15.7	21.7	16.4	2.7	8,313

[1]For definition of median, see preface.
[2]Includes races not shown separately.

varies with its structure. Among lower-class families, Billingsley discerns nine types of basic families with two married adults and no children, nuclear families, attenuated nuclear families with one parent missing. Each of these can be further divided into extended families, subfamilies, or augmented families with non-relatives functioning as intimate members of the household. Size is a fourth important variable that may serve as either a facilitator of achievement or an obstacle, depending on other family characteristics. Fifth is the pattern of decision making, the vanishing patriarchies, the resilient matriarchies, and the expanding equalitarian families. Division of labor is the sixth factor. The segmented relationship, where husband and wife have their separate spheres of activity is probably most common. Collaboration, where there is role flexibility and mutual cooperation between husband and sife, characterizes a significant minority. Finally, attitudes toward authority and socialization of the children are important. Some lower-income black families take very good care of their children, striving to understand and shape their character. An intermediate group functions less well in controlling their children, who may be in and out of trouble. At the bottom, there is the chronically unstable group, whose children are most likely to get into trouble or be neglected.[65]

Finally, the black stratification system can be seen to vary in its expression by region as illustrated in Table 4.1. The urban north contains well over half of all black families; the rural south now contains the smallest number. Both the largest number of upper-income and poor black families, accordingly, are to be found in the urban north.

Social Stratification Processes

Using family income as an indicator of social class, the following picture of inequality in American society can be rendered. Table 4.2 compares the percentage of total income received by each fifth of the population in 1947 and in 1972. As we see, the lowest fifth received 5.1 percent of the aggregate income, and the highest fifth, 43.3 percent in 1947. The upper fifth received over eight times as much income as the lower fifth of the population. In 1972, the comparable figures are 5.4 percent and 41.4 percent, indicating a differential of about eight times. The percentages received by each fifth of the population have not changed very much since the turn of the century. Apparently, the New Deal, Fair Deal, New Frontier, and Great Society have done very little to redistribute income. The most notable changes occurred in the top five percent, whose portion of income declined from 17.5 percent in 1947, to 15.9 percent in 1972. Since income is a very imperfect measure of wealth for this income bracket, it is likely that the figures do not reflect a significant change in the total wealth of the top families.[66]

[65]Billingsley, *op. cit.,* pp. 143–44.
[66]Statistical Abstract, *op. cit.,* 384.

Table 4.2   *Percent of Aggregate Income Received by Each Fifth and Highest 5 Percent of Families and Individuals: 1947 to 1972 (1947–1955 based on grouped data; 1960–1972 on ungrouped data. See source, p. 15, for details on derivation).* (U.S. Bureau of the Census, *Statistical Abstract of the United States: 1974,* 95th edition, Washington, D.C.: United States Government Printing Office, 1974, p. 389.)

Item and Income Rank	1947	1950	1955	1960	1965	1969	1970	1971	1972
Families	100.0	100.0	100.0	100.0	100.0	100.0	100.0	100.0	100.0
Lowest fifth	5.1	4.5	4.8	4.8	5.2	5.6	5.4	5.5	5.4
Second fifth	11.8	11.9	12.2	12.2	12.2	12.3	12.2	12.0	11.9
Middle fifth	16.7	17.4	17.7	17.8	17.8	17.7	17.6	17.6	17.5
Fourth fifth	23.2	23.6	23.4	24.0	23.9	23.7	23.8	23.8	23.9
Highest fifth	43.3	42.7	41.8	41.3	40.9	40.6	40.9	41.1	41.4
Highest 5 percent	17.5	17.3	16.8	15.9	15.5	15.6	15.6	15.7	15.9
Head, white	100.0	100.0	100.0	100.0	100.0	100.0	100.0	100.0	100.0
Lowest fifth	5.5	4.9	5.1	5.2	5.6	5.9	5.8	5.8	5.8
Second fifth	12.2	12.3	12.6	12.7	12.6	12.7	12.5	12.4	12.2
Third fifth	16.9	17.2	17.9	17.7	17.8	17.8	17.7	17.6	17.5
Fourth fifth	22.8	23.5	23.3	23.7	23.7	23.5	23.6	23.6	23.6
Highest fifth	42.6	42.1	41.1	40.7	40.3	40.1	40.5	40.6	40.9
Highest 5 percent	17.4	17.3	16.7	15.7	15.4	15.4	15.5	15.5	15.7
Head, Hegro and other races	100.0	100.0	100.0	100.0	100.0	100.0	100.0	100.0	100.0
Lowest fifth	4.8	3.8	4.0	3.7	4.7	4.8	4.5	4.7	4.6
Second fifth	10.2	9.7	10.3	9.7	10.8	10.9	10.6	10.4	10.0
Third fifth	15.7	17.9	17.8	16.5	16.6	16.9	16.8	16.5	16.3
Fourth fifth	23.6	25.1	25.5	25.2	24.7	24.7	24.8	24.7	25.1
Highest fifth	45.8	43.4	42.4	44.9	43.2	42.7	43.4	43.7	44.1
Highest 5 percent	17.0	16.6	14.3	16.2	15.1	15.2	15.4	15.7	15.8
Unrelated individuals	100.0	100.0	100.0	100.0	100.0	100.0	100.0	100.0	100.0
Lowest fifth	2.9	3.1	2.4	1.7	2.9	3.3	3.3	3.4	3.3
Second fifth	5.4	6.9	7.3	7.3	7.6	7.8	7.9	8.1	8.2
Middle fifth	11.5	13.1	13.4	13.7	13.6	13.8	13.8	13.9	13.8
Fourth fifth	21.3	26.6	24.8	26.0	25.0	24.3	24.4	24.3	23.9
Highest fifth	58.9	50.3	52.0	51.4	50.9	50.9	50.7	50.4	50.9
Highest 5 percent	33.3	19.3	21.9	20.2	20.0	20.7	20.8	20.5	21 4

At the bottom of the income pyramid, the official figures suggest that there has been a significant reduction in poverty. The percentage of the population that falls below the low-income level declined from 22.5 percent in 1959 to 11.9 percent in 1972.[67] While this does reflect some improvement in the status of the poor, it must be remembered that poorest families have moved up to the category of the marginally poor and remain very vulnerable to recessionary fluctuations in the nation's economy. In this marginal position, furthermore, many have been denied the public assistance that they might otherwise have received as officially designated poor

[67]*Ibid.,* p. 389.

persons. While it remains true that the largest number of poor people are outside of our metropolitan areas, the poor occupy about half of the total area of our central cities. (50.8 percent in 1973).[68] The urban poor are more conspicuous because of their concentration.

While the evidence supporting a fairly stable social stratification system in the United States, as well as other industrialized societies, is substantial, the impact of such a system upon individuals is modified by the extent to which it is open to individual mobility and equally accessible to diverse groups within the urban population. In general, rural systems are less open and based more upon ascriptive factors than urban stratification systems.[69] This is in part why the city is often thought of as a place of opportunity, both in developing and industrialized countries.

Two types of studies focus on aspects of the stratification process. The first kind of study concerns itself with the consistency of the process of status attainment within a person's lifetime. To what extent does success in school affect occupational mobility for particular kinds of individuals? The second kind of study focuses on the extent to which parental status determines the status of children. It examines intragenerational mobility.

Status Attainment

Interest in the issue of status attainment has focused around two social problems of inequality: the extent to which the school system promotes mobility, especially among minority groups, and the extent to which women are discriminated against in the labor market. The major studies by Coleman and Jencks concluded that schools generally had less effect upon the mobility of black students than various family variables.[70] A more recent study concludes that when parental status and ability are controlled, blacks give evidence of greater educational attainment than whites. The higher school performance of blacks is attributed to higher self-esteem and aspiration among black students. However, grades and other evidence of superior school performance by blacks is discredited by school officials, especially in racially segregated schools, whereas whites advance through the system in such a way as to allow for a filtering effect for grades. The fact that parental status and ability has a greater effect on white mobility suggests that the whites have access to an "insider's track" which makes them more mobile within the system than blacks with comparable measures of ability.[71] While a number of studies support the importance of educational achievement as a predictor of status attainment, performance in the

[68]*Ibid.*, p. 393.

[69]Joseph Kahl, "Some Social Concomitants of Industrialization and Urbanization," *Human Organization,* XVIII (Summer, 1959), pp. 53–74.

[70]James S. Coleman, *et al., Equality of Educational Opportunity* (Washington, D.C.: United States Government Printing Office, 1966). Christopher S. Jencks, *Inequality: A Re-assessment of the Effect of Family and Schooling in America* (New York: Basic Books, 1972).

[71]Alyondro Portes and Kenneth L. Wilson, "Black-White Difference in Educational Attainment," *American Sociological Review* (June 1976), pp. 414–443.

school system is strongly affected by parental status, because class has been shown to have significant effect upon socialization variables[72] and upon teachers' evaluation of children's performance.[73] Interestingly enough, assignment of youngsters to academic or non-academic forms of secondary education as is done in England produces outcomes that are virtually indistinguishable from those produced by the more open, competitive process in America.[74] Father's occuptional status tends to be perpetuated because family life-styles and values affect the motivation and evaluation of children in the educational system of both countries—though by quite different mechanisms.

Studies examining the status attainment of men and women arrive at mixed conclusions. On the one hand, there is evidence that occupational status depends largely upon educational achievement for both men and women and slightly less so upon social origin.[75] But women generally do different kinds of work than men and are generally paid less. On the other hand, Featherman and Hauser found that sex discrimination accounted for about 85 percent of the earnings gap between men and women in 1962, and about 84 percent in 1973. They also found that women were better educated than men in comparable positions, but that equality of economic opportunity has not followed educational achievement to the extent one would expect. Both men and women were handicapped by having a father who was a farmer, but men suffered more in this regard.[77]

Henretta and Campbell contend that, contrary to some opinion, the status of persons does not decline radically with retirement. They retain status, as measured by income and prestige, despite the large changes which accompany old age.[78]

Occupational Mobility

Comparing industrial societies with agricultural ones, Hazelreg and Garnier concluded that labor-intensive, agricultural economies generally have low rates of father-son status change. They found further that the rate of change in mobility did

[72]Melvin Kohn, *Class and Conformity, op. cit.,*; James D. Wright and S. R. Wright, "Social Class and Parental Values for Children," *op. cit.*

[73]Thomas F. Pettigrew, *A Profile of the Negro American* (Princeton, N.J.: Van Nostrand, 1964).

[74]Alan C. Kirckhoff, "Stratification Processes and Outcomes in England and the United States," *American Sociological Review* 39 (December, 1974), pp. 789–801.

[75]Donald J. Treiman and Kermit Terrell, "Sex and the Process of Status Attainment: A Comparison of Working Women and Men," *American Sociological Review* 40 (April, 1975), pp. 174–200. McKee J. McClendon, "The Occupational Status Attainment Processes of Males and Females," *American Sociological Review* 41 (February, 1976), pp. 52–64.

[76]Barbara Reskin, "Sex Differences in Status Attainment in Science: The Case of the Post-Doctoral Fellowship," *American Sociological Review* 41 (August, 1976), pp. 597–612; Treiman and Terrell, *op. cit.,*; McClendon, *op. cit.*

[77]David L. Featherman and Robert M. Hauser, "Sexual Inequalities and Socio-economic Achievement in the United States: 1962–1973," *American Sociological Review* 41 (June, 1976), pp. 462–483.

[78]John C. Henretta and Richard T. Campbell, "Status Attainment and Status Maintenance: A Study of Stratification in Old Age," *American Sociological Review* 41 (December, 1976), pp. 981–993.

not vary with the measure of the economy's productivity, or its energy consumption.[79] It seems reasonable to suppose that varied mobility rates in industrialized societies are related as much, if not more, to changing occupational distribution, rather than to the changing opportunities such expanding economies provide.[80] If this is so, then a much more detailed examination of occupational specialization is needed to account for different rates of mobility within industrialized societies. It would also seem reasonable to assume that the rate of urbanization would be positively correlated with mobility rates, since the city tends to be the locale in which greater occupational specialization occurs.

Status Crystalization

Max Weber contended that an individual is ranked along multiple dimensions.[81] This seems to be especially true in urban areas, as we have suggested in this chapter. What happens if there is an inconsistency in these rankings? That is, what happens if an individual should be ranked high along one dimension and low along another? Gehardt Lenski coined the term *status crystalization* to refer to situations in which rankings along four dimensions of socio-economic class were consistent. He chose ethnicity, income, occupation, and education as his dimensions of class.[82] Lenski postulated that low status crystalization is directly related to the experience of stress. For example, a black banker would be expected to experience a high degree of stress, because he is low on ethnicity and high on occupation. Lenski was not concerned with pointing out the differences between high and low status crystalization at the top and the bottom of the various dimensions he measured. Rather, he contrasted high and low status crystalization as a horizontal measure of social stratification, which he correlated with psychosocial stress.

It has also been assumed that persons who are low on status crystalization are less likely to be politically active than persons high on status crystalization, regardless of their class position. Lenski also associated status inconsistency with political liberalism.

In a recent study in Australia, Leonard Broom and F. Lancaster Jones found that while status consistency as such had no clear effect on voting behavior, specific types of inconsistency did.[83] They note that Catholics in Australia are more likely than non-Catholics to vote for liberal parties and that the tendency was especially

[79]Lawrence E. Hazelregg and Maurice A. Garnier, ''Occupational Mobility in Industrial Societies: A Comparative Analysis of Differential Access to Occupational Rank in Seventeen Countries,'' *American Sociological Review* 41 (June, 1977), pp. 498–511.

[80]Robert M. Hauser, *et al.*, ''Temporal Change in Occupational Mobility: Evidence for Men in the United States,'' *American Sociological Review* 40 (June, 1975), pp. 279–297.

[81]Max Weber, ''Class, Status, and Party,'' in Bendix and Lipset, eds., *op. cit.*, pp. 21–28.

[82]Gehard E. Lenski, ''Status Crystallization: A Non-verticle Dimension of Social Status,'' *American Sociological Review,* (1954), pp. 405–413; ''Social Participation and Status Crystallization,'' *American Sociological Review,* (1956), pp. 458–464.

[83]Leonard Broom and F. Lancaster Jones, ''Status Consistency and Political Preference: The Australian Case,'' *American Sociological Review* 35 (December, 1970), pp. 989–1002.

marked in the case of Catholics with high achieved status, which confirms Lenski's suggestion. They also note, however, that Australia has been characterized as much less achievement-oriented than the United States, and point out that it will be necessary to determine the specific configurations of status inconsistencies that engender stress in particular cultures.

> Perhaps status inconsistency is most stressful to individuals in societies where most differentially valued statuses are ascribed rather than achieved, and when stress reducing mechanisms are largely ineffective—the example, par excellence, is racial-ethnic status—it is ascribed, visible and irreversible.[84]

While the research on status crystalization seems to have waned momentarily, it seems reasonable to believe that inconsistent ranking does have significant effects on personal behavior, and that its effect upon the urban environment is significant.[85]

Trends

Conventional wisdom in the theory of stratification relies upon an assumed logic of industrialization which contends that in the first instance, industrialization produces similar effects the world over.[86] In Clark Kerr's formulation, a new society, emerging from former "class" and "mass" societies, is the result of this trend. The broad characteristics of this new society are: 1) a reduction in differentiation, with a marked increase in the middle class population; 2) reduction in status inconsistency, as economic rewards and prestige coincide more; and, 3) an increase in social mobility, or movement between social strata.[87]

In contrast to this view, a number of recent observers contend that industrialization is not producing the same kind of stratification system throughout the industrialized world. The Soviet Union, for example, relies much more upon government regulation than it does upon market forces to distribute the resources. It cannot be said to have the same kind of social inequality as a result. In similar fashion, European countries (especially the socialist countries like Sweden) rely much more heavily upon planning than the United States. Berry further notes that the process of urbanization and industrialization in the third world countries has different consequences than in the United States. The "logic of industrialization" fails fundamentally because of these differences.[88]

---

[84]*Ibid.*, p. 1000.

[85]Keith Hope, "Models of Status Inconsistency and Social Mobility Effects," *American Sociological Review* (June, 1975), pp. 322–343, argues that the models previously used to measure status inconsistency are inappropriate statistical models and that his proposed diamond model yields significant results but does not tell us how important status crystallization factors in fact are. The argument continues.

[86]Kerr, *et al.*; Bauer, *et al.*; Inkeles and Bauer.

[87]Kerr *et al.*

[88]Brian J. L. Berry, *The Human Consequences of Urbanization,* (New York: St. Martin's Press, 1973), pp. 164–181.

There are, in addition, a number of empirical studies of the United States which suggest that the generalizations thought characteristic of this country need qualification. In the first instance, while there may be some grounds for asserting a general decline in inequality over a long period of time, there is little evidence of a marked reduction in inequality in the United States since at least World War II.[89] Many studies suggest that there has been an increase in equality, particularly in the case of the lower fifth of the population. This is in spite of official statistics which note a steady decline of the impoverished since the 1960's. Myrdal, for one, points out the tragedy of high unemployment as the result of technological innovation in a society that does not deem it critically important to keep the labor force employed or retrained.[90]

It is commonplace to argue that status inconsistency decreases in industrialized countries. However, there is reason to believe that it will increase as we gain ever more control over our environment and the importance of the controllers increases. Finally, the assumption of increased mobility in industrialized societies like the United States needs to be qualified by recognition of the base from which the individual starts. The poor are increasingly less likely to be upwardly mobile. While there may be some increase in intergenerational mobility, the increasing emphasis upon expertise will make intergenerational mobility less rather than more likely.

In sum, it would seem that there is little logic to industrialization as a worldwide process causing similar patterns to emerge around the world. Both industrialization and urbanization are occurring in different configurations in different parts of the world. Regional history, resources, and culture shape the results. We can at least strongly question the assumption that the millenium has arrived in America. We can also state with conviction that an increase, rather than a decrease in social inequality is likely to occur, at least for the lower segments of the population.

Summary

The apparent complexity of the urban environment is simplified when we stratify the large urban population on the basis of class. Urban locations are determined in part by class distinction and status symbolism. Within these homogeneous enclaves, however, social ranking continues, but on a more personal basis. The urbanite resorts to symbols when he can not know the person.

Social class is related to the life-style of an individual. Class affects everything from the way he raises his family to the way in which he spends his income. Family structure also correlates with social class to such an extent that it makes little sense to speak of "the American family." Social class also affects rates of participation in the political process and in the general health of a population.

[89]Lenski, *Power and Privilege, A Theory of Social Stratification* (New York: McGraw-Hill Book Company, 1966), p. 437.
[90]Gunnar Myrdal, *Challange to Affluence.*

While it was once thought that America was becoming a gigantic melting pot, it is becoming evident that we are moving toward a pluralistic culture in which class and ethnicity play significant roles. This is particularly true in the case of black Americans. They constitute about 11 percent of the population and have been excluded on the basis of their race to such an extent that most observers feel that it is wise to distinguish black and white stratification systems. The characteristics by which persons are distinguished and the advantages enjoyed by most individuals in each system are not truly comparable by class.

While research on status crystalization is currently at a standstill, it is likely that future research will bear out the contention that inconsistent ranking does indeed have significant effects upon urbanites and contributes to the social climate of the urban environment.

Counter to conventional wisdom, we can expect an increase in social inequality, especially between the poor and the middle-class or average man; an increase in status inconsistency, as management roles become more prominent; and a reduction in intergenerational mobility, as we continue to stress the importance of expertise that is not readily obtainable.

chapter 5

Social Participation

The stereotype of urban life-style suggests the inevitability of social ties which are weak, superficial, transitory, and anomic. Family and kinship ties are also portrayed as weak and fragmentary.[1] Even the new suburbs are seen as having a disruptive effect upon family life.[2] Friendship and neighboring ties are pictured as being weakened in the most urbanized areas.[3] The portrait of the work place in urbanized areas, too, is one of generally alienated people.[4] These disruptions of the social structure also spill over to the schools.[5] According to classical theory, most of these disruptions are linked to the overabundance of secondary ties, which are weak and specialized, in contrast to the more intensive primary ties which are supposedly more prevalent in less urbanized areas.

In response to some of the stresses associated with the urban social structure, organizations like settlement houses have grown up in the cities, like the first one in Chicago made famous by Jane Adams (Hull House). Churches and neighborhood organizations also attempt to fill some of the social voids within the most urbanized

[1]See for example: David Schulz, *Coming Up Black,* (New York: Prentice-Hall, 1969); Daniel P. Moynihan, *The Negro Family: The Case for National Action* (Washington, D.C.: United States Department of Labor, 1965); Oscar Lewis, *La Vida,* (New York: Random House, 1965).

[2]Herbert J. Gans, *The Levittowners,* (New York: Vintage, 1967); William H. Whyte, *The Organization Man,* (New York: Simon and Schuster, 1956).

[3]Sylvia F. Fava, "Contrasts in Neighboring: New York and a Suburban County," in William Dobriner, ed., *The Suburban Community,* (New York: Putnam, 1959); also Sylvia Fava, "Suburbanism as a Way of Life," *American Sociological Review,* 21, February (1956), pp. 34–38.

[4]Karl Marx, *Capital,* translated by Ernest Untermann, (Chicago: Charles H. Kerr & Co., 1909); C. Wright Mills, *White Collar,* (New York: Oxford University Press, 1951).

[5]Charles E. Silberman, *Crisis in Black and White* (New York: Random House, 1964); James S. Coleman *et al., Equality of Educational Opportunity,* (Washington, D.C.: United States Government Printing Office, 1966).

Norway. Constitution Day, May
17th. The children's procession
on its way to the Royal Palace in
Oslo. (*The Royal Norwegian
Ministry of Foreign Affairs.*)

areas. Generally, as modern industrial cities developed, there appeared to be a
weakening, or at least a change in the type of social ties, within organizations,
among friends and neighbors, and among informal acquaintances. These social
changes led to the development of new kinds of organizations within urban areas
which were intended to counteract some of these disruptive effects.

In this chapter we attempt to answer several basic questions: (1) What is the
relationship between urbanization and participation in various types of formal social
organizations? (2) How does urbanization effect participation in informal interactions, *i.e.,* with kin, neighbors, work groups, street corner groups, etc? In order to
answer these questions we use extensive examples from studies of social life in
urban areas.

Social Participation

The Concept of Social Participation

Social participation involves interaction at both the individual and group level. The
first type of social participation experienced by an individual is usually with his
family, where he is socialized to perform the various roles and tasks which are

necessary to survive in society. Generally it is recognized that social participation in groups is of two types: formal or informal. Formal organizations are those which have an organized structure, typically with leaders, rules, regulations, membership requirements, etc. Among the various kinds of formal organizations to which people normally belong are churches, clubs, political organizations and unions.

Informal social participation, in contrast, involves participation in less organized groups, which may range from street corner gangs to coffee clatches in suburban neighborhoods. Besides these two general types, informal social participation is also found within neighboring relations, work and school activities, and friendship relations. Most studies by sociologists that deal with participation focus upon voluntary associations such as clubs and organizations which have become more prevalent as the world becomes more organized. In the most urbanized areas, because the family and neighborhood no longer carry out the same functions as they did during less urbanized eras, new types of organizations have sprung up. We have mentioned that the settlement house, such as the Hull House in Chicago, not only provided a place where young and old could enjoy themselves, but also a setting to develop certain values, skills and roles which were necessary to survive in an urban environment. Settlement house programs included citizenship classes, personal counseling and cultural activities. This old version of the settlement house expanded into the modern urban neighborhood organization, which usually focuses on housing problems, unemployment, the lack of city services, and the crime problem in particular neighborhoods. Through the modern techniques of community organization, efforts are made to develop a coalition of citizens based on common needs within a small area. These *locality relevant* concerns may be as basic as demanding that a city government place a traffic light in an area, or as complex as trying to alter an entire urban labor market in order to provide jobs for minorities.[6]

In a similar vein, because of stresses on family structure in an urbanized world, new institutions have also developed. One example is Parents Without Partners, which provides a means of interaction for recently divorced or widowed parents who desire to locate and to interact with others who have common needs and backgrounds. Another organization which was founded to strengthen some of the social stresses associated with one-parent families, is Big Brothers, which provides volunteers to fill some of the paternal role functions which are normally provided by fathers in the two-parent family, often unavailable to single people. A baby sitting co-op in a surburban development is also a relatively recent institution, invented to fill a gap formerly filled by family and kin, who often resided in the same household or close by. One has only to search the daily newspaper to discover additions to the plethora of special function organizations which have developed within cities as a result of the shifts in social structure brought about by urbanization and industrialization.

---

[6]Roland L. Warren, *The Community in America,* (Chicago: Rand McNally & Co., 1972), pp. 167–208.

Status-Conferring and Status-Certifying Elements of Social Participation

While organizations often have specialized purposes which revolve around a single issue (*e.g.*, neighborhood beautification), almost all organizations are characterized by persons from distinctive social strata. Lloyd Warner, in his classic study, *Social Class in America,* developed an index of social status based upon the organizational memberships of families in a community.[7] Indeed, it was possible, based upon the list of organizations in which people participated, to characterize their general position within the local social class structure. For many families or individuals who are in a state of transition from one social class to another (social mobility), membership certifies and strengthens their identity and solidarity with a new social stratum.

Church membership appears to be stratified in terms of denominations and social class. In a demographic study of the major religious groups in the United States, it was found that Jewish, Episcopalian, and Presbyterian groups ranked highest in terms of income and education, in contrast to Methodists and Baptists, which ranked lowest.[8] Membership in different churches, then, not only confers status within a general community, but in certain instances, the socialization process within the church supports certain status conferring values. These values may stress work, obligation to the community, service, or other processes which confer prestige and honor within the local community. Similarly, membership in other types of organizations within the community suggests an individual's place within status hierarchy.

Baltzell, in his classical study of the upper class in Philadelphia (1958), showed that there were great variations, even within the upper class.[9] The most prominent membership, which certified that one was the member of the old upper class in Philadelphia, was membership in the *Social Register,* which first appeared in that city in 1890. Although many people within the upper class in Philadelphia have a great deal of money, education, and prestige within the community, they are often blocked from obtaining membership in the highest strata, because no family member has been in the *Social Register*. Membership is limited principally to families who have had wealth and position within the community for many generations. In the case of the Boston *Social Register,* it is often mentioned that the family of the late president John Fitzgerald Kennedy had not been admitted to the Boston Social Register, prior to his administration.

[7]Lloyd W. Warner *et al., Social Class in America,* (Chicago: Science Research Associates, Inc., 1949).

[8]Bernard Lazerwitz, "Religion and Social Structure in the United States," in Louis Schneider, ed., *Religion, Culture and Society,* (New York: Wiley, 1964).

[9]E. Digby Baltzell, *Philadelphia Gentlemen: The Making of a National Upper Class* (Glencoe, Illinois: The Free Press, 1958).

98

Country Clubs

Also reflecting the prestige of different strata is a hierarchy of country clubs within large communities, the most prestigious of which is limited to the wealthy old families of the upper class. The less prestigious clubs are oriented toward ethnic groups which have more recently reached upper middle-class status. Clubs with a heavy membership base of Jews or Italians are typically more recent entries and rank lower within the highly stratified network of country clubs within a community.

Within the middle strata other organizational memberships prevail, such as the Elks, Moose, Kiwanis and Rotary. In the lower strata, membership may be limited to the church, or labor union, or may reflect no organizational memberships whatsoever.

Labor Unions

Organizational memberships also differ depending upon social status associated with the occupation held by the individual. For the members of trades and crafts, the labor union is a most important organization. In considering labor unions, it is important to note that the labor union not only evolved in urbanized areas but also in rural areas and small towns. The development of labor unions within the coal areas of Pennsylvania in the early 1900's clearly documents the social stresses on which brought about the growth of unions. At the present time when people belong to one or more associations, one of them is usually a labor union. Among working-class individuals, it is typical for their only organizational membership to be a labor union.[10]

Professional Associations

The counterpart of the labor union for professionals is the professional organization. Like labor unions, these are usually not locally based, but rather may operate on a national and regional scale. Like labor unions, bar associations and medical associations within local areas base a great deal of their policy and interests on issues at the national level. Both labor unions and professional associations perform a status-conferring function within local areas, although they do not necessarily provide a social integrative function, because many of their concerns are regional and national in scope.

[10]Wendell Bell and Maryanne T. Force, "Urban Neighborhood Types and Participation in Formal Organizations," *American Sociological Review,* 21 (February, 1956), pp. 25–34.

The Degree of Participation In Formal Organizations

An important concern regarding organizational participation is not only membership, but the extent of the activity with each group. For instance, Chapin (1955) developed a social participation scale, which measures the extent of participation in formal organizations, including not only the number of different groups to which an individual belongs, but also the extent of attendance at meetings and whether a person is an officer or a committee member in each organization.[11] The scale takes into account the tendency for a large number of people to identify with a group, e.g., a church, without being an actual member of the congregation or organization. The result is an overstatement of the amount of participation in formal organizations when simple identification alone is used as criterion of formal organization membership.

Generally, studies of school organization in the United States suggest that slightly over half of the adults are members of formal organizations.[12] The same studies indicate that males are more likely to be members than females. In one recent survey, it was shown that Canadians have a slightly higher degree of affiliation in voluntary associations than persons from the United States.[13] Generally, the more industrialized westernized countries in this survey had a higher rate of social participation. Italy and Mexico revealed organizational memberships which were about half that shown in Canada, the United States, Great Britain and Germany.

Within the United States, whites usually have a somewhat higher degree of participation in formal organizations than blacks.[14] However, when one takes into consideration the class composition of blacks and whites (controlling for social economic status), blacks sometimes have greater social participation than whites.

Hyman and Wright (1971) compared the results of two national surveys and suggest that there was a small increase in the association memberships from 1955 to 1962.[15] Moreover, the increase was not limited to those in the middle or upper classes, but seemed to occur throughout the social strata among both blacks and whites. During this time, blacks became involved increasingly in neighborhood organizations and in civil rights groups, which probably accounted for some of the increase. It is also possible that once people become convinced of the usefulness of formal organizations, they become increasingly more involved. In the case of blacks, the War on Poverty and Model Cities programs emphasized the development of community-based organizations in order to accomplish human and physical

[11]F. Stuart Chapin, *Experimental Designs in Social Research,* (New York: Harper & Row, 1955).

[12]J. Curtis, "Voluntary Association Joining: A Cross Cultural Comparative Note," *American Sociological Review,* 36, October, (1971), pp, 872–880.

[13]*Ibid.,* p. 874.

[14]Marvin E. Olsen, "Social and Political Participation of Blacks," *American Sociological Review,* 35 (August, 1970), pp. 682–697.

[15]Herbert H. Hyman and Charles Wright, "Trends in Voluntary Association Memberships of American Adults: A Replication Based on Secondary Analysis of National Sample Surveys," *American Sociological Review,* 36 (April, 1971), pp. 191–206.

renewal. As blacks learned community organization techniques, they employed them in other areas of urban life.

In sum, several tendencies are suggested with respect to formal organization membership: (1) The less urbanized an area, the higher is the extent of formal organization membership.[16] (2) The higher the social class of the individual or family, the greater is the tendency for membership and participation in formal organizations.[17] (3) Men generally have a higher rate of participation than women.[18] (4) Overall, whites have a higher rate of participation than blacks, but this may be accounted for mainly by the large number of blacks in the lower social strata. When socio-economic status is controlled, some studies indicate that blacks may have a higher rate of social participation than whites.[19]

The Integrative Function of Community Organizations

In the chapter on urban neighborhoods, we discuss the relationship between organizational membership and social integration in different types of neighborhoods. Briefly, we suggest that residential neighborhoods go through a life-cycle. During the first part of this cycle, there is a testing of potential, long-term social contacts, primarily through intensive neighboring and friendship contracts. During this period, organizational membership remains fairly low. During later stages of neighborhood development, however, the pattern reverses. That is, the norm for the neighborhood then involves a focus on more formal relationships through neighborhood organizations and other community-based groups. The intensity of neighboring, manifest in earlier stages, wanes somewhat, as a stable pattern of roles and relationships is worked out. Neighboring, rather than being a way of feeling out potential friendships, now develops into a supportive institution, wherein the "good" neighbor role involves a higher degree of privacy, but also a certain degree of mutual assistance during times of trouble and during other specific times. Patterns of borrowing and helping become institutionalized features of neighborhood

[16]Allan Booth, Nicholas Babchuk, and Alan Knox, "Social Stratification and Membership in Instrumental-Expressive Voluntary Associations," *Sociological Quarterly,* 9 (Autumn, 1968), pp. 427–439; Scott Greer and Ella Kube, "Urbanism and Social Structure: A Los Angeles Study," in Marvin Sussman, ed., *Community Structure and Analysis,* (New York: Thomas Y. Crowell, 1959); Murray Hausknecht, *The Joiners,* (New York: The Bedminister Press, 1962), p. 44; Mira Komarovsky, "The Voluntary Associations of Urban Dwellers," *American Sociological Review,* 11 (1946), pp. 686–698.

[17]Nicholas Babchuk and Alan Booth, "Voluntary Association Membership: A Longitudinal Analysis," *American Sociological Review,* 34 (February, 1969), pp. 31–45; Morris Axelrod, "Urban Structure and Social Participation," *American Sociological Review,* 21 (February, 1956), pp. 13–18; also see Bell and Force, *op. cit.,* Wright and Hyman, *op. cit.*

[18]Babchuk and Booth, *op. cit.;* Wright and Hyman, *op. cit.;* and Hausknecht, *op. cit.*

[19]Nicholas Babchuk and Ralph V. Thompson, "The Voluntary Associations of Negroes," *American Sociological Review,* 27 (October, 1962), pp. 647–655; Marvin E. Olsen, "Social and Political Participation of Blacks," *American Sociological Review,* 35 (August, 1970), pp. 682–697; Anthony Orum, "A Reappraisal of the Social and Political Participation of Negroes," *American Journal of Sociology,* 72 (July, 1966), pp. 32–46.

CARL A. RUDISILL LIBRARY
LENOIR RHYNE COLLEGE

life during this stage.[20] It is obvious that for those living in a frontier area, or an area where farms are widely separated, codes of mutual aid are extremely important. In the more urbanized areas, where a wide variety of public services are available, mutual assistance for protection and survival may become less important, as these functions increasingly are provided as services by the government.

Studies of newly urbanizing areas of West Africa indicate that voluntary associations play quite a different role there. Extensive research done by K. L. Little shows that voluntary associations in new communities serve as mediating groups for newly-arrived migrants coming from traditional villages.[21] Membership substitutes for the traditional extended kinship group of the village by supplying sociability, protection, advice, and a guided introduction to urban life-styles. Some groups maintain traditional culture through music and ritual activities; others follow European organization and thus introduce members to western, urbanized ways. Some train members in modern business and political skills. In all these ways, voluntary associations serve to integrate rural migrants into urban life. In addition, by regulating members' behavior, they serve as mechanisms for social control. Little concludes that two factors are instrumental in the growth of voluntary associations in West Africa: first, the existence of a migrant, unstable, socially heterogeneous urban population; and, second, the adaptability of traditional institutions to modern conditions. Little feels that it is the interrelation of these factors that causes voluntary associations to become important. It will be interesting to see to what extent participation continues as migrants establish family and other primary ties on their own.

The anthropologist Robert Anderson (1971) argues that voluntary associations do not socialize an individual unless broader social forces are favorable.[22] When established in communities not yet swallowed up by spreading urbanization, associations adapt to traditional norms and function informally. As urbanization occurs, they may adapt individuals for participation in the new social order, but they do not initiate social change. Anderson further states that voluntary associations or "sodalities" existed in neolithic societies; they are now wholly an urban phenomenon.

The Function of Voluntary Associations in the Contemporary Community

We have discussed many of the stresses which appear to be inherent in the social fabric of contemporary urban communities. Many of the popular portrayals of urban life emphasize its lonely and alienating impact. Recent books like Hannerz's *Soulside* and Liebow's *Talley's Corner* might lead one to believe that inner city people

[20]Robert A. Wilson, "Anomie in the Ghetto: A Study of Neighborhood Type, Race, and Anomie," *American Journal of Sociology,* Vol. 77, No. 1, (July, 1971), pp. 66–68.

[21]Kenneth L. Little, "The Role of Voluntary Associations in West African Urbanization," *American Anthropologist,* 59, (1957), pp. 579–596.

[22]Robert T. Anderson, "Voluntary Associations in History," *American Anthropologist,* 73 (February, 1971), pp. 209–222.

usually spend an entire lifetime in a neighborhood without even knowing the last names of their friends and neighbors.[23] These studies, however, portray one extreme on a continuum of urban social participation; they do not appear to capture the reality for the vast majority of inner city residents. In fact, most studies indicate that people do have regular primary relationships with friends and kin, although they may see them less frequently than do their counterparts in less urbanized areas.[24] A study by Reis confirms this pattern, finding no differences between rural and urban people in the amount of time spent with kin.[25] The only real difference in rural and urban friendship patterns is that urban friends tend to be more geographically dispersed from the neighborhood residence.[26]

The traditional sociological scenario assumes a weakening of primary ties in urban areas, which is compensated for by membership in formal organizations. However, the real reason for organizational membership in urban areas may be quite different. Fischer maintains that migrants to cities, in spite of their greater participation in group activity may not have an integrative experience:

> . . . studies of these associations suggest that their formal quality is only a veneer (applied often for political purposes) to a set of essentially informal relationships based essentially on ethnicity or village background. For instance, a set of migrants to the city who have come from the same village may wish to participate in the annual carnival parade. In order to do so, they need official recognition from the municipal authorities; so they constitute themselves as a formal club, complete with officers. This kind of group is usually not very formal in the sociological sense . . .

> There are indications that people by and large use their formal associations to cultivate informal personal ties, not as substitutes for ties. Membership in an organization is often valued because the organization provides a place to pursue and develop friendships.[27]

In sum, formal organizations of cities are probably not a substitute for friendship and family ties. Rather, they appear to supplement these ties.[28] Some organizations, however, serve purposes which are particularly important in coping with the specialized problems of urban areas.

Urban Social Action Groups

In the larger urban areas, government must respond to a variety of subcommunities and specialized interest groups which are not present in less urbanized locales. The

[23]Elliot Liebow, *Tally's Corner,* (New York: Little-Brown, 1967); U. Hannerz, *Soulside,* (New York: Columbia University Press, 1969).

[24]Bell and Boat, *op. cit.*; Axelrod, *op. cit.*

[25]A. J. Reiss, "Rural-Urban Status Differences in Interpersonal Contacts," *American Journal of Sociology,* 65 (September, 1959), pp. 182–195.

[26]Joe R. Feagin, "The Kinship Ties of Negro Urbanites," *Social Science Quarterly,* 49 (1969), pp. 661–665; Claude S. Fischer, *The Urban Experience,* (New York: Harcourt Brace Jovanovich, 1976), pp. 106–107; T. Koyama, "Rural-Urban Comparisons of Kinship Relations in Japan," in R. Hill and R. Konig, eds., *Families in East and West* (Paris: Mouton, 1970), pp. 318–337.

[27]Fischer, pp. 106–107.

[28]P. C. W. Gutkind, "African Urbanism, Mobility, and Social Network," in G. Breese, ed., *The City in Newly Developing Countries,* (Englewood Cliffs, N.J.: Prentice-Hall, 1969), pp. 389–400.

same interests are often present in both urban and rural areas. But in rural areas, the number of persons who fall into a category may not be sufficient to form an organization which can mount an effort to lobby, to demonstrate, or to form a formidable voting block. Too, government in urbanized areas usually is manifest as a large, complex bureaucracy which is resistant to the needs of individual citizens.

Although the United States has a history of citizen participation dating back to the frontier era, the kind of grass-roots participation which is exemplified by the New England town meeting is so rare today as to be noteworthy as an oddity. In virtually all communities, lay boards of directors serve as focal points for school systems, hospitals, and cultural or recreational institutions, but in most cases very little decision-making actually is done by the citizen member. Instead, management is presented to the group by professional staff as a series of ready-made options, one of which is recommended by the staff and usually accepted by the board. This process has evolved as the result of the reality that the management of urban government is an exceedingly complex process that requires the day-to-day effort of technicians and professional managers. Intimate involvement by citizens is almost impossible. Moreover, government in most large cities attempts to follow an industrial model, based on the relative costs and benefits of different service systems. While often providing an optimal level of service for the majority of citizens, urban service systems have often been unresponsive to the needs of subcommunities. Examples are the poor, the aged, and most ethnic minorities. Ironically, by becoming more efficient, government lost some of the flexibility to meet specialized needs that was inherent in the old system of ward bosses. For example, the person needing oil during a cold winter must now cope with a bewildering welfare bureaucracy. In contrast, during less bureaucratized times a ton of free coal could be secured by dealing directly with the local ward boss. Today, flexibility in government is secured by organizing a political block which has sufficient clout to demand a change in policy. In order to succeed, enough pressure must be applied to shake the bureaucracy to its foundations. The 1960's witnessed the formation of a number of new kinds of organizations which attempted to secure policy changes from urban government.

One of the earliest organized efforts to cope with big urban governments was generated by neighborhood groups which attempted to influence planning for urban renewal and highway construction.[29] Usually such groups organized with the initial goal of stopping the demolition of an old neighborhood. If successful, some groups remained active for years as neighborhood preservation associations with wide-ranging projects which attempted to improve the social and physical aspects of neighborhood life.

The War on Poverty and the Model Cities Program were both federally funded community improvement programs of the 1960's. A deliberate effort was made to

---

[29]For example, see J. Clarence Davis, *Neighborhood Groups and Urban Renewal,* (New York: Columbia University Press, 1966); also see Jane Jacobs, *The Death and Life of Great American Cities,* (New York: Random House, 1961).

organize neighborhood residents into groups which could provide local input to government programming though neighborhood councils and various task forces which attempted to influence policy on housing, education, health, recreation, and criminal justice systems. Often these groups became so powerful that they posed a threat to the local political establishment. Local governments cut off their funds for organizing and lobbying, thereby alleviating the threat of loss of power. Although the concept of "maximum feasible participation" of the poor in the administration was initially accepted by almost everyone, when the balance of power shifted sufficiently to disrupt local political bureaucracies, federal policy was soon changed to de-emphasize this element of the poverty program. Daniel Patrick Moynihan summed up the degree of dysfunctional conflict by dubbing the eventual result of the War on Poverty as "Maximal Feasible Misunderstanding."[30] One of the results of this era appears to be that urbanites learned the techniques which are necessary to organize communities into political interest groups.[31] The last two decades have witnessed the application of the poverty war's organizational techniques to a much wider spectrum of urban conflicts. Among these have been tenants' rights organizations, womens' rights groups, homosexual groups, anti-school busing groups, and even prostitute organizations.[32]

Thus, the city appears to be not much different from less urbanized areas in the amount of social participation. The functions of voluntary organizations also appear to be the same—to supplement the functions of family and friends, rather than to supplant them. The pattern of voluntary associations in the city appears to differ from its rural counterpart chiefly in that it offers a wider variety of special purpose groups. Some of these have developed into political pressure groups which appear to be the only means of influencing policy in the unwieldy bureaucracies which have become increasingly evident with each increment in the scope of government.

Work as Social Participation

In primitive societies, the differentiation between work and leisure is less apparent than in urbanized, industrialized societies. In hunting and gathering cultures, work and leisure melt in a total pattern of life, encompassing subsistence activities and other traditions which are not often separated conceptually by the members of the culture. Work is usually ritualized to the extent that harvests and hunts become associated with ceremony and with magic or religion. In many primitive

[30]Daniel Patrick Moynihan, *Maximum Feasible Misunderstanding,* (New York: The Free Press, 1969).

[31]Norman I. Fainstain and Susan S. Fainstain, *Urban Political Movements: The Search for Power by Minority Groups,* (Englewood Cliffs, N.J.: Prentice-Hall, 1974); Curt Lamb, *Political Power in Poor Neighborhoods,* (New York: Halstead Press, 1975); David J. O'Brien, *Neighborhood Organization and Interest Group Processes,* (Princeton, N.J.: Princeton University Press, 1975).

[32]Joseph Bensman and Arthur J. Vidich, *Metropolitan Communities: New Forms of Urban Sub-Communities,* (New York: New Viewpoints, 1975).

Manufacturing Television Receivers in a mass production setting. TV broadcasting in Japan was inaugurated in 1953 in black and white. A mere seven years later, color telecasting made its debut. The number of TV sets produced in 1975 totalled 11.5 million, of which 7.5 million were color sets.

cultures, harvesting food is often performed to chanting or singing, which has the effect of integrating the community in a subsistence task and also making the hard work more tolerable.

With the advent of modern industry, work became increasingly more specialized. Not only did individuals now perform a much smaller part of a total production process but increasingly they became less aware of the relationship between their small task and the entire economy which makes it possible for a society to thrive. Work on the assembly line is frequently associated with what Karl Marx called the "alienation of labor," suggesting that a worker not only performs a miniscule task which provides no fulfillment; he also performs it in a way whereby he becomes increasingly disenchanted with the entire production process and industrial society.[33]

Since the worker does not own the means of production, he cannot realize a profit from his investment. He can only sell his services as a "wage slave"— subject to the erratic swings of the supply and demand for labor. This is the major sense in which he is alienated. In the second sense, he does not really comprehend what he produces because he works in such a small part of the entire production process. The product of his labor, therefore, stands over and against him as something alien. The extent to which this alienation occurs has been analyzed in a large number of studies dealing with industry. The field of group dynamics often involves

[33]Karl Marx, *op. cit.*

the study of workers in complex organizations, each of whom performs a minute task, which is necessary in an overall production process and which ultimately results in a production of some technologically complex product.

Industry and government in urbanized countries is increasingly dominated by a complex organization or bureaucracy. Because people's work roles are dependent upon how they can relate to such bureaucracies, the occupational role relates not only to the occupation or its performance, but also to the manner in which the worker interacts with the large corporation which employs him.[34] Even the ''right'' church is tacitly suggested by the organization, also the ''right'' neighborhood, the ''right'' clubs and even the ''right'' hobbies which one needs to engage in, in order to develop into the composite organization man who is on the way up. The modern suburb thus becomes the operational base for organization men and women of several varieties. But one suburb in the megalopolis, having houses costing $50,000, resembles almost exactly similar suburbs a thousand miles away. Families come and go as they are transferred. The organization and the correct progression within it becomes the basis of community, rather than the residential neighborhood or city.

The Protestant Ethic and the Spirit of Twentieth Century Life

The idea of the work ethic that has developed in American sociology can be traced to the ideas expressed by Max Weber in *The Protestant Ethic and the Spirit of Capitalism.*[35] The ideology of capitalism, Weber indicated, was closely associated with certain ideas of European Protestantism. He observed that the growth of the factory system and later modern industry was more prevalent in Protestant cities. The ideas which form the core of the Protestant ethic were extremely prevalent during the growth of America during the first two centuries. The basic ideology of the Protestant ethic is summarized below.

The Value of Self Discipline and Hard Work.   According to the Protestant ethic, work or a ''calling'' is really a matter of predestination. It is impossible to be sure if one is called to heaven or hell, but worldly sucess was often seen as evidence of God's favor and grace. The idea of asceticism, a code of strict self-discipline, meant denial of worldly pleasures, and above all the idea that hard work was necessary for true success. When one is successful, this is a sign of harmony with God. Relief from most anxieties, therefore, could befound in hard work and self-discipline.

The Value of Initiative and Acquisition.   By working hard and disciplining oneself, the results should be an economic advantage over competitors and the acquisition of money or goods. This wealth, of course, was not to be squandered, but rather to be saved or re-invested into other business activity. Fruitfulness was

[34]Whyte, *The Organization Man, op. cit.*

[35]Max Weber, *The Protestant Ethic and the Spirit of Capitalism,* translated by T. Parsons, (London: Allen and Unwin, 1904).

the likely result of faithfully working in God's vineyard and was considered evidence, but not proof, of saving grace.

The Value of Individualism and Competition.   Salvation has most often been seen in Protestant thought as a personal matter. A whole people might be saved by a "righteous remnant," but the remnant was righteous because each individual in it was a faithful and diligent worker. Thus Protestantism has been aptly described as a lonely religion, because it places so little emphasis upon corporate salvation. Competition is a by-product of individual effort.

It is obvious when we examine the core ideology of the Protestant Ethic that the individualism and the competition involved do not focus on large-scale organization, but rather upon the individual. Indeed, the acquisition of wealth and the accumulation of capital, for most individuals of the modern twentieth-century world, is out of tune with the consumption ethic, which stresses the spending of wealth rather, than its acquisition in the form of capital. While the ideas incorporated in the Protestant ethic survive as a dominant American value—particularly that work itself is a virtue—one is no longer thought to be in favor with God if one's occupation is rewarding. Rather, occupation is thought of as a prerequisite to happiness or self-fulfillment which is brought about by the intrinsic rewards within the work process, and also by the prestige of the career within the community. Jobs on the other hand, are important for the income they provide, rather than any intrinsic regard they might have. Jobs are likely to be more alienating than careers.

Occupations in Urban Society

Interpreting participation in the labor force in terms of urban sociology suggests that there are at least two dimensions which are of direct concern. First, there is the occupation in itself—the prestige, its relation to the social structure and the general life-style which is associated with a specific occupation. Second, and perhaps more important, as a current sociological issue, is the relationship of the job to various complex organizations such as large corporations or government. If one works for a corporation and is constantly transferred throughout the country, this pattern in itself must have a direct impact on how one relates to each successive community.[36] If, on the other hand, one enters an occupation with the expectation of having firm roots in a local community over a longer period of time, the implications are different. Although one may join a professional organization which may be national in its interest and character, one is probably more willing to invest oneself in local memberships which have the potential of social investments or social capital over a longer period of time. The capacity to adjust quickly to new locations is not nearly as important when the person expects to reside for most of his lifetime in the same community. But for the mobile bureaucrat, the ability to adjust to find self fulfillment anywhere—becomes paramount.

[36]Eugene Litwak, "Voluntary Associations and Neighborhood Cohesion," *American Sociological Review,* 26, (April, 1961), pp. 258–271.

The new ethic in America? One form of leisure is gambling. Nevada's legalized gambling is licensed and carefully controlled both by state and local authorities. Public confidence in Nevada gaming has never been higher, as attested by 9 million visitors to Las Vegas annually. Here gamblers enjoy action at a baccarat table. (*Las Vegas News Bureau.*)

Social Participation Patterns in Urban Settings

The Upper-Upper Class, (Philadelphia Gentlemen)

Sociologists have not conducted very many studies which focus upon the upper class. One notable exception, however, is the classical study by E. Digby Baltzell, carried out primarily in Philadelphia during the early 50's.[37] The upper class in Philadelphia was identified through its membership in the Social Register, a publication which lists the membership and biographies of families who belong to a national social elite. Baltzell indicates that many of the upper class families listed in the *Register* in the Philadelphia area had maintained their position for over a century in that community. In contrast, families which had acquired wealth, position or power more recently were not as frequently mentioned, nor were the educational elite or other cultural leaders, who were more often listed in *Who's Who in America*.

Baltzell found those who were most frequently members of business elites also served as directors of large banks and corporations in both the Philadelphia area and throughout the United States. These businessmen were over-represented in the *Register*. A much smaller percentage of the *Register*'s members had occupations in

[37]Baltzell, *op. cit.*

politics, media, medicine, architecture, religion, and the cultural arts. Typically the pattern of *Register* membership was that one founding father (in the 1800's) made an outstanding success in business. His descendents usually engaged in occupations outside of business, but retained the family listing in the *Social Register*. From the standpoint of social participation, the *Register* listed for each family a number of upper class organizational memberships, including mens' clubs, country clubs, eating clubs, etc., which signified participation in a limited number of elite organizations. In Philadelphia, for instance, the most prestigious mens' club was the Philadelphia Club. Membership was limited exclusively to members of the *Social Register* and business elite.

Social Register members also limited themselves largely to certain residential neighborhoods within the Philadelphia metropolitan region. One of these was the famous "Main Line." Most of these neighborhoods were in close proximity to the private secondary schools attended by the children of the upper class. They were also near hunt and country clubs, which formed a basis for the social life for the same families.

Certain church memberships also predominated. Most frequently, *Social Register* members were Episcopalians or Presbyterians, with only an extremely small minority in other Protestant churches or Catholic churches, and almost no Jewish members. Although parallel upper class structures existed for Jews and Catholics, in 1940, most members of these groups were not as frequently listed in the *Social Register*. Even the summer recreation areas of the Philadelphia elite suggested an exclusion of other groups. Some of the summer resorts in Maine were populated primarily by members of the *Social Register* from large cities, thereby broadening the social interaction of the national upper class and providing a number of potentially eligible mates from upper-class children.

The Organization Man—A Study of Emerging Upper Middle-Class Patterns

In the 1950's, as the GI bill made it possible for many World War II veterans to achieve a college education, American industry also expanded. This provided a base of employment for engineers, accountants, personnel specialists, advertising specialists, and a large number of new occupational groups, such as computer and systems analysts—a whole array of new specializations which developed with large scale industry and government. This pattern, in itself, brought about many changes in life-styles, documented in *The Organization Man* (1956), written by William H. Whyte, Jr.[38] The ideology of the organization stressed a decline of individualism and Protestant ethic values in favor of an allegiance to the organization, and to success in terms of the organization's goals, rather than through individual acquisition of wealth. In essence, the emphasis on individual productivity was replaced by a

[38]Whyte, *op. cit.*

group ethic, whereby team research, team production and team selling became paramount in the life of the organization man.

Whyte suggested that the litany of the organization man, which is becoming increasingly standard, might go something as follows:

> Be loyal to the company and the company will be loyal to you. After all, if you do a good job for the organization, it is only good sense for the organization to be good to you, because that will be best for everybody. There are a bunch of real people around here. Tell them what you think and they will respect you for it. Don't want a man to fret and stew about his work. It won't happen to me. A man who gets ulcers probably shouldn't be in business anyway.[39]

Interpreting this litany, Whyte suggested that the frontier era of American free enterprise is over. Modern industry functions more to keep things going, rather than develop new products or increase profits. "Unorthodoxy can be dangerous to the organization, in that ideas should come from the group, not the individual."[40]

Whyte also gives advice to prospective employees taking a series of personality tests administered by a large organization's personnel department. There are several rules to follow:

> 1. When asked for work associations or comment about the world give the most conventional, run-of-the-mill, pedestrian answer possible.
> 2. When in doubt about the most beneficial answer to any question repeat to yourself: I love my father and my mother but my father a little bit more. I like things pretty much as they are. I never worry about anything. I don't care for books or music much. I love my wife and children. I don't let them get in the way of company work.[41]

Whyte also testifies to the stresses which large organizations place upon their employees by transferring them frequently. Rather than a stratification system based primarily within the local community, Whyte concluded that the class hierarchy is now transferred to the organization—that is, it is the position the employee has within its organization with respect to management and leadership which determines his class identity.[42] The organization man usually lives in mass-produced community which stresses group membership, in spite of the transiency of the organization families who reside there. Whyte cites a radio advertisement for the Park Forest Development outside of Chicago (November 8, 1952):

> A cup of coffee—a symbol of Park Forest! Coffee pots bubble all day long in Park Forest. The sign of friendliness tells you how much neighbors enjoy each other's company—feel glad that they can share their daily joys—yes and troubles, too. Come out to Park Forest where small town friendships grow and you will still live so close to a big city.[43]

[39]*Ibid.*, p. 129.
[40]*Ibid.*, p. 137.
[41]*Ibid.*, pp. 134–137.
[42]*Ibid.*, pp. 196–197.
[43]*Ibid.*, pp. 284–285.

Even participation in the churches in the areas, which were organized primarily by the inhabitants, suggests the need for new friendships in the "new" areas.[44]

In general, participation in the career within an organization eclipses all other social participation. The friendships and organization memberships of the organization man, at least in Whyte's terms, all revolve around a successful adjustment to the career within a large bureaucracy.

Tally's Corner—A Study of Street Corner Men

In distinct contrast to the Philadelphia upper class and the organization men are the street corner men studied by Elliot Liebow (1967) in Washington, D.C.[45] Liebow's study employs the general anthropological approach of social participation within a urban ghetto—studying interaction with parents, wives, children, girlfriends, employers, brothers, and friends. Liebow indicates that it is the street corner world itself and its friendships which provide both the social participation and the status-conferring apparatus for this group. The work role and all other roles are subservient to the interaction which takes place near a "carry-out" restaurant, where men from the neighborhood gather. A series of cliques develop, which form the basis for friendship. Rather than the organization, neighborhood membership is based upon an informal group which convenes outside or inside the carry-out. The corner group may be relied upon for aid in an emergency, to provide companionship and advice, and to gain information about where jobs might be found. The people on the corner may be relatives, neighbors, fellow workers, or any other people who might gather there. The language of the group stresses a kind of pseudo-kinship relationship where people are called "brother." In the same sense of the organizational memberships which were discussed earlier in this chapter, the street corner provides a group experience. Some interaction at Talley's corner might be characterized as primary relationships, but most may be characterized as secondary. In general, the street group performs many of the social functions which in other settings are carried out by work-associated organizations, churches and neighbors.

The Juvenile Gang

Another classic study focuses on the young men who live in the slums of Chicago.[46] In this research, Suttles shows clearly that the social order of juvenile gangs and young people is determined primarily by two factors: the area which one lives in, and ethnicity. (Specifically whether one is black, Italian, Puerto Rican or Mexican.) Thus, residence, ethnicity, and age limit the associational memberships which a

---

[44]*Ibid.,* pp. 378–379.

[45]Liebow, *op. cit.*

[46]Gerald D. Suttles, *The Social Order of the Slum: Ethnicity and Territory in the Inner-City,* (Chicago: University of Chicago Press, 1968).

person could have. Most of the associations tend to be cliques which "hung out" together and also have certain territorial rights. Gangs and cliques are not formally organized, but act or operated on assumptions about roles which evolve gradually over a period of time. The main function of these ghetto groups, according to Suttles, is to provide a sense of companionship and belonging for members having similar interests, ethnic identity and neighborhood ties. Rather than the universal characteristics associated with job or occupation which are so typical of organization men, success and prestige are limited to that found in the local microcosm. Members are stratified in terms of personal leadership and abilities, such as toughness, fighting, "heart," and loyalty. Leadership is based mainly upon the individuals force of will, the ability to dominate by muscle and shrewdness. Some formal organizations, such as the YMCA, exist in the area, along with churches and labor unions, but most of the young people find little satisfaction in these organizations, because individual roles are not prescribed to a degree which provides the rewards and identity available through the more informal groups.

Conclusion

In this chapter we have provided an overview of the pattern of social participation in groups and in bureaucratic settings, primarily within American urban areas. Social participation varies extensively, depending upon one's position within the social structure and the community of residence. One's occupation probably has the most impact upon overall social participation. This, in turn, affects one's area of residence, neighborhood ties, religious participation, and the pattern of membership in other formal organizations. Similarly, occupation affects one's attitudes towards leisure as well as the symbolism of the local community within which one lives. Organizational membership may provide a necessary buffer against some urban stresses, a function which in previous eras and in less urbanized areas was performed by friends, neighbors and kin. Participation in informal social relationships (friendships, kin, and neighboring) varies principally with the social stratification of the neighborhood and its stage of development in the neighborhood life-cycle.

Finally, a number of new types of voluntary organizations have evolved in urban areas during the last thirty years. The reason for the emergence of many of these appears to be to counterbalance the unwieldy governmental bureaucracies which continue to become larger, more complex, and more resistant to specialized service needs.

part 2

Urban Social Organization

chapter 6

The City
and Family Life

The net impression left by many studies of the city is that it is not a very good place in which to raise a family. This general conclusion is in line with our commonly held conceptions. In America, it seems, cities were established much more for the purpose of getting on with business than for living in them.

However, once we go beyond the general statement we have just made, the issue becomes more complex. What is it about cities that make them poor places in which to raise a family? Or conversely, just what kind of family finds it hard to live in cities in America? It is questions of the latter sort that put our original generality in some context and help us to understand more about cities and families than common sense normally allows.

Urbanization usually refers to the processes of city growth. More precisely, cities have large heterogeneous populations often densely packed together in apartment buildings, condominiums, hotels or boarding houses. The single family dwelling is much more characteristic of the suburbs. Cities change their size and composition rapidly. The process of urbanization within a country has dramatic effects upon rural populations and changes the mix of the city.

At least two other major factors intertwine with urbanization in the growth of cities that also affect family life dramatically. Alex Inkeles and others studying developing countries conclude that modernization is one such factor. Modernization seems to be acquired through encounter with routine procedures of such bureaucracies as the consolidated school, the army, the government bureau, and the large corporation. Adapting to the way things are done in these bureaucracies is associated with greater flexibility and the acceptance of change in a peasant's personality. The large bureaucracies have grown up with our cities.

Industrialization has both contributed to the growth of cities and benefited from

117

"Your friend is more than welcome, dear, but we just want you to know that your father and I didn't do anything funny till after we were married."

Drawing by Modell; © 1972 The New Yorker Magazine, Inc.

it. It shapes the character of a particular kind of bureaucracy—the factory system—and contributes commodities such as the automobile and the pill that change the character of family life. The factory system, especially when it is in the assembly-line mode of operation, requires large numbers of relatively unskilled workers within an hour or so of the factory. Historically, the factory system grew up with the city; now corporations are moving to the suburbs, taking advantage of the improved highway system. The bureaucracy, the factory and its products have effects upon family life that can be distinguished from the effects of other aspects of city life. This will be the focus of the first part of this chapter.

The second portion of this chapter will examine the more recent flight to the suburbs. American suburbs are established, so we often say, because they are "good places to raise kids." To what extent is this so? When considering urban/suburban differences, it must also be remembered that the term "suburb" now covers a number of different types of communities. Working class suburbs, studied by sociologists such as Bennet Berger and William Dobriner, are not the same sort of community as the satellite city or the dormitory suburb.[1] Nevertheless, we will focus upon the dormitory suburb associated with the upper-middle class professional in America and assess its strengths and weaknesses in regard to bringing up a family because, to a considerable extent, the rationalization for life in this suburb revolves around the assertion that the family prospers there.

The final portion of this chapter will look at how design affects human interaction and family life. Does the arrangement of buildings, their interior design, and the way in which they relate to the neighborhood have anything to do with how people live in them? A chief consideration here is how the design manages large numbers of people. We are beginning to understand that there are many ways to measure the density of a neighborhood's population and that good design can offset many of the adverse conditions associated with "high density" housing. How can cities be changed in their design to improve the quality of human interaction and enhance family life? We have no simple answers to these questions, but we can at least begin the exploration.

Urbanization and Family Structure

Assessing the impact of urbanization on family life is a complex task because city growth is intertwined with other processes such as industrialization and modernization. Changes in a population's size, density and heterogeneity (the three most common components of urbanization) have different effects upon family structure and life-style, depending on whether the city is heavily industrialized or not.[2] Indeed, cities are exposed to differing modernizing influences which make their citizens more able to cope with change and adjust to the needs of different kinds of organizations. Further, micro-environments within the city can have a significant impact upon family life independent of the kind of city within which a family might live, as the various ethnic ghettos of the early twentieth century suggest.

Urbanization need not be linked with modernization, although it commonly is. Cities such as Addis Ababa, with over a million inhabitants, have not changed much of the life-style of their inhabitants. They are still essentially villagers. The low profile of the city retains the human scale of the village; most families still live in separate quarters with close relatives living nearby. The extended family functions on a day-to-day, face-to-face basis, so that life, for the average citizen of Addis

---

[1]Bennet Berger, *Working Class Suburb: A Study of Auto Workers in Suburbia* (Berkeley: University of California Press, 1960). William Dobriner, *Class in Suburbia* (Englewood Cliffs, N.J.: Prentice Hall, 1963).

[2]One of the characteristics of cities in developing countries is, of course, that they are not heavily industrialized. Yet the migration to the city exposes the family to a quite different social environment in which, for example, individuals are valued more than families.

Ababa, is not too different in its tone and quality from that of nearby villages. Living in a large city need not of itself change the essential characteristics of a peasant life.[3]

While Addis Ababa seems unusual in this regard, many cities have subcommunities that remain essentially villages for several generations. In cities such as Mexico City or Cairo, Egypt (the world's tenth largest city), many people remain essentially rural in outlook. Herbert Gans dramatized the distinctiveness of such subpopulations in American cities when he called the South Bostonians he was studying "The Urban Villagers."

Oscar Lewis vividly describes the interplay of modernizing and traditionalizing forces in his *Children of Sanchez*.[4] Jesus Sanchez moved from a rural village twenty years before Lewis met him at his apartment in the Casa Grande, a walled apartment compound in Mexico City. Like so many South American cities, Mexico City is surrounded by a growing mass of poor families attracted to the city by the lure of jobs and a more comfortable way of life. In the city, they often live near to shrines, government buildings, hotels, and stores that attract people from all over their country and the world as well. Yet because their immediate neighborhood contains all things necessary to their meager existences, they need not go out into the larger city. Nevertheless, over the years, the children of Sanchez are affected by the urban environment. They come to have more education, higher income, live less under the influence of the old folk religion, speak better Spanish and come to identify themselves more and more with the nation rather than the village from which they came. Much the same thing happens to rural poor who emigrate to the cities from the South or from Appalachia. In the enclaves or locations, as Anselm Strauss would call them, of our inner cities, the poor find some security in the old ways with people like themselves, while they begin to assimilate aspects of cosmopolitan American culture.[5] In the migration from the country, it is rare that an entire extended family moves at one time. Rather, a common pattern is that one conjugal family establishes a beachhead in the city and then houses another conjugal family until the newcomers have time to find a house and get a job.[6] It is abundantly evident, then, that it is possible to have considerable growth in a nation's cities without the immediate destruction of kinship bonds and without immediate modernization of large portions of the urban population.

The impact of industrialization upon family life is yet another thing. The effects of the factory system, in particular, have been amply recorded from its earliest stages in infant mortality, high death rates, child labor statistics and the

[3]William H. Michaelson, *Man and His Urban Environment: A Sociological Approach* (Reading, Mass.: Addison Wesley, 1976).

[4]Oscar Lewis, *The Children of Sanchez* (New York: Random House, 1961).

[5]Anselm Strauss, *Images of the American City* (New York: The Free Press, 1961), pp. 52–67.

[6]Jerome Stromberg, "Kinship and Friendship Among Lower Class Negro Families." Paper prepared for the Society for the Study of Social Problems, San Francisco, August 1967.

disintegration of the family business.[7] Beginning in the late part of the eighteenth century in England, large numbers of people began to move to the city in order to fill the needs of a growing number of factories for a cheap, flexible supply of labor. At the same time, the machine became ever more efficient. Productivity could be increased to meet an expanding market without the immediate necessity to increase the labor force. Women and children could also become machine operatives as easily as men; so for the first time, they truly competed with men for the same jobs. It became common for unscrupulous employers to hire a whole family at the wages formerly paid to a head of household. The results were predictable . . . "infant and child mortality rates rose, the working day lengthened, children were kept out of school, young girls did not learn the necessary domestic arts, and fathers sold their children's labor on harsh terms."[8] Yet Smelzer points out that at an earlier stage in the industrial process, fathers were able to supervise their own children and thus maintain their authority as household heads. When the whole family became employed, this was a much more difficult task.

There is a strong tradition within the sociology of the family to link the conjugal family—a husband, wife and their children—to the factory system under the assumption that it was more functional than the extended family in meeting the needs of the factory.[9] The hunter pursued his game, the modern man pursues his job. In hunting, gathering, and modern industrial cultures, the small conjugal family is common. In the agricultural societies of the world, in contrast, the large extended family predominates. As attractive as this generalization might seem at first, it is by no means established. Goode points out that Japan is a modern industrial nation in which the extended family is still quite strong.[10] The ideology of the conjugal family is present in Japan, but nepotism is common in the large corporations also. Greenfield further suggests that Barbados is a society in which the conjugal family is the predominant family structure, but where there is virtually no industrialization.[11]

Goode suggests, quite reasonably, that industrialization affects poorer families differently from the richer.[12] The richer the family, the more it maintains its integrity in the face of the demands of career or job. Thus the upper class is one of the few places in American society where the large extended family still functions. In similar fashion, wealth allows families to protect themselves from the ad-

[7]See, for example, the account rendered in Francesco Cordasco, ed., *Jacob Riis Revisited: Poverty and the Slum in Another Era* (Garden City, New York: Doubleday and Company, Inc., 1968).

[7a]William J. Goode, *World Revolution and Family Patterns* (New York: The Free Press, 1963), p. 4.

[8]Neil J. Smelser, "Process of Social Change," in Neil J. Smelser, ed., *Sociology: An Introduction* (New York: John Wiley and Sons, Inc., 1967).

[9]Talcott Parsons, "The Stability of the American Family System," in Norman W. Bell and Ezra Vogel, eds., *Modern Introduction to the Family* (Glencoe, Ill.: The Free Press, 1960), pp. 93–97.

[10]Goode, *op. cit.*

[11]Sidney M. Greenfield, "Industrialization and the Family in Sociological Theory," *American Journal of Sociology,* 67 (1961–62): 312–322.

[12]Goode, *op. cit.*

verse consequences of city growth and modernization. Rich families can have a town house or an apartment in the middle of Manhattan where they can take advantage of the city's culture and be close to the heart of its business, and at the same time retire to one or more country estates when they desire. It is, after all, primarily the middle class that has exited from the inner city. Families at this income level cannot afford the luxury apartment protected from the crime and disorder of the streets, nor the tuition for a private school education for all of its children, but they do have enough to move out and buy a home in the suburbs.

Finally, Kingsley Davis distinguishes urbanization from simple city growth.[13] Urbanization, in Davis' understanding, is measured by the ratio of people in a given country who are living in cities as opposed to the rural areas. In advanced industrial countries such as Great Britain and the United States, urbanization, by his measure, has ceased because the farm population no longer contributes to the growth of cities. But cities continue to grow, nevertheless, as a function of natural increase. In the United States, this did not happen until about 1960. Prior to 1960, urban areas in America did not reproduce their numbers and had to rely on immigration from the countryside to provide them their growth. This fact of relatively low urban fertility has been used as an indication of the extent to which cities are perceived of as hostile to family life. Other explanations as to why urban populations have not characteristically been able to reproduce their numbers point to the earlier history of highly unsanitary conditions associated with cities and the extent to which children in cities are less of an economic asset to parents. Farm families depend upon their children to help manage the farm.

Some serious problems occur in countries whose cities are growing more slowly than the population as a whole. In Venezuela, for example, there are about 225 persons trying to eke out a living off each square mile of land.[14] This makes it very difficult for the country to make optimum use of its land resources and results in the necessity to import more food. It seems reasonable to assume that in most cases it would be possible to make better use of the land if the cities could absorb the increase in population growth.

All other things being equal, it seems reasonable to assume that in cities that are growing primarily as a result of natural increase, the conjugal family would be more implanted in a functioning extended family. It would at least be more likely that three generations would remain in contact even if the collateral kin (uncles and cousins) were not tied in. This would be particularly true of the working and lower class, where there would be less tendency to move from city to city in search of better jobs.

Compounded Effects.   Having recognized that urbanization, industrialization and modernization need not occur concurrently, it is now necessary to consider the more common cases in which they do. In countries that are developing today, a common pattern emerges. During the early stages of modernization, improved

---

[13]Kingsley Davis, "Urbanization of the World Population," *Scientific American* (1965).
[14]Davis, *op. cit.*

transportation and communication, increased food supply, improved sanitation, and the introduction of western medical techniques improves the health of the population and dramatically reduces the death rate.[15] These improvements are felt first in the cities.

However, a decline in the death rate does not immediately bring about a reduction in the birth rate. People in developing economies still are tuned to an agricultural economy in which children are decided assets. Since the benefits of reduced mortality are not immediately felt, they tend to produce as many children as possible in order to insure that enough will survive to be of service.

As a result of the rapid reduction in the death rate and a continued high birth rate, the population explodes. Developing countries are rapidly placed in a double bind if they do not bring their populations under control by reducing the birth rate (and most do not). First of all, the number of persons dependent upon the labor force increases dramatically, while the size of this force does not increase appreciably. The needs of these dependents for schools, clothing, housing, and later jobs, would be enormous in and of itself were it not for another factor. As the population of a developing country becomes more urban and more nationalistic (even looking to the international community), its expectations about what constitutes the good life increase. These dependents thus demand more of everything than their parents. The nation as a whole must cope with these rising expectations at the same time that it must accumulate capital in order to increase its industrial production through the building of new facilities. If the nation's agriculture is undeveloped, as in most cases it is, then much capital must be tied up in the improvement of agricultural efficiency.

The major aspects of this transformation of a peasant society into a modernizing one can be summarized in the following points: (1) integration of previously isolated, self-sufficient, rural economies into a single national economy with strong international connections; (2) the increasing dominance of production for sale over production for barter, leading to a monied economy; (3) the technological advance of agricultural techniques involving large-scale capital investments and a reduction in the percentage of the population tied to the land; (4) tremendous growth in the means of transportation and communication which furthers the nationalization and internationalization of the developing country; (5) steady growth of the towns and cities, which become centers of trade and manufacturing; (6) a steady increase in the specialization of life, resulting in an increasing functional interdependence of the population, while at the same time it experiences a breakdown in the traditional means of structuring its society.[16]

This increasing reliance upon the industrial system disrupts the traditional extended family in two primary ways: (1) the conjugal family becomes increasingly

---

[15]A good discussion of the "demographic transition" is found in Nathan Kaylitz, "Population Theory and Doctrine: A Historical Survey," in William Petersen, ed., *Readings in Population* (New York: The Macmillan Company, 1972), pp. 63–65.

[16]Joseph Kahl, "Some Social Concommittants of Urbanization and Industrialization," *Human Organization* XVIII 2 (Summer, 1969), pp. 53–74.

distinct from the extended family network, and (2) the power of the conjugal unit (familism) over its members declines, as women enter the labor force and children find that their parents are becoming less and less influential in guaranteeing them either a job or a status in society. The urban (conjugal) family tends to be composed of a husband, his wife and their children, in which the women have much greater status than in the villages, and the young people enjoy considerably greater freedom to move about, find their own friends, develop their careers and determine their spouses.

The American Experience Since the Civil War.   America's greatest surge of industrialization took place after the Civil War. "If the industrial entrepreneur ever had free reign, it was then—the needs of industry shaped society most notably."[17] During this period, industry drew its supply of labor heavily from immigrants, children and women who were, for the most part, unskilled machine operatives. While the earlier waves of immigrants were largely skilled, those who entered the country between 1883–1917 were largely unskilled and illiterate.

The Northern Experience.   Industrialization in the United States took a somewhat different course than it took in England. The northern experience is further to be differentiated from the southern. In order to fit into the factory system, the immigrant peasant had to learn to be punctual, to acknowledge his dependence upon the employer who owns the machines that he must operate, to be willing to change jobs as machines improved worker productivity, and be willing to move in response to new developments in the job market. Long periods of unemployment were common. Friends and family could not provide employment for the most part, and a sense of belonging and familial security was replaced by increasing reliance upon impersonal contracts.

The impact upon the family was dramatic. The relative isolation of the conjugal family increased; the conjugal family decreased in size (1790 average family size was 5.2; by 1960 this was 3.4). Parents realized that they could not provide all of the good things they wanted for their children if they had many children.[18] The reliance upon the conjugal family increased the emotional intensity between family members and provided the occasion for increasingly likely conflict. Increasing interclass mobility had similar effect upon the extended family as geographic mobility. As conjugal families moved up the status ladder, they left old friends, and often kin, behind.

By the middle of the twentieth century, more married women were in the labor force than single women. In 1975, for example, over 54 percent of all married women with school age children (6–17) were working.[19] Most working women

---

[17]Harold Wilenski and Charles Lebeaux, *Industrial Society and Social Welfare* (New York: The Free Press, 1965).

[18]*Ibid.*

[19]Amatai Etzioni, "The Family: A Look at Possible Dangers of Changing Patterns and Roles," *Washington Post,* January 4, 1976. See also Urie Bronfenbrenner, "The Family," *Washington Post,* January 2, 1977.

provided the needed extra income to maintain their family's status, but an increasing number found personal fulfillment in their work through careers that were intrinsically rewarding. As women gain some degree of economic independence from their husbands through their employment, marriage becomes less of an economic necessity for them. One result is an increasingly high divorce rate.[20] The employment of women further necessitates the redefinition of household roles. As simple as this redefinition might seem from a rational perspective, it is often difficult to achieve in practice because of the hidden assumptions of both partners as to what "good" husbands and wives should do in order to have a happy home.

While the socialization of children could be affected adversely by the employment of mothers, there is increasing evidence that working per se does not have an adverse effect. If adequate substitutes for the mother's care can be found and if the parents spend good time with their children when they have it available, studies indicate that the children are not harmed. Both of these conditions are difficult to realize in practice, but not impossible.[21] Furthermore, in a society changing as rapidly as our own, parents are less significant as socializing agents in their children's lives regardless. Teachers, television, peers, friends and a host of noted authorities compete with the parents for the child's allegiance and certainly inform its developing view of the world to an increasing extent.

At the other end of the life-cycle, the increased isolation of the conjugal family contributes to the isolation of the elderly. In a nation that prides itself on independence, it is difficult for the elderly to accept assistance from their children. While nearly two-thirds of the older Americans over 65 live within about fifteen minutes of at least some of their children, it does not follow that they remain within close association. About one-third of all persons over 65 are living below the officially defined poverty levels.[22] Social welfare measures and private pension plans have not as yet enabled a large number of Americans to retire in reasonable comfort.

The Southern Experience. The southern experience was somewhat different.[23] In the South, urbanization appeared long before industrialization shaped

---

[20]In the nation as a whole there is about one divorce for every two and a half mariages each year. The number of divorces per 1,000 married persons has more than doubled since 1940, in which year there were 25 divorced persons for every 1,000 married persons in the United States; *Statistical Abstract, op. cit.,* p. 66.

[21]Examples of studies in which surrogate mothers are not found to have any harmful effects or are found to have positive effects upon children are: Leigh Minturn and William W. Lambert, *Mothering in Six Cultures* (New York: John Wiley and Sons, Inc., (1964); Leon Yarrow, "Research in Dimensions of Early Maternal Care," *Merril Palmer Quarterly* (April 1963): 101–114; Leon Yarrow, "Maternal Deprivation," *Psychological Bulletin* 58 (1961): 459–490. Studies in which surrogate mothers are shown to have an adverse effect are: Bette Caldwell and Leonard Huseke, "Mother-Infant Interaction During the First Year of Life," *Merril Palmer Quarterly* 10 (April 1964): 119–128. Francesca M. Cancean, "Interaction Patterns in Zincantico Families," *American Sociological Review* 29 (August 1964): 540–550. Rosenthal, M. J. *et al.,* "A Study of Mother-Child Relationships in the Emotive Disorder of Children," *Genetic Psychology Monograph* 60 (April 1959).

[22]*Statistical Abstract, op. cit.,* p. 393.

[23]Rudolf Heberle, "Social Consequences of the Industrialization of Southern Cities," *Social Forces* (1948): 29–37.

urban growth. Northern cities experienced a longer period of industrialization. The typical southern city was a trade center well into the twentieth century. Industries were raw material-oriented (lumber, coal, and iron being leading examples), and tended to be situated in small towns near the major source of their supply. The textile industry developed in the South along with rural electrification and a still dispersed and ample labor supply. As a result, textile factories were set up in the villages rather than the cities and did not much affect urban growth. The dominant trade centers of the nineteenth century South were New Orleans, Mobile, Savannah, and Charlestown. They were supported by much more numerous and smaller centers such as Bogalousa, Monroe and Memphis. A few industrial cities such as Birmingham, Baton Rouge and Beaumont-Port Arthur were partly evolved out of the trading-center type. The more recent its industrialization, the greater the southern city differs from the typical northern city.

An important consequence of the relatively late industrialization in the growth of southern cities is that these cities did not have an extensive working class, and the inner city was not dotted with industrial plants. In the older, smaller cities of the South, the wealthy typically lived just outside the central business district and well within the city proper. This is in marked contrast to the northern experience described by the concentric zone theory. As the city grew, the old families tended to move toward the periphery of the town and their old homesteads typically were converted into tourist homes. In such cities, the poor, who were usually black, tended to live on the periphery of town or on the estate of the wealthy families they served in the cities. Thus the old established families remained longer in the cities and the needs of the factory system were not as evident in the southern experience as in the North. One would not find the high rates of delinquency, the broken homes, the imbalance of poor and unemployed persons distributed in zones around the central business district as in the North. A glance at statistics of this sort would lead one to conclude that the southern city was much more of a desirable place to raise a family—at least for middle- and upper-class persons.

The City of Destruction?

Most studies of the effect of city life upon family life-styles do not distinguish between the different patterns of urbanization and industrialization described above. Urban residence is not typically defined as a variable. In his classic *The Negro Family in the United States,* E. Franklin Frazier entitled one of his chapters "The City of Destruction" because he saw the process of immigration to the city as fundamentally destructive for the black family.[24] It must be pointed out that Frazier was writing from the vantage point of a University of Chicago professor who was primarily examining the effect of the city upon blacks who had left their "forty acres and a mule" and an extensive extended family in the rural South, for the

---

[24]E. Franklin Frazier, *The Negro Family in the United States* (Chicago: University of Chicago Press, 1939).

promise of a better life in the cities of the North. The problems of blacks who were largely unskilled and illiterate in finding good jobs and making a place for themselves in urban society were greatly exacerbated by the fact that the needs of industry for unskilled labor had greatly diminished by the end of World War II. Nevertheless, while at the turn of the century the largest portion of the Negro population in America lived in rural areas, by the 1970 census, 81 percent lived in urban areas, a higher percentage than among whites.[25] Frazier saw city life as a significant factor in the breakdown of the black family because it raised the expectations of what the good life was all about without at the same time providing the opportunity to realize such a life-style. Further, in the city the young were exposed to all of the temptations of street life devoid of the protection of the extended family that would have taken surveillance of their activities in the South.

Much of the concern over the impact of the city upon family life stems from a comparison, implicit or explicit, with what family life is like in contemporary stone-age cultures known to anthropologists.[26] In such societies, the extended family (normally a lineage in which descent, inheritance and succession to office is traced through either the mother's or the father's side of the family) is often the only form of social structure in the society.[27] The family is the government, the school system, the police, the welfare department, and the basis of all community life. As such, it exercises tremendous control over its members because it is the sole means by which a person establishes a place in society. It is often said that those who are "not of the same body"—lineage—are aliens and are to be feared. The placement function of the family is supported by its rights to arrange marriages and determine formal rules of behavior over its members. Marriage serves the important function of uniting previously alien kindreds in reciprocal exchanges, thus cementing the social structure. The family status of another tells one whether she is to be avoided, deferred to, or joked with in many such societies. When children grow up in such villages, hundreds of people who are their kinsmen supervise their everyday behavior, seeing to it that they behave themselves and grow up to be respectable members of the family. Many countries in Africa, South America and Asia have such well-established families before they begin the process of industrialization and urbanization.

Against this background, the impact of moving to the city is tremendous. In spite of the fact that conjugal units that move to the city might remain in contact with their kindred, in comparison to the control exercised by kin in such villages, the conjugal family in the city is isolated indeed.[28] As it becomes increasingly possible for husband and wife to establish their independent residence and raise their

[25]*Statistical Abstract, op. cit.,* p. 17.

[26]See Parsons, *op. cit.*

[27]Claude Levi-Strauss, "The Family," in Harry L. Shapiro, ed., *Man, Culture and Society* (New York: Oxford Press, 1960).

[28]An excellent discussion of the control that lineages exercise over individuals is found in William N. Stephen, *The Family in Cross Cultural Perspective* (New York: Rinehart and Winston, 1969), pp. 102/ff.

children apart from their kinsmen, the old ways are rapidly replaced. Decreasing adherence to traditional kin roles is correlated with increasing rates of urbanization.[29] Kinship terminology decreases in importance and the number of persons that the typical family reckons amongst its kin decreases.[30] Finally, when the urban population is largely immigrant, unstable and socially heterogeneous, fictional kin groups tend to arise as a substitute for actual kinship networks. People who are not related by blood or marriage are given fictive kinship terms such as "cousin," "uncle" or "aunt."[31]

On the other hand, as the power of the lineage and extended family declines, the status of women tends to increase.[32] Husbands and wives become more equal in the conjugal unit.[33] This seems to have quite mixed consequences. As the wife gains in status and power, the conjugal relationship becomes more intense and the stability of the marriage diminishes.[34] The more urbanized a society, the later the average age of marriage and the greater the frequence of nonmarital sexual relationships.[35] Parental control over the children declines along with the decline in the influence of kin.[36] The choice of mate and life-style increasingly becomes matters for the children to determine for themselves.[37] Traditional patterns of marriage and family life tend to disintegrate under the influence of urban life.[38] Overall, while there need not be a correlation between family stability and the degree of urbanization in a country, the more common finding is that family instability is directly associated with increasing urbanization.[39]

[29]J. P. Brewer, "Matrilineal Kinship Among the Kunda," *Africa* 28 (1958): 207–224. Oscar Lewis, *Life in a Mexican Village: Tepotzlan Revisited* (Urbana, Ill.: University of Illinois Press, 1961).

[30]Lewis, *op. cit.,* Philip Garigue, "French Canadian Kinship and Urban Life," *American Anthropologist* 58 (1953): 367–372. Robert F. Spencer, "The Andamese Kinship System," *Southwestern Journal of Anthropology,* (1945): 284–310.

[31]Gallatin Anderson, "Caniparaggio: The Italian God-Parenthood Complex," *Southwest Journal of Anthropology* 13 (1957): 37–53. Kenneth L. Little, "The Role of Voluntary Association in West African Urbanization," *American Anthropologist* 59 (1957): 579–596. Eliot Liebow, *Tally's Corner* (Boston: Little Brown, 1967). David A. Schulz, *Coming Up Black: Patterns of Ghetto Socialization* (Englewood Cliffs, N.J.: Prentice-Hall, Inc., 1969).

[32]Ruth Cavan, *The American Family* (New York: Thomas Y. Crowell Co., 1963): Ernest W. Burgess and Henry J. Locke, *The Family,* 2nd ed. (New York: American Book Co., 1953).

[33] Burgess and Locke, *op. cit.*; Monica Hunter, *Reaction to Conquest* (London: Oxford University Press, 1936).

[34]Burgess and Locke, *op. cit.,* Raymond Firth, "Social Problems and Research in British West Africa," *Africa* 12 (1947): 77–92. Monica Hunter, "The Effect of Contact with Europeans on the Status of Pindo Women," *Africa* 6 (1933): 259–276; Oscar Lewis, *op. cit.*; Clifford Kirkpatrick, *The Family as Process and Institution* (New York: The Ronald Press, 1955).

[35]Murray Groves, "Dancing in Pareporena," *Journal of the Royal Anthropological Institute* 84 (1954): 75–90; Monica Hunter, *Reaction to Conquest; op. cit.*; Thomas P. Mohnanan, "Premarital Pregnancy in the United States," *Eugenics Quarterly* 7 (1960): 133–147.

[36]Burgess and Locke, *op. cit.*; Joan Alduous and Leone Kell, "A Partial Test of Some Theories of Identification," *Marriage and Family Living* 23 (Feb., 1961): 15–19.

[37]Lucy Mair, "Marriage and Family in the Dedza District of Nyasaland," *Journal of the Royal Anthropological Institute* 82 (1952): 1–12.

[38]Bertram Hutchinson, "Some Social Consequences of 19th Century Missionary Activity Among the South African Bantu," *Africa* 27 (1957); 160–177.

[39]Oscar Lewis, *op. cit.*; Burgess and Locke, *op. cit.*

A similar picture emerges when the comparison is made between families with rural residences and families with urban residences in developed countries. In comparison to the rural family, the urban family is also more detached from its kindred, tends to be less self-sufficient and is smaller and more unstable.[40] Marriage is more of a free choice in the urban context, is more satisfying to the wife and is likely to be of shorter duration than in rural areas.[41] It is less likely to regulate sexual relationships between men and women in urban areas. In the city the husband and wife relationship is likely to be more egalitarian, called upon to deal with emotional problems, and likely to end in divorce.[42]

Compared to rural parents, parents in the city have less control over their children.[43] In general, the urban setting produces higher rates of delinquency, especially in the case of boys.[44] However, employed mothers in rural areas are more likely to have delinquent children than employed mothers in urban areas—possibly because of the better facilities for child-care in the city.[45] Parents raise children "by the book" more in the city than in the country.[46]

Alternative Life-Styles

It has become clear that the city provides the occasion for the breakdown of traditional life-styles and the possibility for the emergence of new styles at a very rapid rate. Freed from the control of their parents and kin, urbanites are given greater freedom of movement and the possibility of some degree of economic independence at relatively early ages, subjected to an educational process that permits, when it does not encourage, the critical examination of tradition, and granted an amount of leisure time in which to experiment. Urbanites become caught up in a rapidly changing world that subjects even the most sacred institution of the family to the influence of fads and fashions. While the typical urbanite may well experience his world as made up of people not too different from himself, if he chooses to isolate himself in any one of a number of ways, if he looks about him, the multiplicity of life-styles becomes readily evident. In the city the whole human drama can be fully enacted. To those who are sensitive, it becomes difficult to justify one's own style

[40] Burgess and Locke, *op. cit.*; Wright E. Bakke, "The Cycle of Adjustment to Unemployment," in Norman Bell and Ezra Vogel, eds., *Modern Introduction to the Family* (Glencoe, Ill.: The Free Press, 1960), pp. 112–125; Alexander Lesser, "Evolution in Social Anthropology," *Southwest Journal of Anthropology* 8 (1952): 134–146; Hans Sebald and Wade Andrews, "Family Integrated and Related Factors in a Rural Fringe Population," *Marriage and Family Living* 23–24 (1961–2): 347–351.

[41] William J. Goode, *Women in Divorce* (Glencoe, Ill.: The Free Press, 1956); Alan C. Kirckhoff, "Patterns of Homogamy and the Field of Eligibles," *Social Forces* 43 (Dec. 1964): 287–297.

[42] Burgess and Locke, *op. cit.*; Harold T. Christensen and Hanna H. Meissner, "Studies in Child Spacing: Premarital Pregnancy as a Factor in Divorce," *American Sociological Review* 18 (1953): 641–644. Hunter, *op. cit.*

[43] Burgess and Locke, *op. cit.*; Aldous and Kell, *op. cit.*

[44] Ivan F. Nye, *Family Relationships and Delinquent Behavior* (New York: John Wiley and Sons, 1958).

[45] Nye, *op. cit.*

[46] S. Brody, *Patterns of Mothering* (New York: International Universities Press, 1956).

The mobile American family is no longer as attached to the local community as before. The second home is often mobile.

of marriage and family life as the best when confronted with so many alternatives. This awareness is both exhilarating and anxiety-producing. It remains true, nevertheless, that the other side of the image of the city as the city of destruction is the city as the cornucopia of new ways of living.

Communes. A commune is a group of three or more adults who have taken up common residence for the purpose of trying on a new life-style.[47] The typical commune in America is "urban, internally oriented, pluralistic, non-creedal, private, poor, closed, organic, omnivorous, unincorporated, without industry or business, in a rented house, with partial economic sharing, both sexes, non-monogamous, non-academic, composed of six to eight peers with one or two children under six."[48] By internal orientation it is meant that the group is not intent upon radically changing society, but more intent upon transforming its own members. Since the typical commune is pluralistic, it does not have a single vision, as was typical of the communes in the nineteenth century, but exists in order to

---

[47]Communes are defined in a number of ways. See, for example, Richard Fairfield, *Communes U.S.A.* (Baltimore: Penguin, 1971); Judson Jerome, *Families of Eden: Communes and the New Anarchism* (New York: Seabury, 1974); Rosabeth Kanter, *Commitment and Community: Communes and Utopias in Sociological Perspective* (Cambridge: Harvard University Press, 1972) and Benjamin Zablocki, *The Joyful Community* (Baltimore: Penguin, 1971). See also the discussion of Communes in William M. Kephart, *Extraordinary Groups: The Sociology of Unconventional Life Styles* (New York: St. Martin's, 1976): 283–302.

[48]Judson Jerome, *op. cit.*

promote the maximum amount of variety in life-styles. The "closed" character of the commune means that the typical group restricts its membership to persons it feels can contribute to its life. Diet is an important element of commune life today because many persons find the supermarket fare so repugnant that there is great rejoicing in seeking better ways to live through eating. "Non-academic" simply means that, while a great many communes exist because most of the members are involved in academia, the typical commune is not so involved.

Just as the ethnic ghetto has given distinction to a multitude of life-styles "from the old country," so also sections of our cities are identified with new experimentations. New York's Village, New Orleans' French Quarter, and San Francisco's Haight are a few of the better known. The Haight could be called the cradle of the recent counter-culture. More than any other part of the country, it became linked in the mass media with "beats," "hippies" and "flower children." We will discuss these subcultures in Chapter Eight on community.

Less conspicuous than the ethnic ghetto and the bohemian subculture, but quite dramatic departures from traditional norms, nevertheless, are such alternatives as swinging and various other co-marital sexual arrangements not uncommon in the urban middle class.[49] Swinging can be simply defined as recreational sex. San Francisco's Sexual Freedom League is one of the outspoken advocates of this life-style, but the typical swinger is a very conventional middle-class person in almost all other respects, save his unusual sexual habits. Husbands and wives who swing do so with each other's consent and often together with the understanding that no deep relationship with the sexual partner or partners is expected to develop. More recently, single persons have participated. It has been estimated that about eight million Americans engage in swinging each year.[50]

One group of persons who had begun their sexual adventuring as swingers attempted to establish a group marriage. Known as "Harrod West," the group consisted of six adults and three children at the peak of its development.[51] Its residence was a typical lower middle class bungalow in the suburb of a West Coast city. The adults held very ordinary jobs and maintained their property in quite conventional ways. They simply believed that monogamy was a very destructive form of marriage and that group marriage could provide a much more rewarding life for all. The experiment proved to be too much for them, however.

Cities in America typically have large universities in or near them. University communities have fostered the development of alternative life-styles: the youth commune and "living together." Neither is a distinctive structure, but the academic ethos contributes to the distinctive styles of each. The youth commune, according to Fullerton, can best be described as a kind of half-way house.[52] Young people

---

[49]James Ramey, *Intimate Friendships* (Englewood Cliffs, N.J.: Prentice Hall, Inc., 1975).
[50]Morton Hunt, *Sexual Behavioral in the 1970's* (New York: Dell, 1975).
[50a]Hunt, *op. cit.,* pp. 253 ff.
[51]See Richard Fairfield, *op. cit.,* for a description of this commune.
[52]Gail Fullerton, *Survival in Marriage* (New York: Holt, Rinehart and Winston, 1972), pp. 244 ff.

emerging from the more sheltered environment of their suburban home have a difficult time coping with the complexity of modern urban life. The multiversity they attend and the city they live in both present them with an enormous number of choices and a confusing array of possible careers and life-styles. The youth commune provides them the opportunity to experiment more openly with a wider array of adult roles, to modify traditionally defined sex roles to their own satisfaction, and to determine how they will shape the character of their own intimate environment. They can do this without assuming the full responsibility of adults insofar as they can share this responsibility with their peers. The distinctive characteristic of the youth commune is the unconditional acceptance of its members and an uncommon toleration of deviance. Virtually no one is too "far out" to be accepted.

To be distinguished from the youth commune is the increasingly common practice of living together off campus without benefit of clergy. Studies show that about one-third of all students attending our large (over 15,000 students) universities have experienced a relationship in which they have lived together with a person of the opposite sex for a period of at least three months or more during their four years as an undergraduate.[52a] Persons who so live together typically do not like the communal alternative. They cherish their privacy and cultivate the more personalized intimacy of a dyadic relationship. While some studies show that these couples feel that they have better sexual relationships than their peers, it is sometimes the case that sexual intimacy is not part of the bargain. Indeed, some couples may decide to live together as one way of coping with the demands for sexual competence expected in post-sexual revolutionary days; only they know the truth. Undoubtedly, economic factors are a part of the decision to share "bed and board." It is not yet clear what effect this kind of relationship will have upon the courtship patterns of college students. Is it a new form of engagement? Most do not think of it in this way.

Compared to other students, students who live together generally have better grades, are convinced that they have more rewarding sexual relationships than their peers, are not involved in the drug culture, and are generally well thought of by their universities. One study shows that, while the opportunity of living together in an as yet socially unspecified kind of a realtionship may provide the occasion for greater equality between the partners, students who do in fact live togehter are not significantly different in their attitudes toward equality than students who do not.[54]

Both the youth commune and the practice of living together are more common on large campuses. This is probably so because on these campuses, just as is the case in our large metropolitan areas, there is subcultural support for such experimen-

[53]Dan Peterman and Carl A. Ridley, "A Comparison of Background, Personal and Interpersonal Characteristics of Cohabiting and Non-Cohabiting College Students," Working Paper, The Pennsylvania State University, 1973.

[54]Booke McCauley, "The Effect of Personality Characteristics in the Life Style Choices of College Students," M.A. Thesis, The University of Delaware, 1975.

tation. However daring the student may be, on a small campus he has much more difficulty finding others who can support him in his quest for a better way.

Finally, there are a number of less radical alternatives to monogamous marriage and the conjugal family that are beginning to flourish in our cities. Since the 1960's, industries have begun to cater to the needs of single men and women.[55] The single's complex—a group of apartment buildings arranged around a swimming pool or recreational building, often with its own program director—is a more common feature of cities on the East and West Coasts, but has begun to make inroads in mid-America. Single's bars or "body shops" have long been a feature of the urban scene, but now sophisticated clubs, international tours, even churches that specialize in meeting the needs of single persons have begun to appear. There are over 22 million single persons over the age of 18 and, if present trends continue, increasing numbers of them will never marry. In small town America, the single person could not find the institutions suited to his or her needs, since the community was organized around the assumption that people over the age of 18 ought to get married and begin raising children. In the city this is no longer as imperative.

Only a few of the many alternatives to the traditional conjugal family can be discussed in detail in this text. The point of discussing them at all is to stress the fact that the city life fosters their continued growth and development. Its anonymity, relative affluence, heterogeneity and great numbers, combined with increased education and the opportunity to be exposed to a wide array of life-styles, makes the city a veritable breeding ground for such possibilities. The opposite face of destruction is indeed the cornucopia of possibility. The city appears in both guises, depending on the values of the observer.

The Suburbs and the Quest for Familism

Many studies do not make the distinction between urban and suburban residence when examining the effect of the city upon family life. This complicates the interpretation of the findings somewhat because the dormitory suburb of the middle class was founded largely on the rationalization that it was good for the family. The suburbs grew as various modes of transportation enabled first the professional class, then the working class, to live a considerable distance from their jobs.

In contrast to the city itself, most suburbs are more homogeneous in age stratification because they are dominated by families in the child-bearing years. The young singles and the older Americans live elsewhere. The poor, the ethnically different, the skid-row dropouts until quite recently were left behind in the inner city as the suburban exodus grew. During working hours, the homogeneity of the dormitory suburb increases as working adults—still mostly men—leave for their place of

[55]Rosalyn Moran, "The Singles in the Seventies," in Joanne Delora and Jack Delora, eds., *Intimate Life Styles* (Pacific Palisades, California: Goodyear Publishing Company, 1973).

work. The older children may even leave the community to go to school, leaving the community inhabited predominantly by women and younger children. Working-class suburbs tend to be formed around industries that have moved to the outskirts of the cities and even rarer ethnic suburbs emerge. Sometimes this results from an older community comprised mainly of a single ethnic group becoming encapsulated in urban sprawl. In some cases, such communities are composed of blacks who at one time made up the domestic labor force for the wealthy suburbanites of northern cities. In this section, however, we will focus on the dormitory suburb of the upper middle-class professional as a distinctive metropolitan environment in which to raise families.

The design of the typical dormitory suburb centers around the single family home. To the extent that such suburbs have been planned or reflect zoning ordinances, the value of this home varies by neighborhood. Americans can and do make "status choices" in which they select a home that is recognizably priced above value because of its neighborhood, or they make "good buys" in which they try to get the most home for their money. The house with its conspicuous garage (sometimes with fake extra doors) has become a major status symbol in America. As the cost of construction soars, it is becoming increasingly difficult for most Americans to buy a new home and very difficult for many to purchase a home of their own. Nevertheless, since World War II, the suburban home has been the dream of most Americans and the realization of most in the middle class. The desire for privacy and the display of wealth have contributed considerably to the homogeneity of the suburban environment.

But privacy often means loneliness in a spacious suburb. This is particularly true in the case of the housewife who must stay at home with preschool children. Who is she to talk to? Her husband's world revolves around his career and its advancement. The family's budget has been strained to its capacity in the purchase and maintenance of the home and the now necessary two cars to provide the family with adequate transportation. Mass transportation does not serve a dispersed population efficiently, at least not to the present time.

The physical separation of the husband's place of work from the home has far reaching effects. The husband lives in a quite different world from his wife. His circle of friends and acquaintances, unless consciously catered to by his wife, are not likely to be known by his wife. His interests and energy are tied up in different activities that occupy his mind and demand his attention even when he is not on the job. The average professional male, for example, spends only a few minutes a day with his children. It requires great skill for a husband and wife to manage their marriage when it is being pulled between these two worlds.

In the traditional marriage, the wife characteristically sacrifices her interests for his. The development of his career is seen by both as critical to the family's advancement and it is given proper priority. If and when he succeeds, she may be able to develop her talents and interests. In the more recent understanding, the dual career family, the suburban home may present too many problems to negotiate and an apartment or condominium in the city is preferred. When women want independence and autonomy and a home in the suburbs, something has got to give. Purchasing the domestic services normally provided by the wife is one relatively simple, but expensive, alternative. The decision not to have children is becoming an increasingly popular option. Only the very affluent can manage to realize the traditional dream of raising a family in the suburbs and giving the wife the opportunity to fully develop on her own.

Young people who are forming communes and seeking alternative life-styles typically come from suburban middle class families. To these youth, the suburb is a bleak environment indeed. The family for which the move to the suburbs was made seems lacking in intimacy. Often the problems of modern suburban living fill it with conflict. Increasingly, we have come to recognize that juvenile delinquency is not merely an urban problem, but a suburban one as well.[56] Over half a million youth leave home each year to become part of a growing population of wandering nomads in search of a better way.[57] In part, this restlessness of youth reflects the idleness of affluence and may recede when the effects of the recession have been more widely felt, but it also testifies to the dissatisfaction of the younger generation with the dormitory suburb their parents thought of as heaven.

Urban Design and Family Living

The physical characteristics of a community can have an effect upon the style of family living as the American suburb and the ethnic ghetto have demonstrated. So also can the design of the housing itself. For example, consider three community studies undertaken in the middle of the 1950's. Park Forest, Rockland County, and Old Harbor were all inhabited by middle class persons, yet they had quite different patterns of social interaction.[58] In part, this is to be explained by the nature of their housing.

Park Forest was envisioned by its designers as providing housing for families in all stages of the life-cycle.[59] However, the dream was never fully realized. When the study was made, the single family home intended for couples whose children were in school and whose incomes had stabilized were only a small part of the housing in the community; almost no couples in the post-child rearing stages were living in the community. The bulk of the activity centered around the apartments that tended to be inhabited by the young junior executive on his way up. These apartments were arranged around courts, which each took on a distinctive pattern of interaction peculiar to the families that "originally" lived there.[60] Child care, barbecues, evening cocktails and "back fence gossiping" took place in the courts.

---

[56]*Statistical Abstract, op. cit.,* p. 149.
[57]Jane O. Reilly, "Notes on the New Paralysis," *New York Magazine* (Oct. 26, 1970) p. 28.
[58]William H. Whyte, *The Organization Man* (Garden City, New York: Doubleday, 1956); A. C.
[59]White, *op. cit.,* p. 314.
[60]Whyte, *op. cit.,* pp. 338–39.

The intensity of interaction was so great that it became necessary to establish internal signals (such as the closed window shade) to indicate that one wanted privacy. Normally, neighbors entered each other's apartments without knocking at almost any hour of the day. Oddly enough, this high level of court activity was also proclaimed as the greatest protection against extramarital affairs since the chastity belt. Everyone's activities were so closely scrutinized that no one felt they could step out of line and get away with it. (In the case of singles complexes in the 1970's, however, the higher rates of social interaction go along with higher rates of sexual encounters because the norms of the courts are quite different.[61]

In contrast, the exurbanites living in Rockland County, New York, were slightly higher up the status ladder and somewhat further out of the commuter line from the city than Park Foresters, but were essentially middle class, nevertheless. The ex-urbanites lived in single family dwellings situated on two- to five-acre lots. The pattern of daily social interaction in the community was greatly reduced. Most wives felt isolated and lonely. Their frustrations were increased because they could not count on any help from their husbands or neighbors during the day. If the plumbing wouldn't work, if Johnny broke his arm, or if Suzie swallowed some turpentine, there was no one but mother to take care of it. If the crisis was serious— requiring hospitalization, for example—the father might not know about it until the child was in the hospital and the wife could get free to phone. As a result of trying to cope with their loneliness, these wives typically tried an affair, started drinking, or dreamed of going back to work. Most were not able to go back after their years of absence while raising children. Whereas Park Foresters were actively involved in the politics of their community, the ex-urbanites were not. The ex-urbanites longed for the city. They preferred to walk its streets rather than the tree-lined lanes of Rockland County. In many ways, they were aliens in the suburbs; but they refused to make the move back to the city. It somehow signified defeat. They were thus "thirsty when their cup was full."

Still another suburban setting for middle class families is provided by Old Harbor, Connecticut. Old Harbor was a small fishing village founded in colonial times. The suburbanites surrounding it were post-World War II. The interests and attitudes of the suburbanites contrasted sharply with those of the old timers. The suburbanites lived in Old Harbor because they felt it was a good stopping-off place enroute to much greater affluence. Their single family dwellings on the outskirts of town were large and comfortable, but they had no intent of long-term residence. They voted for the school bonds because they saw education as a critical factor in their children's success. The old timers felt that the school was good enough as it was. The old timers supported the church, the suburbanites tended to ignore it. Suburbanite interest in politics tended to be limited to national elections. Old timers dominated the local scene. In spite of their common interests, the suburbanites of Old Harbor found their friends through their vocations and outside interests rather

[61]Moran, *op. cit.*

than through their neighborhood. Their friends were typically dispersed throughout the country and the world.

Family Interaction and Density.   One of the major differences between the three suburban settings mentioned above is density. Park Forest was far denser than either Rockland County or Old Harbor. This was reflected primarily in the fact that it was predominantly apartment dwellings, while the latter two were exclusively single family dwellings. The much more intense interaction in Park Forest was a partial function of this density, though it need not be, as many lonely apartment dwellers can testify. The problem of urban density has been studied most commonly from the perspectives of what to do with the poor. Public housing has often taken the form of high-rise apartments in the inner city for the alleged reason that such accommodations are more economical. Characteristically the people who live in public housing would prefer their own house with a back yard and some privacy, but they cannot afford it.

Michelson summarizes a lot of research on ethnic ghettos which supports the observation that these life-styles are sustained by the intense interaction amongst the members and that this is possible because of the design of the communities which encourages such interaction. He states the proposition thusly: "Intense family interaction is congruent with low separations of people from other people."[62] Often these communities are called disorganized because the intense interaction that occurs within them is organized in ways that middle-class researchers do not recognize as organization. Boston's West End was a case in point as studied by Whyte in *Streetcorner Society.*[63] St. Louis's Near North Side is another, as indicated in Lee Rainwater's *Behind Ghetto Walls.*[64] In both these studies, families were very much involved in each other's lives and were able to maintain much of their distinctive life-style as a function of such interaction. However much kin may be recognized as important, for example, it is nevertheless true that a number of studies have found that when families are separated, interaction of all kinds decreases (including writing, phone calls, etc.).

An interesting study of the effects of separation is provided by Young and Wilmott's study of the Londoners who were moved to the new town of Greenleigh.[65] Not only did the interaction with "mum" decrease, but also the community life was less intense. When the families were uprooted from the East End, where they had gotten to know their neighbors well over many years, and placed in new less crowded housing, one indication of their greater separation from their neighbors was the fact that much attention was given to the furniture of incoming families. Not knowing the new families, residents looked for clues as to the family's

[62]William H. Michelson, *Man and His Urban Environment: A Sociological Perspective* (Reading, Mass.: Addison Wesley, 1976).

[63]William F. Whyte, *Streetcorner Society* (Chicago: University of Chicago Press, 1943).

[64]Lee Rainwater, *Behind Ghetto Walls* (Chicago: Aldine, 1971).

[65]Michael Young and Peter Willmott, *Family and Kinship in East London* (Baltimore: Penguin Books, 1957), pp. 121–169.

status and they gave serious thought to the possessions as a reliable indicator. In London, status was much more a function of personal knowledge and therefore much more widely assessed. A person could have status, for example, because she was a good story-teller, or he was a true gentleman. The mum-centered style of life returned to Bethnal Green after a generation (when the daughters who moved had daughters of their own), but it was far from the dominant mode of interaction in the new setting. In large measure, this was because the housing did not facilitate such close interaction between mothers and daughters.

In short, the following hypotheses relating family life-style of environment are supported by the literature: (1) intense, frequent association with a wide range of relatives diminishes involuntarily in areas of low density; (2) the dormitory suburb is most compatible with an emphasis on the nuclear family; (3) people with "cosmopolitan" life-styles desire more physical separation from neighbors and place emphasis on proximity to facilities and services than do people whose interests are "local."

Conclusion

The city is often cited in research as having a negative effect upon family life. Much of this research is colored by the assumption that the proper form and the most functional form of family is the conjugal family of the middle class. (This family structure is adversely affected by city life in most studies.) The suburbs, indeed, were formed in some measure as a means of fleeing the city of destruction and recapturing the centrality of the conjugal family. The most adverse effects upon the conjugal family life-style is most probably to be seen in the industrial cities of the North. The southern experience was much less destructive of family life, since there was a lesser degree of segregation of higher income people in the suburbs. Jobs and neighborhoods remained intact for much longer periods of time as a result of the residential patterns more common in the South.

It becomes readily apparent that the design of an urban environment does affect the nature of the social interaction. In the 1960's, there was great optimism about our ability to solve urban problems such as juvenile delinquency and vandalism simply by changing the design of the neighborhoods in which people lived. While this was much too optimistic, it is readily recognized that ethnic ghettos and bohemian subcultures alike depend upon daily interaction of like-minded persons, which is supported or made more difficult by the physical design of the urban environment. Apartments built around courts encourage interaction; houses built on two-acre lots discourage it. However, people with more cosmopolitan views expect and normally achieve a greater degree of privacy than "locals."

chapter 7

The Neighborhood

This chapter focuses on residential neighborhoods. The student of sociology soon discovers that an enormous number of studies have been conducted in small areas commonly labelled ''neighborhoods.'' The locales vary from the most pathology-ridden metroplitan slum to affluent suburban developments. The sociological interactions analyzed in these studies range from primary group relationships among inner city youth gangs to coffee clatches among suburban housewives. It is generally acknowledged that people having common demographic characteristics form distinctive residential clusters. Group qualities, however, the systematic interaction that differentiates one neighborhood from another, have generally remained obscure. The ecologist has sketched a wide panorama of urban neighborhoods, showing quite graphically that distance and space are intimately connected with the socio-economic mixtures of neighborhood populations, as well as their ethnic compositions, age structures, median incomes, crime rates, mental illness rates, and a host of other indicators of social pathologies. In contrast, the participant-observer has concentrated on values, norms, and life-styles, producing a vivid portrait of a subculture in a single small area. Neither, however, has as yet successfully formulated a theory which effectively relates the ecological processes of the greater urban area to the subcultural patterns which are peculiar to the individual neighborhood.

There are a number of key sociological issues concerning neighborhoods with which the student should attempt to become familiar. Some of the most important questions are listed below.

139

A Definition of Neighborhood

What is a neighborhood? The neighborhood is a small group of people living in the same geographical area who recognize common social bonds. They acknowledge a set of roles, statuses, social processes, customs, and social controls which differentiate their group from other geographically-based groups. This is a purely sociological definition of a neighborhood; it delimits a specific group which is based upon geographic proximity. There are, of course, other non-sociological definitions of neighborhoods which are based upon geographic, economic, ethnic, administrative, and political considerations. Many of these definitions overlap with the sociological definition, but as the reader will confirm later in this chapter, the methods of defining, studying, and utilizing these other concepts, does not hinge primarily upon the analysis of social interaction.

Why is the neighborhood concept important? The sociologist has traditionally viewed urban life as being more disorganized and more anomic than life outside of the city. Although few will dispute the fact that urban life can be more chaotic than life in rural areas, the urban residential neighborhood may actually provide a retreat from these stresses—a safe haven among friends and relatives. On the other hand, in some instances, the urban neighborhood may magnify the harsh reality of street life, thriving on a norm of exploitation which extends even into one's own household.

The function of the neighborhood in either moderating or magnifying the general processes of urbanization now, more than ever, presents the sociologist with a crucial ideological dilemma. Specifically, are neighborhoods worth preserving? Particularly if they preserve and transmit values which are antithetical to modernization and development?

Other theoretical and conceptual issues regarding neighborhoods linger. What distinguishes a neighborhood from other sociological groups, such as communities, primary groups, or subcultures? What is the best way to study a neighborhood—as a participant-observer within the area, or as a survey researcher or demographer looking in from the outside? This chapter addresses all of these issues, questioning the usefulness of the neighborhood concept in the field of sociology.

The Neighborhood in the Great Society

If there is one idea which has had a great impact on urban social policy during the last twenty years, it is the concept of neighborhood. This trend is traced to a consensus among policy makers that many urban social problems stem from a lack of community and that the neighborhood should be a meaningful subcommunity for inner city residents. Two massive federal programs which came into existence during the 1960's both placed a strong emphasis upon developing the inner city neighborhood, by fostering neighboring, and developing local leadership. The first was the War on Poverty, which through its Community Action Programs emphasized participation of inner city residents in decision-making groups. These groups, often

"This neighborhood sure has changed since I was a kid."

Drawing by B. Tobey; © 1956 *The New Yorker Magazine, Inc.*

organized at the city block level, planned and administered neighborhood efforts, such as social service centers, detached worker programs, and food cooperatives. More recent than the War on Poverty was the Model Cities Program, which aimed not only at the renewal of the physical neighborhood through the development of better housing and neighborhood facilities, but also stressed social renewal through neighborhood-based social service and education programs. Model Cities placed great stress upon the involvement of local residents in planning and setting funding priorities. The underlying theme of both the War on Poverty and Model Cities Program was that the heavy concentration of social problems found in inner city areas was not due primarily to poverty, but rather to a lack of self-determination, leadership, and community organization within urban neighborhoods.

But urban residents appeared to be unable to alter the disastrous course of ecological forces affecting their neighborhoods.[1] Both the War on Poverty and Model Cities programs have been all but eliminated from the federal budget. Al-

[1]Daniel P. Moynihan, *Maximum Feasible Misunderstanding* (New York: The Free Press, 1969).

though millions of people were aided by both programs, most of the problems of the inner city neighborhood persist. It was probably most unrealistic to believe that once people's lives were upgraded, that they would remain in the same residential areas which had previously been so symbolic of their failure to come to grips with American life. To many, the slum is seen not only as a kind of exploitive jungle, but also as an area where local pride, local identity and responsibility are nearly extinct. To many, the inner city neighborhood is symbolic of personal failure. It is not a place that one identified with. It is a place to escape in order to build a better life.

Efforts to remedy the negative image of the urban neighborhood have been mounted, most notably by public television. Since orientations and interaction modes are developed through socialization processes which begin at birth and continue throughout life, young children soon learn the realities of urban life. If this life-style is to be modified, an alternative must be learned during early childhood. The public television program, "Sesame Street" attempts to foster a positive neighborhood orientation by featuring a number of familiar neighborhood characters in a positive light. In one familiar presentation, people who work in the neighborhood are presented to young viewers and readers in this way:

(Bert, Ernie, and Oscar the Grouch—three puppets, who live on Sesame Street, a mythical inner city neighborhood)

Ernie: Gee, Bert, I guess everybody feels happy like I do, and sad, and all.
Bert: Oh sure, Ernie, I bet even Oscar is happy sometimes.
Ernie: How about it, Oscar? Do you ever feel happy?
Oscar: Nah, never. Well, maybe sometimes I'm glad to live in the neighborhood.
Ernie: Do you know some of the people in your neighborhood?
Bert: A grocer sells things you eat, like cereal and cheese and meat.
Grocer: Whatever food you're looking for, you're sure to find it in my store.
Narrator: A doctor works the whole day long to keep you feeling well and strong.
Doctor: But if by chance you're feeling sick, I'll try to make you well real quick.
Narrator: The doctor and the grocer are people in your neighborhood. Here are some other people in your neighborhood. Policeman, hair-dresser. Construction men. Window washer.
Ernie: Hey, Mr. Hooper, you're one of the people in the neighborhood.
Mr. Hooper (who is a grocer): Sure I am. And I like my job, too, running the candy store. Sometimes, though, I think about all the other jobs people do. Just think! What would it be like to be somebody else? Like a fireman! Or a spaceman! Or maybe a skindiver![2]

[2]Children's Television Workshop, *The Sesame Street Book of People and Things* (Boston: Little, Brown, and Co., 1970).

Vignettes such as the one above are offered and repeated regularly, with the hope that inner city children will develop and sustain the perception that the neighborhood is their home, that it is (or should be) warm and friendly. A clear neighboring role is presented to the young viewers, stressing certain rights, obligations, duties, and privileges, which if learned, should foster an atmosphere of security and warmth. But, if such an alternative role is to be widely adopted by inner city residents (indeed, residents of any area) the alternative role must be realistic enough to compete with other inner city life-styles. It must be attractive enough to entice people to begin with; together with its supportive institutions (like the family, school, and church), it must be strong enough and enduring enough to persist. Obviously, this result is too much to expect from a single television series alone. Roles and institutions can be shown in a favorable light on television, but they must be experienced as warm and secure to some degree in everyday life for us to feel that a significant change has occurred. This often takes hard work over a long period of time. But a start must be made somewhere. Nevertheless, values do shape reality. Children learn, in part, through patterning their behavior after others who become models for them. Bert, Ernie and the Sesame Street gang are models for some children and the neighborhood may change as a result.

The Idea of Neighborhood

The idea of "neighborhood" has been related to a number of sociological conceptual frameworks. Each sociological usage has a specific meaning that sometimes differs from everyday usage.

Historical Roots

The word "neighborhood" has usually been cast in a human, if not romantic, image.[3] In reviewing the early American sociological literature, it is evident that the neighborhood is perceived typically as a repository of warm, *primary* relations.[4] This tradition is rooted in nineteenth century German sociology and is probably best represented in Tonnies's conceptualization of *Gemeinschaft* (community).[5] Following this early trend, the neighborhood concept is modeled after the rural settlement, which in turn is based on the tribe or extended family. Thus, according to the classical sociological theory, if one were to describe the sociological characteristics of a neighborhood, the usual adjectives employed to characterize a primary relationship would also apply to the neithborhood. Neighborhood interaction would be

---

[3]Ephraim M. Mizruchi, *Success and Opportunity: A Study of Anomie* (New York: The Free Press, 1964).

[4]Charles H. Cooley, *Social Organization* (New York: Charles Scribner's Sons, 1920), p. 24.

[5]Ferdinand Tonnies, "Gemeinschaft and Gessellschaft," E. P. Loomis, trans. and ed., *Fundamental Concepts of Sociology* (New York: American Book Co., 1940).

Nothing new under the sun? Some emergent lifestyles reveal a primary group quality that resembles the extended family. *(Bonnie Freeman/Photo Researchers.)*

described as "spontaneous," "free," "intimate," "deep," "extensive," and "satisfying," very much like the relationship usually portrayed among family members, lovers, some work groups, sports teams, and teenage gangs.

This conceptualization of the neighborhood seems most appropriate in describing the rural village or small town. Beginning with the development of large industrial cities, however, observers noted major changes in the pattern of community organization. Simmel (1950), in his treatise on *The Metropolis and Mental Life,* was one of the first to describe the atomization of urban social life.[6] Following in this European tradition, Wirth was the earliest of the American sociologists to emphasize the "superficiality, anonymity, and the transitory character of urban social relations."[7] Thus, with the development of modern cities, sociologists observed changes in the social relationships among urbanites which were associated with rapid industrialization and urbanization. These relationships are usually characterized as *secondary* relationships, a residual category including patterned social interaction in associations, work, school, and all the other situations of life.

Building on this European tradition, the urban sociologists of the University of

[6]Georg Simmel, "The Metropolis and Mental Life," Kurt Wolff, ed. and trans., *The Sociology of Georg Simmel* (New York: The Free Press, 1950).

[7]Louis Wirth, "Urbanism as a Way of Life," *American Journal of Sociology,* 44 (July, 1938), pp. 1–24.

Chicago produced a plethora of studies documenting the ills and describing the characteristic life-styles of that city's neighborhoods.[8] The classical statement of the Chicago school's position is found in Louis Wirth's "Urbanism as a Way of Life." Urbanism, according to Wirth, is a function of a population's size, density, and heterogeneity. The ultimate sociological consequence of urbanization is an amorphous social structure, characterized by weak, transitory, and superficial social ties.[9]

The most convincing evidence of this dismal image of the city is not, however, found in the sociological writings, but in the popular literature of the era, which abounds with descriptions of the wicked city. Dreiser's (1900) earthy chronicle of Sister Carrie's encounters in Chicago and New York provides a vivid description of the evils of the large city.[10] In contrast, the farm, the small town, and the rural village are pictured as the moral heartland of America. The social-class inequities of Lynd's Middletown (1929) seem minor in comparison with those of large cities described in popular literature and in the early sociological writings.[11] Even Sinclair Lewis's description of Babbitt's home town, Zenith,[12] seems genteel in comparison to Zorbaugh's description of *The Gold Coast and the Slum* (1929).[13]

Prior to the 1940's, both the city and its neighborhoods were pictured by American sociologists as "disorganized" social structures. During this period, it became fashionable to analyze the social disorganization found in the various kinds of neighborhoods of the large cities. To the sociologist, the word "disorganization" implied not only the presence of a concentration of social problems, *e.g.,* juvenile delinquency and alcoholism, but also the absence of a viable network of social relationships. The inner city neighborhood was perceived not primarily as an area with a distinct subculture, but as an area lacking in culture. This missing culture is, of course, that of the mainstream, the great American middle class, the absence of which, among lower class people, was linked with personal and social disorganization.

[8]The following comprise the Chicago Studies most commonly cited: Robert E. Park, Ernest W. Burgess, and Roderick D. McKenzie, *The City* (Chicago: University of Chicago Press, 1915); Frederic M. Thrasher, *The Gang* (Chicago: University of Chicago Press, 1927); Lois Wirth, *The Ghetto* (Chicago: University of Chicago Press, 1928); Clifford R. Shaw, F. M. Zorbaugh, H. D. McKay, and L. S. Cottrell, *Delinquency Areas* (Chicago: University of Chicago Press, 1929); Harvey W. Zorbaugh, *The Gold Coast and The Slum* (Chicago: University of Chicago Press, 1929); Paul G. Cressey, *The Taxi Dance Hall* (Chicago: University of Chicago Press, 1932); Franklin E. Frazier, *The Negro Family in Chicago* (Chicago: University of Chicago Press, 1932); Walter C. Reckless, *Vice in Chicago* (Chicago: University of Chicago Press, 1933); Norman S. Hayner, *Hotel Life* (Chicago: University of Chicago Press, 1936); Robert E. L. Faris and H. Warren Dunham, *Mental Disorders in Urban Areas* (Chicago: University of Chicago Press, 1939); Nels Anderson, *Men on the Move* (Chicago: University of Chicago Press, 1940); Robert E. Park, *Human Communities* (New York: The Free Press, 1952).

[9]Louis Wirth, "Urbanism as a Way of Life," *American Journal of Sociology,* 44 (July 1938).

[10]Theodore Dreiser, *Sister Carrie* (New York: Doubleday, Page, and Company, 1900).

[11]Robert S. Lynd, *Middletown: A Study in Contemporary American Culture* (New York: Harcourt, Brace and Company, 1929).

[12]Sinclair Lewis, *Babbitt* (New York: Harcourt, Brace and Company, 1922).

[13]Zorbaugh, *The Gold Coast and the Slum.*

Beginning with Whyte's study of the *Street Corner Society* (1943), social scientists became increasingly aware of the inner city neighborhood as a subculture. Whyte was able to capture the strong ethnic traditions of lower class Italian neighborhood, as well as analyze the organization and cohesiveness of its teenage peer group. Several other researchers, focusing on the culture of the inner city, also identified neighborhood subcultures. Probably the most famous of these works of the 1960's was Gans's *The Urban Villagers* (1962).[14] Living in a Boston working-class neighborhod as a participant-observer, Gans was able to capture the institutionalized quality of neighborhood life. Describing a life-style based on both Italian cultural patterns and working-class norms, Gans identified the development of a unique life-style in this culturally isolated area within the city of Boston. More recent works testify also to the presence of neighborhood subcultures: Elliott Liebow's *Talley's Corner* (1967), Gerald Suttles's *The Social Order of the Slum* (1968), and Joseph T. Howell's *Hard Living on Clay Street* (1973). These studies emphasize the importance of ethnicity and social class in the understanding of neighborhood life-styles.[15]

It seems plausible that the structure of a neighborhood's social system is ultimately bounded by elements which are fixed by the overall social system of the community and larger society (*e.g.*, social class, societal values, communication media, and the political structure). However, the larger community merely sets the limits within which a neighborhood social system may develop. Thus, the social structure of the larger community may not be necessarily the major factor in determining the form of the social system of the neighborhood, but may merely define its boundaries. The internal social process of the individual neighborhood may be the more salient factor in the generation and maintenance of certain norms, values and sentiments. Sometimes neighborhood values prevail against seemingly overwhelming odds in the political arena, as when the residents of Boston's Brookline-Elm district prevented an expressway from being built through their neighborhood.[16] At other times, neighborhood interests lose out, as happened in the Ocean Hill-Brownsville battle over neighborhood control of the schools in New York City.

Neighborhood as an Ecological Concept

It has been traditional in American sociology to view the neighborhood as a part of an ecological system encompassing a much larger urbanized area. Probably the clearest example of this position is found in the early writings of Park, Burgess, and McKenzie (1925).[17] According to this outlook, the human ecology of an urban area

---

[14]Herbert J. Gans, *The Urban Villagers* (New York: The Free Press, 1962).

[15]Eliot Liebow, *Talley's Corner: A Study of Negro Streetcorner Men* (Boston: Little, Brown and Co., 1967); Gerald D. Suttles, *The Social Order of the Slum: Ethnicity and Territory in the Inner City* (Chicago: The University of Chicago Press, 1968); Joseph T. Howell, *Hard Living on Clay Street: Portraits of Blue Collar Families* (Garden City, N.Y.: Doubleday, 1973).

[16]Gordon Feldman, *The Deceived Majority* (New York: Transaction Books, 1973).

[17]Ernest W. Burgess, "The Growth of the City," in Robert E. Park, Ernest W. Burgess, and Roderick D. McKenzie, *The City* (Chicago: University of Chicago Press, 1925).

is treated as an organized whole. The human organisms within this whole are in a competition for life-space. Since this competition is based on the reality of economics, the residential land use pattern of cities reflects a social class distribution. Thus, the poorest people usually reside in the least desirable areas of the city, the most deteriorated of which Park and Burgess call the *zone in transition*. This is the area bounding the center of the city, a zone of changing land use, a locale with an unstable social organization and a high concentration of social pathologies. Proceeding outward from the core of the city and the central business zone, the status of residents continuously rises; in contrast, the prevalence of various social pathologies shows a decrease. A large number of sociological studies verify this gradient pattern, focusing on a wide variety of social pathologies, including crime and delinquency, mental illness, illegitimacy, physical health, suicide, prostitution, and almost every other conceivable pathology which is related to social class.[18] Following the principles of the Park and Burgess scheme, several modifications of the original zonal theory are made, taking into consideration the natural features, topology and differential land use patterns of cities.[19]

Reacting to the over-simplification of the gradient-concentric zone theories, still other ecological techniques were developed in the 1950's and 1960's. The most comprehensive of these methods is *social area analysis,* developed by Shevky and Bell (1949, 1955).[20] This method, which produces a ranking of census tracts or other kinds of land areas, employs three indices: social rank, segregation and urbanization. According to the authors, each of these indices measures an independent dimension of the social organization of an area. (See Chapter 3 for a more extensive discussion.)

Neighborhood As a Social Organization Concept

It should be pointed out that American sociology is rich with studies which have been carried out in various types of neighborhoods, but whether it is a neighborhood socialization process which actually causes behavior to occur is a question which usually remains unanswered. Geographic clusters of persons with similar socio-economic and ethnic characteristics have been found to reside, almost invariably, within clearly identifiable areas of the city. However, it has not been determined whether individual characteristic (*e.g.*, the social attributes of individuals, such as class or ethnicity) cause people to act in a certain manner, or whether some institutional characteristic of a neighborhood has the greatest impact on their behavior.[21]

[18]George A. Theodorson, *Studies in Human Ecology* (New York: Harper and Row, 1961).

[19]Homer Hoyt, *The Structure and Growth of Residential Neighborhoods in American Cities* (Washington Federal Housing Administration, 1939); Chauncy D. Harris and Edward L. Ullman, "The Nature of Cities," *Annals of the American Academy of Political and Social Science,* 242 (November, 1945), pp. 7–17.

[20]Eshref Shevky and Marilyn Williams, *The Social Areas of Los Angeles* (Los Angeles: University of California Press, 1949). Also see: Eshref Shevky and Wendell Bell, *Social Area Analysis* (Palo Alto, California: Stanford University Press, 1955).

[21]Rudolf Herberle, "The Normative Element in Neighborhood Relations," *Pacific Sociological Review,* 3 (Spring, 1960), pp. 3–11.

In short, similar kinds of persons may be drawn to an area because of a preconceived image of the social character of a neighborhood. Hence, the demographic and attitudinal consistencies of urban areas may be actually the result of anticipatory socialization which takes place prior to the move, rather than socialization which occurs after arriving in a neighborhood.

The literature of urban sociology testifies to a wide variety of neighborhood types, each having a different form of social organization.[22] American neighborhoods have been found to vary widely in the intensity and frequency of neighboring.[23] In a historical study of the neighborhoods of Boston, Firey (1945) showed, however, that the same areas evoked similar sentiments and symbolic imagery over a period of many generations.[24] In an earlier study, Shaw and McKay (1942) found that the same Chicago areas retained similar delinquency rates for several generations, suggesting that neighborhoods have the potential to preserve and transmit subcultural values.[25]

Many studies, however, actually emphasize the limitations of the neighborhood as a sociological unit. Several authors describe the "neighbor" role as basically one of mutual aid and assistance, informal visiting, and exchange of advice.[26] The neighbor may be one from whom another borrows tools or food, or relies upon to take care of children during emergencies, but in a more serious crisis of life, relatives and friends are called upon. In some neighborhoods, there is an overlap of the roles of relative, friend, and neighbor, because these persons are one and the same. In general, there appears to be an absence of studies focusing upon the neighborhood as a social system which generates and maintains norms, roles, and institutions which are unique to the individual neighborhood.

The Current Status of Neighborhood Theory

It is not unexpected that the sociologist should seek out patterned interactions between people in developing his conceptualization of neighborhood. Historically, his tools have included a core of concepts which analyze the relationship between

[22]Suzanne Keller, *The Urban Neighborhood: A Sociological Perspective* (New York: Random House, 1968), pp. 87–123.

[23]Sylvia Fava, "Suburbanism as a Way of Life," *American Sociological Review* 21 (Feb 1956), pp. 34–38. Also: Scott Greer, "Urbanism Reconsidered: A Comparative Study of Local Areas in a Metropolis," *American Sociological Review*, 21 (Feb., 1956), pp. 19–25. Also: Joel Smith, William H. Form, and Gregory P. Stone, "Local Intimacy in a Middle-Sized City," *American Journal of Sociology*, 60 (Nov., 1954), pp. 276–284.

[24]Walter Firey, "Sentiment and Symbolism as Ecological Variables," *American Sociological Review*, 10 (April, 1945), pp. 140–148.

[25]Clifford R. Shaw and Henry D. McKay, *Juvenile Delinquency and Urban Areas* (Chicago: University of Chicago Press, 1942).

[26]Suzanne Keller, *The Urban Neighborhood: A Sociological Perspective* (New York: Random House, Inc., 1968), p. 31. Also: Eugene Litwak and Ivan Szelenyi, "Primary Group Structures and their Functions," *American Sociological Review*, 34 (Aug., 1969), pp. 465–481.

the individual and the group. It, therefore, is most predictable that the sociologist should look at the neighborhood in terms of status, roles, norms, values, and attitudes. Looking at the individual neighborhood, the sociologist asks the question: What kind of a social group (if any) do these people represent? He then compares them with other neighborhoods in terms of a sociological entity.

Although it is this question which has provided the underpinning for most sociological studies, planners and administrators have usually concerned themselves not only with the social neighborhood, but also with the economic, physical, and political areas. That is, areas may be classified as neighborhoods for administrative purposes which have little to do with its social fabric. Summarizing the various uses of the word "neighborhood," Keller identifies four major classifications.[27]

First is the ecological neighborhood. This is a larger area which has a distinctive identity, due to geography and land-use patterns. Often, certain "natural" areas, as identified by the Chicago School, had special functions. Dock areas, skid rows, medical services districts, and automobile rows fall into this category.

Second is the area of neighborhood resources. This is an area containing specific physical resources, such as stores, schools, and housing, that differentiate an area from those with other land use patterns. Of course, these facilities may be used by people who reside in the area or by outsiders. The question of who uses the neighborhood resources is often a predominant factor in the quality of life of an area.

Third is the symbolic or ideological neighborhood. An area may suggest a symbolic image only for those who reside or work there, or for those who do not reside there, or for the entire community. Buildings may be neighborhood landmarks, much as the corner drug store used to be in small-town America. From either within or without, certain areas evoke an image of values like political or religious cohesion, social position or power, immorality, sedateness, or alienation. What is important in this conceptualization is the consensus of people as to where such areas are located and what they symbolize, rather than the fact that what is symbolized is true.

Fourth is the subcultural or sociological neighborhood. Often ecology, ethnicity, and history interact with a host of social and economic factors to form a distinctive quality of life in area. The important idea here is that there are certain institutionalized characteristics of the neighborhood as sociological entity which strongly affect the behavior of the individuals who live and work there. Reciprocally, the individuals contribute to that institutional fabric through their individual choices, preferences, and decisions, which may reinforce institutions or change them, gradually or abruptly. In these terms, the old ethnic neighborhood, where generation after generation has remained, is clearly different from the slum or the highly transient suburban neighborhood. But all three areas have in common the fact that the quality of social life persists over decades, despite the fact that actors die,

[27]Keller, pp. 91–92.

move in and out, or grow older. The task for the sociologist, then, is explaining neighborhood stability and change, rather than describing interaction at a specific point in time.

These four major approaches clearly overlap, both in terms of underlying theory and ideas, as well as in the method of analysis. Besides being non-exclusive, the list is also non-exhaustive in the sense that it falls far short of detailing all of the major conceptualizations of "neighborhood" found in the social sciences. These four major approaches have, however, been used most predominently in the analysis of theoretical and applied issues. Each method is discussed in more detail in the following sections.

Applying the Ecological Approach

The most important question asked in applying an ecological approach to the study of an individual neighborhood is: How does this local area relate to the larger urbanized area? In the study of human ecology, an organic analogy is applied which analyzes the function of the neighborhood as it relates to the ongoing operation, continuity, and stability of the community. Thus, the individual neighborhood is constrained by the social structure and process of the greater community and region, but at the same time develops a localized social structure rooted in its own unique social organization. Most ecology studies of neighborhoods trace their methodology to the work of Park, Burgess, and McKenzie (1925).[28] In this pioneering work, and in later ecological studies, the methodological emphasis is on mapping different land use patterns throughout an urban area.

As mentioned previously, land costs are regulated by economic competition, which has a direct impact on the accessibility of both residential and commercial property. The classic studies of the Chicago School focused on neighborhoods in lower class residential areas, and skid-rows, Chinatowns, and urban slums. This zone is also known as the "zone in transition," signifying that the two innermost zones are expanding into this area, causing land values to increase as the predominant pattern shifts from residential to commercial. From an ecological standpoint, the dynamics of neighborhood life in the zone of transition may best be explained by the upheavals in the neighborhood social structure which are brought about by the invasion and succession process. In thinking about neighborhood life in these terms, one might ask why it is that the lower-class residential area always appears to receive the brunt of the social disruptions brought about by invasion and succession. If the entire city is expanding, in terms of the organic analogy, should not the other zones also experience similar strains and stresses of social change? The answer is that the other areas, of course, are also subject to social disruptions brought about by an expanding ecology. But the shifts in the outlying zones do not encompass a fundamental change in land use—from residential to commercial.

---

[28]Park, Burgess, and McKenzie, *op. cit.*

Rather, the outlying zones undergo a more gradual change—from middle class residential to lower class residential.

A recent ecological theory developed by Shevky, Bell, and Williams (1949, 1955)[29] from studies of Los Angeles County represents the most recent trend in ecological theory. Analyzing several hundred census tracts of this large urbanized area, it was found that they could be classified into three theoretically and mathematically distinct types. Shevky *et al.* examined the data through a mathematical technique known as *factor analysis* and found that three groups of variables clustered together. These three clusters were social rank, segregation, and urbanization.

Social rank was described with data on the occupational structure and educational level of an area. Segregation gave the degree of ethnic or racial segregation of the smaller area compared to the greater area. Urbanization consisted of an index of the fertility ratio, the proportion of women in the labor force, and the proportion of single family, detached dwelling units (compared to apartments or other multiple family units).

These three measures, according to Shevky and Bell, are merely indicators of a more complex, underlying dynamic ecological process. This particular process differs from those described by the University of Chicago group. The Chicago theorists described concentration, segregation, centralization, invasion and succession as the concentric zones expand. In contrast, social area analysis emphasizes inferences about patterns of social organization in individual neighborhoods based upon indicators of social rank, segregation, and urbanization. Like most social indicator techniques, social area analysis provides a cue as to where the social action is, but leaves the explanation to the investigator, who must explore a wide range of social and cultural factors to get at the cause of the action. Thus, social area analysis, as a sociological approach, provides a general framework from which to identify locales for more intensive analysis. Usually extremes in one or all three indices are studied (*e.g.*, very segregated areas, neighborhoods high or low in social rank, locales at extremes on the urbanization index). Social area analysis also makes possible a comparison of ecological units from different cultures, or allows the comparison of entire regions or cities, besides allowing a comparison of individual neighborhoods. One of the best known applications of social area analysis in the study of neighborhoods was carried by Wendell Bell (1959).[30] In this research, several urban neighborhoods were classified, using the Shevky-Bell urbanization index. The results clearly indicate that a difference in the demographic profile of the neighborhoods may account for vivid differences in life-styles.

The ecological approach has the advantage of elegant simplicity. The accessibility of data on a census tract (and now even on a city block) along with detailed area maps which are available through local government make possible all four of

[29]Shevky and Bell, *op. cit.*; Shevky and Williams, *op. cit.*
[30]Bell (1959).

the ecological methods of analysis. It is practical to compare urban neighborhoods through this broad-brush profile. Once a particular pattern is evident in the ecological analysis, however, it may be advantageous to undertake an in-depth attitudinal study or a participant-observation study in order to gain a more systematic understanding of the social process of a particular neighborhood.

Applying the Neighborhood Resource Approach

From the standpoint of the economist, resources of a local area are usually divided into physical and human components. Physical resources would include not only the land itself, but also any natural features like navigable rivers, and of course, the man-made features of an area. These include buildings, roads, public utilities, schools, hospitals, police stations, sewer and water systems, and solid-waste disposal systems. Beyond these physical components are what the economist calls the human resources of an area. These include its labor force, political organization, type of governmental structure, degree of poverty or wealth, collective health, educational level, and other social organizational factors which contribute to the relative self-sufficiency of an area. All of these physical and social components are crucial both to planning for the future development of neighborhoods in administering the services which are required.[31]

The planner, in assessing the service requirements of a city's neighborhoods, typically creates a profile of various planning areas. Neighborhoods are compared in terms of the adequacy of housing, schools, transportation, parks and recreation facilities, police and fire protection, etc. A neighborhood which revelas a high concentration of youth may become the target area for more intensified youth gang control efforts by police. An area which reveals a high incidence of whooping cough among children may become the focal point of a stepped-up immunization campaign in the public schools. The major point is that, in the resource approach, local areas are classified in terms of service requirements and problem intensity. The boundaries of the city's service areas need not, however, correspond with social neighborhoods or natural ecological areas. A fire company or a police precinct may include within its service area a number of diverse commercial and residential neighborhoods. The boundaries of municipal service districts within a city are frequently based on cost-effectiveness criteria, rather than the preferences of the residents of a distinctive social area or neighborhood. Often, service area boundaries are the focal point of political conflict between neighborhood groups and service agencies, particularly with respect to health, education, and social services. The costs and benefits of incongruity between service areas and neighborhoods have not commonly been calculated, however.

---

[31]For a good example of the resources approach see: *Youth in the Ghetto* (New York: New York Opportunities Inc., 1964).

   As mentioned in the beginning of this chapter, the urban residential neighborhood has become the basic unit for the planning and administration of many social services. The fundamental question relates to which services are appropriately offered at the neighborhood level, and whether the administration should be under the control of neighborhood residents. From the perspective of cost effectiveness, there are economic models which clearly indicate the optimal service areas for garbage and trash collection (sanitary districts), bus routes, and even hospital service area boundaries.[32] Effectiveness in terms of economic costs, however, is often considerably different from effectiveness in terms of social costs. From the perspective of the hospital planner, the large centrally located hospital with quick ambulance access is far more efficient than a series of outlying clinics and neighborhood facilities. For residents of a poverty area with limited access to private physicians, however, the neighborhood clinic is an important source of treatment for common illness and the only source of preventative medicine, such as immunization and early breast cancer detection. Add to this the invidious comparison of the emergency room of the municipal hospital, (where all "walk-in" patients are received), with the neighborhood clinic staffed by neighborhood residents; the social costs and benefits become even more clear. Locally controlled planning and administration of other services, such as police and schools, becomes a much more difficult problem.[33] Fundamental questions here relate to whether the administration of justice should be tailored to the preferences of a local subculture, or whether the education and socialization of children should be under control of the total community or the local area. The researcher, in examining the adequacy of neighborhood resources, must employ some standard. It is much easier to point up the existence of a problem with this comparative technique than it is to propose a viable solution to social problems, because the latter invariably involves making value-ladened policies in lieu of truly universal criteria.

   A common resources approach employed by social planners is the *neighborhood resource inventory*. The planner selects an administrative area, usually one previously classified for urban planning purposes and proceeds to list the social services available in the area (if possible, providing a demographic description of the service clientele of each resource). Services are classified into health, education, counselling, and recreational groups. Through a comparison of the extent of services offered to specific age and economic groups, it is possible to assess the various social service gaps, overlaps between agencies, and unfulfilled service needs of a neighborhood. This technique should combine a demographic profile with various social pathology indicators, such as crime rates, infant mortality rates, school drop-out rates, poverty indices, etc.[34] When the resource inventory and social pathology

[32]Martin Beckman, *Location Theory* (New York: Random House, 1968). Also: George P. Schultz, "Facility Planning for a Public Service System," *Journal of Regional Science,* 9, #2 (1969).
    [33]J. Clarence Davis, *Neighborhood Groups and Urban Renewal* (New York: Columbia University Press, 1966).
    [34]*Youth in the Ghetto* (New York: Harlem Youth Opportunities Inc., 1964).

indicators reveal a basic disjunction, *e.g.*, when there is a high rate of gang-related delinquency, but few related social service programs, this signals a severe service gap. The manner in which a service is planned and directed toward a particular problem is usually the subject of a more intensive planning and community organization process.

The neighborhood resource approach is currently the most common method of determining "need" for social service programs. This method will quickly uncover inequities in a neighborhood's social services (as compared to those of other areas). Used in conjunction with demographic social pathology indicators, this process will help agencies make arguments and develop proposals for program funding. Like most ecological techniques, however, neighborhood resource analysis will tell us that a program is needed and possibly that a program has suceeded or failed, but will not provide a systematic model for design and administration of the program. This is a far more complex process, which requires an in-depth understanding of the target population and a precise simulation of program impact before implementation. Setting up an effective program, among other things, entails an understanding of the culture and ideology of the neighborhood.

The Symbolic or Ideological Approach

People draw mental maps of neighborhoods. These maps often have more to do with culture andlife-style than with actual physical elements. Geographers have recently demonstrated that people tend to have fairly uniform preferences for certain areas. These mental maps are dependent upon both geographic proximity and the set of information and imagery which is conveyed by them.[35] Neighborhoods signify values and imagery both to the persons who reside there and to the outside community. Some of these images are national and even world-wide in scope. Few educated adults in the United States are unfamiliar with such names as Telegraph Hill, Shaker Heights, Central Park West, or Georgetown. Nor are they unacquainted with Haight-Ashbury, South Side (Chicago), or the Bowery.

Looking at a neighborhood from the perspective of two groups—those who reside (or work) within, and those in the outside community, the two sets of images interact with each other. First, is the perception of the neighborhood people themselves, their image of their own neighborhood. Second, there is the perception of outsiders. Third is the perception of those in the neighborhood toward outsiders, the way in which neighborhood people think others view them. Fourth is the way outsiders think the neighborhood people view themselves. All of these perceptions are the result of personal interaction, as well as imagery conveyed by the communications media. An important point is that, while the formation of this imagery is a

---

[35]Peter Gould and Rodney White, *Mental Maps* (Baltimore, Md: Penguin Books, 1974).

moderately complex process, the process is visable and readily subject to analysis. In short, we know how to find out how mental maps are formed.[36]

History plays a very important part in the understanding of neighborhood imagery. Some neighborhoods persist, in the face of suburbanization, as upperclass areas. Such is the case with Beacon Hill in Boston, which co-exists with several slum neighborhoods. Firey (1945), in his classical article on the Beacon Hill district, stressed that neighborhood space is frequently associated with values that have dominated the area over a period of time.[37] Sentiments may be far more important in locational decision than economic considerations. Firey never emphasized the role of negative sentiments regarding certain urban space. It is probable, however, that some of the overzealous bulldozing of slum neighborhoods during the 1950's and 1960's (despite the fact that the housing stock was structurally sound) was also the result of negative sentiments.

The stress on neighborhood symbolism is viewed by many as the theoretical opposite of the ecological theories. Usually, the critics attribute a high degree of ecological determinism to the zonal theories, which is traced, in turn, to the supply and demand factors affecting the price of land. But land prices are also influenced by sentiments and symbolism. Demand is generated or diminished by the prestige factor.

The symbolic approach to neighborhood is important to sociologists primarily as an explanatory theory. It is grounded in the symbolic interaction tradition of the founding fathers of the discipline, Cooley, Thomas, and Meade. According to this approach, the key to understanding the differences between neighborhoods is rooted in a powerful set of internalized symbols which guide behavior.[38] The symbolic interactionist studying a neighborhood attempts to discover these symbols, the manner in which they develop, and the reason why different neighborhoods appear to have different symbolic references. These different images concern not only the neighborhood itself, but also a wide range of attitudes and life-styles.

It has been found, for instance, that in inner city neighborhoods, the degree of anomie and militancy vary substantially, depending upon the type of neighborhood.[39] Most neighborhoods reinforce norms, values, and attitudes which apply to issues that go far beyond local concerns. Some suburban areas also manifest a

[36]For a discussion of cognitive perception from this perspective see: Roger Brown, *Social Psychology* (New York: The Free Press, 1965), pp. 656–679.

[37]Walter Firey, "Sentiment and Symbolism as Ecological Variables," *American Sociological Review,* 10 (April, 1945).

[38]Charles H. Cooley, *Social Organization* (New York: Scribner, 1909); W. I. Thomas, *The Child in America* (New York: Knopf, 1928); George H. Mead, *Mind, Self, and Society* (Chicago: University of Chicago Press, 1934).

[39]Robert A. Wilson, "Anomie in the Ghetto: A Study of Neighborhood Type, Race, and Anomie," *The American Journal of Sociology,* Vol. 77, No. 1 (July, 1971). Robert A. Wilson, "Anomie and Militancy Among Urban Negroes: A Study of Neighborhood and Individual Effects," *The Sociological Quarterly,* 12 (Summer, 1971), pp. 369–386.

distinctive set of beliefs and attitudes. Kramer and Leventman, in a famous study of middleclass Jewish neighborhoods, christened these areas "gilded ghettos," because of their physical and sociological isolation.[40] The main issue involving attitudinal uniformity of certain neighborhoods is the degree to which these orientations are the result of a neighborhood socialization process. Persons with certain beliefs and life-styles may be drawn to a neighborhood because of a preconceived image of the kind of people who already reside there. Thus, the neighborhood merely acts to reinforce certain preferences which already exist.

The two notions—of a neighborhood socialization process and of a selective migration—are not mutually exclusive. There is some evidence that persons with similar social characteristics and preferences are drawn to similar neighborhoods. In the instance of the average person drawn to the suburbs, his orientation may merely relate to buying the best house for the least amount of money.[41] In other instances, the attitudinal uniformity of urban neighborhoods may be explained by the fact that they are often populated by a concentration of people who are all in the same phase of the life-cycle. Elderly people, for instance, are not only coping with the same problem of aging, but also have collectively undergone a similar set of experiences, simply by being born into similar age cohorts.

Thinking of groups in terms of the symbolic or ideological approach, it can easily be concluded that the values and attitudes of each group are not only contingent upon a neighborhood socialization process, but also are the by-product of a national social structure which specifies a set of roles and statuses grounded in social class, ethnicity, and age.

The Subcultural or Sociological Approach to Neighborhood

Although the previous three approaches to the study of neighborhood are frequently applied by sociologists, they do not, by themselves, explain the neighborhood as a social group. The concept of the group, at minimum, infers some form of patterned interaction between two or more individuals. Underlying this interaction is always a set of norms, values, statuses and roles. When one thinks of these group characteristics in terms of the neighborhood, it is sometimes difficult to separate the roles of friends, neighbors, and kin.[42] While a great deal may be required of kin in terms of personal sacrifice and inconvenience, the friendship role emphasizes mutual tastes, entertaining, comradeship, and limited helping, borrowing, babysitting, etc. The neighbor role, in contrast, is much more constricted than either the friendship or kinship roles. It is different from the other two in that geographic proximity is the primary basis for the relationship. Also, while the kinship role is rooted in a set of

---

[40]Judith R. Kramer and Seymour Leventman, *Children of the Gilded Ghetto* (New Haven: Yale University Press, 1961).

[41]Herbert J. Gans, "Urbanism and Suburbanism as Ways of Life," Arnold Rose, ed., *Human Behavior and Social Process* (Boston: Houghton Mifflin, 1962), pp. 625–648.

[42]Eugene Litwak and Ivan Szelenyi, "Primary Group Structures and Their Functions," *American Sociological Review*, 34 (Aug., 1969).

well-defined cultural norms, and the friendship relationship is dependent upon a social contract between two individuals, the neighbor role is dependent upon the norms of the local neighborhood. The upshot of this division of labor among kinship, friendship, and neighboring roles is that the neighbor role musttake up the slack where the other two fail to provide certain functions. Neighboring is, by necessity, far more important in a rural frontier than it is in a city saturated with social services of all types.

Several researchers have attempted to pinpoint differences in neighboring patterns in different locales. Fava (1968) employed a series of questions, known as the *Wallin Neighborliness Scale,* and found that surburban residents manifested a higher degree of neighboring than did inner city residents from either the boroughs of Manhattan or Queens.[43] The Wallin Scale (1953) measures not only frequency and intensity of interaction between neighbors, but also activities such as entertaining and personal problem solving, which go far beyond the normal neighboring role.[44]

In another study focusing on the intensity of neighboring, Foley (1952) looked at a middleclass area of Rochester, New York and concluded that neighboring was not as frequent or important to most people as it was several decades previously.[45] Neighboring tended to be limited to families who lived next door to each other and was far more prevalent in the summer than the winter.

Neighboring also tends to develop between individuals of the same age and sex, rather than the whole family. Evidence relating to fundamental changes in neighboring patterns over the last half-century is inconclusive. Gans, in his study of Levittown, New Jersey, a suburban development, found no evidence to indicate that persons moving there engaged in any more or less neighboring than in their previous residences.[46] Gans adds the valuable insight that a great deal of adult neighboring is the result of relationships between young children who must live and play in the neighborhood. Despite the increasing distance between home and work, home and leisure, and home and church, the children's primary play relationships continue to be based in the neighborhood. Women's coffee groups also stay closest to home. In the *Organization Man,* a study depicting suburban life during the 1950's (1956) Whyte depicted the middleclass housewife as being concerned primarily with her husband's career, upward mobility, home management, and child-rearing.[47] Whether this pattern has changed radically as a result of the emergent women's liberation movement has yet to be documented. The suburb, however, continues to dominate growth in urban areas. A new type of social cohesion appears to be developing in suburban areas, despite the high degree of residential transiency. Fellin and Litwak (1963) suggest that many suburban neighborhoods are developing

[43]Sylvia Fava, *Urbanism in World Perspective* (New York: Crowell, 1968).
[44]Paul Wallin, "A Guttman Scale for Measuring Women's Neighborness," *American Journal of Sociology,* 59 (Nov., 1953), pp. 243–246.
[45]Donald L. Foley, *Neighbors of Urbanites* (Rochester: University of Rochester, 1952).
[46]Herbert J. Gans, *The Levittowners* (New York: Pantheon, 1967).
[47]W. H. Whyte, Jr., *The Organization Man* (New York: Simon and Schuster, 1956).

a set of well-defined customs and formal organizations which serve to integrate the transient into the local setting quickly and efficiently. That is, transiency may not be as serious an impediment to integration of a suburban neighborhood as previously believed.[48] In fact, upward social mobility and geographic mobility may have become so interrelated in the dominant ethos of most suburbanites that the family who stays too long in a neighborhood is perceived as having failed, *i.e.*, having terminated its upward mobility.

Voluntary Associations and Neighboring

Most associations between people, like neighboring, are informal. The relationships are not structured through an organization with an official structure and process. There are also a large variety of formalized relationships which may emanate from *voluntary association*. These associations are termed "voluntary," in that the individual is free to decide whether he desires to participate or not. Voluntary associations, then, range from civic and neighborhood associations to fraternal and church groups. The spectrum of possible interaction may be divided into voluntary associations, informal associations, and work-related associations (which are almost mandatory by virtue of a person's occupation). When one analyzes the social fabric of the urban neighborhood, it is important to explore the interrelationship between the various types of relationships and associations. The type of neighborhood and its relationship to the overall urban setting has a vast influence on which groups perform which functions and in what way. An urban area which has a large number of voluntary associations ranging from Weight Watchers to nude sensitivity groups, provides far more sociological options than are typically found in less urbanized settings.

National surveys have generally indicated that the proportion of urban dwellers who are members of voluntary organizations is greater in smaller cities than in larger ones.[49] In cities over 250,000 in population, 47 percent of the adults were members of one or more associations; while in counties with all communities under 10,000, 68 percent reported voluntary association membership. Village and farm areas averaged 55 percent. Studies have also indicated that low-income blacks are commonly not involved in voluntary associations (Pettigrew 1964),[50] while middle-class blacks are (Frazier, 1957).[51] Also, studies have consistently reported that a higher proportion of Protestants and Jews are participants than are Catholics and non-affiliates. Also, persons having higher education, professional occupational training, and higher annual income are more likely to be participants than

---

[48]Phillip Fellin and Eugene Litwak, "Neighborhood Cohesion Under Conditions of Mobility," *American Sociological Review,* Vol. 28, No. 3 (June, 1963), pp. 364–374.

[49]Herbert H. Hyman and Charles R. Wright, "Trends in Voluntary Associations of American Adults," *American Sociological Review,* 36 (April, 1971), pp. 191–206.

[50] Thomas F. Pettigrew, *A Profile of the Negro American* (Princeton: Van Nostrand, 1964).

[51]Franklin E. Frazier, *Black Bourgeoisie* (New York: The Free Press, 1957).

those on the lower end of the socio-economic range. Finally, several studies have concluded that the longer a person resides in an area, the more likely he is to be a member of one or more voluntary associations.[52]

Most of the research cited above, however, does not relate the purpose of the voluntary associations to the functioning of the member's neighborhood. While some organizations, such as civic associations and churches, are clearly neighborhood-oriented and contribute to the social solidarity of an area, others like professional organizations and leisure groups, may not contribute, and in fact may detract from concentration on neighborhood issues.

Toward A Theory of Neighborhood Social Interaction

A comprehensive theory of the neighborhood as a social group should explain the social interaction patterns of various local areas. Such a scheme should take into account not only the voluntary association pattern, but variations in informal inter-action, including neighboring, teenage gang activity, and couple visiting. All of these interaction patterns, of course, should interrelate to the neighborhood sub-culture (if one exists) in terms of values, norms, and attitudes.

It is quite clear from the previous research cited that the invasion and succes-sion cycle has a major impact on neighborhood social life. In work done by Wilson (1971), it was found that three lowerclass urban neighborhoods in varying stages of the invasion-succession cycle revealed vastly different attitudinal and interaction patterns.[53] For example, it was found that in a poverty-stricken black ghetto, the level of militancy and anomie was considerably lower in two more affluent, inte-grated neighborhoods. These attitudinal differences were related, in turn, to dif-ferences in neighboring and voluntary association participation. In the ghetto, anomie was associated with a low level of participation in associations and a high degree of neighboring. In the outlying neighborhoods, the reverse pattern prevailed. Anomie was correlated with a low degree of neighboring and uncorrelated with participation in voluntary associations. This pattern suggests that the "appropriate" mode of social integration may be a function of the invasion and succession cycle. Contrary to sociological convention, ghetto residents who were very high in neighborliness were also very high in anomie. Unlike respondents with lower neighborliness scores, those with very high scores indicated: (1) that they had been inside more than four of the neighbor's homes; (2) that they had attended movies, picnics, clubs, or other events with their neighbors; and (3) that they had exchanged or borrowed items from their neighbors. In short, too much neighborliness in the ghetto proved to be a source of malintegration; while in the newer neighborhoods, the only way of integrating one's household was to reach out in the most neighborly

---

[52]Amos H. Hawley and Basil Zimmer, *The Metropolitan Community: Its People and Government* (Beverly Hills: Sage Publications, 1970), pp. 31–33.
[53]Wilson, *Anomie in the Ghetto* and *Anomia and Militancy Among Urban Negroes* (1971).

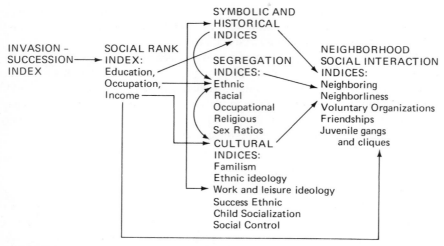

Figure 7.1 Model predicting a neighborhood's social interaction patterns.

fashion possible. If this pattern can be generalized, it suggests that modes of social interaction in the individual neighborhood are set in phase by the invasion-succession cycle.

In essence, if a comprehensive sociological theory of neighborhood is to be developed, any one of the three previously presented approaches (ecological, re-sources, and symbolic) would be inadequate by itself to explain social interaction within a small area. Although each approach contributes to the understanding of the local social process, the operation of all of these factors over a period of time must be considered in order to place a neighborhood within a broader, comprehensive typology of neighborhoods. From such a typology, a series of hypotheses about social interaction patterns of different neighborhoods could be constructed. Based upon the knowledge we already have, a simplified model directed toward explaining neighborhood social interaction is shown in Figure 7.1.

This scheme suggests a causal ordering which effects the mixture and intensity of social interaction found in a neighborhood. The invasion and succession pattern underlying most land use is fundamental, controlling the social rank of an area (determining average educational, occupational, and income levels of those who reside there). It also should be noted that social rank has both a direct and an indirect effect on neighborhood social interaction. That is, it has an important effect which is independent of symbolic and historical factors, the degree of segregation, and various cultural indices. In short, the neighborhood's location in the community's and society's social structure has a direct impact on social interaction which is not effected by the norms of the individual neighborhood. A Cadillac is a Cadillac, no matter where one lives. Being on welfare is being on welfare, no matter what the neighborhood. On the other hand, social rank and cultural indices interact differently in different neighborhoods and produce an indirect effect on social interaction patterns. Being on welfare has a different meaning in a black ghetto than in a Polish ghetto. A Cadillac has more prestige in a show-business community than in an academic community. These interactions, in turn, have an effect on social interaction patterns.

The symbolic and historical character of an area also intervenes between social rank and neighborhood socialization. Living in an old prestigious area, or a historic district, even if the area's social rank index has changed, affects social interaction. Similarly, residence in segregated areas—black ghettos, WASP areas, Jewish neighborhoods, or singles' apartment areas, has an effect which interacts with social class, producing different neighborhood social interaction patterns. Finally, cultural or ideological factors relating to work and leisure, success, child socialization and social control contribute to the specific pattern of social interaction in a neighborhood.

We have defined social interaction in fairly conventional terms, determined by the amount of contact between neighbors, attitudes toward neighbors, and whether the neighboring role of an area also includes interactions which normally might be considered more appropriate for friends, rather than neighbors. Social interaction, as used here, also refers to the degree of participation in voluntary organizations, whether these organizations are neighborhood-based, or a by-product of work, school, or religious participation outside the neighborhood. Beyond the conventional adult interactions, there are of course, the associations of young children and teenagers. One of the most important of these is the teenage gang found in a vast variety of delinquent and non-delinquent forms. The extensive literature on delinquency suggests that it is the neighborhood social context, including its collective social class, its degree of segregation, and its stage of the invasion-succession cycle, which has the greatest impact upon the type of gangs found in an area. The fighting gang, the drug-using gang, and the non-delinquent gang are each found in different areas of the city.[54] In reading the criminology literature, one gains the impression that the neighborhood is far more important in influencing juvenile crime than adult crime. This may be due to the fact that younger children are often virtual captives of the neighborhood (particularly the surburban area), while adults are not.

Conclusion

In this chapter, we have raised many issues about the neighborhood concept and its usefulness to sociologists. We have described a number of approaches for defining and analyzing neighborhoods. We have suggested a comprehensive model of neighborhood interaction, based largely upon what we already know about cities

[54]Richard A. Cloward and Lloyd E. Ohlin, *Delinquency and Opportunity: A Theory of Delinquent Gangs* (New York: The Free Press, 1961).

and neighborhoods. We have failed to demonstrate to our own satisfaction that the neighborhood is powerful with respect to either socialization or in influencing attitudes or life-styles. But we are confident the neighborhood is, and will remain, a crucible of social interaction as an area where there is a consciousness of kind, and even at times the epitome of the ideal community.

chapter 8

The Community

Numerous studies have called our attention to our intense need for a sense of belonging and a widespread nostalgia for the small town. A recent Gallup Poll found that 56 percent of the respondents preferred living in a small town, even though two-thirds of them were in fact living in cities. On the other hand, a Wisconsin study found that about 85 percent of the respondents, while expressing a preference for living outside a city, preferred to live within about 30 miles of a city. This study also discovered that about half of the non-metropolitan respondents preferred to live near a large city.[1] It seems as though the metropolitan environment's commuting range defines the preferred location for most of us. The typical commuter range easily includes several hundred square miles around a major city, and it is within this area that most Americans live and work.[2] Whatever we and our children will know of community will most likely be defined by the quality of life that we fashion here.

This chapter examines the city and its environs as an expression of community. It sees the city both from the perspective of the individual city dweller and as a sociological entity. It is, of course, proper to ask in what sense urban populations can be considered communities at all? When the neighborhood seems to be declining in importance and is no longer the traditional base of community for most of us, what holds the urban population together? The answer often provided is *functional*

[1]J. J. Zuiches and G. V. Fuguitt, ''Residential Preferences: Implications for Population Redistribution in Non-Metropolitan Areas.'' Paper presented at the meeting of the American Association for the Advancement of Science, Philadelphia, December 1971.

[2]Report of the Social Science Panel in the Significance of Community in the Metropolitan Environment to the National Research Council, *Toward an Understanding of Metropolitan America*, (San Francisco: Canfield Press, 1974), p. 11.

163

interdependence. Most urbanites are so highly specialized in their occupation, so narrowly adapted to their world, that they are utterly dependent upon thousands of other persons to provide them with their daily needs. Most of these persons, along with the persons living next door or down the hall, are not known, even if recognized.

Yet, the evidence suggests that communities of shared sentiments and interests are also to be found in our metropolitan regions, both within the central cities and in its surrounding suburban fringe. The set of relationships that binds the heterogeneous populations living within the city and its spheres of influence is complex indeed. By focusing first upon a distinction between *location* and *locale,* the coexistence of two distinctive kinds of life-styles within the urban mosaic can be discerned. One is based on similarities, the other on differences among the inhabitants. The homogeneous locations come closest to our understanding of what community once was (and some think, ought to be again). The heterogeneous locales suggest the nature of a new type of community yet to be fully expressed.

An examination of the different types of basic social bonding will further suggest that the urban population is held together by much more than shared sentiments. Utilitarian and coercive bonds also unite urbanites and these bonds are complex and ever-changing.

With these distinctions in mind, the basic models of urban integration will be examined, considering first what was understood to be "little communities," then moving on to metropolitan communities. Then we will describe new possibilities of urban social integration that are not widely acknowledged. The chapter concludes with a brief description of the city as an "open society."

Locations and Locales

The mere fact that things are spatially close does not imply that they are in any way bound together. They can be simply an aggregate of objects such as a pile of rocks. Although this may be more apparent for physical objects than for people, it should not be assumed that just because people live together in close proximity they have much to do with each other. Indeed, cities have become known the world over for their urban anonymity.[3] People living together in an apartment complex who do not know most of the people in their building or even on their floor are not, however, in the same state of "togetherness" as an aggregate of rocks. The apartment provides the minimal basis of their togetherness if only because they, for whatever reasons, all chose to live in it. By virtue of this fact, they have a number of common ecnomic and political interests, may share same or similar shopping and recreational areas, and are likely to brush up against each other quite frequently, even if they do not interact on a more personal basis. Should the building catch fire, suffer a power

³*Ibid.,* p. 55.

The old-fashioned neighborhood. Is life the same as it was in the "good-old days?" (U.S. *Information Agency.*)

failure, or be confronted with some other external threat, it is quite likely that a new sense of "togetherness" would emerge: "We're all in the same boat!"

In vivid contrast to this urban anonymity, we find the almost frenzied interaction of other apartments. Whyte made us aware of the intensity of urban neighboring in his coverage of court life in Park Forest, a suburban development outside of Chicago.[4] Park Foresters were Americans "on their way up." They were studied in 1955 when the economy seemed to be expanding and people were on the move. Park Foresters were joiners, interested in clubs and other voluntary organizations. They participated in political parties and reformed the churches in their neighborhood. In addition to their organizational involvement, there was an intense day-to-day interaction that occurred in the courts around their apartments. Park Foresters were mostly in the child-rearing stage of their life-cycle, and small children played continuously in the courts, supervised by mothers sitting in deck chairs or drinking their morning coffee. It was assumed proper to enter apartments without knocking, and most families enjoyed their life in a fishbowl. If one wanted privacy, a commonly recognized signal to gregarious neighbors was a closed windowshade.

These two brief illustrations should give some indication that the modes of social interaction in metropolitan areas are many and varied. Whatever model we

[4]William H. White, *The Organization Man* (Garden City, N.J.: Doubleday Anchor Books, 1956).
[5]Herbert J. Gans, *The Urban Villagers* (New York: The Free Press, 1962).

develop to mirror this interaction must be placed in the context of such variation or it will completely distort the reality of urban life. Therefore, we will begin our discussion with a few concrete examples of differing patterns of urban life. Four descriptions will be of various urban locations—places in the city where people have been together long enough to develop distinctive styles of living and where they feel free enough to be themselves.

Urban Villagers

The fact that the city is not totally without a community of sentiment is documented by Herbert Gans in his 1955 study of Boston's West End, entitled the *Urban Villagers*.[5] The area was populated by a great variety of ethnic groups, mainly Italians, Jews, Poles and Irish. Gans chose to study the dominant group, the Italians, which constituted 42 percent of the West End population. His study was an early attempt to distinguish the slum from viable forms of community (like the West End) so that urban planners could have a better perspective on what parts of cities could be torn down without disrupting viable social networks, and which portions of the city (though physically debilitated) should be retained because of their viable social structure and sense of community. Gans distinguished between what he called the "urban jungle" and the "urban village." The jungle was "populated largely by single men, pathological families, people in hiding from themselves or society, and individuals who provide the more disreputable of illegal-but-demanded services to the rest of the community." The village was an area "in which European immigrants—and more recently Negro and Puerto Rican ones—try to adapt their non-urban institutions and cultures to the urban milieu."[6] Despite the appearance of the urban village, Gans argued, it is really not a slum or skid row.

The West Enders' social structure was comprised of family, peer groups, and the larger community. The family was usually extended and included numerous relatives in daily interaction with conjugal family members. As in most working-class families, the conjugal roles were segregated so that peer groups were segregated by sex.

Italian West Enders typically had a strong sense of loyalty to their family. Men's groups and women's groups provided the context within which most adult entertainment took place outside of the family. The community was defined in social terms and included institutions and organizations used by the West Enders to perform functions that cannot be taken care of within the peer group society."[7] The fact that most of these institutions were located in the same area provided social accessibility for West Enders and should not be taken as evidence of a strong attachment to the spatial area. In fact, only after the West End was threatened with demolition did a strong sense of attachment to the area develop.

[6]Derek L. Phillips, ed., *Studies in American Society: II* (New York: Thomas Y. Corwell, 1967), p. 181.

[7]*Ibid.*, p. 182.

The West End community was comprised of the following specific institutions: the parochial school; the church; formal social, civic and political organizations, some of them church related; and some commercial establishments. The outside world—referred to by West Enders as "they" or "them"—was made up of institutions largely imposed on West End life. "These include work, education, health services, welfare agencies, government, and the mass media of communications."[8]

The social interaction of West Enders typically extended outward from family members, to peer group members, to members of other peer groups and institutions in the community, to the outside world. The church reinforced family, peer, and community relationships by providing the major schooling (and hoped-for discipline) for the children of the West End, by sponsoring clubs and activities for the peer groups, and, through its clergy and nuns, providing physical expression of an ideal male and female image (with the notable exception of the church's stand on chastity for which the clergy are venerated, but not followed). The priest was the court of first resort for the young delinquents. Persistent misdeeds called for the patrolman to take him to the precinct house and from there into the juvenile court system.

Leadership was actively sought in the West End, because it provided the occasion for individual expression, but it was regarded with suspicion for much the same reason. Leadership required a measure of detachment from a group, but detachment lent itself readily to charges of seeking personal gain. Even clergy were not exempt from suspicion. In the sacred realm, their leadership was not questioned, but when they spoke out on civil matters, they were on their own. Gans contends that the West End, probably more than most places, had "too many chiefs and not enough Indians."

The social clubs declined in importance during the late fifties, but Gans observed that there was indeed a "college boy"—"corner boy" distinction to be noted in the West End, just as Whyte had observed it in Boston's East End. The college-boy clubs served as a focal point for college-educated young people who had moved away, a place to keep in touch. The corner-boy clubs, in contrast, were quite cohesive and supportive of members who stayed behind.

The picture presented of the Italian community within the West End neighborhood is clearly that of an organized, relatively cohesive group of people who support one another and find meaning in their social institutions.

Satmar: An Island in the City

An even more cohesive urban village is described by Israel Rubin in his account of an Hasidic Jewish community in Brooklyn, New York.[9] The Satmarer are a particular segment of a larger complex Hasidic Jewish community in Brooklyn called Williamsburg.

---

[8]*Ibid.*, p. 184.
[9]Israel Rubin, *Satmar: An Island in the City* (Chicago: Quadrangle Books, 1972).

Clearly, the beliefs of Hasidic Judiasm constitute the core of the Satmar culture. The flavor of the community can be conveyed through a description of the social hierarchy, which is based on relative prestige, not necessarily on relative power. At the top of the social hierarchy is the *Rov,* in a class by himself. He is rabbi, the religious and political leader of this small community. There are some members of the Satmar who, by virtue of occupation, pedigree, or self-definition, are a bit above the average in status. The status of these members derives from their religious functions; they are the scribes, rabbis of sattelite congregations, and scholars. Another group in this upper strata are descendents of rabbis. The rank-and-file in Satmar consider themselves a bit above the common man because Satmar is an elite community. Just being average has status. At the bottom of the strata are two kinds of individuals: those whose substandard conduct had disgraced them, and those who are not full members in Satmar.

Although the family is the chief social institution, the congregation is the basic organizational structure of Satmar. The Torah consists of 613 laws, 365 proscriptions, and 258 prescriptions that govern almost every aspect of everyday life. The clothes one wears, the food one eats, the way one goes about the business of earning a living are all directed by thr religious law. Of critical importance is the prohibition on education beyond high school for the rank-and-file. Other religious communities such as the Hutterite and the Amish, which maintain equally distinctive cultures in our society, have also felt it necessary to live in relative isolation in small rural communities. Unlike these, however, the Satmarer have remained insular in the midst of a metropolis. Moreover, contrary to the European Orthodox saying of "Be a Jew in your home and a human being on the street," Satmarer often conduct their religious ceremonies in the street, blocking traffic in the process. They live next door to sometimes hostile ethnics, who have nevertheless come to consider their distinctiveness a part of the normal life of the neighborhood.

Satmar is a community bound together by religious norms. The social control at its disposal is as viable as the more common economic bonds. However, the fact that Satmarer increasingly aspire to upper middle-class economic status and must strive to achieve this by virtue of only high school education has created some unresolved tensions within the community that have tended to increase since World War II. This community of over a thousand families has, furthermore, lost its leader, Rov Teitelbaum. This will lead to inevitable fragmentation unless a replacement can be found. The social function of *Rov* was great. He was consulted in all matters of import by members of the community, and his word was regarded as final in arbitration of disputes. Because he was regarded by his followers as virtually infallible, and because he lead a rigorous and virtuous life, he will be exceedingly difficult to replace.

But the continued existence of Satmar (and the resurgence of interest and commitment to orthodox Judaism as well) amply demonstrates that it is indeed possible to lead distinctively different life-styles in America. Satmar has retained the essential elements of an eighteenth-century religious culture well into the twentieth, and for over sixty years has been successful in the struggle to preserve its cultural heritage in the midst of a modern metropolis. Thus Satmar and the Orthodox community continued as outstanding examples of the viability of a pluralist culture.

The Dormitory Suburb

Another distinctive urban location is the middleclass dormitory suburb. The growth of the suburbs since World War II is a testimony both to our increasing affluence and to the tendency of the middle class to flee from the problems of the inner cities. The green suburbs with their single family dwellings on comparatively spacious half- to one-acre lots were enthusiastically developed as a ''good place to raise the kids.'' When the inner cities became populated by blacks and other minorities, the white middle class took flight to the suburbs. The families that left the inner city were not only comparatively affluent, but were also more likely to be in the child-rearing stage of their development. Couples without children who were just beginning their families and the elderly who had watched their children leave the nest tended to remain in the city. Therefore, the dormitory suburb is usually age-segregated. Because most of these suburbs are strictly residential, the working members of the household—still most often the husbands in this group—must leave during the day and work elsewhere. During the day, the dormitory suburb is also strongly sex-segregated. The community is made up predominantly of mothers caring for their younger children.

And yet within the dormitory suburbs there is significant variation in the character of the localized social interaction or neighboring patterns. In places such as Park Forest the interaction is intense. But in other settings like the more affluent Rockland County, New York, described by Spectorsky in the *Exurbanites,* there were no coffee klatches.[10] The houses sit back from the street in wooded lots that offer privacy and foster the sense of isolation amongst the women left behind. In such settings obsessive participation in voluntary organizations is resorted to in order to drive off the boredom and find self-fulfillment.

The problems of these suburban communities are increased by the fact that public transportation is not readily available. The family automobile (commonly two of them) must provide much of the transportation. This means that much of the wife's time must be spent driving the other members of the family to and from their appointments. In settings like Rockland County, even the children must make appointments with each other in order to play.

The effects of age and sex segregation in such settings mean that the children grow up with quite restricted adult role-models and miss the opportunity to be guided and ''spoiled'' by doting grandparents. Neither birth nor death becomes a common part of their experience. Protected also from the devastations of poverty

---

[10]A. C. Spectorsky, *The Exurbanites* (New York: J. B. Lippencott Company, 1955).

and isolated from the conflicts of the workaday world, the suburban child is likely to perceive life as superficial and relatively impersonal. We should not be surprised that the children of the counter-culture grew up in the suburbs and that young people flee from this environment in large numbers. What seemed initially to be a good place in which to raise the kids turns out to be a very unsatisfying environment for large numbers of teenagers and young adults.

Since 1960, there has been a steady increase in the number of multiple dwelling units being built in the suburbs. The percentage of home ownership has also declined steadily. These facts suggest a trend toward greater heterogeneity as young people without children and persons over sixty-five increasingly find the suburbs a good place to live.[11]

The three patterns of urban life described above—Boston's Italian West End, Satmar, and the dormitory suburbs—fit Anselm Strauss' concept of location, as opposed to that of locale. Strauss summarizes his concept of location as follows:

> At a location, the physical segregation of the people of a social world is maximized. Here they can openly indulge in ceremonial and ritual gestures, here they may speak a foreign language without shame. For it is here that an urban world is seen in the form of relatively widely shared symbols. It is here, too, that the outsider really knows that he is an outsider, and if he wishes to become an insider, he knows that he must learn the appropriate ways of this world.[12]

In contrast to locations, *locales* are characterized by heterogeneous populations. Locales like Fifth Avenue in New York are essentially places where people pass each other by. Locales may provide an occasion for the public display of self, but in the context of strangers who do not have very much in common. The "orbits" of many different kinds of people intersect in locales and the segregation of the urban world is at a minimum. Locales are the setting for cosmopolitan life-styles to be put on display and they are the settings that, above all others, tend to give the city its distinctive flavor.

> A street like Rush Street in Chicago, for example, is a locale where in the evening one may find—on the street and in the many restaurants and bars—a variety of customers, servicing agents, and visitors. Rush Street has its own atmosphere, as many people have observed, compounded of all these people and all these institutions. It is one of the glamour streets of Chicago. There one can see, if one has an eye for them, prostitutes, pimps, homosexuals, bisexuals, upper-class men and women, university students, touts, artists, tourists, businessmen out for a good time with or without girl friends, young men and women dating, people of various ethnic backgrounds, policemen, cabbies—the entire catalogue is much longer. Rush Street is a locale where people from many different urban worlds, with many styles of urbanity, pass each other, buy services from each other, talk to one another, and occasionally make friends with one another.[13]

[11]Report of the Social Science Panel, *op. cit.,* p. 18.
[12]Anselm L. Strauss, *Images of the American City* (New York: The Free Press, 1961), p. 66.
[13]*Ibid.,* p. 65.

Locations maximize the similarities between residents; locales maximize their differences. Locations and locales co-exist in city life, each location or locale different from the next, each exhibiting its special characteristics, and all creating the richly varied tapestry of the urban social fabric.

Social Binding

In analyzing the nature of a community, anthropologists have always given considerable weight to the role of normative values in binding members together. Thus, in spite of their awareness of how non-normative considerations bind people together, and of how actual behavior departs from desired behavior, much of what they record is an account of preferred behavior, or how people ought to be.

This tendency has been carried over into other social sciences, particularly sociology. The social system is seen as comprised of roles and institutions that embody widely shared social expectations of appropriate or preferred behavior. It is no surprise, therefore, that when sociologists and anthropologists go about trying to delineate a community or a society, they seek to establish the existence of a value consensus. Since there is little apparent consensus in an urban area, this makes it difficult to study the urban environment and leads to much of the pessimism of "Chicago Sociologists."

Political scientists, however, assume that the principal mode of social organization is some form of government. Further, the base upon which all government finally rests is the power to take life. Coercion is thus assumed to exist in all social groupings to some extent, and this is the basic bond most likely to suggest itself to them. This orientation to the subject of social integration has produced a host of studies on community power.

Finally we can conceive of utilitarian bonds that hold people together in all societies. Economic transactions are the chief concern of economists who have been least of all influenced by the other social sciences. However, the influence of economic analysis can be seen in sociology and more recently in political science, with the introduction of exchange theory. In this context, social relations are thought of as profitable, and therefore continued, if they are perceived of by the participants as having benefits which exceed their costs. The most common medium of exchange is money. But it must be admitted that what may seem to be a purely economic exchange can often involve other, more fundamental, human costs and benefits.

In offering his basic classification of social bonding, Etzioni suggests that we can think of their essential elements in the following ways. *Normative* bonds entail shared values and norms. In them, the participants treat each other as "goals" and their mutual commitments are non-rational. *Utilitarian* bonds involve complementary interests. The participants treat each other as means and their mutual commitments are rational. Finally, *coercive* bonds involve the threat of violence by one participant against the other.[14] Participants treat each other as objects, and the commitment may be rational or nonrational. It is common in social relationships for one type of bonding to dominate. For example, the parent-child bonding is typified by the normative bonding; "normative" here describes both an ideational and an emotive component. The interaction transpiring between two trades is primarily utilitarian, and the relationship that obtains between a criminal and his victim is primarily coercive. The social network is never to be thought of as being composed of pure types of relationships, however. An understanding of urban society demands a sensitivity to the interactive nature of social bonding and to the complexity of the situations of urban life.

Basic Models of Urban Integration

When we approach the issue of social integration from the perspective of the basic bonds, our focus is much closer to the individuals that comprise the social fabric. When, however, we turn to an examination of various models of social integration that may be appropriate to the city, we are looking at the urban population as some kind of whole. In this context, we expand our vision by examining the social bonds in the context of their networks or "systems." Thus we must consider the primary locus of utilitarian bonds to be in the economic exchanges of the people, commonly called "the market." The primary locus of coercive bonds must be examined within the context of the power struggles of government, and normative bonds primarily within the context of community. It becomes even more obvious when we do this that our models are grossly simplified. We know that no market exists without some degree of normative consensus and coercion, that no government survives for long without some kind of constitution that modulates the distribution of benefits, and that a community, however defined, is considerably more than a normative consensus. Be that as it may, the market and the problems of government are discussed in separate chapters, and we will here focus upon the problem of the urban community as a network of social bonds.

The Little Community

Let us first try to grasp what exactly we mean by the term "community." Anthropologists studying contemporary Stone Age villages such as Chan Kom on the Yucatan peninsula or a small peasant village in Europe are inclined to consider them as some kind of whole to which the term "community" is often applied. The multitude of objects, activities, customs, and beliefs are thought of as somehow hanging together in a more or less distinctive culture. Thus Robert Redfield described the "little community," for which Chan Kom was the prototype in a

---

[14]Amitai Etzioni, *The Active Society* (New York: Free Press, 1968), p. 96ff.

number of different ways. He suggested that it could be studied as an ecological system, well adapted to the cultivation of maize in fields cleared from the semi-tropical rain forest. All of the activities, beliefs, and institutions of the village could be meaningfully related to this adaptation. The whole of this community could also be seen through an analysis of its social structure (the roles and institutions of the village life). It could be grasped by a typical biography, or the presentation of a typical outlook on life, or the unraveling of events that comprise the history of the village. The same whole could be approached and understood through these apparently diverse points of entry.[15]

An anthropologist such as Raymond Firth defines a community as "a body of people sharing common activities, bound by multiple relationships in such a way that the aims of any individual can be achieved only by participation in action with others."[16] He concludes that there are at least four essential elements to social existence in a community: 1) social alignment or social structure, in the narrow sense of the grouping and grading of people for carrying out the activities demanded by the common existence; 2) social controls, thought of here as principally a system of beliefs and procedures by which activities are guided; 3) social media, made up primarily of material goods and language which make activity possible and serve as reservoirs of effort against future needs; and 4) the social standards or values of a society by which objects are assigned preference or priority. In Firth's notation, values have both an ideational component and an emotional charge.

The term "community" is widely used in social science literature. One study estimates that there are at least 94 different meanings attributed to this term.[17] In spite of the great diversity of meanings, there are common threads, and it is helpful to examine these before specifying more precisely what we shall mean by "community." In keeping with common understanding, "community" refers primarily to a group of individuals who are assumed to have had a prolonged history of interaction. Prolonged interaction is necessary for commuity in our common understanding, because it is only through repeated encounters with others that we feel we can learn to "count on them."[18]

To call a group a community normally implies something about the quality of the relationships as "primary," meaning that they are based on face-to-face interaction and involve a higher degree of trust, openness and interdependence than we normally experience in society at large.[19] The essence of community, in any case, is

---

[15]Robert Redfield, *The Little Community* (Chicago: University of Chicago Press, 1955).

[16]George A. Hilley, Jr., "Definition of Community: Area of Agreement," *Rural Society,* 20 (June, 1955), pp. 111–123.

[17]*Ibid.*

[18]A notable exception to this generalization is the use of the term "community" to define the outcome of intensive (and massive) 2–4 day group encounter. See, for example, Jack R. Gibbs, "The TORT Community Experience as an Organizational Change Intervention," in W. Warner Burke, ed., *Organization Development: Conceptual Orientation and Intervention* (Washington, D.C.: National Training Laboratory, 1972), pp. 109–126.

[19]Charles Winck, Dictionary of Anthropology (New York: Philosophical Library, 1956), p. 126.

the family-like relationships between members. This close association between "community" and "family" is well depicted in communes.[20]

Less frequently we use the term "community" to refer simply to an area such as a village or neighborhood. In this fashion we say that so and so came from the small community of Bland, Missouri, or we ask, "What brings you back to the old neighborhood?" When used in this fashion, "community" is normally shorthand for the assumed relationships thought to prevail in such areas when they are relatively stable and homogeneous. Historically, closeness of residence has been a prerequisite for the development of primary relationships, though the term is sometimes applied when the relationship no longer obtains. When referring to a geographical area as a community, it is often assumed that the people living in this area are functionally interdependent. They use the same public utilities, respond to the same governmental agencies, and make use of common doctors, newspapers, and recreational centers or gathering places.

"Community" is also often used to signify a shared set of values or experiences, as in reference to the "black community." The assumption often made in this usage is that even though people do not live together or do not share the same social class, there is enough common interest (derived in this case from their common heritage and common treatment by whites) to unite an otherwise heterogeneous people in a common cause. Thus, neither propinquity nor primary relationships may typify such a community.[21]

Metropolitan Communities

In the urbanized world of today, the association between a sense of community and a geographic area is becoming less intense.[22] It is becoming more common for people to have viable, intimate relationships with persons who do not live nearby. Conversely, people who live crammed together in large apartment complexes or in urban row houses may not exhibit a high degree of interpersonal interaction. Even a strong sense of identification with a region or neighborhood may not signify a high degree of intimate interaction with the persons who live there. Finally, persons who may live many miles apart are becoming increasingly interrelated through their functional dependence upon certain facilities such as the power grids that span our country. Indeed, with the advent of the atomic age, it is becoming obvious that the whole world is affected by the actions of a few people. Interdependence is becoming increasingly characteristic of the world's population as a whole as captured in the slogan "spaceship earth."

Some social scientists have stretched the term "community" to correspond with city. Roland Warren is one such social scientist, and he includes metropolitan areas in his broad definition of "community":

[20]Rosabeth Kanter, *Commitment and Community* (Cambridge: Harvard University Press, 1972).

[21]Stokey Carmichael and Charles Hamilton, *Black Power* (New York: Random House, 1967).

[22]Suzanne Keller, *The Urban Neighborhood: A Sociological Perspective* (New York: Random House, 1968).

Washington Square outdoor art show. Is this community? A semi-annual event (late spring and early fall), this legendary happening turns Greenwich Village into a huge open-air art gallery. *(New York Convention and Visitors Bureau.)*

> We shall consider a community to be that combination of social units and systems which perform the major social functions having locality relevance. This is another way of saying that by ''community'' we mean the organization of social activities to afford people daily access to those broad areas of activity which are necessary in day-to-day living.[23]

He considers these basic functions to be: 1) the production, distribution and consumption of goods and services which finds best expression in the corporate institution; 2) socialization as exemplified in the school; 3) social control as manifested most directly in government; 4) social participation such as provided by the churches; and 5) mutual support as provided by the family, relatives, and public welfare.

In order to make this definition useful for the study of entire metropolitan areas, it is necessary for Warren to assert that communities differ in the manner and extent of the provision of these services. He proposes that the primary dimensions of difference are: 1) the extent of a community's autonomy or self sufficiency; 2) the extent to which its service areas (shopping centers, churches, schools, utilities, etc.) coincide or fail to do so; 3) the extent of psychological identification with a particu-

[23]Roland Warren, *The Community in America* (Chicago: Rand McNally, 1968), p. 9. Report of the Social Science Panel, *op. cit.,* p. 2.
[24]Warren, *op. cit.,* p. 24.

lar community; and 4) the strength of the functional relationships between various local units (individuals and social systems).[24]

In sum, "community" has been commonly used to refer to a group of persons normally thought of as living close together, depending upon common services and resources, and manifesting at least some of the characteristics of primary relationships such as those commonly meant by neighborliness and having a more or less strong sense of identification with a particular area. "Community" must also be seen as embodying a widely shared human hope for mutually satisfying relationships with others, and for many urbanites, it is an emotionally loaded word.

Community, Communion, and Society

Herbert Schmalenbach has pointed to an enduring set of contrasts between community, communion, and society that can help us further place the term "community" in context. Community is based upon natural bonds most commonly reflected in blood ties or prolonged proximity. The social institution that most clearly reflects community bonds is the family. Historically, family structure was the dominant social structure. When family is expressed as lineages, a complex social order can be maintained.[25] The rights and privileges of diverse social roles are transmitted through lineages; property and descent are likewise regulated. In such societies, persons are born into their social roles. Because everyone knows his or her place, the social order is not often threatened; daily behavior is rigidly specified; individual freedom and autonomy is sacrificed for the benefits of community. Persons who find themselves in society by means of their birth into a family can and do take their social obligations for granted to a considerable extent. Weber would say that authority in such communities was based on tradition and the whole effort of the society is directed toward representing the patterns of the past.[26]

Communions, on the other hand, are based on emotional bonding. The feeling of encounter and acceptance into the brotherhood often dramatized by ritual rites of passage is central to the experience of communion. Religious groups provide the best examples of such social relationships, particularly those in the modern world that Troelsch would characterize as sectarian.[27] The Holy Rollers, Jehovah's Witnesses, Hari Krishna Movement, the followers of Mehr Baba, Rev. Moon, and others come readily to mind. Authority in such groups is characteristically based on the charisma of particular leaders who have become messiahs for their followers. While much of the activity of the sect may not involve the members in an emotional orgy, conversion experiences are central to the life of the group and highly valued by all. In some regards, the encounter movement among middleclass Americans has become very much like these sects, in that the experience of encounter within

[25]Claude Levi-Strauss, "The Family," in *Man, Culture and Society*, Harry L. Shapiro, ed. (New York: Oxford University Press, 1966).
[26]Max Weber, *The Theory of Social and Economic Organization* (Glencoe, Ill.: The Free Press, 1947).

the group itself becomes self-validating. Rather than finding in the experience the means to improve one's relationships in other aspects of one's life, the central concern becomes the quest for encounter.[28] It is clear that this kind of social relationship based on feelings is most unstable. Our emotions have a tendency to wax and wane. Charismatic leaders rarely are able to find successors adequate to the task of following in their footsteps. Communion relationships, therefore, most often characterize a phase in a person's experience or a group's history.

Society is characterized by relationships that are intentionally entered and left. Rational-legal authority, symbolized by the contract, prevails. The economic system and the market place best represent these types of relationships. Marketing relationships are normally perceived of as mutually beneficial and utilitarian. It does not matter how one feels about them; it does not matter if one is not related to the contracted partner (indeed normally this is not the case); it does not even matter if one knows the person with whom one is entering into a contract. The law provides the "court of last resort" before whom grievances can be brought. It thereby guarantees the stability of the relationship should one or the other suddenly desire to break it before its terms have been met. Contracts attempt to specify precisely the nature of the mutual obligations and rights for this very reason. The less ambiguous, the less likely they are to be broken.

Contracts are normally for a specified time and cease to make demands upon the parties when their terms have been met. It should also be evident that contracted relationships depend to a considerable extent upon some willingness on the part of all parties to the contract to tolerate the ambiguities that cannot be eliminated. The marriage contract is least characteristic of contracts per se, but most illustrative of this reliance upon non-legal elements of the relationship. The marriage contract is more symbolic of a proposed life-long commitment to each other than a rational-legal guarantee that the terms of the contract will be fulfilled. This is very evident in the case of divorce. The court cannot effectively force a husband to honor his alimony or child support payments since he can always choose to become a beachcomber or leave the country. He must be willing to cooperate.

Urban people experience all three types of social relationships (those characterizing communities, communions and societies), but the most dominant form of relationship is the societal, or rational-legal. We contend, along with numerous others, that the dominant evolutionary trend in human social relationships has been from community toward society. There are notable exceptions to this general rule, such as in Israeli *kibbutzim* and the new alternative of communal living in America, but these involve only a small fraction of the population of either nation. It is evident that there is much dissatisfaction with modern urban societies because of an enduring nostalgia for the security of community and a deep thirst for communion.

[27]Herman Schmalenbach, "The Sociological Category of Communion," in Talcott Parson, *et al.,* eds., *Theories of Society,* Vol. I (Glencoe, Ill.: Free Press, 1961), pp. 332–347.

[28]Kurt Back, *Beyond Words: The Story of Sensitivity and the Encounter Movement* (New York: Russell Sage Foundation, 1972).

Eclipse of Community

Although few of us experience a sense of community in large cities, we have little difficulty perceiving small towns and villages as communities. What changes occurred as cities grew in size that caused the eclipse of "community"? Do these changes rule out altogether the possibility of a true urban community? Increasing division of labor produced specialization and functional interdependence of persons living in urban communities, as illustrated in the production, transportation, processing, packaging, distribution and consumption of food. A differentiation of interests and associations, develops, wherein family members find themselves pursuing divergent interests and associations most of their waking hours. Warren warns that such secondary associations cannot replace the support and mutuality of primary relations, should these be weakened beyond their endurance. Increasing bureaucratization and impersonalization stress a rational-legal, matter-of-fact approach to life. In caricature, it can be seen as red tape, inflexibility and lack of imagination in our response to problems, but within certain specific contexts, represents at least an increase in narrowly defined economic efficiency. Many functions have been transferred to profit enterprises and to government. As an individual specializes, he depends on others to perform the functions he gives up. These functions become standardized—get into the price system—as the individual must pay others to perform these tasks.

There is increasing concentration of persons in urban and suburban areas. Changes in basic values have taken place, such as the increasing acceptance of governmental activity in an increasing number of areas, a gradual decline in the moral interpretation of human behavior, and increasing reliance upon planning rather than moral reform. There is decreasing emphasis upon work, in favor of enjoyment and consumption. The great change can be described differently as far as its impact upon different kinds of urban communities, but the overall effect has been to produce what Warren calls "the community problem."[29]

Warren defines the community problem as primarily twofold: 1) a loss of community autonomy, and 2) a lack of identification with a community, which can be seen in the increasing apathy, alienation, anonymity, and delinquent behavior. Indeed, most of us lament that one of the major problems of urban life is that most people do not feel that they belong to a community. While there may be temporary islands of community or neighborhoods in which people are good neighbors, city life is experienced by many as alienating, anxiety-producing, and lonely.

Urban Social Integration

The central meaning of community seems to lie on the quality of family-like relationships thought to obtain between the members, and it seems wise to restrict the

[29]Warren, *op. cit.*

178

term to this focus. If community, after Schmalenbach, is to mean essentially the natural bonding once thought to have been expressed in the large extended family and conveyed by the term "blood," then it is unlikely that cities will ever be characterized as communities, though it may be possible to discover locations within them that could be properly so called. The family, as we have seen in Chapter 6, is not likely to exercise the power it once did over the individual ever again. However, we need not conclude that modern urban life can never provide adequate support for persons living in large, heterogeneous, complex populations. Rather we must simply look for different manifestations of support on the one hand, and consider the conditions under which community might be manifested in cities on the other. Unfortunately, we have given little thought to what desirable alternatives there might be. In this section we will begin to speculate about some possibilities.

Why does it appear that so much of our lives are characterized by isolation, loneliness, anomie, and a quest for communion and community? Why can't we seem to find enough of these relationships in the abundant and complex society we have created? The answer is possibly to be found in the fact that we have no real experience as yet with a truly pluralistic society in which it is not only possible, but expected, that persons will meet their need for community and communion in a wide variety of relationships and life-styles valued because of their differences, not simply tolerated because we do not have the coercive power to eliminate them. The problem the urbanite must face is to learn how to satisfy his quest for communion while permitting others to do likewise in other locations where the values are different from those that thrive in the city. This can be done in part by a dedication to rational-legal societies where the law establishes the right to be different. But the law cannot be called upon to establish a community.

Urban Integration as a Statement of Possibilities

Much confusion in our thinking about cities results from the fact that we do not as yet have an adequate image of what an urban society can or should be. The model of the little community cannot be applied to the whole metropolitan complex though it has some utility when describing locations within it. Various models describing the functional interdependence of selected elements of a metropolitan complex—such as Roland Warren's—seem to minimize the importance of the interpersonal relationships so central to our understanding of both community and communion. But where do we as individuals fit into such images of the city?

The Pretense of Pluralism. There is much talk today about our pluralist culture. From a celebration of "America, the melting pot," so common in the rhetoric of the first half of this century, we now commonly speak as though we delight in our ethnic, racial, and intentionally chosen differences. The violence of the late 1960's and the reaction of the right in the 1970's should tell us otherwise. In fact, we tend to accommodate differences in values, life-styles, and cultures until we can find a way to eliminate them through assimilation or repression. Such differences persist in spite of our sentiments, not because of them. The culture that encourages us to celebrate these differences has not yet appeared in the human experience. But only a broad-scale cultural affirmation of the intrinsic value of diverse life-styles can guarantee the actual autonomy of each. Only then can we speak without pretense of a pluralist society.

We have heard Lewis Mumford speak of the city as the only stage upon which the full human drama can be enacted. We have listened to Anselm Strauss romanticize about the intrigue of urban locales such as Chicago's Rush Street. We have spent a number of pages describing in detail some of the differences in life-styles discernible in our cities. These differences are real, they help account for the color of the metropolitan mosaic, but they are not celebrated. In political debate, we still seek consensus more than cooperation. Simple slogans like "God, Guns and Guts Made America Great—Let's Keep All Three," clutter our collective self-image and justify our imperialism. We still struggle to recapture the conviction that American democracy and American technology do indeed determine the future of the world. In the administration of public welfare to the poor and in the reconstruction of our cities, bulldozers and bullheadedness in planning for others speak more eloquently of our need to bring all things to a common level than a respect for what others find to be of value. As many observers have pointed out, our worship of money in a market economy is the great leveler of values and the great creator of classes.

The False Dichotomy.   A widely shared value caricatured as "rugged individualism" promulgates a false dichotomy between the individual and his/her group and helps to preserve the pretense of pluralism. Individuals pitted against each other in the competition of free enterprise or the open market place, hardly value each others differences, though out of a sense of strategy they may "respect" them. More importantly, however, the emphasis upon individualism presupposes that not only is it valuable for individuals to struggle against each other, but that they cannot do otherwise. A somewhat ameliorative position would contend that individuals can escape from freedom into the conformity of an "in" group. In which case, the struggle is carried on between groups rather than simply between individuals.

There can be no doubt that we do indeed pit ourselves against one another individually and in ever larger groups. But, the question remains, is this now either inevitable or desirable? There are other images available which seem more compelling. Before we can examine them it is necessary to understand why the dichotomy is false—or, better, why its half-truth is no longer preferable. If we understand anything about the human animal, we understand that to be human is to be social.[30]

---

[30]Indeed, to use the word "social" in the currently accepted understanding of the term in the social sciences, is to recognize that the human infant does not achieve humanity through simple maturation. Others "call him forth" through an interaction we call socialization. Left alone or abandoned, the human infant would probably not survive, or, if physical survival were possible, would hardly be recognizable as a human being. Certainly severely deprived children show few marks of personhood such as language, intelligence beyond a rudimentary level, emotional flexibility and the like.

This is not simply the bias of sociologists, but well enough established on an interdisciplinary basis. The romanticism of Rousseau and his fabled state of nature in which the state was formed by means of autonomous rational individuals entering into a mutually agreed upon contract does not allow for this interdependence.

At the other end of the so-called "dichotomy," there is no known society that has completely socialized the individual so that everyone wants the same things, believes the same things, behaves in essentially the same way. Paul Radin, among others, testifies to the unique contributions of individuals in the most collectivized little communities. The reality we must acknowledge is a complex interdependence between the individual organism and its cultural and social environment. As Peter Berger has put it, "Men are in society, and society is in men." How strange that our current images of community do not give adequate recognition of this simple observation.

A Preferable Prefigurement of Pluralism. Karl Popper has argued eloquently for the open society as a model of a pluralist society.[31] The seeds of the open society have been planted long ago in our tradition, but they have yet to fully germinate. Pericles declared in his famous funeral oration in the fifth century before Christ:

> Our city is thrown open to the world; we never expel a foreigner . . . we are free to live exactly as we please, and yet we are always ready to face any danger. . . . We love beauty without indulging in fancies, and although we try to improve our intellect, this does not weaken our will. . . . To admit one's poverty is no disgrace with us; but we consider it disgraceful not to make an effort to avoid it. An Athenian citizen does not neglect public affairs when attending to his private business. . . . We consider a man who takes no interest in the state not as harmless, but as useless; and although only a few may originate a policy, we are all able to judge it.[32]

Karl Popper considers the open society to be constantly struggling with various forms of totalitarian societies which he labels as "closed." In his view, little communities are "closed" societies. The notion of the intimate interface between public and private worlds, the assertion that all are able to judge a policy (though only a few may originate it), the freedom to live exactly as one pleases expressed in the above oration can be seen as central concepts in western democratic thought. But, while Pericles spoke of them as realities of his Golden Age of Athens, it is unlikely that things were in fact as he thought of them. The image of the open society rests on the assumption that no one can unambiguously discover the truth. In Socratic dialogue, individuals may come closer to it, but the dialogue is a continuing conversation, not a precise method for the discovering of unchanging truths. In contrast, totalitarian societies are based on the assumption that truth is manifest in history and that there are precise methods for discovering it. Popper wrote his *Open Society* as his "war effort" in the 1940's, because he was convinced that western

---

[31]Karl Popper, *The Open Society and Its Enemies* (Princeton, N.J.: Princeton University Press, 1962).

[32]Quoted in Popper, *op. cit.,* p. 186.

democracies were threatened by Nazism. He argued that the Nazi's believed that they and they alone knew what was best for Europe and the world because of the popularity of Hegelian thought in Germany. Hegel asserted that it was possible to build a precise model of reality, and further that history could be shown to follow exact laws in the realization of that model.

The philosophical debate is intricate and demanding.[33] It need not concern us in detail here beyond the apparently simple observation that if you believe that history has a truth or meaning, it is very likely that you also believe that you have discovered it—or are surely on the way to doing do. The notion of a "chosen people" is one clear example of this conviction in western experience. It is quite incompatible with a pluralist or open society, for the reason that if one is chosen, someone else is not. At best, the chosen can treat the non-chosen benevolently, or pastorally as Christians claim to treat pagans. At worst, such a view leads to the creation of concentration camps.

Aside from the totalitarian threat to the open society, Popper envisioned a more subtle threat characteristic of our modern society. He called it the "abstract society" and thought of it as a kind of degeneration of the open society. At the same time, he believed that all open societies were to some degree abstract.[34] He used the term "abstract" because he felt that the society loses its organic character and its identification with a concrete or real group of persons. In exaggerated terms he suggested . . .

> We could conceive of a society in which men practically never meet face-to-face—in which all business is conducted by individuals in isolation who communicate by typed letters or by telegrams, and who go about in closed motor cars. (Artificial insemination would allow even progapation without a personal element.) Such a fictitious society might be called a completely abstract or depersonalized society. Now an interesting point is that our modern society resembles in many of its aspects such a completely abstract society . . . There are many people living in a modern society who have no, or extremely few, intimate personal contacts, who live in anonymity and isolation, and consequently in unhappiness. For although society has become abstract, the biological make-up of man has not changed much; men have social needs which they cannot satisfy in an abstract society.[35]

To consider the abstract society thusly is to consider the cost of transition from the closed society, or little community. But there are also benefits to consider in the transition.

> Personal relationships of a new kind can arise where they can be freely entered into, instead of being determined by the accidents of birth; and with this a new individualism

[33]In his assessment of the debate, Popper considers the "friends" of the open society to be Heraclitus, Socrates, Pericles, Kierkegaard, Kant, among others, and the enemies to be Plato, Aristotle, Hegel and Marx, among others. The central issue in the debate was formulated by Kant in terms of our inability to know anything at all about the "thing in itself." In contrast, Platonic "recollection" enabled the soul to know the true forms because it saw them clearly before birth. In recollection, it merely recaptures the vision of "treeness," etc. However, in Plato, only the philosopher-kings had this knowledge.

[35]*Ibid.*, p. 175.

arises. Similarly spiritual bonds can play a major role where the biological or physical bonds are weakened . . . our modern open societies function largely by way of abstract relations, such as exchange or cooperation. (It is the analysis of these abstract relations with which modern social theory, such as economic theory, is mainly concerned. This point has not been understood by many sociologists, such as Durkheim, who never gave up the dogmatic belief that society must be analyzed in terms of real social groups.)[36]

Janet Abu-Lughod makes the same point somewhat differently in her conceptualization of "tertiary" relationships.

If a primary relationship is one in which the individuals are known to each other in many role facets, whereas a secondary relationship implies a knowledge of the other individual only in a single role facet, then a tertiary relationship is one in which only the roles interact. The individuals playing the roles are interchangeable and, in fact, with the computerization of many interactions, are even dispensible, at least at the point of immediate contact. What are in interaction are not individuals in one role capacity or another, but the functional roles themselves. Such tertiary relationships can only be maintained under conditions of physical isolation; once supplemented by physical contact they tend to revert to the secondary. Thus, the isolation of different communities within urban regions promotes role and life-style sterotyping via perceptions created by mass media imagery, particularly television, and many people behave to others as if these perceptions are correct.[37]

With the introduction of the notions of "abstract society" and the "tertiary relationship," the image of the metropolitan complex can be clarified. From the point of view of the whole society, we become concerned about the nature of stereotyping and the images of other groups presented by the mass media, since these assume critical import in defining many personally unknown "others" for modern urbanites. They become the basis of tertiary relationships between different groups. The social sciences play a particularly critical role in the creation of these abstract images, since social science data feeds into the media images, as well as exerting an independent effect through professional publications and conventions. In particular, it seems critical that stereotyping, as such, not be downplayed, but the rigid adherence to stereotypical generalizations seen as a threat to the stability of pluralist societies—particularly when the "other" is labeled as "enemy."

It would seem advisable that the possibilities for cooperation between groups be sought out and presented as well as the potentialities for conflict. It would be wiser to stress the fact, for example, that poor Americans of whatever color generally desire to participate in the mainstream of the American way of life, than to conceive of them as cut off in a culture of poverty, or simply dedicated to various forms of separatism (which is another element in the matrix). Cooperation between peoples of different heritage and aspiration is clearly possible without consensus on many values and without uncontrollable conflict. Presenting images favorable to this end is both a matter of the interpretation and the selection of data about

[36]*Loc. cit.*

[37]As interpreted by Brian J. L. Berry, *The Human Consequences of Urbanization* (New York: St. Martins, 1973), p. 58.

particular groups in the urban complex. It is not simply a matter of accurately describing any particular group "as they are," or letting the data speak for itself.

Synergistic Societies.   Ruth Benedict coined the term *synergistic* to describe little communities in which individuals were rewarded for what they were personally proud of doing.[38] One would think that in view of the extreme homogeneity of such communities it would be difficult to find societies that were non-synergistic. Nevertheless there were certain "surly" societies, in her opinion, in which individuals were terrorized by their own cultural creations (as in Dobu). Other societies such as the Tiv of Africa rewarded constant warfare between members and between cultures. Others simply made competition for scarce items (such as money, prestige, power) a "zero sum" game in which all wins were at the loser's expense. This is most common in our own experience in the west.

In contrast, synergistic societies strive to set up situations in which everyone is a winner. Amongst the examples from the little communities, are the Zuni Indians from our own Southwest. In examining our own society, Benedict tentatively concluded that we ought to be considered a "mixed" example. There were some situations in which team work necessitated that individual specialties be incorporated into the large effort in order for everyone on the team to win. Examples from sports such as football and basketball come readily to mind, but industry task forces are becoming increasingly common. Whole laboratories, and to some extent industries, in their research and development sectors depend upon their ability to reward specialized skills in the context of a group effort to realize common objectives. Indeed, any situation in which superordinate goals are present would seem to offer the possibility for synergistic effort.

However, other aspects of our society, such as the pursuit of a professional career, seem to be based on zero-sum models in which one person's advance is at the expense of another. Surprisingly, the evidence of sibling rivalry suggests that we structure the child-rearing process in our society in such a manner that children from a very early age compete for parental affection. Sibling rivalry is not natural to the child-rearing process, but culturally prescribed. Societies vary considerably in the extent to which it is present.

Notice that the possibility for synergistic cooperation amongst large numbers of persons depends not simply upon the awareness of functional interdependence. Most of us are aware of the extent to which we are dependent upon each other in an emergency such as a fuel shortage. Synergistic cooperation also depends upon the feeling of belonging to a group and the consequent willingness to accept responsibilities within it. It would also seem that it is critical for all members of a synergistic effort to believe that the reward they strive for will be adequate if realized or that the value of participation is sufficiently great in itself to maintain the collective effort. The reward world must thus be perceived of as abundant, rather than scarce, as our common economics would have it. Reward, of course, can be symbolic or material and must, when considering the dimension of abundance, be

---

[38]Recorded by Abraham Maslow.

relative to the felt needs of the participants in a synergistic effort. It goes without saying that it is highly unlikely that a society of 200 million people can under any economy, meet the criteria of material abundance for everyone on the surface of a finite planet over any extended period of time. Therefore, symbolic rewards must play an increasingly critical role. Abstract relationships as defended in courts of law and recognized in the marketplace are not antithetical to community in modern metropolises. They are, however, pre-conditions for new forms of synergistic development.

Clearly, synergistic effort is impossible between persons excluded from a common effort because of unacceptable differences. Interest-group liberalism would resolve this problem by reconceptualizing society as a large number of competing groups, and by asserting that the common interest is realized through the competition of these diverse groups. In the give-and-take of everyday politics, this school of thought would have it, it all balances out. The common good, the common interest, therefore, is nothing more than the sum total of the interests realized through competition over time. The optimists here contend that no group is ever likely to be unjustly excluded for long. The pessimists simply accept the inevitable of someone being left out. Both see the result as just. Cooperation between individuals within groups and between groups resulting in synergistic effort presupposes the intrinsic value of the differences between them.

Self-Actualizing Individuals

Popper's conceptualization of the open society affirms the individual's role as a citizen who must participate in the process of government, not simply in order to give consent to his being governed by others, but because, in a fundamental sense, his judgment is needed. But is the citizen role enough to establish a viable community? From the point of view of the individual urbanite in community, one becomes concerned about the ratio of primary, secondary and tertiary relationships that makes up an individual's daily pattern of interaction. The emphasis on the rational role of decision-making restricts the secondary and tertiary relationships of open societies to a rather narrow aspect of interpersonal interaction.

Popper, being a classical rationalist, further contends that a part of the price we must pay for being human in a modern urban society is to forego some of our emotional needs.

> The strain of civilization . . . is still felt in our day, especially in times of social change. It is the strain created by the effort which life in an open and partially abstract society continually demands from us—by the endeavor to be rational, to forego at least some of our emotional social needs, to look after ourselves, and to accept responsibility. We must, I believe, bear this strain as the price to be paid for every increase in knowledge, in reasonableness, in cooperation and in mutual help and consequently in our chances of survival. . . . It is the price we have to pay for being human.[39]

[39]Popper, The Open Society, *op. cit.*, p. 176.

The implications of the open society for policy makers confronting the problems of governing our cities will be considered in Chapter 13. The strength of Popper's arguments seem to lie in this direction. Here, however, we must consider his weakness and ask: Must we pay this price—this sacrifice of emotional needs—in order to live in a modern urban society?

There is mounting evidence to suggest that this is a much higher price to pay than Popper suspected. The evidence that culturally induced somatosensory deprivation is a fundamental cause of violence is well summarized by a leading neurophysiologist, Dr. James Prescott.[40] In Prescott's view, we do not give each other enough concrete strokes, do not touch and allow ourselves to be touched enough. We should cultivate child-rearing practices such as breast feeding, nudity in the home, cuddling and carressing as a constant part of parent-child interaction because of the increased amount of skin contact and direct stimulation of bodily pleasure involved. We should encourage nonmarital sexual pleasuring between persons who are affectionate and caring. He observes,

> When viewed in connection with the cross-cultural evidence on physical deprivation, the violence, and warfare associated with monogamy (involving exclusive sexual rights in the spouse), the need to create a more pluralistic system of marriage becomes clear. We must seriously consider new options such as extended families comprised of two or three couples who share values and life-styles. By sharing the benefits and responsibilities of child-rearing, such families could provide an affectionate and varied environment for children as well as adults, and thereby reduce the incidence of child abuse and runaways.[41]

He sees further implications of the data for women's rights.

> Because power and aggression are neutralized through sensual pleasure, man's primary defense against a loss of dominance has been the historical denial, repression and control of the sensual pleasure of women. The use of sex to provide mere release from physiological tension (apparent pleasure) should not be confused with a state of sensual pleasure which is incompatible with dominance, power, aggression, violence and pain. It is through the mutual sharing of sensual pleasure that sexual equality between women and men will be realized.[42]

The emotive element in the normative integration of any society cannot be denied. But we inherit a work ethic which makes the conscious pursuit of pleasure very difficult for most of us in spite of our efforts to have a "fun time." It begins to appear more and more important for us to incorporate the conscious pursuit of bodily pleasure into the pattern of our lives, not in order to mimic Roman debauchery, but in order to reduce the aggressive feelings that may well end our civilization in our time. "Make love, not war," begins to assume substance beyond mere rhetoric.

---

[40]James W. Prescott, "Body Pleasure and the Origins of Violence," *The Bulletin of Atomic Scientists* (Nov., 1957), pp. 10–20.

[41]*Ibid.*, p. 11.

[42]*Ibid.*, p. 19.

While technology makes it increasingly possible to live without much emphasis upon primary and secondary relationships, the cost to the individual and to the society is great when the process is carried too far. We know this from social psychology and are made constantly aware of it through the widespread concern about the impersonality and alienation of modern urban man. The stress and strain of modern life is increasingly evident. But how far is too far? What is the best ratio of primary, secondary, and tertiary relationships? One wonders if the basic human needs for acceptance, love and belonging can be adequately fulfilled without primary relationships beyond the family? Or does the increasing complexity of modern life demand that other intimate friendships be established because the relative power of the familial relationships diminishes in a world in which tertiary relationships play an increasingly central role? Or is it perhaps possible to improve the quality of familial relationships in order to increase their effectiveness in meeting these basic human needs? There are supportive data on both sides of this issue. At the center of the issue is the debate over the nuclear family crises. Whatever conceptual clarity we may obtain, it seems reasonable to assume that the character of primary relationships in families will continue to change. The apparent direction of this change is toward the incorporation of intimate friends into the primary erotic network of relationships. The disagreement amongst researchers is mainly over whether this is a thing to be encouraged or not.

Finally, in the approach of humanistic psychologists, the synergystic society contributes to the generation of self-actualizing persons.[43] Self-actualizing persons are not rugged individualists, nor intellectual elites. They are productive members of an abundant society, who find joy in their lives and do not sharply distinguish between work and play. Because they are able to realize more of their own potential, they are able to contribute more to the commonwealth. Such persons are integrated into urban society because they are fully aware that they could not realize their own potential unless their society was able to provide them with enough safety, and security, enough food and material comforts, enough love and acceptance to enable them to adequately meet their deprivation needs. They, furthermore, cannot realize their unique potential unless significant numbers of others are able to do likewise. Having met their own deprivation needs, they are in a position to increase the abundance of their world for others.

Such synergistic societies and self-actualizing individuals are possibilities that have been realized in varying degrees in the human adventure. Yet, they speak more of future possibilities than past realizations. They clearly are not possible in any society in which the political system is not open to the citizenry, in which the rich diversity of the human experience is not celebrated, and in which the symbolic culture does not help to create a world of abundance.

---

[43]See, for example, Abraham A. Maslow, "Toward A Psychology of Being," (New York: Van Nostrand Reinhold Company, 1968). Of special interest is the chapter, "Some Basic Propositions of a Growth and Self Actualizing Psychology," pp. 189–215.

chapter 9

The Suburbs and Beyond

From the standpoint of urban sociology, the suburbs are a residual category. Historically, studies have focused upon the social structure and process of inner cities or those of rural areas and small towns. The suburbs constitute the neglected middle ground between these two ideal types. Whether the notion of an urban-rural continuum, with the suburbs somewhere in the middle, actually reflects social reality, is highly questionable. Rather than a point on an urban-rural continuum, the suburbs may represent qualitative departure from both inner cities and rural areas. Suburbs may manifest subcultures which cannot be explained by urbanization alone.

The sheer demographic importance of the American suburbs is suggested by the density of the population which lives there. It is not the large number of people, however, which gives rise to the sociological import of suburbs, but the social organization and stereotypic life-styles.

Two orientations have characterized the writing and research on American suburbs. First is the analysis of the *life-styles*. Second, suburbs have been analyzed in terms of the overall *metropolitanization process,* an area of study which has also received a great deal of attention from regional economists.

The first approach (life-styles) centers around the study of certain sterotypes. These are related primarily to the upper-middle class—familism, child-centeredness, single-family houses, the separation of the place of work from the home, memberships in organizations, and the informal life-style which is man-ifested through neighborliness, cocktail parties, extra-marital affairs, and an overall permissiveness in life. This exotic image of the suburbs appears to have evolved in the late 1940's, with new housing developments which departed radically from the old traditional city houses and the attendant life-style. The mid-forties marked a new

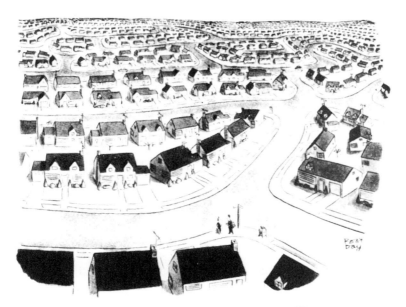

"I'm Mrs. Edward M. Barnes. Where do I live?"

Drawing by Robt. Day; © *1954 The New Yorker Magazine, Inc.*

generation of suburban dwellers, principally young World War II veterans with their young families. The same economic boom and technological development which was fostered by World War II resulted in the rapid growth of large corporations. They employed many suburbanites as engineers, technicians, accountants, computer operators, and an entire range of new jobs which confirmed the fact that the technological age had arrived. This economic surge, in turn, generated a new affluent life-style marked symbolically by the two-car family and the new housing developments. Mortgages and credit were easy to obtain, particularly GI and FHA mortgages. Easy credit made it possible for people to use more of their incomes for consumer goods and recreation than had been possible in any previous generation. Overall, the suburbanites stood out like a sore thumb, presenting distinct contrast to the small town life-style, which had prevailed since the days of the Great Depression.

Books like Robert C. Wood's, *Suburbia* (1958), and William H. Whyte's, *The Organization Man* (1957), preserved the image.[1] Read widely by the American public as popular social science, paperbacks like the *Split Level Trap* (1961), stamped the suburban culture as a deviant life-style, and contributed to the stereotype of the suburbs as too fast-moving and too concerned with status symbols,

[1]Robert C. Wood, *Suburbia—Its People and their Politics* (Boston: Houghton Mifflin, 1958); William H. Whyte, *The Organization Man* (New York: Doubleday, 1957).

compared to the conservative life-style which still persisted in small town Ameri-ca.[2] In short, the early works on the suburbs described them as affluent, upper-middle-class, young, credit-oriented, family-oriented. Even in the 1940's, this rep-resented an inaccurate portrayal. It is this image, developed over three decades ago, which provides a base from which to begin our examination of the suburbs.

This chapter addresses seven basic questions about the suburbs:

(1) What are the suburbs?
(2) What is the suburbanization process?
(3) What are the demographic shifts which have accompanied suburban growth?
(4) What is the social, economic and political structure of the suburbs?
(5) What is a meaningful sociological typology of suburbs?
(6) How do suburbs relate to the inner city, the overall metropolitan area, and the hinter-land?
(7) What is the prognosis for the suburbs and the accompanying personal and public choices and policies which must be made?

The Origins of American Suburbs

One convenient way to define the suburbs is to consider them as the territory within a standard metropolitan statistical area which is not included in the central city. By this definition, forty million Americans lived in the suburbs in 1950, about sixty million in 1960, and over seventy-six million in 1970. Testifying to the growth of these areas, most projections suggest about half of the American population will reside in suburban areas by the year 1985.

The Nineteenth Century

American suburbs began to develop in substantial numbers soon after the Civil War. A small number of people began commuting from outlying villages or country homes in the latter part of the nineteenth century. Many of these early suburbs existed previously as small towns, although almost no one commuted to the center city to work. Gradually, many summer country homes were converted to year-round residences. This early commutation was made possible by the development of railroad lines. People were attracted to these rural suburbs because of their relatively healthy environment—an unpolluted water supply, access to fresh farm foods, and freedom from the congestion and disease of the larger cities.

In the late nineteenth century, the street-car came into wide use, permitting an increasing proportion of the middle class to live further out from the city. At first, street-car lines transversed wide areas of open country. Gradually, the street-car lines themselves spurred population growth. The functional boundaries of the city

[2]R. Gordon, K. Gordon, and M. Gunther, *The Split Level Trap* (New York: Geis, 1961).

(if not the corporate boundaries) expanded along these transportation arteries. As suburban villages developed, some areas sought annexation to the larger cities in order to gain police protection, water supplies, sewage systems, and other municipal services. For many suburbs, however, the city represented a politically corrupt bastion, which was badly mismanaged, or not managed at all. Many suburbs sought to detach themselves as completely as possible.[3]

The Nineteen Twenties

Suburban growth in the 1920's was primarily dependent upon the street-car and railroad expansion. After World War I, the automobile came into wide use and provided the dominant influence on suburban growth which has prevailed until the present time. The number of cars on the American highways increased from nine million in 1920 to twenty-six million in 1930. Cars evolved from open-roofed contraptions, plagued with frequent tire blow-outs, to the popular and inexpensive Model T Ford, which made it possible for the average American family to own a car for under a thousand dollars. At the same time, the street-car suburbs, primarily on the eastern coast, continued to grow.[4]

Although the technological advances in automobiles were achieved rapidly, highway systems developed at a much slower pace. During the 1920's, there was no federal mechanism for funding interstate highways, nor was the amount of state funds allocated for highway construction sufficient to meet the demand of the American public. Some states advanced faster than others. In the 1920's, Governor Gifford Pinchot of Pennsylvania put an unemployed public to work building paved roads—many of which still exist in the rural areas in their original form. Most states, particularly those in the South, lagged in highway construction. The maze of highways, rail lines, and street-car lines continued to develop outside of the incorporated cities. Land-use planning and zoning were rare, almost non-existent.

The result was the beginning of the suburban sprawl, with its accompanying eye-sores—strip developments, incompatible land-use patterns, and non-zoning, all reflecting the prevailing American belief that unregulated free enterprise alone would provide an efficient and acceptable land-use pattern. Land speculation with accompanying political corruption, became a preoccupation of many men. Corruption was particularly evident in the rapid-growth areas such as Los Angeles, where the combination of rapid population growth and an emerging governmental structure created opportunities for political corruption which made the Tammany Hall politics of the east coast seem minor in comparison.

[3]See Carol E. Hoffecker, *Wilmington, Delaware: Portrait of An Industrial City 1893–1910* (Charlottesville, Virginia: University Press of Virginia, 1974).

[4]Sam B. Warner, Jr., *Streetcar Suburbs* (Cambridge, Mass.: Harvard University and M.I.T. Presses, 1962).

1930—1944

The Great Depression began in 1929. It resulted in a gradual stoppage of national economic growth and an accompanying cessation of suburban growth. Businesses retrenched. Speculation in real estate development ceased; fortunes were lost; mortgages were foreclosed; a negative psychological climate caused people to conserve their savings and to avoid investments in any new ventures. Millions were unemployed. Although some federal projects to conserve land and build parks were mounted (the Civilian Conservation Corps is an example of one of these), relatively little was done toward the development of a nationwide highway system.

During the latter part of the 1930's, state and federal government began to invest in planning and development of parkways, over-passes and elaborate freeway systems. This vision of the future was presented in the General Motors exhibit in the New York's World's Fair in 1939. As America emerged from the Depression and began to tool up for a wartime economy, the invention of the clover-leaf intersection and the multi-lane highway became ingrained in the American imagination, indeed in the American expectation for the future. The ground work had been laid, but as the 1930's ended and the birth rate began to climb, a consensus developed that the business at hand was the inevitable American involvement in World War II. Suburban development during this period recorded a modest growth, mostly around street-car lines and rail lines which already existed. The real suburbanization existed mostly within people's minds as a vision of the future.

1945—1960

World War II (1941–1945) was marked by a tremendous housing shortage in the United States. With the exception of military housing, construction of new units almost ceased. Although there had not been a severe housing shortage during the war, the demand for new housing was accentuated following the war, when millions of new households were formed by the returning veterans. These men and women, many of whom had been teenagers at the beginning of the war, formed an instantaneous housing market beginning in 1945. Demographically, this group represented a young, middle working-class population with a high fertility potential. Many returning veterans attended college, using the generous benefits of the GI Bill. A high proportion of the college GI Bill population was married. Colleges scrambled to create "temporary" housing for veterans. Typically, these units were huts which sometimes had been used previously by ROTC and other officers candidate programs during the war. As soon as the graduating veterans joined the labor market, there was a greater demand for higher-cost housing. The mass-produced suburban developments were made possible by low-interest loans under the Veterans Administration and through the Federal Housing Administration. With a few hundred dollars down payment, it was possible to buy a modern suburban house, complete with appliances and young neighbors.

No, it's not a modern inter-state highway - it's the General Motors Exhibit at the 1939 World's Fair (New York), called the Futurama. It anticipated with almost total accuracy the kind of highway system that makes suburbs possible. *(General Motors Corporation.)*

Before 1945, suburban areas were usually developed piecemeal. New houses were added as individuals contracted to have each one built. Now, primarily because of government subsidized mortgages, it was possible to design an entire development and to build houses on a speculative basis, knowing that the market was there, and that the houses would be sold, even though they had not been ordered by specific individuals. Early suburbs of this era offered three-bedroom houses with shiny new appliances and a promise for a modern life-style. Best known among these were Levittown, New York; Drexelbrook, near Philadelphia; Park Forest, near Chicago; Parkmerced, in the San Francisco area; and Lakewood, just outside of Los Angeles. All were the forerunners in the mass-produced developments as we know them today. The post-war period affirmed the American love of the single-family, detached dwelling unit. The preference was for a suburban house with a large lawn, and an informal suburban life-style, where people lived casually without household help, and an emphasis upon the nuclear family, all stressing an underlying faith that things were good now and would get better as people became more successful. One's first suburban house signified but a start in a long succession of suburban houses.

The idea that the suburban life-style was infinitely better than the traditional one found in the cities prevailed. A new generation of children who had never lived in cities or small towns was born. The automobile and the suburban shopping center became the dominant reality for millions of Americans. It is this stage which provided the stereotype of the American suburb which persists today.

1960—1969

The most recent period of suburban development involves an elaboration of different kinds of suburban developments, ranging widely in price. The result is that the suburbs reflect a wider spectrum of social strata than in previous periods. At one end of the social spectrum are "blue-collar suburbs" made up of workingmen's homes; at the other end of the social strata, there are upper-middle class suburbs with more expensive housing. As the World War II generation advanced in their occupations, many abandoned their first suburban locations and moved outward into more expensive and more elaborate housing, leaving their original units as "starter" houses for still another group.

Suburban housing developments tend to be stratified along price lines whereby households of similar incomes and life-cycle stages tend to live within similar areas.[5] A person who is employed in a certain level of management within a large corporation will probably live in a development with others of similar circumstance. Few suburban developments have a wide range of house prices; marketing dictates that people will buy houses at the same upper limit of their financial capacity, attempting to disassociate themselves from housing and households they perceive as being lower in status. The result is often a remarkable income and life-style homogeneity within new developments. Some reflect predominately blue-collar occupations, and might be classified as working-class suburbs, while others consist predominantely of the highest level of professionals and managers, *i.e.*, physicians and upper-level management.[6] Thus, the homogeneity of the surburban development has been the result of mass production of developments, most of which cater to persons within a narrow income range.

Although some developers like Levitt created total planned communities, within which schools, shopping centers, and recreation areas were included in the overall design, most developers concentrated on finding cheap land for developments, without a great deal of thought about the necessary services. Often the cost of installing and supplying these new services caused high public indebtedness, which was borne not only by the residents of the new development, but by the older residents as well. Planning and zoning were often neglected, or totally ignored, resulting in strip developments along highways and other incompatible land usages.

During the 1960's, many of the residents who had previously lived in cities and small towns began to move to the suburbs. Large and middle-sized cities began to lose population, principally, white middle-class families. Stores, doctors, dentists, and other businesses also began to move to the suburbs, because the chief buyers of services lived there. As a result, the cities suffered a declining tax base and an abandonment of housing. Because of the declining tax revenue, urban government

---

[5]Thomas L. Van Valey, Wade C. Roof, and Jerome E. Wilcox, "Trends in Residential Segregation: 1960–1970," *American Journal of Sociology*, Volume 82, No. 4, (January, 1977) pp. 826–844.
[6]*Ibid.*, pp. 800–804.

made up for lost property taxes in the form of new kinds of taxes: business taxes on corporate headquarters, factories, insurance companies, as well as income taxes on suburban residents working in the cities. Soon, many businesses found that it was cheaper to move to the suburbs than to remain in the city. Even the federal government began to move into the suburbs. The suburban area surrounding Washington, D.C., in Virginia and in Maryland, contains a large number of federal administrative and research offices which lease space from commercial developers. The move of business and government to the suburbs completed the decentralization which had begun many decades earlier.

In the late 1960's, the country began to move into an economic recession, marked by a high unemployment rate and a high level of inflation. Some economists refer to this era as the era of stagflation, indicating that there is a stagnant economy (a period of non-growth), with a great deal of inflation. Because of the inflation, housing costs soared enormously, brought about by high land costs, high interest rates and the high cost of labor. The housing boom that had prevailed during the entire 1960's ceased. By 1975, the typical house in the metropolitan area sold for approximately $40,000. A new "rule-of-thumb" as to the household income required to qualify for a mortgage developed. Rather than the old guideline that a house's cost should not exceed two and a half times a family's annual income, the new guideline suggested that a house should not cost more than *two* times a family's annual income.

In order to buy the typical $40,000 house, a family had to have an income of $20,000. But the typical family in the United States had an income of about $13,000. Compounding this problem, less mortgage money was available through FHA and the Veteran's Administration, requiring many families to assume conventional mortgages. In 1976, buying a house required that a family put approximately one-quarter of the value of a house in a down-payment, thereby requiring an average of ten thousand dollars before qualifying to buy a home. These factors culminated in the typical American family being priced out of the market for the averagew house.

Developers began to seek ways of satisfying the demand for single-family, detached dwelling units. Condominiums and mobile homes provided an alternative to the traditional single-family home for many people. Now, the nation is slowly emerging from the recession of the early 1970's. The boom days of the suburban developments of the 1950's and 1960's seem a distant memory.

Underlying Factors in Suburbanization

The suburbs discussed in this chapter are almost exclusively those of metropolitan United States and Canada. But suburbs are also evident in western Europe, particularly in England, Germany, France, Italy, and the Scandinavian countries. The European pattern is not as pronounced as that of the United States, although highway systems and railway networks are equally evident. The extensive sprawling suburbs have not occurred abroad to the degree that it has in the United States. It should be stressed that not even in the United States do all middle-class metropolitan people prefer to live in suburbs.

In fact, in all large cities, there are substantial numbers of upper- and upper-middle class people who prefer the cosmopolitan life-style and convenience of the city. In the area surrounding Central Park in New York, one such concentration of upper-middle class city dwellers is found. It is comprised of apartment houses with rents in excess of a thousand dollars per month. The inhabitants of Central Park West could clearly live in the suburbs much more cheaply if they preferred. San Francisco also contains a substantial upper-middle class population which has chosen to remain in the city. Chicago and Boston also contain large populations of upper-middle class residents who prefer the life-style of the city over that of the suburbs. This pattern has persisted to an even greater degree in most of the European cities such as Paris, London, and Amsterdam. Although government subsidized mortgages spurred suburban growth in Europe, the evidence suggests that people in Europe and England prefer the life-style of the cities because of cultural tradition.

Comparing the United States with Europe, it is evident that until the twentieth century, America's population was concentrated mainly in rural areas and in small towns. Although there was an urban tradition for many, the predominant middle-class ethic stressed the goodness of small town life and the distastefulness and evil of cities. These earlier rural orientations have slowly been transformed into the open space ethic of the suburbs, a predominant preference for single-family detached dwelling units which becomes manifest through the demand for suburban housing. Underlying the economic policies which have fostered suburban growth in the United States is a cultural ethic which stresses the inherent goodness of life away from the city.

Suburban Scale

The development of mass transportation and of modern highway systems has extended the life-space for the majority of Americans. It is now common to commute to a workplace—employing a car to get to the railroad station, then undertake a forty-minute train ride, and then take a subway or bus to work. Shopping is commonly done within an area of a thousand square miles. Children often require up to a half-hour to be "bused" to school. The life-space of Americans has increased enormously as a result of this technological evolution. Economic theories stress that the limits of commuting are imposed mainly by the time and costs of transportation.[7] During the last two decades, because the work-place itself has moved to the

[7]See the discussion on economic location theory in the chapter on ecology. A more extensive discussion may be found in Werner Z. Hirsch, *Urban Economic Analysis* (New York: McGraw Hill, 1972) and William Alonso, *Location and Land Use* (Cambridge, Mass.: Harvard University Press, 1964).

suburbs, transportation costs have often been reduced. Although the costs of energy and fuel have increased, income has kept up with these demands and the rapid development of four-cylinder engines has made travel more economical. Because of this quantum leap in the functional living space in the overall metropolitan area, the idea of the suburb as sociologically distinct from what we used to call "the city" appears to be an obsolete concept. Probably, we should think in terms of metropolitan regions rather than suburbs and cities. Reviewing the factors which have brought about the increase in scale, we must consider the vastness of the land area in the United States and the relatively rapid development of rail and highway systems. The increase in suburban development was further bolstered by a deliberate federal policy to subsidize suburban housing through low-interest mortgages, as well as a policy of generous highway subsidation, while ignoring mass transit systems. In sum, while a suburbanization was inevitable, given long-term factors of urbanization and modernization, the values held by Americans provided the political impetus for transportation and housing subsidies which spurred the suburban housing boom period.

Racial and Ethnic Factors

During World War II, American blacks migrated in large numbers to the metropolitan areas of the United States to work in the war industries. Desegregation began in the armed services and spread to other public institutions—schools, government agencies, and later in residential communities. As blacks began to move to cities, the patterns of invasion and succession became more accentuated then previously. Increasingly, inner cities became the primary domain of lower-class blacks and other visible minority groups. Because of the growing concentration of poverty-stricken minorities in ghettos, these areas experienced an increase in social problems: crime, health problems, and the usual array of pathologies cities had always suffered. Because these pathologies were vividly concentrated among lower-class blacks who resided in the inner city, blacks became symbolic of inner city problems.

Working and middleclass whites attempted to escape from the encroaching conflicts by fleeing to the suburbs. The result was that the inner city became increasingly black, while the suburbs became more than ever the domain of middle-class white persons, excluding even middle-class blacks. Also, following World War II, the influx of increasing numbers of Mexican-Americans and Puerto Ricans, accentuated the ethnic polarization of city and suburb. Suburbs were segregated not only economically but racially. Moreover public housing was also built principally within the cities, because of heavy resistance by suburban areas. The result was a further isolation of poverty and racial segregation within the city.

The Dynamics of Suburban Social Organization

Ideology and Culture

If there is a suburban culture, it is probably close to what we might call the national American culture. This culture is not "local," but what might be described as "sub-local," in that suburbanites tend to be home-oriented rather than community-oriented. Gans, in his study of Levittown, New Jersey, concludes that the reason most people moved to Levittown had little to do with its social climate, but rather because the housing presented the best alternative to what might be found elsewhere: *i.e.,* the attractiveness, the new appliances, the easy financing, and most importantly the cost.[8] In short, the packaging which could be provided only through American industrial methods was what drew most people to Levittown. Most buyers knew little of the social structure of the community, nor did they appear to care. What they were looking for was a total housing package, fairly good access to the workplace, good schools, and other supporting institutions which are necessary to lead the "good life." If there is a set of values with respect to life-styles which is important to suburbanites, Gans believes it is conveyed through the mass media, particularly through television. Gans suggests,

> The impact of the media is most apparent among children; they are easily impressed by television commercials, and mothers must often fight off their demands on shopping trips.[9]

As to the sub-local quality of life in Levittown, Gans continued,

> Unlike the aristocrat or the intellectual who was once able as an individual to influence the national society and still attempts to do so, the Levittowners come from a tradition and from ancestors too poor or too European even to conceive the possibility that they could affect their nation. And unlike the cosmopolitans of today, they have not yet learned that they ought to try. As a result, the Levittowner is not likely to act unless and until a national issue impinges directly on his life. When this does happen, he is as frustrated as the cosmopolitan about how to be effective. All he can really do is voice his opinion at the ballot box, write letters to his Congressman, or join protest groups. In times of crisis none of these can change the situation quickly enough, and this of course exacerbates the threat of hysteria and the utge toward mob action or scape-goating.[10]

In another study of Levittown, Dobriner notes the decline in the number of males in white-collar jobs between 1950 and 1960 (down from 62 percent to 50 percent).[11] Within this ten-year timpe span, there was a corresponding rise in the proportion of blue-collar workers. The two groups, according to Dobriner, manifest

---

[8]Herbert J. Gans, *The Levittowners* (New York: Random House, 1969) pp. 31–41.

[9]*Ibid.,* p. 192.

[10]*Ibid.,* p. 192.

[11]William M. Dobriner, "Local and Cosmopolitan as Contemporary Suburban Character Types," in Dobriner, ed., *The Suburban Community* (New York: Putnam, 1958), pp. 132–143; also see Dobriner, *Class in Suburbia* (Englewood Cliffs, N.J.: Prentice-Hall, 1963).

different values. The white collar workers (who are predominantly middle-class) appear to stress privacy, initiative, and upward mobility. In contrast, the blue collar group is more concerned with living for the moment, rather than planning for the future. In its leisure time, the middle class emphasizes reading more than television (although this pattern may have changed), while the working class stresses television viewing. The middle class does more entertaining and visiting with co-workers and people outside of Levittown. Among the blue-collar group, entertaining of relatives seem to be the predominant social outlet.

In a more recent study of the values of suburbanites, Zelan (1968) surveyed the graduating class of American colleges in 1961, a total sample of more than 33,000 respondents.[12] Zelan wanted to know whether those who had grown up in the suburbs of metropolitan areas differed in "anti-intellectualism," compared to those raised in large cities. He found little difference in these attitudes based on where the respondents had grown up. But the responses concerning where graduates wished to live in the future showed that those who desired to live in the suburbs showed much higher anti-intellectualism than those who preferred to live in the city. As expected, the married students also preferred suburban residences. Probably most important, most of those who had lived in the suburbs during their growing-up years wished to live in the suburbs in the future, irrespective of their orientation toward intellectualism.

Fava (1975) also describes most suburbanites as "local" in her analysis of suburban attitudes.[13] Their span of interests is limited principally to their immediate residential locale, in contrast with those who live in the cities, who more often manifest interests in national and world affairs. Fava concludes that suburbanites are likely to have neighboring relationships with those who live in the same area and that, in general, their involvement with local concerns is greater than city dwellers. The reason for this local orientation, according to Fava, is that suburbanites typically manifest demographic characteristics such as age, ethnicity, home-ownership, and family-cycle which are associated with high levels of local orientation. Young home-owners with children in school have a more direct interest in local concerns, as distinct from the problems of mankind. Thus, it is not the suburban subculture, but rather the aggregate characteristics of suburban individuals which spurs these attitudes. Individual attitudes, of course, are accentuated by what sociologists call a contextual effect. The concentration of large numbers of people having similar values and concerns magnifies and supports the attitudes of the individual. The least important reason for suburban attitudinal orientations is the ecological argument that the location of the suburbs and their low population density create greater costs of engaging in non-local activities than local activities.

In a study of several suburbs of Chicago, Bell documented the emphasis on the

---

[12]Joseph Zelan, "Does Suburbia Make a Difference: An Exercise in Secondary Analysis," in Sylvia F. Fava, ed., *Urbanism in World Perspective* (New York: Thomas Y. Crowell, 1968), pp. 401–408.

[13]Sylvia F. Fava, "Beyond Suburbia," *The Annals,* Vol. 422, November, (1975) pp. 10–24.

nuclear family, the focus upon life goals, joint activities around the home, and raising children.[14] This family orientation is in distinct contrast to the alternative orientations toward career or conspicuous consumption. Since American values stress both career and consumership, as well as family, it can be seen that there must be trade-offs among the energies and resources focused in each area. In the Chicago suburbs studied by Bell, eight out of ten respondents indicated that they had moved from the city because it was healthier for the children in the suburbs, that there was a better social environment for the children, that there were better schools, and that the area provided greater security than the city. A much smaller percentage of respondents indicated that they had moved to the suburbs as a manifestation of success in their jobs or other reasons associated with upward mobility. In short, the newer studies of the suburbs suggest that the move, during the 1960's, was not a part of the ''Organization Man'' syndrome, which stresses the house and neighborhood as a status symbol, but instead is an attempt to provide better housing and better environmental circumstances for the entire family, particularly for the children.

The development of new school systems in the suburbs during the earlier stages of suburbanization often presents severe problems. The older districts, upon which the affluent suburbs are often superimposed, are typically more conservative in their appraoches to spending, borrowing, and paying teachers and administrators. In the development of Gans' Levittown, for instance, the new school system spurred considerable conflict. In later stages of suburbanization, the infusion of working-class and blue-collar households often prompts friction as to the overall philosophy and the extent of resources which are employed in the funding of schools. Cleavages between the old political bosses and the new constituents also emerge. These same frictions between the older residents and the new are manifested in changes in old churches, or when people establish new churches in their suburban communities when differences cannot be reconciled.

Ecological Forces

Most of the classical ecological theories focus upon the city. Suburban areas are accommodated simply by putting a suburban ring around the outer-most zone of the city. This extension stems from the idea of the Park-Burgess concentric zone theory, but as discussed in the chapter of ecology, large urbanized areas usually have multiple nuclei and consist of a number of subareas, thereby making the idea of a single urbanization gradient inaccurate. Particularly within the huge areas where older cities and suburbs are fused into giant regions of the nation, gradient theories are inadequate for describing the ecological mosaic. Also, because of long-distance commuting (and reverse commuting) to and from various centers within the

---

[14]Wendell Bell, ''Social Choice, Life Styles, and Suburban Residence,'' in Dobriner, *The Suburban Community.*

megalopolis, the older ecological theories which described areas of residence (but not work places), are obsolete. Beginning with the 1970 census, data was made available which permitted an analysis of both the residential and work addresses of individuals. Berry (1971) suggests the concept of Daily Urban Systems (DUS), each of which has a radius of 75 to 80 miles, which now comprise an ecology including all but the most sparsely settled parts of the United States.[15] These DUS's encompass the daily routines and travel of nine out of ten Americans. The DUS, as conceived by Berry, is not bounded by county or census tract, but also includes cross-counry patterns. The area which is commonly called the hinterland (beyond the suburbs) can be clearly established through a mapping of DUS's.

Political and Legal Aspects of Suburban Growth

In a classic study focusing on suburban politics, Zikmund (1975) summarizes a number of principles and hypotheses. Suburbs which develop in sparsely settled rural land, as compared to those which originate in a small town, typically display different political organization. Suburbs which form in sparsely settled rural land manifest issues and conflicts around incorporation and the general form of local governments. Stress develops as political dominance passes into the hands of the new suburban residents, and as the new communities incorporate. During the early stages of massive suburbanization, issues of zoning and schools tend to dominate the political process.

In contrast, in suburban communities which originate from the suburbanization of small older towns, political conflict between established politicians and representatives of the new areas will persist for some time, but generally will end with the victory of the new suburbanites. Zoning and schooling issues also predominate during this transition period.

Suburbanization of large existing satellite cities suggests still different patterns. The political style will already be set, and will be more formal and less personal than in the other patterns discussed previously. Decision making is more likely to occur in a public forum rather than in private. Political polarization in the form of "conflict blocks" will already be established. Significant political conflicts will occur between established groups who are already present in the community and the new suburbanites. The probability, according to Zikmund, is that the new group will assimilate itself into the old, instead of winning a clear victory. In satellite cities, the primary issues of conflict are likely to involve expansion of present facilities, in contrast to the development of new facilities.

Another political factor which already affects the national political process is that increasing numbers of Congress people are from suburban areas. This means

[15]Brian J. L. Berry, "Population Growth in the Daily Urban Systems of the United States, 1980–2000," in *Population, Distribution, and Policy,* Sarah Mills Mazie, ed., Vol. 5 of the Commission on Population Growth and the American Future Reports (Washington, D.C.: United States Government Printing Office) p. 142.

that Congress will have to deal increasingly with the policy positions and demands of suburbanites. These power blocks will become more organized and compete more directly with the cities for resources. Already, suburban areas are receiving large federal revenue sharing grants which rival or exceed those allocated to cities.

Several recent federal court decisions have required cross-busing of public school students between city and suburbs. School desegregation has been closely linked by the courts with housing segregation in suburban areas. Discussing the persisting dilemma of racial segregation, Taeuber (1975) concludes:

> It has become somewhat fashionable to recognize hese linkages only to use them as an excuse. Segregated schools are said to depend on segregated housing, which depends on black poverty, which depends on occupational discrimination, which depends on earlier discrimination in southern schooling, which depends on antebellum social institutions. This kind of logic rests on a specious reading of social science evidence. There is indeed a "certain unity of the negro problem," as Gunner Myrdal noted more than thirty years ago, that unity may be expressed in the present tense, not only as a historical residue of slavery.[16]

Beyond the changes in Congress and the school desegregation issues, which are pressing in the late 1970's, there are other obvious economic and political tradeoffs between cities and suburbs. The costs of new suburban growth must be borne not only by those who are moving into the suburban areas, but must be shared by those who already live in the suburbs. Thus, there are substantial costs of growth. The building of new sanitation and water systems, highways, streets, schools, electrical power grids and the provision of police services is expensive. Economic studies have shown that massive population growth does not allow the purchase of these services at a wholesale rate, but rather the reverse occurs.[17] Typically, the more densely settled the urban area, the greater the per-capita costs to each individual taxpayer in the area. Also, with increasing urbanization, comes inevitably an increase in urban pathologies and the costs of controlling these problems. For example, suburban crime during the last five years has increased at a much higher rate than crime within the cities.[18] This suggests that many more resources will have to be poured into the suburban criminal justice system.

Classical Sociological Studies of the Suburbs

Working-Class Suburbs

One of the characteristics of the middle-class suburbanite is supposedly that of joining—belonging to churches, clubs, civic groups, and other social organizations.

---

[16]Karl E. Taeuber, "Racial Segregation: The Persisting Dilemma," *The Annals,* No. 422, November, (1975) p. 96.

[16]Robert F. Minnehan, *Costs of Growth* (Volumes A, B, and C) (Newark, Delaware: University of Delaware, College of Urban Affairs and Public Policy, 1975).

[17]*Crime in the United States: Uniform Crime Reports* (Washington, D.C.: F.B.I., U.S. Department of Justice, 1975).

Studies of working-class suburbs, however, suggest that this pattern may not prevail in these areas. In a study of a working-class suburb of California, which was populated by many automobile workers, Berger found seven out of ten men did not belong to a single club or organization other than the automobile workers union.[19] Informal visiting among neighbors was also rare, unless the neighbors happened to be relatives. Only half the families even attended church. Another myth which was dispelled by this study was that upon moving from the city to the suburb, voters tend to change their political affiliation from Democratic to Republican. Among Berger's working-class suburbanites, more than eight out of ten continued to vote Democratic. Nor did the working-class suburbanite become enamoured with the middle-class success ethic, which stresses upward social mobility. The group expressed little hope of getting ahead in their job, unlike the earlier organization men. For this group, the suburb was not perceived as a temporary stopping place on the upward road to success, but was seen instead as a lifelong place of residence. In essence, it was the characteristics of the individuals which shaped the life-style and attitudes, rather than the contextual character of the suburban area. The working-class ethic persisted, despite the move to a suburban environment. Supporting this research, in another study carried out by Cohen and Hodges in the San Francisco area (1963), no differences were found between urban and suburban blue-collar workers in self-concept, status striving, family loyalty, and attitudes toward sex.[20]

Crestwood Heights— An Upper-Middle-Class Suburb

A classical study of an upper-middle class suburb is presented by Seeley, *et al.* (1956), in his study of Crestwood Heights.[21] Probably, this suburb comes closest to the image of the suburb as portrayed in the movies like *The Graduate,* and as originally suggested in the *Organization Man.* It is an affluent area, complete with upper level executives, swimming pools, cocktail parties, and children attending private schools. Behavior centers around status striving. Parents are viewed as passing on a spirit of competition to their children; the idea of upward social mobility is seen as paramount. Outside experts are used constantly to provide indications of children's progress and for guidance in health and in school. The home is perceived primarily as a status symbol rather than a place to enjoy and use. Crestwood Heights, however, is in an outlying area of Toronto. Whether the findings of this study represent those which might reflect on all middle-class suburbs remains open to question.

---

[18]Bennet M. Berger, *Working Class Suburb* (Berkeley and Los Angeles: University of California Press, 1960).
[19]Albert K. Cohen and Harold M. Hodges, Jr., "Characteristics of the Lower Blue-Collar Class," *Social Problems,* Volume 10, No. 37, Spring (1963).
[20]Sim R. Seeley and E. Loosley, *Crestwood Heights* (New York: Basic Books, 1956).

Black Suburbs

Although the predominant black population growth remains within center cities, there is a trend for the growth of the black population in the suburbs. The absolute number of blacks involved in suburbanization is relatively small. But a definite move into the suburbs is evident around the larger cities: Chicago, Los Angeles, New York, Cleveland, Newark, and Washington, D.C. Between the 1960 and the 1970 census, the number of blacks in Los Angeles suburbs increased by 124,000. In Washington, D.C., the increase was 84,000 and in New York, the increase was 77,000.[22] Not unexpectedly, studies based on the 1970 census indicate that the social economic status of the black suburbanites exceeds that of central city blacks.

Formerly, blacks residing outside of cities tended to be of lower socio-economic status than central city blacks. The issue which arises is whether middle-class blacks will continue to move into the suburbs as they assimilate into the great American middle class. If they move into the suburbs in massive numbers, will blacks settle in white communities, or form separate middle-class black communities by themselves? So far, blacks who have moved to the suburbs have lived mostly in areas which contain a disproportionate number of blacks. One study (Sternlieb and Lake, 1975) indicates that blacks moving from the cities move first into the older suburbs or inner suburbs, rather than into the suburban fringe. Blacks who are moving into these areas are mostly upwardly mobile middle-class, who are seeking to leave the central city. Sternlieb and Lake conclude,

> While black suburbanization is increasing in some localities, however, black demand appears to be below the level expected based on income. In suburban home purchase, the availability of equity associated with previous home-ownership may be a better index of buying power than current income. Historical limitations on black home-ownership thus continue to limit suburban home purchases. Public policy initiatives are needed to counteract these trends, facilitate middle-class black migration, and contribute to the viability of the inner suburbs.[23]

In another statement on the progress of blacks moving into the suburbs, Siembieda concludes,

> The suburbanization of ethnics of color made slow progress during the 1960's. . . . During this period, the nation continued its long-term trend towards dual societies. Only one major metropolitan area, Los Angeles, was able to double the number of ethnics of color (blacks and Mexican-Americans) living outside the central city. However, the central city still became blacker, browner, and poorer. The ethnics of color who migrated to the suburbs were middle-class and had a high propensity toward home-ownership. Rises in real income, and available housing supply, a lessening of discrimi-

[21]U.S. Bureau of the Census, Census of Population and Housing: 1970, *General Demographic Trends for Metropolitan Areas,* 1960 to 1970. Final Report PHC (2)-1 United States (Washington, D.C.: United States Government Printing Office, 1971).

[22]George Sternlieb and Robert W. Lake "Aging Suburbs and Black Home-ownership," *The Annals,* no. 422, November (1975), pp. 105–117.

[24]William J. Siembieda, "Suburbanization of Ethics of Color," *The Annals,* no. 422, November, (1975), p. 118.

nation practices in an economically differentiated metropolitan area are variables that help explain the Los Angeles experience. Ethnics of color did not suburbanize in a random manner. They tended to locate in selected suburban communities . . . Most lived in segregated suburban areas—the goal of an integrated society still far into the future.[24]

Missing Links in Suburban Research

"Suburbs are but one part of the picture of the general trend toward population movement out of the cities," says *Time Magazine* (March 15, 1976).[25]

Americans are moving out of the big cities; where once Americans thronged to the bit cities and their immediate suburbs in search of jobs, education and excitement, they are now moving to smaller cities and towns. Between 1970 and 1974, over 1.7 million more Americans left the big metropolitan areas than moved into them. Through migration, the New York area alone lost one half a million people more than it gained; similarly, Chicago lost one quarter of a million. Of the sixteen metropolitan areas that have more than two million people each, eight have lost population since 1970. Besides New York and Chicago, there are Los Angeles, Philadelphia, Detroit, St. Louis, Pittsburg and Newark. In 1973 and 1974, three others lost population; Boston, San Francisco and Long Island's Nassau-Suffolk. Significantly, the big suburbs are no longer growing as fast as they did in the 1960's. Some, like New Jersey's Bergen County and New York's Westchester County have lost population since 1970.[26]

Thus, Americans are still moving out of the big cities in significant numbers to the countryside—specifically to cities of under 50,000 population. Rural counties in the West had an unusually high growth rate between 1970 and 1974. And during the same period, Mississippi and Alabama had a net immigration to their states, a dramatic reversal of the trend which prevailed during the 50's and 60's. In New England, New Hampshire grew by over 10%, Maine by 11% and Vermont by 6%. Americans are leaving the Northeast area—the old industrial areas of St. Louis and Chicago, Philadelphia and Boston—and moving toward the South and West. The fastest growing states in the country are now Florida, Nevada, Arizona, Idaho and Colorado. These areas are known as the Sun Belt, which stretches from southern California into the Carolinas. Part of this move has been sparked by industry moving to the South and Southwest because taxes are low, unions are relatively unorganized, energy costs and other housing costs are comparatively low, too.

Whether this trend which has been reported through the news media represents more than a short-term trickle, or an accurate long-term projection of a general migration to the South and to the West, remains unknown. Moreover, how long these refugees from the megolapolitan areas can escape the same adverse circumstances which drove them out of the more urbanized areas in the first place is

[25]*Time*, March 15, 1976, p. 50.
[25]*Ibid.*, p. 50.

questionable. In any event, studies of exurbs and people who have fled to less urbanized areas are remarkably sparse in social science journals.[27]

Smaller cities, (under 50,000), like their larger counterparts, also have suburbs. Most of the studies which have been cited in this chapter have been conducted in the suburbs of large metropolitan areas. Whether suburbs of smaller cities differ from suburbs of larger cities remains largely an unknown. Probably, people who have fled many of these smaller cities have not done so because of an influx of lower-class blacks, increased crime, higher taxes, poor schools, or the other standard problems which plague larger cities. The rationale for their move and their general value structure remains unstudied.

Most studies of the development of suburban areas employ economic theory or ecological models. Ecological theories (whether of the gradient variety, or of the more recent social area type) usually ignore a very important determinant of people's residential preferences, namely that of life-cycle stage. Gans, in his criticism of Wirth's original ecology, stresses life-cycle stage as an overwhelming determinant of the characteristics of residential areas. Most of the literature on suburbs stresses the fact that these areas are excellent places for people with young children to live. If life-cycle stage were considered as one of the key independent variables explaining residential location and sub-cultural characteristics, a great deal more evidence might be assembled on the overall sub-culture of the suburbs. Open space, lots of room, and good schools, seem more important for people in the early child-bearing years than at later stages.[28]

The Future of Suburbanization

We conclude by hypothesizing a number of trends, from both a demographic and sociological perspective, which will probably take place in the future suburbanization of America.

Increase in Scale

The overwhelming factor affecting suburban growth will be an increase in social and economic scale. That is, as the lifespace for people becomes extended because of technological advances in communication and transportation, the suburbs will continue to extend into the hinterland. As noted by Shevkey and Bell in their original theory, this increase in scale will result in more differentiation in terms of

[26]For one of the few sociological discussions of exurbanites, see A. C. Spectorsky, *The Exurbanites,* (Philadelphia: Lippincott, 1955).

[27]Herbert J. Gans, "Urbanism and Suburbanism as Ways of Life," in Arnold M. Rose, ed., Human Behavior and Social Process (Boston: Houghton Mifflin, 1962) pp. 625–648.

the resources or income of the people living within difficult areas.[29] There will also continue to be an increase in racial and ethnic residential segregation, unless the federal government adopts a radically different policy. Increasingly middle-class families will tend to become more segregated in suburban areas. Single people, in contrast, will remain in the inner areas and in singles ghettos in the suburbs, as will the elderly, the poor, and broken families, who will congregate in multiple-dwelling units, such as apartments and condominiums. As housing costs increase, mobile homes will prove to be a viable alternative to increasing numbers of households.

The federal government will probably continue to subsidize suburban housing in several forms: subsidized mortgage payments, income tax deductions for interest on mortgages, and the development of highway and sewer and water systems for suburban areas.

The movement of more women into the labor force, along with the redefinition of the female role, which will include greater participation in activities outside of the home, will prompt Americans to prefer smaller houses which require less maintenance. These smaller housing units, which will be located both within larger cities and within suburban areas, will probably resemble modernized row houses or town houses. They will be designed to require minimal maintenance; they will have fewer rooms than the standard four-and-a-half bedroom and the two-and-a-half bath homes which were so popular during the 1970's; they will also have smaller yards which require less care.

Because of stabilization of the American labor force and the occupational structure, people will not expect the inevitability of upward mobility to the degree common during the era following World War II. Reflecting this reality, people will typically retain housing units of similar status (and costs) for a relatively long period, rather than moving consecutively to a series of more prestigious houses, each of which has a higher mortgage. With the decline of the success ethic, the work ethic may also decline. During the same period, there will be a corresponding increase on leisure activities and an emphasis on self-fulfillment and inner happiness. This trend will probably result in people spending less of their total money and time on housing than previously.

An increasing proportion of the total population will no longer live in "standard family" households (mother, father and children). The divorced, separated, single and elderly will make up an increasing proportion of the suburban population. As the result of this emerging market, new housing (probably apartments and condominiums) will be constructed for these groups. Moreover, the elderly will become more powerful politically as they assume a larger proportion of the electorate. Because of the political pressures inherent in numbers, greater subsidization of housing and services for the elderly in suburban areas will occur.

[29]Eshresf Shevky and Wendell Bell, *Social Area Analysis* (Palo Alto, California: Stanford University Press, 1955).

Many policy issues will center around some of the hidden costs of suburbanization. As mentioned previously, as new suburbs are developed, high costs are incurred in developing and sustaining services: building and servicing schoos, police and fire departments, electric power, sewage, and water systems. Whether costs will be subsidized by taxes, or whether they will be financed by just simply increasing utility bills and school taxes will be crucial. Conflicts will surely continue around the racial segregation and desegregation of housing and schooling in the suburban areas. The key public policy issue will center around the degree of federal involvement in racial desegregation and socio-economic desegregation, probably through federal regulations on suburban housing developments. Finally, policy choices will have to be made regarding the future of public housing in suburban areas, which had heretofore been practically non-existent.

The public policies which will affect the suburbs are tied directly to the future of the inner city. Future decisions on whether to subsidize new housing in suburban areas will involve a deliberate choice of using limited resources in suburbs, rather than building in cities, or redeveloping and preserving older residential neighborhoods in cities and towns.

Policies surrounding the subsidization of highways and automobile travel, as opposed to mass transit systems, will also play a crucial role in urban planning. This issue, of course, is closely tied to the general energy supply problem, particularly as this relates to the supply of oil. The size and type of housing will also be related to the availability and cost of energy. Smaller houses will probably come into vogue, not only because they are easier to maintain, but more importantly because they cost less to heat. Solar heating, as a supplement to regular heating will probably become common within twenty years. (See Figure 000.)

The concept of metropolitan government and how it is developed will be even more important in the future. Overlapping levels of government will probably be reduced to some extent in many areas. Metropolitan police, fire departments, and certain kinds of services, such as health services, will be consolidated. In the long term, metropolitan government will probably develop piecemeal, service-by-service, rather than through dramatic reorganization of total government in a large metropolitan area.

The further growth of the suburbs appears inevitable. There will probably be no significant move back to the city. As in previous generations, the principal problem will be the planning for orderly growth—specifically, long-range planning, rather than short-term profit. The federal government may carry out a key role in establishing a process for orderly growth by establishing and enforcing guidelines. Such standards might encompass the type and quality of housing, and the kind of services including schools, parks, recreation, police, sanitation systems that areas must have in order to qualify for federal subsidies.

Looking toward the future in terms of the broadest perspective of the urban sociologist-planner, the central issue is the functions which will be performed by suburban areas, vis-à-vis the city, within the metropolitan area. Possibly, with a

University of Delaware Solar 1, an experimental solar house.
(Courtesy University of Delaware Institute for Energy Conversion.)

continuing increase in societal scale, the areas of the old center cities which formerly contained housing may be used increasingly for specialized business, cultural activities, and entertainment. Low-income housing, in turn, would be dispersed into other areas throughout the metropolis. In short, increases in scale should lead to increased functional specialization; certain areas within the metropolis would perform more highly specialized functions than before; *i.e.,* governmental, industrial management, heavy industry, shopping, schools, recreation, etc. Viewed in this perspective, planning for the metropolitan area should work in harmony with increases in scale. Invasion and succession would be planned, rather than trying to counter this trend with rigid and rarely followed planning and zoning policies.

part 3

Urban Social Issues

chapter 10

Housing

> Burt and Nan and their brother and sister, Freddie and Flossie, lived in a large white house with a white picket fence on a street with lots of trees. They lived with their mother and father and their 'man' and their maid.[1]

When many Americans grew up, they developed a conception of the ideal home based on books like the *Bobbsey Twins* series. Socialized at a very early age to value the large white house in the suburban or rural area, several generations of Americans translated these perceptions into marketing desires. The large white house was pictured in children's series, complemented by adult magazines, such as the *Saturday Evening Post,* and constantly reinforced by movies and later television portrayals of the middle-class American family.

Although the economic recession of the 1970's has severely limited the housing available to the American family buying its first home, sociologists have focused upon housing mainly as a social problem affecting the poor. Substandard housing is viewed as a social pathology in itself. Like the values regarding the meaning of poverty, the conceptualization of adequate housing has many facets. Banfield, writing in *The Unheavenly City Revisited* (1974), stresses that a clear distinction must be made between urban problems which are based upon cognitive uneasiness (relative deprivation) and those problems which pose a threat to health, safety, and general welfare.[2] The fact that the media portray the norm for housing as a house costing $60,000, located in an affluent suburb, and that many people feel that such a life-style is a necessity, does not imply that a social problem exists when

[1] Adopted from Laura Lee Hope, *Bobbsey Twins' Big Adventure at Home* (New York: Grosset and Dunlap, 1930).
[2] Edward C. Banfield, *The Unheavenly City Revisited* (Boston: Little, Brown, and Company, 1974).

213

such a lofty standard is not reached. There is no question but that housing is one of our most important status symbols. This gap between the symbolism and the reality of life provides an important theoretical underpinning for sociological studies.

In this chapter we focus upon four questions: (1) What is adequate housing? (2) What is the relationship between housing and other social problems? (3) What are the patterns of residential segregation and the implications for public policy? In particular, what are the issues relating to the "opening up" of the suburbs? (4) What should be the role of the urban sociologist in housing policy formulation?

The Housing Problem

Policy issues relating to housing in the United States seem to center around the standard for adequate or inadequate housing. Urban sociologists usually conceptualize the adequacy of housing in at least three ways: as *shelter,* as a *status symbol,* and as an *ecological pattern.* It is the first of these elements (shelter) which has caused the most difficulty with respect to setting standards of housing adequacy. Urban areas usually have many more governmental services of all kinds than rural areas. In fact, many of the services furnished by cities are totally absent in rural areas. Thus, the water supply problem faced by the average farmer is not even conceived of as potential problem by a city dweller. Water supply, sewage, and police protection are rarely acknowledged as "urban problems." The maintenance of streets, the provision of electric power, even the availability of commercial services such as stores, hospitals, libraries, movies, and recreational facilities are usually considered environmental service problems rather than issues which are related to housing. Moreover, a house which is structurally sound from an engineering or health standpoint may be quite unattractive in the eyes of the family who must live there. Newer housing units, irrespective of structural soundness, when compared to the castle-like qualities of earlier dwellings may be much more appealing. In sum, the physical adequacy of housing (usually considered in terms of structural soundness) may not correspond with the value of housing as a status symbol or simply as a pleasant place in which to live.

Many sociologists have explored the status of housing environments. In both the inner city and in the suburbs, sociologists have clearly identified a hierarchy of neighborhoods having different prestige. Typically, housing within a neighborhood is fairly congruent with respect to cost and appearance. Particularly in suburban neighborhoods, developers usually build houses within a fairly narrow price range, thereby attracting a class of owners who are similar in occupation, education, and income. As a result, the social strata of a given suburban neighborhood appears to be remarkably consistent (particularly during the early stages of development). The manner in which people come to choose houses in various neighborhoods and how they decide to move have been the subject of a number of studies, few of which deal with the structural adequacy of housing per se. Most sociological studies of housing choice focus on housing as a status symbol, looking at differences in people in various social strata and life-cycle stages.

In this book we have previously considered housing as an ecological pattern. The various ecological zones show a great deal of internal consistency with respect to the quality of housing within a given zone. In a nation with democratic principles such as the United States, the divergency in life-styles between various housing zones gives rise to a great ideological debate. The debate, however, has hardly altered this pattern. What it does is to furnish a continuous ideological issue among planners regarding the ideal social class and ethnic makeup of new neighborhoods.

Substandard Housing: How Do We Measure It?

Because housing quality encompasses both subjective (attitudinal) and objective dimensions, it follows that information used to assess housing conditions ought to be multi-dimensional. Hartman, commenting on the data base which is available to measure housing conditions, indicated some of the difficulties in securing information.

> If we can describe housing needs as a multi-dimensional package, it then follows that information by which to assess housing conditions and the scope of housing goals and programs ought to be equally comprehensive. In both areas, however, reality falls woefully short of the ideal. Available data on housing conditions, even notions of the kinds of data that are important, are but a small part of what we need to guide social policy. Moreover, the quality in reporting frequency for those items which are surveyed are extremely inadequate. A precise, reliable description of the nature and magnitude of the U.S. housing problem is not possible, and ideas based on the data that are available significantly understate the problem.[3]

The only comprehensive data source for the nation as a whole is the United States Housing Census, which was initiated in 1940.[4] Because this survey is administered on such an infrequent basis, it is impossible to use it to gauge the extent of the housing problems or to develop research-based policy. In the latter part of each decade, census data become inaccurate and obsolete because of changes in the housing stock. Obviously, if census data are to be used for policy purposes, there is a need for more frequent censuses, possibly employing sampling techniques or some other continuous monitoring systems which are more economical than complete enumerations.

Another problem relates to the inaccuracy of the United States housing census format. Until the 1960 census, housing quality was evaluated by census enumerators through a combination of visual inspections and interview techniques.

[3]Chester W. Hartman, *Housing and Social Policy* (Englewood Cliffs, New Jersey: Prentice-Hall, 1974) p. 5.

[4]See, for example, U.S. Bureau of the Census, (1970) *Census of Housing: 1970 Detailed Housing Characteristics*. Final Report (HC(1)-A1. U. S. Summary.

But the enumerators received only minimal training and as a result were inaccurate in detecting the many structural and environmental deficiencies of housing that should be taken into consideration. Because of this unreliability in the evaluation technique, housing condition ratings ("sound," "deteriorated" or "delapidated") were eliminated entirely from the 1970 census. Only two housing factors remained in this 1970 census—ratings of plumbing facilities and overcrowding. Because many of the measures of the fundamental quality of housing, particularly indicators relating to health and safety (*e.g.*, electrical wiring, building foundation weaknesses, defects in heating equipment) cannot be assessed on the basis of a cursory visual inspection, the census no longer makes an attempt to estimate the incidence of these defects.

Local housing code enforcement data, in contrast to national census data, might provide a more comprehensive picture of local standards and defects. Many cities have adopted housing codes which specify minimal standards for the following: kitchen and plumbing facilities, water supply, hot water and heating systems, electrical systems, ventilation, space standards and space usage, entrances, insect and rodent control, garbage and rubbish disposal, and sewer systems. These local housing codes, however, vary substantially in both their content and in their enforcement. Moreover, data relating to code violations is collected and analyzed with varying degrees of reliability. Thus neither code enforcement data nor census data provide an accurate overview of the condition of the housing stock in urban America.

Overcrowding

The overcrowding concept implies a standard which specifies the ideal number of occupants of a housing unit according to the space which is available. Hartman states:

> There is reason to believe that the effects of overcrowding on mental health in family life may be more severe than the effects of physically substandard conditions, and that we ought to devote more effort to ameliorating the housing plight of families overcrowded in physically separate units. Among the more serious effects of overcrowding are increased stress, poor development of a sense of individuality, sexual conflict, interfamilial tensions and lack of adequate sleep, which contributes to poor work and school performance.[5]

The present overcrowding standard is extremely crude and probably understates the extent of the overcrowding. The United States census uses a ratio of 1.01 or more persons per room, excluding bathrooms, hallways and porches, as the point at which people in a household are classified as living in overcrowded conditions. The census classifies a ratio of 1.51 persons per room as severe overcrowding. This measure, however, does not take into account the household composition (age, sex,

---

[5]Hartman, *Housing,* p. 7.

and relationships) or the overall layout and design of the house. In one study, Greenfield and Lewis (1969), found a great discrepancy between census standards for overcrowding and a more sensitive measure which they developed.[6] Employing their new measure, they found a 12 percent overcrowding rate, as compared to a 2 percent overcrowding rate as measured by Census Bureau criteria.

Substantial cultural variations exist with respect to the housing and lifespace which people are socialized to expect. In some Asian cities, there is a great deal more tolerance for living in close proximity to others than exists in Western cities. Both mental health definitions and social relationships are largely culturally determined. The overcrowding concept, too, appears to be grounded in the individual culture. Culture, however, is real and cannot be changed in the short run. To say that overcrowding standards are culture-bound should not imply that we can safely ignore the adverse consequences of substandard housing within any culture.

Structural Deterioration and Overcrowding

Because the 1970 census did not generate indices of the structural quality of American housing, only limited comparisons can be made with the 1960 census. According to 1970 census, there were 4.7 million housing units which lacked adequate plumbing facilities (or 7 percent of the total housing stock). In comparison, in 1960, there were 15.2 million delapidated units—26 percent of the housing stock—which lacked adequate plumbing facilities or were structurally deteriorating or delapidating. In 1970, 8 percent of all households, 5.2 million families, had a ratio of over 1.01 persons per room. In 1960, the corresponding figure was 11 percent of all households, or 6.1 million families living in a ratio of over 1.01. Thus, within the 5.2 million overcrowded households in 1970, most (4.4 million) were living in houses that had inadequate plumbing facilities. In sum (using nonoverlapping counts), in 1970 there were 9.1 million households in the United States—one out of 7 families—living in substandard housing conditions.[7]

Most of the housing units without adequate plumbing, however, are located in rural areas. Only about one-third are found in standard metropolitan statistical areas (SMSA's), and within the SMSA's, less than half of the deficient units are located in the central cities. Not unexpectedly, employing plumbing facilities as a measure of housing adequacy suggests that cities are comparatively better off than rural areas in this respect. Plumbing, water and sewage systems, however, are more a characteristic of the municipality than its housing stock. Perhaps it is better to think of these census measures as a measure of general environmental adequacy rather than as an indicator of the quality of the housing within that environment.

Several studies have developed more comprehensive measures of the adequacy of housing. In 1965 a special Census Bureau survey was administered in the Watts

[6]R. J. Greenfield and J. F. Lewis, "An Alternative to a Density Function Definition of Overcrowding," *Land Economics,* 45 (May 1969).
[7]Hartman, *Housing,* p. 9.

area of Los Angeles following the riots of 1965.[8] The result showed that within a five-year period, the proportion of substandard housing in Watts had risen by over 10 percent. During the same period rents had risen from an average of $63 to over $75. In New York City, a task force appointed by Mayor John Lindsay found that the number of unsound housing units in New York City increased from 420,000 to 525,000 during the five-year period. For tenants, the average rent accounted for over 20 percent of family income, as compared to 18 percent five years earlier.[9] A study conducted in Boston by the Boston Redevelopment Authority indicates that between 1960 and 1965 deteriorated and delapidated housing increased by 5 percent—from 21 percent in 1960 to 26 percent in 1965.[10] From these limited studies in major cities it is apparent that the quality of housing stock in the inner city area may be deteriorating both physically and in terms of the proportion of income which must be applied by the typical family. Commenting on the effects of high housing costs, Hartman cites the work done by the M.I.T.-Harvard Joint Center for Urban Studies.

> Perhaps the most serious form of deterioration of housing conditions in the last decade is the rapid rise in the cost of housing of any kind, as the Watts area and New York City studies suggest. Good studies of changing rental levels are infrequent, but a 1970 study of the Boston area by the M.I.T.-Harvard Joint Center for Urban Studies is probably indicative of what is happening in almost all large urban areas. The survey showed that from 1960 to 1970 median rents have risen 66 percent, from $78 a month, including heat and utilities, to $130. At the same time, there was only a 33 percent rise in median family income and a 27 percent rise in the cost of living index (which includes rent) for the Boston area. One out of every three Boston families now pays more than 30 percent of its income for housing, including nine out of every 10 families with annual incomes of less than $3,000.[11]

The elderly are the single group in the United States which appears to suffer most from rising housing costs, primarily because they are on fixed incomes. Recently a United States Senate Committee on Aging found:

> Millions of older Americans—whether they live in congested cities or sparsely populated rural areas—now find themselves in a "no man's land" with regard to housing. Hundreds of thousands are being driven from their homes because of prohibitive property taxes and maintenance costs . . . yet it is becoming increasingly difficult to locate suitable alternative quarters at rents they can afford. Although a high proportion of elderly persons have paid off their mortgages, property taxes continue to increase rapidly.[12]

The same Senate study showed that more than 8,000 aged Wisconsin home owners whose annual income was under $1,000 annually paid 30 percent of their incomes

---

[8]U.S. Bureau of the Census, *Special Census Survey of the South and East Los Angeles Areas: 1966 Series* P-23, No. 17 (Nov. 1965), p. 1–10.

[9]Hartman, *Housing,* p. 10.

[10]*Ibid.,* p. 10.

[11]*Ibid.,* p. 11.

[12]U.S. Congress, Senate, Special Committee on Aging, *Economics of Aging: Toward a Full Share in Abundance.* U.S. Senate Report Ms 91–1548 (Dec. 1970).

The roaring, raucous legend of ''The Unsinkable Molly Brown,'' heroine of the Titanic disaster, lives here in her Denver mansion, where she entertained dukes and duchesses and occasionally splintered the woodwork with impromptu pistol shooting exhibitions. Molly, coldly snubbed by Denver's 400 but warmly received by royalty and heads of state throughout the world, was the wife of Johhny Brown, who struck it rich in the gold-veined mountains of Leadville, Colorado. Following a $20 million gold strike, Molly and Johnny built a house in Leadville with inlaid silver dollars imbedded in the concrete flooring.

for property taxes alone.[13] Moreover, the problems of maintaining a home often become more difficult as a person ages, necessitating the use of contractors to perform routine maintenance. The aged living in cities are also particularly vulnerable to the rise in urban crime. The crime phenomenon, whether based on objective measures on the crimes committed in the neighborhood or upon the fear of crime, yields the same conclusion. Environmental conditions of many of our large cities affect housing negatively, particularly for the elderly, creating an increasingly large

[13]*Ibid.*, pp. 25–29.

number of persons over 65 who lead a lonely, barricaded existence. In a study conducted in Delaware, it was found that the elderly living in cities generally resided in houses which had far superior physical characteristics than their counterparts who lived in rural and suburban areas.[14] Also, the many services concentrated in cities—shopping, health social services and entertainment—on the surface appear to make the city a far better place for the elderly to live. Despite the obviously superior resources available in cities, the elderly living in urbanized areas were far more negative and generally pessimistic about the overall quality of housing. They cited the general atmosphere, the fear of crime, the actual number of crimes, and a number of aspects of the social climate of urban areas which made the city more undesirable in the eyes of the elderly who lived there. This discrepancy between objective and subjective standards of housing bears out the serious inadequacies of census data (focusing primarily on overcrowding and plumbing facilities for gauging the overall quality of housing) as a housing quality indicator.

Social indicator models which examine housing adequacy should employ multidimensional criteria. Among these should be measures of structural soundness and general physical adequacy, along with infrequently measured qualities such as lighting, outside sitting areas, electrical outlets, and even temperature. Beyond these physical standards should be measures of overcrowding, price-to-income ratios, tax-to-income ratios, etc. Subjective standards might also be employed. These standards would measure the adequacy of housing in terms of some hypothetical reference group against which the aging homeowner would compare himself. Included in this battery of questions could be items on feelings of safety, happiness, opportunities for social interaction and other items which provide assessments of the subjective qualities of housing.

Housing and Social Problems

It is axiomatic that inadequate housing and social problems are highly correlated. Yet whether poor housing causes social problems in the sense that if we provided good housing, social problems would not occur or would be remedied, remains questionable. Because housing is primarily an economic "good," it reflects both the social class and the income of the consumer. Whether inadequate housing is a cause of social problems, in the same sense as poverty, is doubtful. It is more likely that housing should be viewed only as part of the overall context of highly urbanized areas, particularly the inner city. It is the overall environment which fosters such problems as crime and delinquency, mental illness and a plethora of other urban pathologies.

Recalling Wirth's (1938) classical theory of urbanism, we are reminded of the

[14]Bernard L. Dworsky and Robert A. Wilson, "Social Indicators for the Aged," *The Social Welfare Forum: National Conference on Social Welfare* (New York: Columbia University Press, 1972).

three major factors of the theory (size, density, and heterogeneity. Density is the single quality which is most highly related to urban housing.[15] Not only in terms of the number of inhabitants per room, but also in terms of the number of inhabitants per area, density fosters greater interaction within a small space, causing (in theory) social acts of all types to increase in frequency, deviant as well as normal.

In one index of urbanization created by Shevky and Bell, it will be recalled that the urbanization index consisted of three subcomponents: females in labor force, fertility ratio, and single-family, detached dwelling units.[16] Several studies of deviance employing the Shevky-Bell method have found that the dwelling unit index is the only one of the three urbanization subindices which accounts for increased deviance in areas which are highly urbanized.[17] The implication, when explaining deviancy from an ecological perspective, is that deviance brought about by changes in family structure (signified by decreasing fertility ratio and increasing proportions of women in the labor force) is not as strongly related to crime and drug abuse as increases in density. However, some theories of urbanization suggest that more "unconventionality" exists in urban places, and that this factor is usually related to the overall number of people in an area, as opposed to the density of residential settlement or where people reside.[18] Possibly, density is most highly related to crimes associated with lower-class inner city areas, while sheer numbers of people are linked with "middle-class" deviancy such as drunken-driving and "swinging."

Public Housing and Deviant Behavior

The general consensus is that public housing policy in the United States has been unsuccessful. Most of the problems with the concept seem to relate to the fact that public housing is equated with welfare housing. As a result, a stigma is placed upon individuals who are tenants in projects; tenants, in turn, internalize this stigma and act out their adverse self-image through deviant and destructive behavior. The classical statement of the problems with public housing is found in a study of the Pruitt-Igoe Project in St. Louis, a public housing project consisting of 33 eleven-story buildings with approximately 2,800 apartments, initially occupied in 1954.[19] Within five years, Pruitt-Igoe had become a national scandal because of the severe problems of crime and vandalism. The project was physically unappealing, in fact ugly, by almost any aesthetic standard. In 1970, the decision was made to partially

[15]Louis Wirth, "Urbanism as a Way of Life," *American Journal of Sociology,* 44 (July 1938).

[16]Esref Shevky and Marilyn Williams, *The Social Areas of Los Angeles* (Berkeley and Los Angeles: University of California Press, 1949).

[17]Dennis Wenger and Robert A. Wilson, paper presented at American Sociological Association, *An Ecological Analysis of Drug Use Among High School Students: Evidence from Social Area Analysis of School Districts,* San Francisco, 1975.
Theodore R. Anderson and Lee L. Bean, "The Shevky-Bell Social Areas: Confirmation of Results and a Re-interpretation," *Social Forces,* 40 (Dec. 1961).

[18]Claude S. Fischer, *The Urban Experience* (New York: Harcourt Brace Jovanovich Inc., 1976) pp. 154–169.

[19]David A. Schulz, *Coming Up Black* (Englewood Cliffs, New Jersey: Prentice-Hall, Inc., 1970).

demolish the project and to renovate some of the buildings. By 1973, fourteen years after its inception, Pruitt-Igoe was totally demolished as a result of a decision of the St. Louis Housing Authority. The failure of the project received widespread publicity, including major coverage by *Time* Magazine. Pruitt-Igoe, in the eyes of the American public, stands for the problems associated with public housing.

Lee Rainwater and his associates studied Pruitt-Igoe over a period of ten years.[20] About two-thirds of the households were female-headed; the ratio of women to men in the project was over 2.5 to 1. Only 45 percent of the families were economically self-sufficient; the average annual family income was under $2,000. Almost all of the project's tenants were black. Most of the original tenants had migrated from areas which had been cleared for urban renewal.

Rainwater argued that the serious problems of Pruitt-Igoe did not result from its physical qualities. The problems were social. In interviewing one tenant, Rainwater elicited the following appraisal:

> The elevators are dangerous . . . bottles and other dangerous things are thrown out of windows and hurt people . . . little children hear bad language all the time so that they don't realize how bad it is . . . the laundry areas aren't safe; clothes get stolen and people get attacked . . . the children run wild and cause all kinds of damage . . . a woman isn't safe in the halls, stairways or elevators.[21]

The primary problems, then, Rainwater deduced, did not stem from the architectural design or the physical environment of Pruitt-Igoe. The problems, Rainwater concluded, were racial discrimination, lack of economic opportunities, compounded by the fact that "lower-class people are constrained to live among others who are equally marginal in economic terms, and in the community that grows up in this situation, a premium is placed upon the exploitation and the manipulation of peers."[22]

Schulz (1970), in an analysis of the family life in Pruitt-Igoe, found exploitation to be rampant.[23] He cites one case in which an ambulance crew arrived to take an injured resident to the hospital. A large number of tenants gathered in the apartment of the injured person. After the crowd had departed, it was discovered that a large number of articles had been stolen by the same people which had purportedly gathered to "help" the injured tenant. Suttles, in another analysis of public housing, indicates that because there is no status differentiation among residents, a great deal of anonymity results.

> Public housing also provides a ready temptation for those who are already eager to disassociate themselves from their families. Particularly among teenagers whose parents might be regarded as "country" or "square, there is a strong tendency to escape the

---

[20]Lee Rainwater, *Behind Ghetto Walls: Black Family Life in a Federal Slum* (Chicago: Aldine, 1970).

[21]*Ibid.*, p. 10–11.

[22]*Ibid.*, p. 371.

[23]Schulz, *Coming Up Black,* 1970.

household lest it "cramp" their style. Much of the same thing may happen with adults who have learned that a double life only doubles their pleasure.[24]

Suttles continues:

> In project neighborhoods, however, the conditions of residency provide public testimony to the universal importance of fellow residents. If someone has economic resources, "connections," or "clout," there is no reason for him being in public housing . . . complementing these grounds for disregarding each other's role as a potential benefactor, there are others which encourage project dwellers to regard each other as potential predators. It is common to take material deprivations as an omen of opportunism, ignorance, irrationality, and resentment. All slum residents must live with this oppressive view of their neighbors. Only project dwellers, however, have it on best of evidence that everyone around them is subject to such deprivations.[25]

Housing Segregation

Segregation, in sociology, generally infers a concentration of a certain social group within an ecological or residential area. departing from the distribution of that group within an overall population. Thus, a residential neighborhood may be segregated in terms of its economic status, its religious status, its racial status, or even if it has a preponderance of persons within a certain age group. Most studies of segregation, however, have explored racial or ethnic segregation. Usually the consequences of segregation have been viewed adversely. Residential segregation is linked with school segregation, which, in turn, has been associated with inferior schools. Religious segregation is often thought of in terms of intolerance or discrimination. The most extreme form of segregation is *apartheid,* whereby laws mandate housing segregation within an area. Apartheid is still the law in the Union of South Africa, where blacks are prohibited from living in the same areas as whites.

In the United States, a ghetto is usually thought of in terms of an area populated by lower-class blacks who live in a state of poverty and social disorganization. While most studies have borne out the fact that the black ghetto is poverty-stricken, many do not support the theory that the ghetto is socially disorganized.[26] The cause of segregation of blacks in the ghettos has been traced by some to restricted opportunities for housing in outlying inner city areas and suburban areas.[27] On the whole, however, descriptive studies of the amount or degree of segregation prevail, describing segregation within various areas, but adding little in the way of explanation as to the reason for the segregation or the consequences of segregation. A discussion of housing segregation studies follows.

[24]D. Suttles, *The Social Order of the Slum: Ethnicity and Territory in the Inner City* (Chicago: University of Chicago Press, 1968) p. 167.
[25]*Ibid.,* p. 168.
[26]Robert A. Wilson, "Anomie in the Ghetto: A Study of Neighborhood Type, Race, and Anomie," *The American Journal of Sociology,* 77 (July 1971).
[27]Bonnie Bullough, "Alienation in the Ghetto," *American Journal of Sociology* 72 (March 1967).

American Attitudes on Race and Housing

In a 1973 study of both black and white attitudes towards housing problems, Pettigrew focused upon changes in outlooks.[28] The attitudes of American whites toward open housing have become increasingly favorable over the past generation. This trend appears to be the result of factors other than housing per se, in particular, racial desegregation in other spheres of life. The implementation of fair housing legislation over the past twenty years has also influenced the trend toward more open attitudes. The attitudes of blacks favoring open housing have remained the same over the past twenty years. Blacks are apparently reluctant to move into previously all-white areas, even after they have increased their social status, primarily as a result of fear of a hostile white reception. Pettigrew concludes that,

> Desegregation is a cumulative process for both races: the more optimal intergroup contact you have had, the more you favor and seek it in the future. Behavior change, then, typically precedes rather than follows attitude change. The practical implication of this principle and an effective way to alter opposition to interracial housing, white and black, is to have them live successfully in such housing.[29]

But what constitutes "successful" desegregation? How does one achieve it before the attitudes are altered? Millen (1970), summing up the factors affecting racial mixing in residential areas, provides a number of generalizations as to the factors which make racial mixing possible.[30] First, stable racial mixing is more easily achieved in rental housing than in areas of entirely owner-occupied housing, provided that management supports it. Second, racial mixing is feasible at all price or rental levels, but stable and substantial mixing is most likely in the middle-price range. Third, good quality and value for money are means of overcoming resistance to racially mixed housing. Fourth, location and neighborhood facilities are a major factor in housing choices and will influence the success of racial mixing. Fifth, the market for racially mixed housing is not restricted to those with very distinctive social characteristics or racial attitudes. Sixth, stable racial mixing is most easily achieved where residents from the different races are of corresponding socioeconomic level.[31]

Opening Up the Suburbs

Anthony Downs (1973), in a classic analysis of urban development in the United States, maintains that the primary housing problem in America is the inherent injustice in the absence of housing opportunities in suburban areas for low-income house-

[28]Thomas F. Pettigrew, "Attitudes on Race and Housing: A Social-Psychological View," *Segregation in Residential Areas* (Washington, D.C.: National Academy of Sciences, 1973).

[29]*Ibid.*, pp. 79–80.

[30]James S. Millen, "Factors Affecting Racial Mixing in Residential Areas," *Segregation in Residential Areas* (Washington, D.C.: National Academy of Sciences, 1973).

[31]*Ibid.*, pp. 156–166.

holds. This problem is rooted in the absence of opportunities for moderate-income households to move into "new growth portions" of suburban areas. The fundamental difficulty, Downs, contends, is found in the "trickle-down" process, whereby older neighborhoods continuously deteriorate.[32]

Downs describes the trickle-down process in this way:

> As time passes, the new housing units in . . . a neighborhood become older and less stylish compared to newer units. . . . Design changes, like family rooms, built-in appliances, and bathroom countertop sinks also hasten the obsolescence of older units. Eventually their increasing age generates higher maintenance costs, too. At the same time, the real incomes of many households initially living in this neighborhood increase. Many move to even newer housing units that are even larger, more stylish and in "fancier" neighborhoods. Gradually the edge of settlement moves father out, leaving this neighborhood surrounded by other urban developments. This makes it relatively more central but also more hemmed in and subject to higher traffic congestion. In addition, relatively lower-income households continuously move into the housing in the area. They are larger and tend to use the housing more intensively. For most incoming households, this housing represents an improvement over the older units from which they have moved. As more time passes, the once new housing becomes less and less desirable compared to the newest and best in society, even if it is well maintained. Because it is occupied by a succession of *relatively* lower and lower income groups, it eventually houses groups with *absolutely* much lower incomes than the first who lived there. As long as the occupants have incomes high enough to maintain their properties, the neighborhood may remain in good physical condition. But in time, the annual cost of such maintenance becomes fairly high, while the occupants' annual incomes become quite low. Then the housing begins to deteriorate significantly. Households with alternative choices move elsewhere. Finally, the housing becomes occupied by the lowest income groups in society and falls into extreme disrepair. At this point this housing has "trickled down" through society's income distribution from near the top to the bottom.[33]

The upshot of this trickle-down is that for the poorest residents of metropolitan areas, the cycle is an on-going disaster that perpetuates the pattern of those with lowest income in concentrated urban slums. It is this concentration which has a "critical mass" effect that multiplies the negative impacts of poverty, creating entire neighborhood environments dominated by the social conditions of inadequate income. The results are "crises ghettos" marked by high prevalence of crime, vandalism, broken families, mental illness, delinquency, and drug addiction.

Downs cites several reasons for opening up the suburbs. First is better access to expanding suburban job opportunities for workers in low- and moderate-income households—especially the unemployed. Second, there are greater opportunities for such households to upgrade themselves by moving into middle-income neighborhoods, thereby escaping from crisis ghetto conditions. Third, higher quality public schooling is available for children from low-income households. Greater opportunity for the Nation to reach its officially adopted goals for low and moderate-income households is fourth. Fifth is fairer geographic distribution of the fiscal and social

[32]Anthony Downs, *Opening Up the Suburbs: An Urban Strategy for America* (New Haven: Yale University Press, 1973).
[33]*Ibid.*, pp. 4–5.

costs of dealing with metropolitan area poverty. Sixth is elimination of concentration in poverty-stricken minorities in metropolitan areas. Finally, there are greater possibilities of improving ghetto areas without displacing urban decay to adjacent neighborhoods.[34]

Downs claims that there are two lessons to be learned about the viability of neighborhoods from the American experience. "The first is that most urban neighborhoods containing relatively high concentrations of low-income households are neither economically nor socially viable. The second is that the upgrading desired by low- and moderate-income households and the protection of neighborhood quality desired by middle- and upper-income households can be achieved simultaneously in the same neighborhoods if a significant number of low- and moderate-income households live there, providing that middle-class dominance is maintained. 'Middle-class dominance' means that the preponderant majority of persons living in a neighborhood and interacting in most institutions serving it (such as public schools) are from middle- and upper-income households. 'A preponderant majority' is a sufficiently high percentage (well over 50 percent) so that middle-class mores and behavior remain prevalent. From these two lessons comes the following corollary: In most cases, keeping an urban neighborhood economically and socially viable requires maintaining middle-class dominance there."[35]

According to Downs, a viable neighborhood should exhibit the following characteristics. Crime rates are low enough so that most people consider it safe to walk on the streets at any time during the day and some of the time at night. Housing and other structures are maintained in good physical condition. Neighborhood schools are considered adequate or more than adequate by most local residents. The streets are reasonably safe from trash, abandoned automobiles and other debris, and local public services are considered adequate by most residents. The area is reasonably convenient to normal urban facilities (such as shopping, employment centers, and churches) and is served by public transportation to a degree enabling its residents to accomplish their major movement goals. (In many suburban areas this does not require any public transportation.) Most people who live in the area or who are considering living there believe the above conditions are likely to persist for an indefinite period—at least for five years.[36] The result of Downs' work, then, according to him, is the conclusion that most deteriorated residential neighborhoods of the inner city, should not be allowed to survive. Their populations shoulld be dispersed throughout the greater metropolitan area, leaving the central city areas to be developed for other purposes. Just what these purposes should be is left unspecified.

The Future of Housing Segregation

The key question regarding housing segregation—both racial and economic—is whether there will be a higher or lesser degree of concentration in the future.

[34]*Ibid.*, p. 26.
[35]*Ibid.*, p. 87.
[36]*Ibid.*, pp. 88–89.

Notice the curtains in this houseboat. In Amsterdam one age-old technique for beating the housing squeeze is to live in a houseboat. Would this work in American cities?

Demographic trends comparing the most recent federal censuses suggest that there will be less ethnic and racial segregation in the second half of the twentieth century.[37] While there may be generally less segregation, the phenomenon of the crisis ghetto with its concentration of pathology-ridden, poverty-stricken lower-class ethnics will probably remain. Thus, segregation will probably remain, but find its locus more in class and economic criteria rather than race. Until the critical shortage of housing funds which developed during the mid-1970's is alleviated, it is doubtful whether any major changes in housing trends will appear.

Housing Policy: Past and Present

Throughout this chapter we have documented the fact that government at all levels in the United States has had a dramatic impact upon housing patterns. Federal government, in particular, since World War II, has affected the patterns of both private and public housing through a number of programs which subsidize home-owners and renters in various ways. In this final section, we review a number of these programs and look at some of the policy decisions which must be made in the future.

[37]Karl E. Taeuber and Alma F. Taeuber, *Negroes in Cities* (Chicago: Aldine, 1965).

The federal government stepped into the housing business with the creation of the Federal Housing Administration in 1934 and its original housing program, begun under the National Industry Recovery Act in 1933. The Model Cities Program is not discussed here due to the fact that it is only marginally a housing program. Less than 10 percent of the funds allocated under the Model Cities Act have been devoted to housing and these mostly for establishing local development corporations, organizing tenants and hiring counselors. Also not included is a major discussion of urban renewal, which has been largely a de-housing program in that it has been responsible for the demolition of large numbers of houses without accompanying redevelopment. In short, urban renewal established under the 1949 Housing Act was principally slum clearance, used primarily by local governments to reappropriate land which was occupied by the poor for commercial purposes. As a result, over half a million households, most of them non-white and poor, were forceably removed from their neighborhoods. In the late 1960's, however, there were some changes in the urban renewal law which restructured the program to help meet some of the needs of low- and moderate-income households. Unfortunately, the trend has again shifted with the emphasis upon revenue-sharing grants, which allow municipalities to return to the old style demolition and bulldozing of urban areas occupied by the poor.

Income Taxes as a Housing Subsidy

Hartman, in his analysis of government housing program states, "By far the largest subsidy given to housing comes through the workings of the Internal Revenue Code, even though in the peculiar American folk logic 'tax breaks' usually are not regarded as subsidies."[38] The savings that result from allowing owners to deduct mortgage interest costs and property costs from their taxable income and to exempt from taxation the imputed rental income from owned houses are in the neighborhood of seven billion dollars annually. This is

> ... equivalent to a reduction in the price of housing to home-owners that results in benefits to them approximately equal to the tax savings. The savings the income tax system provides to home-owners represent a substantial portion of their housing costs: at 1965–67 tax rates the typical home-owner offset about 12 percent of his housing costs through interest and property tax deductions. Another way of expressing this is that property tax and interest deduction were worth a mere one dollar to the average family that earned less than $3,000, $45 to the average family that earned $7,000 to $10,000, $166 to the average family that earned $15,000 to $20,000, and $1,082 to the average family that earned over $100,000. The major feature of the federal income tax system that favors home-owners is exclusion of the implicit rental value of an owner-occupied home from the tax base. That is, the person who invests in stocks and bonds must pay taxes on the earnings from the investment; the person who invests the same amount in a home for his family and receives his "return" in the form of housing services does not have to pay taxes on his investment.[39]

[38]Chester W. Hartman, *Housing and Social Policy* (Englewood Cliffs, New Jersey: Prentice-Hall, 1974) p. 108.
[39]*Ibid.,* pp. 108–109.

Public Welfare as a Housing Subsidy

Most public assistance programs are not perceived as housing programs; but public welfare provides more direct subsidy for housing costs among low-income families than all the other housing programs combined. Persons receiving Aid to Dependent Families with Children (ADFC), old age assistance, and aid to the disabled, all receive federal and state subsidies, a part of which is budgeted for housing. These subsidies, however, are woefully inadequate. The central problem is money.[40] The welfare system does not provide nearly enough assistance for families to secure decent housing. A HEW Report notes that "For more than three million recipient households (that is, for almost all welfare households at the time), the average allowance for housing is less than $400 per year ($33 per month). This amount is grossly inadequate for either rental housing or home ownership." The problem of welfare households is exacerbated by the fact that few are fortunate enough to get into public housing. Only 7 percent of families receiving public welfare in 1967 were living in public housing.[41]

Public Housing

In America, the federal public housing program was started in the early 1930's as part of the Roosevelt Administration's economic and job creation approach to economic recovery from the Depression. To date, the program has produced nearly 1.2 million public housing units, about 200,000 of which were still under construction at the end of 1971.[42] Most public housing programs are run by local public housing authorities. The basic decisions in each city regarding public housing are made by these administrations—whether to build units, how many to have, where they should be built, and what type of construct. These decisions are made by a public body which is made up of local businessmen, lawyers, government officials, etc. In short, public housing authorities are made up of conservative members of the community's middle class. Also, because they are politically appointed, local housing authorities are quite sensitive to the location of public housing. As a result, almost all has been built in slum areas which are most universally located in center cities where land values are high. As a consequence, because of limited land acquisition funds, public housing has been forced to build upward, creating high-rise buildings such as the ones described by Rainwater in the analysis of the Pruitt-Igoe project.

New Ideas in Public Housing

A number of new techniques for providing public housing have been introduced during the last decade. Among these is the "turnkey" project. Here, a builder

[40]*Ibid.*, p. 110.
[41]*Ibid.*, p. 111.
[42]*Ibid.*, p. 114.

229

arranges to construct a development to the specifications authorized by the housing authority. After completion, he turns the units over to the authority at a negotiated price. Leasing or renting units from a private landlord for occupancy by public housing tenants is another means. Purchase and rehabilitation of substandard buildings by the public housing authority is a third mode. Fourth is acquisition of existing housing, sometimes those which have had mortgages foreclosed by FHA or VA. Last, programs allowing tenants to gain ownership is a promising concept.[43]

Subsidizing Home Ownership

In 1968, in Section 235 of the Housing Act, the American Congress established a program of home ownership subsidies for families who are unable to purchase housing within the private housing market. This program is the largest single subsidized housing effort. By 1971, Section 235 accounted for 29 percent of the almost 500,000 units produced under federal subsidy programs.

Housing Allowances

Housing allowances are the latest idea of the 1970's.[44] The central idea is to provide direct subsidies either in cash or vouchers, like certificates of rent, to housing consumers and then to allow them to make their own decision with respect to housing on the private market. This process is in lieu of subsidizing housing or the production of housing through the elaborate bureaucratic structure which is necessary to allocate housing units to the poor. The rationale is that almost all middle- and upper-income people live in good housing because the market, aided by various income tax features, provides for them the income which is necessary for adequate housing. If poor people had enough money, they would make their own decisions regarding housing which would presumably be "good" decisions. They would not spend their money on luxury items, but rather would make intelligent decisions with respect to housing.

The idea of housing allowances was supported by the Nixon Administration. It was propagated under the idea that the major advantage to the consumer would be expanded choice. Rather than being limited to public housing, the family would be free to make any decision to live in any unit they chose within their rent limitations. The housing allowance notion, however, assumes that the major cause of inadequate housing is inadequate income.

This idea ignores the major problem—the great shortage of moderate- and low-income rental housing in most urban areas, particularly for large families. The experience in New York has indicated that increasing housing subsidies through housing allowances does not cause landlords to correct code violations after they

[43]*Ibid.*, pp. 120–121.
[44]*Ibid.*, p. 153.

receive increased rent.[45] The major issue, then, is whether adequate housing can be expanded by increasing the supply of decent housing, thereby increasing the funds which are available to secure housing through housing allowances. In sum, governmental subsidies to housing have been mainly successful for middle- and upper-income home buyers. Programs designed to help the poor have done little to remedy their housing situation. In the main, this problem is due to inadequate incomes, but it is also due in part to the general hesitancy of housing administrations to create adequate housing in areas other than center cities. Public housing in suburban and rural areas is almost nonexistent. Moreover, the housing which has been built has not made an effective dent in the great need for adequate housing by the great majority of poor people.

Future Policy Issues

We have reviewed a number of issues relating to housing policy in the United States. Most of the decisions which we face in the future seem to relate to six major dilemmas. Each of these is discussed below.

Preservation vs. Urban Renewal

Much of the housing stock in inner city areas is still structurally sound. Neighborhoods have deteriorated for the reasons discussed in this chapter and other chapters. The decision lingers whether these older units should be torn down and other land uses developed. Probably if a neighborhood is viable, in the sense that a significant number of its residents and potential residents are willing to preserve the housing in the area, the decision may be made to supply federal and state funds to aid in the preservation of the neighborhood.

Transportation vs. Inner City Development

One of the areas of subsidies which was not discussed was that of the public highway and other forms of mass transit in major metropolitan areas. By making it possible through building superhighways and mass transit systems for people to move further out from the city, local governments have actually subsidized the development of suburban areas. In many European cities these elaborate highway networks are simply not available, thereby making it unfeasible for most people to commute long distances. Whether tax funds should be used to continue this trend and thereby foster the deterioration in center city residential areas is another crucial dilemma which must be faced in the last half of the twentiety century.

[45]*Ibid.*, p. 156.

Public vs. Private

We have discussed in detail the idea of providing through a voucher system a form of subsidy whereby people can purchase or rent homes in the private market, rather than live in public housing. If public housing does survive into the twenty-first century, we must somehow integrate tenants into the community as a whole. Possibly, scattered-site public housing, wherein units are located throughout the community may be the answer to this problem.

Social Indicators of Housing Quality

We have spoken earlier in this chapter about the difficulties in developing objective and subjective indicators of housing quality. Although housing may be up to standard in terms of health, safety and decency, its amenities and symbolic qualities may cause people to look unfavorably upon it. The extent to which public policy should be based upon this notion of relative deprivation will be one of the key issues facing sociologists exploring housing policy.

Housing the Elderly

The birthrate in the United States has declined substantially. Increasingly, the large numbers of persons who were born in the 1950's will be moving into middle age, and beginning in the year 2000, will be retiring from the labor force. As this age group reaches maturity, providing housing and services for this group will become the dominant problem of public housing policy.

The Great American Dream vs. the Actual American Reality

We began this chapter by describing the Bobbsey Twins' house. It was white, large, and had a picket fence and two servants. Because of the energy crisis of the 1970's, America's love affair with the large car is rapidly becoming a part of the past. Americans, like Europeans, are driving smaller four-cylinder cars. Will the four-bedroom, two-and-a-half bath suburban house go the same route as the eighty-cylinder car? The answer is probably yes, but not for the reason that the car changed. Americans, in their wisdom, are becoming increasingly leisure-conscious. The time and effort involved in maintaining large suburban houses, coupled with the cost of construction, may cause many persons who have the option to choose units which are less difficult to maintain—such as townhouses, mobile homes, condominiums, or rehabilitated houses in urban areas. Whatever the genesis of this change, we already see indications that the typical American family can no longer afford the large suburban house. The policy decisions which we face relate to the subsidy of housing, and if so, what kind to subsidize. Whatever decisions are reached, there will be a major shift in the old life-styles which have been prevalent since World War II and an accompanying rationalization of the shifting value structure. Urban sociologists will monitor and explain this changing housing pattern as it relates to social structure and social process. Hopefully, as the options are considered, some of the sociological dimensions will figure into the policy-making process. Most important will be the assessment of policy relating to different population segments, *i.e.,* the different classes, the elderly, women, teenagers, and different ethnic groups. Urban sociologists will probably be helpful in this policy-making process.

chapter 11

Urban Crime: Issues of Social Deviance and Social Control

"Crime in the streets" is usually thought of as the foremost urban problem. Throughout modern history, the city has suffered from an image which has portrayed it as a repository of social problems of all kinds. Particularly during the 1960's and 1970's, violent crimes committed in cities received prominent news coverage. Next to the war in Southeast Asia, crime was the problem most often which became a political issue. In the mind of the American public, the crime problem was linked with the concentration of disreputable people found in the cities—criminal types, the poor, particularly minority groups who could not "make it" legally and thus resorted to crime. Crime was also associated with a range of environmental problems in the cities, including blight, decay, overcrowding, and a host of other images which pictured the city as a problem-infested, dismal place. The urban crime wave is verified by data from the criminal justice systems which indicate that the problem is real, not a figment of the popular imagination. The nature of the problem and what to do about it, however, remains an emotional arena, despite the massive federal programs which have attempted to alleviate urban crime.

In this chapter we attempt to focus several sociological questions regarding the urban crime problem. Specifically, we discuss the following questions: (1) Is urban crime a social problem? (2) What is the extent of urban crime? (3) What causes urban crime? (4) What can be done to control urban crime? (5) What should be the strategy for the future?

Crime as a Social Problem

American cities have always attracted a diverse group of immigrants who moved in an attempt to better themselves. Particularly in the United States, large cities served as a port of entry for immigrants, many of whom were seeking an escape from poverty, religious persecution, and political persecution in their native lands. Immigrants not only lived under conditions of filth and squalor, but were often exploited in a newly developing industrial system. The same trend continues today. Large numbers of migrants from Puerto Rico, Mexico, and rural parts of the United States flow into larger cities seeking a better way of life. The usual point of entry is the center city slum, which has undergone successive waves of immigrants of different ethnic stock—the Germans, the Irish, the Polish, the Italians—still later the blacks and the Puerto Ricans.

Urban slums have typically manifested a high incidence of social problems of all kinds—crime, mental illness, poverty, alcoholism, drug abuse, and various forms of sexual deviancy. Suburbs and rural areas have manifested social problems, too, but the intensity in the inner city areas of the metropolis has always been much greater.

Over the last century, the United States has become one of the wealthiest nations in the world. Wages are high; the life-style is replete with more conveniences and status symbols than in any other nation in the world. When an individual assesses his own well-being, he compares himself with an implicit "reference group," a standard by which he judges himself in comparison with those around him.[1] If the standard by which one judges himself evolves from watching television, he will find that the average family is portrayed as having a $100,000 house, two new cars, extravagant vacations, an expensive wardrobe, and an abundant supply of liquor and food. If one accepts this image as a standard for self-assessment, in many instances tremendous dissatisfaction and stress will result. Banfield (1968) has characterized much of this malaise as a by-product of our rising expectations brought about by the increasing emphasis upon the upper middle-class consumption style.[2] That is, people exhibit the symptoms of social stress because there is a great discrepancy between the life-style which they think they should lead, compared to that which they are actually capable of sustaining.

Relative deprivation is not a new idea, either in sociology or in other social sciences. The classical sociological theory on relative deprivation was stated by Robert Merton.[3] Merton theorized that social deviancy was a by-product of a differential access to the institutionalized means for achieving cultural goals. According to this theory, most people aspire to certain cultural goals, most of which focus

---

[1]Robert K. Merton, *Social Theory and Social Structure* (Glencoe, Illinois: The Free Press, 1957). pp. 225–280.

[2]Edward C. Banfield, *The Unheavenly City Revisited* (Boston, Toronto: Little Brown and Company, 1968), pp. 127–147.

[3]Merton, *Social Theory,* pp. 131–194.

235

upon economic success. Since many people do not have access to the legitimate means for achieving these success goals, stress develops, which often results in people adapting socially deviant ways of achieving goals. In other words, America, in Merton's conceptualization, suffers from an overabundance of the Horatio Alger spirit—the ideal that everyone, given enough hard work, can achieve success. In reality, however, people are often blocked and frustrated in their goal-striving efforts, resulting in social stresses and disruptions.

Poverty-stricken residents of the inner city are particularly vulnerable to this discrepancy between the ideal and the real. Social pressures which result because of these differentials in the "opportunity structure" are often associated with deviancy or mental illness.

Other social theorists have focused not so much on this discrepancy in life styles, but have attempted to trace the genesis of urban alienations to the methods of mass production, the political bureaucracy, and the business oligarchy.[4] Mills follows in the Marxian tradition, attributing the alienation of urbanites not so much to the structure of the urban community but rather upon the built-in facets of the industrial society, especially the "military-industrial complex," which has gradually evolved into a configuration of power and wealth within a relatively small elite. In the traditional urban sociology, however, it has been more common to attribute social deviance to the disorganization which is inherent in both urbanization and industrialization. Following the tradition of the Chicago Schools, particularly Louis Wirth (1938), social disorganization is linked to "anonymity," "superficiality" and the "transitive" nature of social life in a highly urbanized society.

Urban sociology was dominated until the 1940's by sociologists having a rural, middle-class, Protestant orientation.[5] This conceptualization stressed the goodness of small town and rural life, centered around the primary associations found in the family, the neighborhood, the church, and the work place. In contrast, social relationships in urban areas were characterized as secondary, based upon the specialized social relationships in almost all areas of life. Social problems were seen as stemming from the overabundance of secondary relations of urbanized society. Because of the absence of an integrated social structure and the accompanying social control, urban areas were vulnerable to social disorganization, which typically manifests itself through urban social problems.

The term *social problem* usually implies a very general concept, referring to almost any kind of human difficulty. Sociologists have developed a set of more specific concepts which define a social problem. When we consider urban crime, all of these elements are present.

It is generally acknowledged that a situation must meet three criteria for it to be

---

[4]C. Wright Mills, *The Power Elite* (New York: Oxford University Press, 1956).

[5]Roscoe C. Hinkle, Jr. and J. Gisela Hinkle, *The Development of Modern Sociology* (New York: Random House, 1954), p. 3.

considered a social problem.[6] First, a social problem is manifest among people who are frustrated because they fail to meet certain criteria of their society, or among people who anticipate failing to meet such criteria. Second, a social problem involves people's attempts to deal with their frustration, in particular, their attempts to surmount a problem through the organized institutions and mechanisms of their community and their society. Finally, the attempt to cope with the problem arouses concern among other members of the society who are not directly affected by the social problem. The urban crime problem, then, may be seen as the attempts by a social group or groups to cope with their life situation. The problem is social in nature, because it is a collective dilemma of urban residents, and because it attracts the attention of other members of the society.

Social problems create waves, ripples and aftereffects throughout the entire society because they reflect social conflicts between various groups. The greater these conflicts, the greater the passion which is aroused.[7] For example, when we consider the ''drug crisis'' of the late 1960's, we observe that the conflicts centered around different life-styles and values evident in younger groups, in contrast to the more traditional styles of older, middle-class members of the society. The stereotype of the drug subculture evokes the image of the unshaven hippie whose overall life-style is the antithesis of the middle-class work ethic. Although the drug problem was acknowledged as a serious medical problem prior to World War II, it was the defiance of the middle-class norms and values by large numbers of persons which caused it to be redefined as a social problem.

Most urban crime is directed toward the property—robbery, vandalism, auto theft, etc. Although crimes against property cause a great deal of economic distress, only infrequently do they result in physical injury. Yet urban crime is typically perceived in terms of violence—mugging, rape, murder. Urban crimes, in the popular view, stand for an alien way of life. Not only should urban criminals be punished, the theory says, but they must be rehabilitated in a manner in which their values are restructured. They must be brought into the mainstream of society. By punishing criminals, we also affirm our own values, symbolically indicating the evil of alien values and life-styles. Although criminologists generally acknowledge that the death penalty as punishment, for example, has little impact in deterring others from committing murder, the punishment may have a great impact upon society itself. By affirming the fact that justice has been done and that right has triumphed, society reunites itself symbolically in fighting the forces of evil. Thus, in affirming punishment, society goes through a ritual whereby the demons are expiated; evil is driven off; the society collectively cleanses itself. In fact, while such efforts to alleviate social problems often have little impact upon the basic problems them-

---

[6]H. C. Bredemeier and J. Toby, *Social Problems in America* (New York: Wiley, 1960), pp. 145–146.

[7]Irving Tallman and Reece McGee, ''Definition of a Social Problem,'' in Erwin O. Smigel, ed., *Handbook on the Study of Social Problems* (Chicago: Rand McNally and Company, 1971), p. 42.

selves (witness the War on Poverty), the fact that something is being done about a problem often helps to resolve the social conflicts which cloud in the perception of the issue. The combination of collectively perceiving a problem and collectively doing something about it are important social processes which help to maintain the structure and function of the society. In the last ten years, the United States government has focused upon several urban social problems. Large-scale funding has been aimed at poverty and crime. While few of the programs appear to have had a significant impact, the process of confronting problems has united many urbanites in a common political and social process. People have learned methods by which they can cope with problems in the future. Whether these methods of community organization will actually have an impact upon the urban crime rate remains an unanswered question.

The Extent of Urban Crime

Clearly more crimes are committed in urban areas than in rural or suburban areas in the United States. Both crimes against property and crimes against persons have been concentrated in urban areas. Although this pattern reflects itself year after year, the general relationship between crime and urbanization as a process is more complex. There is some evidence to indicate the amount of crime in urban areas peaks during times of rapid growth and development. Ferdinand (1967), in his work on Boston found that the arrest reports for seven major crimes examined between 1849 and 1951 showed a continual decrease.[8] Murder, manslaughter, forcible rape, robbery, assault, burglary, and larceny each revealed a distinct downward tendency. Robbery and burglary, in contrast, seem to peak during war and severe depressions. Only forcible rape showed a continual increase over the one hundred year period that Ferdinand studied. Possibly, changes in attitudes toward sexuality and the status of women had more impact on this crime than has had urbanization. Ferdinand traces the decline in overall crime to the assimilation of the recently migrated Irish and Italians into the overall population, the development of an expanding and stable middle class, and a gradual rise in the overall quality of life. These changes in urban crime may reflect social stress and social disorganization during times of rapid urbanization. Supporting this contention, a study by Lodhi and Tilly (1973) showed a similar trend in France.[9] Crimes against property between 1831 and 1931 decreased steadily; in contrast, crimes against persons revealed almost no change within the one hundred year period. In summary, crime is universally higher in urban areas than in rural areas; urban crimes appear to peak during periods of rapid industrialization and urbanization and to stabilize somewhat as the social structure of the society adapts to these new conditions.

[8]Thomas N. Ferdinand, "The Criminal Patterns of Boston Since 1849," *American Journal of Sociology*, 73 (July 1967).

[9]A. Q. Lodhi and Charles Tilly, "Urbanization Crime, and Collective Violence in France," *American Journal of Sociology*, 79 (Sept., 1973).

Recent Crime Trends in the United States

The most frequently cited source of crime information in the United States is the *Uniform Crime Report* issued by the Federal Bureau of Investigation.[10] Published annually, this series is based upon data reported by the police throughout the United States. During the last twenty years, the FBI has reported a continuous increase in both the number of crimes and the crime rate (based on the number of crimes per 100,000 population). The FBI also computes a crime index, based upon seven serious crimes—murder, non-negligent manslaughter, forcible rape, robbery, aggravated assault, burglary, larceny of $50 and over, and auto theft. Urban crime rates for the most recent periods are shown in Table 11.1. For four of the last five years, both the total crime index and each of the individual crimes have increased substantially in the United States. It is important to emphasize, however, that the majority of crimes goes unreported. Surveys show far more persons report being victimized by crimes than the FBI Uniform Crime Report reveals. The important unanswered question here is whether crimes known to the police and the FBI are increasing at the same rate as crimes which are not reported. Most evidence suggests that in urban areas crime continues to increase.

The Extent of Unreported Crime[11]

Although the police statistics indicate a lot of crime today, they do not begin to indicate the full amount. Crimes reported directly to prosecutors usually do not show up in the police statistics. Citizens often do not report crimes to the police. Some crimes reported to the police never get into the statistical system. Since better crime prevention and control programs depend upon a full and accurate knowledge about the amount and kinds of crime, the President's Commission on Law Enforcement and Administration of Justice (1967) initiated the first national survey ever made of crime victimization. The National Opinion Research Center of the University of Chicago surveyed 10,000 households, asking whether the person questioned, or any member of his or her household, had been a victim of crime during the past year, whether the crime had been reported and, if not, the reasons for not reporting.

More detailed surveys were undertaken in a number of high and medium crime-rate precincts of Washington, Chicago, and Boston by the Bureau of Social Science Research of Washington, D.C., and the Survey Research Center of the University of Michigan. All of the surveys dealt primarily with households or individuals, although some data were obtained for certain kinds of businesses and other organizations.

---

[10]*Crime in the United States: Uniform Crime Reports* (Washington, D.C.: Federal Bureau of Investigation, U.S. Department of Justice, 1973).

[11]Adapted from *The Challenge of Crime in a Free Society: A Report by the President's Commission on Law Enforcement and Administration of Justice* (Washington, D.C.: U.S. Government Printing Office, 1967), pp. 20–25.

Table 11.1 *Uniform Crime Reports (Source: Uniform Crime Reports, March 30, 1977. Issued by Clarence M. Kelley, Director, Federal Bureau of Investigation, United States Department of Justice, Washington, D.C. 20535, Advisory: Committee on Uniform Crime Records, International Association of Chiefs of Police) (1976 Preliminary Annual Release)*

The volume of Crime Index offenses reported to law enforcement agencies during 1976 showed no change when compared to 1975. The only Crime Index offense showing an increase was larceny-theft, with an increase of 5 percent.

Reported violent crime decreased 5 percent, with murder and robbery each down 10 percent and aggravated assault down 1 percent. Forcible rape showed no change. Property crimes increased 1 percent, with larceny-theft up 5 percent. Burglary decreased 5 percent and motor vehicle theft decreased 6 percent.

Crime in the Northeastern States increased 5 percent, with the Western States up 1 percent. Crime in the North Central States decreased 3 percent and the Southern States 1 percent.

As each quarter is viewed individually, January–March and April–June each experienced a 3 percent increase in reported crime. The three month period of July–September experienced an increase of less than 1 percent, while October–December decreased 6 percent.

Crime Index Trends (Percent change 1976 over 1975, offenses known to the police)

Population Group and Area	Number of Agencies	Population in Thousands	Total	Violent	Property	Murder	Forcible Rape	Robbery	Aggravated Assault	Burglary	Larceny-theft	Motor Vehicle Theft
Total all agencies	9,271	192,392	—	− 5	+ 1	−10	—	−10	− 1	− 5	+ 5	− 6
Cities over 25,000	998	95,813	—	− 6	+ 1	−10	− 1	− 9	− 1	− 5	+ 5	− 8
Suburban area	4,015	68,070	—	− 3	—	−12	+ 3	−12	+ 1	− 6	+ 4	− 5
Rural area	1,743	24,763	+ 1	− 5	+ 1	−10	+ 3	−16	− 3	− 4	+ 5	+ 3
Over 1,000,000	6	17,990	+ 3	− 3	+ 5	− 4	− 7	− 4	− 2	—	+10	− 3
50,000 to 1,000,000	20	12,943	− 3	−10	− 2	−14	− 2	−15	− 2	− 6	+ 2	−10
250,000 to 500,000	32	11,275	− 1	− 6	—	−17	+ 5	−13	+ 1	− 7	+ 6	− 8
100,000 to 250,000	109	15,726	− 1	− 8	− 1	− 9	+ 1	−14	− 4	− 7	+ 4	−11

			Total	Violent	Property	Murder	Forcible Rape	Robbery	Aggravated Assault	Burglary	Larceny-theft	Motor Vehicle Theft
50,000 to 100,000	263	18,188	—	−6	−8	−13	+2	−14	−1	−6	+4	−6
25,000 to 50,000	568	19,690	+1	−5	−10	−8	+3	−10	+4	−5	+5	−6
10,000 to 25,000	1,395	21,902	+2	−4	−13	−8	+4	−12	—	−4	+5	−3
Under 10,000	4,653	18,107	+2	−6	−5	−13	+4	−13	+2	−6	+6	+2

Crime Index Trends by Geographic Region (Percent change 1976 over 1975)

Region	Total	Violent	Property	Murder	Forcible Rape	Robbery	Aggravated Assault	Burglary	Larceny-theft	Motor Vehicle Theft
Northeastern States	+5	−2	+6	−8	−4	−4	—	+1	+12	−6
North Central States	−3	−10	−3	−10	−4	−16	−3	−10	+1	−7
Southern States	−1	−8	−1	−13	+2	−17	−3	−9	+5	−12
Western States	+1	+2	+1	−5	+5	−2	+5	−2	+3	—

Crime Index Trends (Percent change 1969–1976, each year over previous year)

Years	Total	Violent	Property	Murder	Forcible Rape	Robbery	Aggravated Assault	Burglary	Larceny-theft	Motor Vehicle Theft
1970/1969	+9	+12	+9	+8	+2	+17	+8	+11	+9	+6
1971/1970	+6	+11	+6	+11	+11	+11	+10	+9	+5	+2
1972/1971	−4	+2	−5	+5	+11	−3	+7	−1	−6	−6
1973/1972	+6	+5	+6	+5	+10	+2	+7	+8	+5	+5
1974/1973	+18	+11	+18	+5	+8	+15	+8	+18	+21	+5
1975/1974	+10	+5	+10	−1	+1	+5	+6	+7	+14	+2
1976/1975	—	−5	+1	−10	—	−10	−1	−5	+5	−6

Table 11.2   *Comparison of Survey and UCR Rates (per 100,000 population)*

Index Crimes	NORC Survey 1965–66	UCR Rate for Individuals 1965*	UCR Rate for Individuals and Organizations 1965*
Willful homicide	3.0	5.1	5.1
Forcible rape	42.5	11.6	11.6
Robbery	94.0	61.4	61.4
Aggravated assault	218.3	106.6	106.6
Burglary	949.1	299.6	605.3
Larceny ($50 and over)	606.5	267.4	393.3
Motor vehicle theft	206.2	226.0	251.0
Total violence	357.8	184.7	184.7
Total property	1,761.8	793.0	1,249.6

*"Uniform Crime Reports," 1965, page 51. The UCR national totals do not distinguish crimes committed against individuals or households from those committed against businesses or other organizations. The UCR rate for individuals is the published national rate adjusted to eliminate burglaries, larcenies, and vehicle thefts not committed against individuals or households. No adjustment was made for robbery.

These surveys show that the actual amount of crime in the United States today is several times that reported in the UCR. As Table 11.2 shows, the amount of personal injury crime reported to NORC is almost twice the UCR rate and the amount of property crime more than twice as much as the UCR rate for individuals. Forcible rapes were more than 3½ times the reported rate, burglaries three times, aggravated assaults and larcenies of $50 and over more than double, and robbery 50 percent greater than the reported rate. Only vehicle theft was lower, and that by a small amount. (The single homicide reported is too small a number to be statistically useful.)

Even these rates probably understate the actual amounts of crime. The national survey was a survey of the victim experience of every member of a household based on interviews of one member. If the results are tabulated only for the family member who was interviewed, the amount of unreported victimization for some offenses is considerably higher. Apparently, the person interviewed remembered more of his own victimization than that of other members of his family.

The Washington, Boston, and Chicago surveys, based solely on victimization of the person interviewed, show even more clearly the disparity between reported and unreported amounts of crime. The clearest case is that of the survey in three Washington precincts, where, for the purpose of comparing survey results with crimes reported to the police, previous special studies made it possible to eliminate from police statistics crimes involving business and transient victims. As the following figure indicates, for certain specific offenses against individuals, the number of

Estimated Rates of Offense[1]
Comparison of Police[2] and BSSR Survey Data

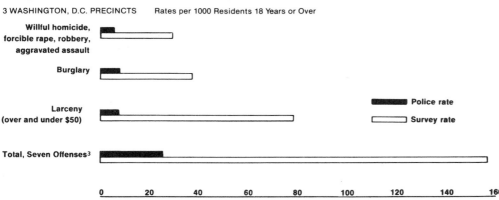

Figure 11.1

[1]Incidents involving more than one victim adjusted to count as only one offense. A victimization rate would count the incidence for each individual.

[2]Police statistics adjusted to eliminate nonresident and commercial victims and victims under 18 years of age.

[3]Willful homicide, forcible rape, robbery, aggravated assault, burglary, larceny (over and under $50), and motor vehicle theft.

offenses reported to the survey per thousand residents 18 years or over ranged, depending on the offense, from 3 to 10 times more than the number contained in police statistics.

The survey in Boston and in one of the Chicago precincts indicated about three times as many crimes as the police statistics, in the other Chicago precinct about 1½ as many. These survey rates are not fully comparable with the Washington results because adequate information did not exist for eliminating business and transient victims from the police statistics. If this computation could have been made, the Boston and Chicago figures would undoubtedly have shown a closer similarity to the Washington findings.

In the national survey of households, those victims saying that they had not notified the police of their victimization were asked why. The reason most frequently given for all offenses was that the police could not do anything. As Table 11.3 shows, this reason was given by 68 percent of those not reporting malicious mischief, and by 60 or more percent of those not reporting burglaries, larcenies of $50 and over, and auto thefts. It is not clear whether these responses are accurate assessments of the victims' inability to help the police or merely rationalizations of their failure to report. The next most frequent reason was that the offense was a private matter or that the victim did not want to harm the offender. It was given by 50 percent or more of those who did not notify the police for aggravated and simple assaults, family crimes, and consumer frauds. Fear of reprisal, though least often cited, was strongest in the case of assaults and family crimes. The extent of failure

Table 11.3 *Victims' Most Important Reason for Not Notifying Police* (In Percentages)*

Crimes	Percent of Cases in Which Police Not Notified	Reasons for Not Notifying Police				
		Felt it Was Private Matter or Did Not Want To Harm Offender	Police Could Not be Effective or Would Not Want To Be Bothered	Did Not Want to Take Time	Too Confused or did Not Know How To Report	Fear of Reprisal
Robbery	35	27	45	9	18	0
Aggravated assault	35	50	25	4	8	13
Simple assault	54	50	35	4	4	7
Burglary	42	30	63	4	2	2
Larceny ($50 and over)	40	23	62	7	7	0
Larceny (under $50)	63	31	58	7	3	(*)
Auto theft	11	20[2]	60[2]	0[2]	0[2]	20[2]
Malicious mischief	62	23	68	5	2	2
Consumer fraud	90	50	40	0	10	0
Other fraud (bad checks, swindling, etc.)	74	41	35	16	8	0
Sex offenses (other than forcible rape)	49	40	50	0	5	5
Family crimes (desertion, non-support, etc.)	50	65	17	10	0	7

SOURCE: NORC survey

*Less than 0.5%

[1]Willful homicide, forcible rape, and a few other crimes had too few cases to be statistically useful, and they are therefore excluded.

[2]There were only 5 instances in which auto theft was not reported.

to report to the police was highest for consumer fraud (90 percent) and lowest for auto theft (11 percent).

The survey technique, as applied to criminal victimization, is still new and beset with a number of methodological problems. However, the Commission has found the information provided by the surveys of considerable value, and believes that the survey technique has a great untapped potential as a method for providing additional information about the nature and extent of our crime problem and the relative effectiveness of different programs to control crime.

Trends in Crime

Trends in Crime.   There has always been too much crime. Virtually every generation since the founding of the nation and before has felt itself threatened by the spectre of rising crime and violence.

A hundred years ago, contemporary accounts of San Francisco told of extensive areas where "no decent man was in safety to walk the street after dark; while at all hours, both night and day, his property was jeopardized by incendiarism and burglary." Teenage gangs gave rise to the word "hoodlum;" while in one New York City area near Broadway, the police entered "only in pairs, and never unarmed." A noted chronicler of the period declared that "municipal law is a failure. . . . we must soon fall back on the law of self-preservation." "Alarming" increases in robbery and violent crimes were reported throughout the country prior to the revolution. And in 1910, one author declared that "crime, especially its more violent forms, and among the young is increasing steadily and is threatening to bankrupt the Nation."

Crime and violence in the past took many forms. During the great Railway Strike of 1877, hundreds were killed across the country and almost two miles of railroad cars and buildings were burned in clashes between Pittsburgh strikers and company police and the militia. It was nearly a half century later, after pitched battles in the steel industry in the late thirties, that the nation's long history of labor violence subsided. The looting and takeover of New York for three days by mobs in the 1863 draft riots rivaled the violence of Watts, while racial disturbances in Atlanta in 1907, in Chicago, Washington, and East St. Louis in 1919, Detroit in 1943 and New York in 1900, 1935, and 1943 marred big city life in the first half of the twentieth century. Lynchings took the lives of more than 4,500 persons throughout the country between 1882 and 1930. And the violence of Al Capone and Jesse James was so striking that they have left their marks permanently on our understanding of the eras in which they lived.

The fact that there has always been a lot of crime, however, does not mean that the amount of crime never changes. It changes constantly, day and night, month to month, place to place. It is essential that society be able to tell when changes occur and what they are, that it be able to distinguish normal ups and downs from long-term trends. Whether the amount of crime is increasing or decreasing, and by how much, is an important question—for law enforcement, for the individual citizen who must run the risk of crime, and for the official who must plan and establish prevention and control programs. If it is true, as the Commission surveys tend to indicate, that society has not yet found fully reliable methods for measuring the volume of crime, it is even more true that it has failed to find such methods for measuring the trend of crime.

Unlike some European countries, which have maintained national statistics for more than a century and a quarter, the United States has maintained national crime statistics only since 1930. Because the rural areas were slow in coming into the system and reported poorly when they did, it was not until 1958, when other major changes were made in the UCR, that reporting of rural crimes was sufficient to allow a total national estimate without special adjustments. Changes in overall estimating procedures and two offense categories—rape and larceny—were also made in 1958. Because of these problems, figures prior to 1958 and particularly those prior to 1940, must be viewed as neither fully comparable with nor nearly so reliable as later figures.

For crimes of violence the 1933–1965 period, based on newly adjusted unpub-

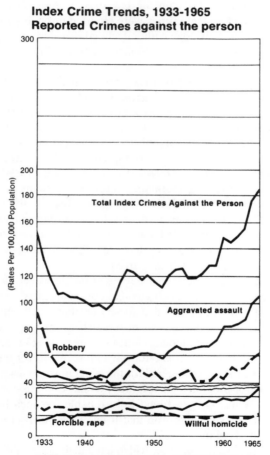

Index Crime Trends, 1933-1965
Reported Crimes against the person

NOTE: Scale for willful homicide and forcible rape en-
larged to show trend.
Source: FBI, Uniform Crime Reports Section; unpublished
data.

Figure 11.2

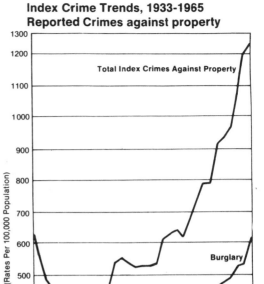

Index Crime Trends, 1933-1965
Reported Crimes against property

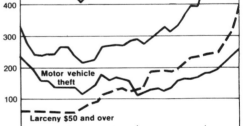

Figure 11.3

NOTE: The scale for this figure is not comparable with that used in Figure 3.

Source: FBI, Uniform Crime Reports Section; unpublished data.

lished figures from the UCR, has been, as Figure 11.2 shows, one of sharply divergent trends for the different offenses. Total numbers for all reported offenses have increased markedly. The nation's population has increased also—by more than 47 percent since 1940. The number of offenses per 100,000 population has tripled for forcible rape and has doubled for aggravated assault during the period, both increasing at a fairly constant pace. The willful homicide rate has decreased somewhat to about 70 percent of its high in 1933, while robbery has fluctuated from a high in 1933 and a low during World War II to a point where it is now about 20 percent above the beginning of the post-war era. The overall rate for violent crimes, primarily due to the increased rate for aggravated assault, now stands at its highest point, well above what it has been throughout most of the period.

Property crime rates, as shown in Figure 11.3, are up much more sharply than the crimes of violence. The rate for larceny of $50 and over has shown the greatest increase of all Index offenses. It is up more than 550 percent over 1933. The burglary rate has nearly doubled. The rate for auto theft has followed an uneven course to a point about the same as the rate of the early thirties.

The upward trend for 1960–1965 as shown in Table 11.4, has been faster than the long-term trend, up 25 percent for the violent crimes and 36 percent for the property crimes. The greatest increases in the period came in 1964, in forcible rape among crimes of violence and in vehicle theft among property crimes. Preliminary reports indicate that all Index offenses rose in 1966.

Arrest rates are in general much less complete and are available for many fewer years than are rates for offenses known to the police. They do, however, provide another measure of the trend of crime. For crimes of violence, arrest rates rose 16 percent during 1960–1965, considerably less than the 25 percent increase indicated by offenses known to the police. For property crimes, arrest rates have increased about 25 percent, as opposed to a 36 percent increase in offenses known to the police during 1960–1965. Figure 11.4 compares the 1960–1965 trend for arrests and offenses known for both crimes of violence and property crimes.

Prior to the year 1933, shown in Figures 11.2 and 11.3, there is no estimated national rate for any offenses. UCR figures for a sizable number of individual cities, however, indicate that the 1930–1932 rates, at least for those cities, were higher than the 1933 rates. Studies of such individual cities as Boston, Chicago, New York, and others indicate that in the twenties and the World War I years, reported rates for many offenses were even higher. A recent study of crime in Buffalo, New York from 1854 to 1946 showed arrest rates in that city for willful homicide, rape,

Table 11.4 *Offenses Known to the Police, 1960–1965 (Rates per 100,000 Population)*

Offense	1960	1961	1962	1963	1964	1965
Willful homicide	5.0	4.7	4.5	4.5	4.8	5.1
Forcible rape	9.2	9.0	9.1	9.0	10.7	11.6
Robbery	51.6	50.0	51.1	53.0	58.4	61.4
Aggravated assault	82.5	82.2	84.9	88.6	101.8	106.6
Burglary	465.5	474.9	489.7	527.4	580.4	605.3
Larceny $50 and over	271.4	277.9	296.6	330.9	368.2	393.3
Motor vehicle theft	179.2	179.9	193.4	212.1	242.0	251.0
Total crimes against person	148.3	145.9	149.6	155.1	175.7	184.7
Total property crimes	916.1	932.7	979.7	1,070.4	1,190.6	1,249.6

SOURCE: FBI, Uniform Crime Reports Section, unpublished data.

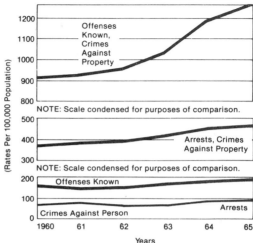

Figure 11.4   Source: FBI, Uniform Crime Reports Section; unpublished data.

and assault, reaching their highest peak in the early 1870's, declining, rising again until 1918, and declining into the forties.

Trends for crimes against trust, vice crimes, and crimes against public order, based on arrest rates for 1960–1965, follow a much more checkered pattern than do trends for Index offenses. For some offenses this is in part due to the fact that arrest patterns change significantly from time to time, as when New York recently decided not to make further arrests for public drunkenness. Based on comparable places covering about half the total population, arrest rates during 1960–1965 rose 13 percent for simple assault, 13 percent for embezzlement and fraud, and 36 percent for narcotics violations, while for the same period, the rates declined 24 percent for gambling and 11 percent for drunkenness.

The picture portrayed by the official statistics in recent years, both in the total number of crimes and in the number of crimes per 100,000 Americans, is one of increasing crime. Crime always seems to be increasing, never going down. It may be up 5 percent this year, 10 the next, and the Commission's surveys have shown there is a great deal more crime than the official statistics show. The public can fairly wonder whether there is ever to be an end.

This official picture is also alarming because it seems so pervasive. Crimes of violence are up in both the biggest and smallest cities, in the suburbs as well as in the rural areas. The same is true for property crimes. Young people are being arrested in ever-increasing numbers. Offense rates for most crimes are rising every year and in every section of the country. That there are some bright spots does not change this dismal outlook. Rates for some offenses are still below those of the early thirties and perhaps of earlier periods. Willful homicide rates have been below the 1960 level throughout most of the last few years. Robbery rates continue to decline in the rural areas and small towns, and arrest rates for many non-Index offenses have remained relatively stable.

Because the general picture is so disturbing and the questions it raises go to the very heart of concern about crime in the United States today, the Commission has made a special effort to evaluate as fully as possible the information available. It has tried to determine just how far this picture is accurate, to see whether our cities and our countryside are more dangerous than they were before, to find out whether our youth and our citizens are becoming more crime-prone than those who were in their same circumstances in earlier years, to see what lies behind any increases that may have occurred, and to determine what if anything this information tells us can be done to bring the crime rate down.

What is known about the trend of crime—in the total number of offenses, the ratio of offenses to population, and the relationship of crime trends to changes in the composition of the population—is almost wholly a product of statistics. Therefore the Commission has taken a particularly hard look at the current sources of statistical knowledge.

The cause of the increase in crime in urban areas varies, depending upon the type of crime which we are considering. We must constantly remember that most murders are committed by relatives or friends. Theories of societal alienation and anomie do not appear to be adequate causal models for crimes of passion. Individual stresses and family pathologies appear to be far more helpful in explaining the increase in the murder rate than do theories of relative deprivation. Another crime which has shown a considerable increase over the years is auto theft. But we must also remember that auto theft rates are developed in terms of the number of persons in the population rather than the number of vehicles. Thus, the auto theft rate may reflect the opportunity to steal, rather than any deep, underlying social stress.

The number of police in American urban areas has also increased substantially. The implication here is that if more are on the street to apprehend criminals, then crimes known to the police may increase, thereby increasing the crime rate. Another possible explanation for an increase in the crime-rate is that people are now more prone to report crimes than they were during previous eras. In the days before the telephone, it was a major task to report a crime. With the advent of radio cars and central data processing, crimes are far more likely to be reflected in statistics than previously.

Irrespective of changing communications technology, or reporting systems which may cause a "paper" increase in the crime rate in urban areas (see Table 11.5), certain factors remain prominent. Murder has increased dramatically over the

Table 11.5   *Reporting System Changes UCR Index Figures Not Comparable with Prior Years*

Name of City	Years of Increase	Amount of Increase (Index Offenses)		
		From	To	Percent Increase
Baltimore	1964–65	18,637	26,193	40.5
Buffalo	1961–63	4,779	9,305	94.7
Chicago....................	1959–60	56,570	97,253	71.9
Cleveland	1963–64	10,584	17,254	63.0
Indianapolis	1961–62	7,416	10,926	47.3
Kansas City, Mo............	1959–61[1]	4,344	13,121	202.0
Memphis	1963–64	8,781	11,533	31.3
Miami	1963–64	10,750	13,610	26.6
Nashville...................	1962–63	6,595	9,343	41.7
Shreveport	1962–63	1,898	2,784	46.7
Syracuse	1963–64	3,365	4,527	34.5

[1]No report was published for Kansas City, Mo., for 1960.
SOURCE: "Uniform Crime Reports," 1959–1965.

last twenty years; murder is a crime which is almost invariably reported. Reported insurance claims in urban areas have risen dramatically, affirming the fact that property crimes are really on the rise. As a totality, these crime indicators corroborate each other, affirming the fact that urban crime indeed has risen dramatically during the last twenty years. But the FBI Uniform Crime Report, in emphasizing the phenomenon, gives little insight into the causes of crime. The FBI assesses crime from the perspective of the law enforcement officer. The policeman is seen both as a deterrent to crime and corrective agent once the crime has taken place. Few other solutions are offered. Criminological theory, however, offers a series of causal models which explain the genesis of urban crime; but it, too, offers little in terms of a tested model of prevention or correction.

Sociological Explanations of Urban Crime

In sociological theory, historically there are two major methodological approaches to crime—*structural-functionalism* and *social ecology*.[12] Structural-functional theories assume that deviant behavior may be traced to the social system or social environment in which people live. Stresses within social systems may result in situations which cause people to play a deviant social role. Sometimes, an entire

[12]Tallman and McGee, *Handbook,* p. 33.

deviant subculture may develop which allows people to pursue a life-style in conflict with the dominant middle-class culture. Social ecology, in contrast, usually attempts to explain deviance in terms of a more general relationship of people and their environment. There are many other explanations of urban crime, most notably psychological orientations based upon Freudian psychology, but the two former approaches have been most characteristic of urban criminology.

Structural Functional Approaches

Exploring the history of social thought, one generally discovers that Durkheim, in his classic work on suicide (1897), was instrumental in documenting the effect of social structure upon deviant behavior.[13] Showing that those political subdivisions in Europer which had the highest rate of suicide were the least integrated socially, Durkheim argued that the differences in suicide rates were dependent upon integration of the social structure within ecological areas. In certain areas, it was more difficult for people to relate to each other and to become integrated into the community. When the social structure and social process were blurred or in a state of rapid change, people often lived in a state of normlessness or anomie. According to Durkheim's conceptualization, the anomic person is detached, lives in a state of social limbo which, taken to an extreme, may result in suicide or other socially deviant acts. Anomie has been causally linked with delinquency, mental disorder, drug addiction, and alcoholism.[14]

Anomie, in contemporary sociology, is generally viewed as a form of alienation whereby people are cut off from the mainstream of society. Building upon Durkheim's tradition, Louis Wirth (1938) described the breakdown of primary relationships in the city:

> ... the superficiality, the anonymity and the transitory character of urban social relations make intelligible... the sophistication and the rationality generally ascribed to city-dwellers. Our acquaintances tend to stand in a relationship of utility to us, in the sense that the role which each one plays in our life is overwhelmingly regarded as a means for the achievement of our own ends. Whereas the individual gains, on the one hand a certain degree of emancipation of freedom from the personal and emotional controls of intimate groups, he loses on the other hand the spontaneous self-expression, the morale, and the sense of participation that comes with living in an integrated society. This constitutes essentially a state of *anomie,* or the social void to which Durkheim alludes in attempting to account for the various forms of social disorganization in technological society. The segmental character and utilitarian accent of interpersonal relations in the city find their institutional expression in the proliferation of specialized tasks which we see in the most developed form of the profession.[15]

[13]Emile Durkheim, *Suicide,* George Simpson, Trans. (New York: Free Press, 1951).
[14]Marshall B. Clinard, ed., *Anomie and Deviant Behavior* (New York: Free Press, 1964).
[15]Louis Wirth, "Urbanism as a Way of Life," in *Urbanism in World Perspective: A Reader,* Sylvia Fava, ed. (New York: Thomas Y. Crowell Company, 1968), p. 53.

Thus, the anomic lifestyle was brought about, according to Wirth, not only by this heterogeneity (in the sense of people being drawn from many cultural traditions), but also by the size and density of an urban settlement. When a large number of people act and view each other as objects, it is relatively easy to make the logical leap to the explanation of deviance and crime in an urban society. Following Wirth and his colleagues at the University of Chicago during the 1920's and 1930's, a large body of literature evolved based upon the structural functional theories of Durkheim and his successors.

Social Ecological Theories

Ecological theories are based upon the notion of conflict and competition within a society. Because land use patterns are determined by the economic forces of the market, certain people are relegated to different areas of the city—for work, for play, and for recreation. Overall life-styles reflect this competition for life space. Social problems are usually concentrated in areas where most of the people reside who have lost out in this competition. Although overall land costs may be high in center city (the same areas where the problems are concentrated), large numbers of persons drawn from lower social strata still reside here because these are the only places where they can find housing. The most severe problems are found in a ring or area near the center of the city or surrounding the center which is known as the *zone in transition*. More extensive review of ecological theories of deviance is found in the chapter on urban ecology.

Subcultural Theories of Urban Crime

Studies of crime are usually conducted in urban areas. Approximately five times more crimes are reported in standard metropolitan areas than in smaller cities and rural areas.[16] Most studies of crime, however, have not identified precisely what characteristics of urban areas cause the crime rate to be so much higher there than in other areas. The tendency is to assume urbanization as a constant factor—to assume that there is something inherent in the urban environment (in contrast to its rural counterpart) which causes crime. Most recent explanations of crime derive from a series of subcultures which have been identified in urban areas. Although criminal subcultures also exist in rural areas, they have received far less attention from criminologists.

In American criminology, most subcultural theories are traced to the work of Edwin H. Sutherland.[17] Known as *differential association theory,* Sutherland's work rests on a number of principles and/or assumptions. First, criminal behavior is

---

[16]*Crime in the United States: Uniform Crime Reports* (Washington, D.C.: F.B.I., U.S. Department of Justice, 1975).

[17]E. H. Sutherland and D. R. Cressey, *Criminology* (Philadelphia: J. B. Lippincott Company, 1970).

learned. Second, it is learned in interaction with persons through a process of communication. Third, the learning of criminal behavior occurs within intimate social groups. Fourth, when criminal behavior is learned, the lessons include: techniques of committing the crimes and the specific direction of the motives, drives, rationalizations and attitudes. The specific direction of motives is learned from definitions of legal codes, favorable and unfavorable. A person becomes delinquent because of an excess of definitions favorable to the violation of law as compared to definitions unfavorable to violation of law. Differential associations may vary in frequency, duration, priority, and intensity. The process of learning criminal behavior by association with criminal and anticriminal patterns involves all of the mechanisms that are involved in any other kind of learning. Although criminal behavior is an expression of general needs and values, it is not explained by these general needs and values, since non-criminal behavior is an expression of the same needs and values.

In essence, Sutherland theorizes that criminal behavior is learned through a cultural transmission process. Although Sutherland's theory explains how criminal behavior is transmitted once it becomes implanted into a society, it does not explain the genesis of criminal behavior nor why criminal behavior appears to be more prevalent in urban areas than in rural areas.

Albert K. Cohen.   In his work *Delinquent Boys,* Cohen continues in Sutherland's tradition, tracing crime to a delinquent subculture.[18] The subcultural concept, as used here, holds that a group has the capacity of developing, transmitting, and perpetuating certain deviant values and norms (at least for a period of time) which cause delinquency to persist. According to Cohen, a delinquent subculture is characterized by behavior which is "non-utilitarian," "malicious," and "negativistic." By non-utilitarian, Cohen means that much of the behavior of delinquent gangs is irrational, in that it does not relate to a goal. Rather, delinquent behavior is a form of rebellion, or a kind of "reaction formation" against the middle-class norms of society. The behavior of delinquent boys is also "malicious," in that it results in a destruction of property or causes bodily harm. Finally, delinquent behavior is "negativistic" in that it challenges symbolically the values of middle-class society—particularly those which relate to the sanctity of property. To Cohen, gang behavior represents a striking out against a social order which is irrelevant and beyond the reach of boys in the delinquent subculture. Cohen's theory implies a kind of sour-grape mechanism, whereby youthful energies are vented against the establishment, particularly when other social controls and goals are not present which function to direct adolescent energy into more productive channels.

It should be emphasized that there is nothing in Cohen's theory which is explicitly urban. Implicitly, however, since Cohen suggests that there are large

[18]A. K. Cohen, *Delinquent Boys: The Culture of the Gang* (Glencoe, Illinois: The Free Press, 1955).

concentrations of lower-class youth in cities, there is a tendency for urban groups to gravitate to the delinquent subculture.

Cloward and Ohlin. Building a structural functional tradition, Cloward and Ohlin (1961) in their book, *Delinquency and Opportunity,* trace delinquency to dysfunctions in the urban social stratification system. Because of the inequities in the opportunity structure, some boys are prone to delinquent adaptations, as suggested by Merton.[19] Building on Merton's theory, Cloward and Ohlin suggest that the middle-class success goals of American society are often a source of frustration for youths living in deprived urban environments. Because of the absence of legal opportunity to attain middle-class success, young men often turn to illegal means or retreat into a drug subculture, where they may find a respite from the reality of their hopeless position. This frustration arises because of the discrepancy between internalized American success goals and the means which are available for achieving such goals. According to Cloward and Ohlin, blocked goals may result in three kinds of delinquent adaptations or subcultures, all of which are prevalent in slum areas of large cities.[20] The three subcultures which Cloward and Ohlin describe are the *criminal,* the *conflict,* and the *retreatist,* each of which is found in a different type of urban neighborhood.

The Conflict Subculture. This group thrives in the highly transient neighborhood—one in which there is a great deal of residential instability—rapid migration both in and out. This neighborhood appears to be the classic "disorganized neighborhood" in which anomie is the dominant orientation. In this type of neighborhood, people are deprived of both the conventional and criminal opportunities to achieve success. Social controls, in the form of parental guidance and other authority, are quite weak, resulting in a volatile atmosphere. Youth residing in these areas are prone to violence—street fighting, gang wars, and generally disruptive behavior. In essence, adolescents in these disorganized areas turn to violence and physical competition in search of status within their limited social sphere.

The Retreatist Subculture. This pattern, in contrast, is found in a neighborhood where the youth have turned to both drugs and alcohol. Retreatism, in this instance, is the result of the rejection of both the cultural goals and the institutionalized means of achieving these goals. Retreatist youths are a double failure. They have rejected both the goals of the middle class and the means of achieving these goals. In their definition of retreatism, Cloward and Ohlin stated:

> Retreatism arises from continued failure to near the goal by legitimate means and from inability to use the illegitimate route because of internalized prohibitions, this process occurring while the supreme value of the success goal has not yet been renounced. The conflict is resolved by abandoning both precipitating elements, the goals and the norms. Escape is complete, the conflict is eliminated and the individual is asocialized.[21]

[19]Merton, *Social Theory,* 1957.
[20]R. A. Cloward and L. E. Ohlin, *Delinquency and Opportunity: A Theory of Delinquent Gangs* (New York: The Free Press, 1955), p. 152.

Retreatist behavior occurs in neighborhoods where adolescents have grown out of gang-fighting, sports and other kinds of competitive activities. They have given up. Thus, the conflict subculture and the retreatist subculture may coexist in the same disorganized neighborhood. The principle difference between the two is that those who join the retreatist group are older and have given up street fighting and dropped out of competition.

The Criminal Subculture.   As portrayed by Cloward and Ohlin, this exists in the most organized type of inner city neighborhood, one in which organized crime plays a much more important part than in the disorganized neighborhoods described previously. Residing in this area are large numbers of people who have successfully entered into criminal careers—gambling, drugs, and loan sharking. In this area, too, are a large number of successful criminal role models, people who have "made it" in organized crime. Gradually, youths living here may transfer their reference group to more sophisticated boys who are experienced criminals or racketeers. In fact, a kind of apprenticeship system exists in organized crime neighborhoods, whereby boys must prove their worth, first by committing a large number of destructive acts, then entering into petty thefts, then becoming involved with "the organization"— helping with policy operations, selling drugs and engaging in other kinds of organized crime. The organized crime neighborhood, as described by Cloward and Ohlin, requires both residential stability and continuity in leadership in order to sustain its organization and social integration, even along these illegal lines.

Much of the literature and research dealing with urban crime focuses upon juvenile gang activity. Adult crime, although far more prevalent in urban than in rural areas, has been assumed to be the direct byproduct of an apprenticeship or experience in juvenile crime. The assumption is when once a juvenile is socialized into a delinquent subculture, there is a high probability of a subsequent entry into the world of adult crime. Most of the literature emphasizes that once an individual has come into contact with the corrections system that socialization into criminal behavior is even more accentuated. Overall, the emphasis in explaining crime is given to the early socialization processes, which, according to the theories, result in life-long encounters with the criminal justice system. This tendency (to view crime patterns as being "set" in childhood) is further stressed in the work dealing with pre-delinquents, such as that conducted by the Gluecks (1956), which suggests that pre-delinquent patterns can be recognized in children as early as seven years of age.[22] This theory emphasizes the inability of families to adequately socialize the child as the primary factor which causes youth to begin a lifelong pattern of contact with criminal justice and welfare agencies. Unfortunately, this research does not

[21]Cloward and Ohlin, *Delinquency,* 1960, p. 181.

[22]S. Glueck, "The Home, the School, and Delinquency," in S. and E. Glueck, *Ventures in Criminology: Selected Recent Papers* (London: Tavistock Publications, 1964); S. and E. Glueck, *Unraveling Juvenile Delinquency* (Cambridge, Mass.: Harvard University Press, 1950); S. and E. Glueck, *Family Environment and Delinquency* (Boston: Houghton Mifflin Company, 1962); S. and E. Glueck, *Toward a Typology of Juvenile Offenders: Implications for Therapy and Prevention* (New York: Grune and Stratton, Inc., 1970).

identify the factors, both personal and social, which cause the majority of individuals who grow up in urban poverty areas to remain law-abiding citizens throughout their lifetimes.

The Subculture of Violence

There are a large number of criminological theories dealing with lower-class subcultures. Wolfgang, in a recent book, suggests that there are many elements which are accentuated in the life-styles of inner city areas which predispose people toward violence.[23] The expectations regarding the world as a whole are such that it is seen as a violent place in which to live. Fighting, stabbings, shootings, and murders are seen as the inevitable outcome of the interplay of forces in everyday life, which are beyond the control of the individual. Men are socialized into a role where one's manhood must be constantly proved by aggressive behavior, an ethic which is known in the Latin subculture as *machismo*. As these expectations of violence are translated into reality, life in inner city slums becomes very dangerous. Violence, in short, is seen as a solution to problems and as a problem in itself. The popular stereotype of the inner city as a dangerous place is supported by a subcultural ethos which too often results in acting out behavior and is manifested in the high murder rates and high rates of aggravated assault in the inner city.

The Subculture of Poverty

One group of theorists suggests that a "culture of poverty" causes crime. The poverty culture manifests a set of values and norms which predispose persons toward certain types of crime.

In delinquency research, one theory states that a lower-class culture exists which has certain "focal concerns."[24] According to Miller, these concerns emphasize values and actions which are inherent in lower-class life. Prominent among these focal concerns are an emphasis upon "trouble," "toughness," "smartness," "excitement," "fate," and "autonomy." For men, "trouble" usually involves fighting or sexual adventures while drinking; for women, "trouble" involves sexual involvement with disadvantageous consequences.[25] Thus trouble, in terms of the culture of poverty ethos, is what life gets you into. Toughness, for men, involves physical prowess, skill, and masculinity, the opposite of which is weakness, femininity, and ineptness. Lower-class culture also places a deal of emphasis upon "smartness," which stresses the ability to outsmart, dupe, con, or gain money by one's wits, shrewdness, adroitness, and tricky repartee. The opposite of smartness

[23]M. E. Wolfgang and F. Ferracuti, *The Subculture of Violence: Towards an Integrated Theory in Criminology* (London: Tavistock Publications, 1967).

[24]W. B. Miller, "Lower Class Culture as a Generating Milieu of Gang Delinquency," *The Sociology of Crime and Delinquency,* Wolfgang, Savitz, and Johnston, eds., (New York: John Wiley and Sons, Inc., 1970), p. 353.

[25]*Ibid.,* p. 353.

is slowness, dull-wittedness, verbal maladroitness, or boredom. Also, there is a cultural emphasis upon "excitement," "thrills," "risks," "danger," and change, which is contrasted with "deadness," "safeness," "sameness," or "passivity." Most of the literature on lower-class cultures strongly emphasizes the notion of fate—that one is favored (or not favored) by fortune or being lucky, and that one has little control over life. This overall orientation results in an inability to defer gratification, to plan, to save, or results in behavior which leads a person to drift into other kinds of troubles. Finally, there is an emphasis upon autonomy—freedom from external constraint—the idea that a person should be independent. This orientation results in a challenge to any kind of recognized authority, particularly the police, and explains many of the conflicts which develop in the slum areas. It is not only the police, however, which are seen as authorities. Teachers, judges, bosses, and other functionaries who have political or business authority are also perceived of as a threat to autonomy.

Besides the attitudinal manifestations of the culture of poverty, Lewis (1966) stressed the lack of involvement in the basic institutions of the society—schools, government, industry, etc.[26] Members of the culture of poverty are "over-represented" in the regulatory and caretaker institutions of the society—police, courts, prisons, armed services, the welfare system, and in primary public education. According to Lewis, the family structure of the culture of poverty is unstable and disorganized, resulting in the absence of prolonged and protected childhood, early initiation into the sexual activities, free unions or consensual marriages, abandonment of wives and children, female-centered families, sibling rivalry, and competition for limited resources and maternal affection.

From a psychological perspective, the members of the culture of poverty are assumed by Lewis to possess a weak ego structure, confusion of sexual identification, lack of impulse control, little ability to defer gratification and to plan for the future, resignation and fatalism, belief in male superiority, tolerance for a psychological pathology, provincial and local orientation and very little use of history.[27]

The difficulty with Lewis' conceptualization of the culture of poverty relates to whether it is a culture or a subculture. That these conditions co-exist with poverty is undeniable. However, whether parents teach their children these ideas, whether these norms are passed from generation to generation as "values," seems highly questionable.[28] The main question is: Do people develop these kinds of characteristics after they become poor, while living among other poor people, or is there a self-perpetuating set of values and institutions which an anthropologist might call a culture?

[26]Oscar Lewis, *La Vida: A Puerto Rican Family in the Culture of Poverty: San Jaun and New York* (New York: Random House, 1966).

[27]*Ibid.*, pp. XLII–XLVIII.

[28]Charles A. Valentine, *Culture and Poverty: Critique and Counterproposals* (Chicago: University of Chicago Press, 1968), pp. 113–120.

The student of urban sociology should not forget that poverty is more prevalent in rural areas than in urban areas. It happens, however, that poverty is both more concentrated and more visible in urban slums than in rural areas, thereby drawing our attention. Probably, a culture of poverty, as such, does not exist. It is more likely that people who are poor make adaptations to their poverty and develop rationalizations about their values and norms by virtue of necessity.[29] But these values and life-styles are also reinforced by living among others who are poverty-stricken, particularly when people are concentrated in city ghettos.[30] When a poverty-stricken urban neighborhood is isolated, its norms and attitudes are reinforced by constant interaction among people in the same dilemma. The result may be an accentuation of attitudes which were originally somewhat blurred. These same pessimistic attitudes have effects on other kinds of social deviancy besides crime, such as mental illness, sexual deviancy, suicide, health practices, and attitudes toward education. Because these norms and life-styles are often in conflict with those of the middle class, they are frequently the focal point of social conflict. If lower-class behavior is at all threatening to the dominant social values of the dominant middle-class culture, then it is usually viewed as an appropriate target for external social control.

The Criminal Justice System and Social Control

The criminal justice system includes the police, the courts, and the prisons, both juvenile and adult. These traditional institutions have often been blamed for the urban crime problem. The crime problem, however, as identified by nation'wide opinion surveys focuses upon the "fear of crime," rather than the actual probability of becoming a victim.[31] Citizens of suburban and rural areas perceive the city and its environs as an area where bodily harm may be inflicted. The inner city, moreover, is perceived as an area of desperate persons who are bent upon murder, robbery, rape, and other acts which are beyond the mental purview of the majority of non-urban middle-class citizens. No doubt, this image has been accentuated by the fact that violent crimes make news, and that many middle-class citizens have fled the inner city to suburbs. The objective probability of becoming a victim of crime in urban areas, however, is relatively low. The incidence of crime in most city areas is comparable to that of suburban and rural areas. Thus, the perception of the urban crime problem seems to be mainly based upon unfounded fears. These fears have been accentuated by an increasing isolation into single-class suburban communities of most members of American society. That an urban crime problem exists is

---

[29]Hyman Rodman, "The Lower Class Value Stretch," *Social Forces* 42(1960), pp. 205–215.

[30]Robert A. Wilson, "Anomie in the Ghetto: A Study of Neighborhood Type, Race, and Anomie," *The American Journal of Sociology,* 77 (July 1971).

[31]L. Harris, *The Public Looks at Crime and Corrections* (Washington, D.C.: Joint Commission on Correctional Manpower and Training, 1968).

unquestionable. But the fears revealed through opinion polls appear to be unjustified.

As central metropolitan areas become less a part of the experience of most people living within the overall metropolitan complex, they gain the semblance of enemy territory, a strange land which is outside the orbit of most Americans. As this isolation increases, middle-class persons become less aware of the motivations and overall life-styles of people who live in cities. Consequently, they are perceived as outsiders, even as enemies, and as such, subject to social control rather than integration into the overall social system.[32]

Conclusion: Sociological Solutions to the Urban Crime Problem

By now, the reader should be aware that the authors believe there are at least two parts to the urban crime problem—the fear of crime and the consequences of crime. In the frontier society, which probably existed up until the early 1900's, criminality, even violence, was expected and often revered. Within a highly organized society, however, many of the old social patterns, particularly crimes against persons, present serious problems. We stress the fact that a "social problem" represents primarily a value conflict. Urban crime appears to reflect a value conflict, because many of the illegal actions of urban residents are actually justified, in terms of the social conditions under which the urban residents live. We also recognize some of these patterns as long-term or even permanent, in that they are traced to the socialization of individuals at a very early age. But we also recognize that in reacting to the urban crime problem, suburban residents have actually overstated the downtrodden position of people living in urban slums. Most Americans are aware of the fact that Scandinavia and England have very minor urban crime problems in comparison to those of the United States. However, most are also unaware of the resources which are employed in solving the educational, medical, and social problems of citizens in these other countries.

The cost of the long-term solution to the crime problem is too well known. It involves trade-offs between short-term social control and long-term elimination of the causes of crime. In other words, in the view of these authors, the ultimate solution to the urban crime problem is generally acknowledged, in that it involves the restructuring of both opportunities and constraints for citizens of inner cities. In some cases, the constraints may include the removal of children from families in situations where the prognosis for a law-abiding life is negative. This, of course, is a short-term control; the long-term solution is to bring the life-chances of all families up to a point where crime is an irrelevant alternative. Unfortunately, however, we rarely think in the long term. Pragmatically, Americans look at the realities of life within a short time span. Realistically, policies within the short time period relate more to systems of social control than to removal of the causes of social problems like crime.

[32]H. S. Becker, *Outsiders: Studies in the Sociology of Deviance* (Glencoe, Illinois: The Free Press, 1963).

chapter 12

Minority Groups

Urban sociologists have studied ethnicity and race mainly from the perspective of the segregation and concentration of certain ethnic groups in urban areas. As urbanization increases, many ethnic groups, such as blacks, Chicanos, and Puerto Ricans, have tended to become more segregated during the 1960's and 1970's. Although this pattern is a continuation of a long-term trend, evident even during the colonial era, many social problems and policies have centered around this ecological pattern during the last two decades. The inequalities which have been associated with concentrations of poverty have been magnified and made more visible as a result of the segregated neighborhoods which have proliferated in our cities. The ghetto riots of the 1960's and the continuing conflicts surrounding school busing have forced policy-makers to an awareness of the theories and issues which were formerly the province of the social scientist alone.

The United States is not alone in facing the social issues associated with race and segregation. With the decline of colonialism in Africa and in Latin America, the rigid caste systems which had been institutionalized over the centuries have almost disappeared within a few decades. In South Africa, where a large group of whites still retain political power, the pressures for revolutionary change are constantly brought to our attention. In Latin America and in Africa as well, large numbers of rural peoples continue to migrate to the primary cities. Many migrants are peasants who have been pushed off the land. Still others come voluntarily to the cities hoping to find work. The press of these masses of humanity has caused severe administrative problems in providing employment, education, health services, as well as basic municipal services associated with street development and maintenance, water supply, sewage disposal, police service, and fire protection. Social scientists have analyzed and proposed alternative urban policies and remedies, but the magnitude of the problems associated with large numbers of people migrating to cities in Latin America and Africa go beyond short-term economic and technical solutions.

This chapter addresses the following questions: (1) How do sociologists define the concept of minority group? (2) What are the forces which have given rise to a concentration of minority groups in urban areas? (3) What are the historical trends in American segregation patterns? (4) What is the relationship of ethnicity and certain kinds of inequalities and discrimination in urban area education, income, and housing? (5) What are the prospects for the future?

The Sociology of Ethnic Minorities

Minority Groups

Although most people can name a number of minority groups, based largely on their own operational definitions, sociologists and anthropologists have gone beyond naming in order to develop research and theory in this area. Generally, specialists in minority groups have settled on a definition based on five characteristics offered by Simpson and Yinger:[1]

(1) Minorities are subordinate segments of complex societies;
(2) Minorities have special physical or cultural traits which are held in low esteem by the dominant segments of the society;
(3) Minorities are self-conscious units bound together by the special traits which their members share and by the special disabilities which these bring;
(4) Membership in a minority is transmitted by a rule of descent, and is capable of affiliating succeeding generations even in the absence of readily apparent special cultural or physical traits;
(5) Minority peoples commonly, by choice or by necessity, marry within the group.

Probably the most complex form of social organization is an urban society within which persons having specific physical or cultural traits are not only held in low esteem, but many times set off in ghettos or in quarters restricting most of their movement. From a sociological perspective, minorities are a group in the sense that they are self-conscious about their minority status and therefore share a sense of disability or inequality which accentuates the group's solidarity. Our definition also notes that not all minority groups may be identified by physical characteristics, but are often self-sustaining through cultural or structural factors, which may cause the minority group to persist for generations. From a cultural perspective, this continuity is enhanced by the fact that minorities frequently marry only within the group, either by choice or necessity, thereby perpetuating and magnifying the qualities of the group.

---

[1]George E. Simpson and J. Milton Yinger, *Racial and Cultural Minorities* (New York: Harper and Row, 1965), pp. 18–19.

Drawing by Koren; © *1970 The New Yorker Magazine, Inc.*

The original typology proposed by Louis Wirth (1945) is based upon the ultimate objectives of minority group culture.[2] Wirth distinguishes four patterns.

First is pluralistic, a minority which generally expresses peaceful existence and cooperation. For the most part, pluralism is the norm rather than the exception in urban areas. Pluralism implies a tolerance of racial, cultural, linguistic or religious differences. This pattern usually prevails in areas where political and economic equality have been achieved or promised. In American cities, ethnic groups like the Irish and the Polish best represent the pluralistic concept.

Wirth's second pattern is assimilationist. In this instance, the minority desires absorption into the dominant society; when the majority accepts this concept, assimilation may occur even to the point where the minority group can no longer be identified. Assimilation has been most common among European minorities in the United States. However, many groups are often divided as to the desirability of pluralism or assimilation. A good example are the American Jews, who have lived in the United States for many generations. Although the first groups were likely to be assimilationist, more recent groups were likely to be pluralistic.

The third pattern is secessionist. A group which desires both cultural and political autonomy is secessionist. When pluralism or assimilation fails, some minorities develop a movement devoted to complete independence. Generally, such groups have experienced disenchantment with the notion of pluralism or assimilation. Probably the best example of a secessionist group is expressed by a Garveyite movement for a separate nation of blacks and more recently in the separatist ideology of the Black Muslims.

[2]Louis Wirth, "The Problem of Minority Groups," in Ralph Linton, ed., *The Science of Man in the World Crisis* (New York: Columbia University Press, 1945), pp. 354–363.

The last pattern is militant. Sometimes minority groups go beyond the desire for participation and equality to the extent that they wish to dominate other groups. Some groups became convinced of their own natural superiority. The Germans during World War II sought to dominate the Czechs and Slovaks; after Britain withdrew from Palestine, the Arabs and Jews attempted to establish dominance. Similarly, in the continuing conflict in Asia and Africa, various groups now attempt to reverse their previous minority status.

The American Dilemma

Probably the most important study of the minority status and the inequalities facing the American black was published in 1944.[3] In *An American Dilemma,* Gunnar Myrdal documented the plight of the American black in a white nation and studied the black social structure. In his introduction, Myrdal emphasized:

> The American Dilemma, referred to in the title of this book, is the ever-raging conflict between, on the one hand, the valuations preserved on the general plane which we shall call the American creed, where the American thinks, talks and acts under the influence of high national and Christian precepts, and, on the other hand, the valuations on specific planes of individual and group living, where personal and local interests; economic, social, and sexual jealousies; considerations of community prestige and conformity; group prejudices against particular persons or types of people; and also some miscellaneous wants, impulses, and habits dominate his outlook.[4]

Considering the social inequality in the black community, Myrdal documented the existence of a deliberate policy of discrimination and pointed out the viability of American blacks as a minority group. Myrdal's work helped to create an awareness and consensus of a need for action.

Later, during the 1940's and 1950's, American behavioral scientists focused upon the attitudinal manifestations of the white majority toward the black minority. Gordon Allport, in his seminal work, *The Nature of Prejudice* (1954) emphasized that prejudice was the primary force which propelled white America to discriminate against blacks and other minorities. Allport defined the word *prejudice* as evolving through three stages.[5] To the ancients, *praejudicium* meant a *precedent*—a judgement based on previous decisions and experiences. Later, the term in English acquired the meaning of a judgement formed before due examination and consideration of the facts—a premature or hasty opinion.

Finally, the term acquired its present emotional flavor of a favorableness or an unfavorableness that accompanies a prior, unsupported statement. Allport concluded that prejudice is an avertive or hostile attitude toward a person who belongs

---

[3]Gunnar Myrdal, *An American Dilemma* (New York: Harper and Row, 1944).
[4]*Ibid.,* p. LXXI.
[5]Gordon W. Allport, *The Nature of Prejudice* (Cambridge: Addison-Wesley, 1954), p. 7.

to a group, simply because he belongs to that group, and is therefore presumed to have the objectionable qualities as ascribed to the group.[6]

It is now over thirty years since the publication of *An American Dilemma*. During the intervening decades, a great deal of effort has focused on eliminating stereotypes and prejudicial attitudes which result in discriminatory behavior like segregation. During this period, groups like the National Conference of Christians and Jews attempted to foster a spirit of community and tolerance which would allow white and black people to work and live together. Although these early efforts accomplished a great deal toward alleviating some of the prejudices and misconceptions about minority groups, segregation and inequality have endured into the 1960's and 1970's.

During the 1960's the "War on Poverty," the Model Cities Program, and other federally assisted programs which aimed principally at improving the position of urban minorities were designed and funded. In retrospect, it appears that these massive federal aid programs evolved only after a consensus was reached that a focus on the attitudinal and cultural aspects of the problem did not lead to a resolution of institutionalized economic and social patterns. Moreover, a philosophy of assimilation, or even pluralism, was not well established in the law or social policy. Supreme Court decisions voided some of the most blatant aspects of discrimination, particularly with respect to school desegregation and restrictive housing covenants. But these decisions, while recognizing the problem, did not lead to easy solutions. Housing is still largely segregated by race, as are public schools. Although the *Brown vs. Board of Education* decision established the legal principle that separate education for blacks and whites is inherently unequal, the nature of that inequality and its policy implications still remain in doubt today.[7] In short, no consensus has evolved as to the desirability of the assimilation of minorities into a single American culture. Although the notion of the American city as a great "melting pot" has prevailed, a careful look at the evidence suggests that the concept may be more myth than reality.

The Urban Melting Pot—Fact or Fiction

The idea of a common, homogeneous, American culture based on generations of assimilation and accommodation is apparently both unrealistic and inaccurate. Unlike some European and Asian countries with a common linguistic and social structure which has persisted for centuries in a constant, self-maintaining population, the United States is made up of a large number of ethnic minorities. The American city has traditionally been th epoint of entry for new minorities. New York epitomizes the conglomeration of ethnic groups and races which have migrated to the New World. In their famous study of the melting pot concept in New York, Glazer and Moynihan

[6]*Ibid.*, p. 8.
[7]347 U.S. 483 (1954), (May 17, 1954).

(1963) examine the Negroes, Puerto Ricans, Jews, Italians and Irish of that city.[8] They offfer:

> The assimilating power of American society and culture operates on immigrant groups in different ways, to make them, it is true, something they had not been, but still something distinct and identifiable. The impact of assimilating trends on the groups is different in part because the groups are different—Catholic peasants from southern Italy were effected differently, in the same way and at the same time, from urbanized Jewish workers and merchants from Eastern Europe. We cannot even begin to indicate how various were the characteristics of family structure, religion, economic experience and attitudes, educational experience and attitudes, political outlook that differentiated groups from such different backgrounds. Obviously some American influences worked on them in common and with the same effects. Their differences meant they were open to different parts of American experience, interpreted in different ways, used for different ends. In the third generation, the descendants of the immigrants confronted each other and knew they were both Americans, in the same dress, with the same language, using the same artifacts, troubled by the same things, but they voted differently, had different ideas about education and sex, and were still, in many essential ways as different from one another as their grandfathers had been.[9]

In American cities, particularly in the larger metropolitan areas, immigrant groups settled and maintained different neighborhoods. Although the city was made up of persons from varying backgrounds, the atomistic, anomic qualities of the cultural polyglot which Wirth described probably rarely existed.[10] For most immigrants, the reality of the Little Italy, the Polish neighborhood, the Negro ghetto, and the Puerto Rican barrio offered an organized, often tightly knit sociological unit. There was assimilation into general middle-class culture, but many of the subcultural elements—like language, child rearing patterns, leisure patterns and above all, consciousness of ethnic heritage persisted. Thus, the concept of the "melting pot" was not really one in which the ingredients melted into a whole at all; rather, the result might be characterized more aptly as a kind of chowder, having one common flavor, but also having a number of ingredients which have unique flavors, textures, tastes, and identities.

Ethnic Groups in America

The largest single ethnic group in the United States is comprised of American blacks. As of 1970, blacks constituted 11 percent of the national population, or about twenty-three million people. In size, this is a population larger than Canada's. When the first American census was taken in 1790, however, blacks made up 19 percent of the total. The proportion declined during the nineteenth century, not

---

[8]Nathan Glazer and Daniel Patrick Moynihan, *Beyond the Melting Pot* (Cambridge, Mass.: The M.I.T. Press, 1963).

[9]*Ibid.*, pp. 13–14.

[10]The original position is stated in Louis Wirth, "Urbanism as a Way of Life," *American Journal of Sociology*, 44, (July, 1938), pp. 1–24. For further discussion, see the chapter on neighborhoods.

because the black population failed to reproduce itself, but because of the large number of European immigrants. However, the influx from Europe was greatly curtailed by the immigration laws of the 1920's. Starting in 1930, the black population began to increase in proportion to the total American population. American blacks continue to have a higher fertility rate than white Americans. Demographic estimations generally suggest that American blacks will total between 30 and 34 million by year 2000.

Prior to the Civil War, the black population was largely rural, reflecting the fact that slaves were used primarily as agricultural laborers. After the war, during the Reconstruction Era, there was little change in geographical distribution. Even as late as 1910, nine out of every ten blacks still lived in the South, predominantly in rural areas.

Beginning in World War I, many blacks moved from the South to the North because of a need for workers in the war industries. Large numbers of European immigrants were no longer available, and blacks provided a cheap source of labor, forming the necessary human capital for development of American industry. Black migration was further spurred by widespread mechanization of farming and by the fact that cotton production was no longer limited to the Old South, but had moved to the newly developing areas in the Southwest.

The Great Depression of the 1930's caused a virtual cessation of industrial development throughout the United States. Black movement from the South ceased. But beginning in 1941, when America began to tool up for World War II, American industry again recruited large numbers of blacks from the South. This migration continued into the 1950's and 1960's. The result was that between 1910 and 1960, about five million blacks left the South, arriving mostly in the larger cities of the industrial East and Midwest. Although from a historical perspective this was certainly a large migration, there is often a tendency to exaggerate its magnitude. In comparison, almost nine million Europeans migrated to the United States in one decade, between 1901 and 1911.[11]

The migration of the blacks from the South has now largely ceased. There are not enough rural southern blacks remaining to have a substantial impact even if they all migrated to the northern areas. In contrast, foreign immigrants continue to come into the United States, approximately 400,000 annually. The American metropolitan area is still largely the domain of immigrants and their offspring. But the recent population growth which has occurred among blacks in American cities is due largely to natural increase, a high rate of fertility.

In 1970, while approximately half of the black population of the United States still lived in the South, four out of five blacks were urban dwellers. The overwhelming reality is that in less than a century, blacks have been transformed from a principally rural people to one of the most urbanized minority groups in America. Even in the South, blacks comprise the most urban part of the population. In fact, in

[11]J. John Palen, *The Urban World* (New York: McGraw-Hill, 1975), p. 212.

some American cities (Atlanta, Gary, Newark, and Washington, D.C.), blacks comprise the majority of the population; and in nine other cities (Baltimore, Birmingham, Charleston, Detroit, New Orleans, Richmond, Savannah, St. Louis, and Wilmington), four out of ten of the population are black. It must be remembered, however, that a disproportionate number of the blacks in the urban areas are in the younger age group. As a result, in all these cities, the majority of the public school population is black.

The proportion of the black population living in major cities continues to increase. The 1970 census indicated that about six out of ten blacks lived in central cities, as compared to about four out of ten in 1950. This concentration is further accentuated by the flight of the white population to outlying areas.

The most recent evidence suggests that, although the overall number of blacks living in cities continues to increase, the degree of segregation within inner city neighborhoods has actually decreased somewhat between 1960 and 1970.[12] Palen points out, however, that the white population of Detroit declined by over 300,000 between 1960 and 1970.[13] Chicago lost over one-half a million whites during the same period. This was a pattern in most of the nation's cities. If this trend continues, along with limited migration of American blacks into suburban areas, many of the nation's largest cities will consist of a majority of black inhabitants by the year 2000. It must be remembered, however, that the larger metropolitan areas which contain these cities have often grown, while the cities' population has actually declined. Thus, although the old municipal boundaries of cities remain, the larger areas expand. The result is that relatively small areas containing large numbers of blacks have become blacker, a pattern which is highly visible. The larger metropolitan area, however, is also expanding, but not so conspicuously. The result is an undue emphasis on the highly visible, highly concentrated, black population of the center city. By using the simplest measures of segregation and concentration, the true patterns of the urban regions are often obscured by looking only at comparisons of central cities in various time periods, without considering the expansion of outlying suburban areas and the urban fringe.

Segregation Process and Trends

Much of the controversy regarding segregation in the United States has revolved around the involuntary segregation of blacks in American cities. While it is common to conceptualize segregation in terms of housing patterns, segregation has also been apparent in school systems, in the work place, and in community facilities like swimming pools. It is housing or residential segregation, however, which urban sociology has emphasized. In the United States, some residential segregation has been the by-product of deliberate policies, formal and informal, followed by realtors

---

[12]Thomas L. Van Valey, Wade C. Roof, and Jerome E. Wilcox, "Trends in Residential Segregation: 1960–1970," *American Journal of Sociology,* 82:4 (January 1977), pp. 826–844.
[13]Palen, *Urban World,* p. 214.

and land developers. Some residential segregation of American blacks is also voluntary, in the sense that individuals prefer to live with members of their own group, apart from those who are perceived as indifferent or hostile in some respect. Some researchers have described the barriers, both psychological and real, encountered by blacks attempting to move from the ghetto.[14] These difficulties constitute not only an encounter with gatekeepers, such as real estate agents and others who control real estate, but also encompass attitudinal barriers encountered by persons moving from a familiar place into a territory which they consider to be bewildering and hostile. In sum, if a minority regards another group with fear or hostility, it is unlikely that they will attempt to move into the same neighborhood unless they are forced to do so.

Involuntary Segregation

Involuntary segregation occurs in two ways. First, individuals may be required by law or social tradition to live in a specified area, or they may be prevented by law or tradition from residing in areas occupied by other groups who are different in certain respects, such as race or caste. In India, some of the lower castes have long been relegated to specified areas of the city and countryside. Second, involuntary segregation may take place through the operation of economic forces, because individuals live in areas which commonly contain others of the same economic circumstances. This pattern of segregation has long been evident in the large cities and is probably best exemplified by the classic University of Chicago studies, discussed in the chapter on Urban Ecology.

Whatever the cause of segregation, whether voluntary or involuntary, it affects the social process of the entire community. People living in segregated areas tend to develop different life-styles and to perceive people as different and to act differently toward other persons than they do towards people who live within their own area. Sometimes, as in the case of the classical European Jewish ghetto, the social and cultural isolation which is already present is reinforced by intensive interaction among others within the same locale. Thus, the more people are segregated, the more they may interact in a way that reinforces their minority values and life-style, which may have given rise to the segregation in the first place.

In Raymond Mack's work on an industrial port located on Lake Erie (1954), he found that the heavy immigration of Swedes and Finns during the late nineteenth century caused them to become categorized collectively by the community as "the Swedes."[15] The group lived in an area called "Swedetown," which was located near the docks and railroad repair area. Later, as Italians arrived in the succeeding wave of immigrants, they, too, moved into the same area. This caused the Swedes to continue the process of invasion and succession, moving out into an adjacent area

---

[14]Bonnie Bullough, "Alienation in the Ghetto," *American Journal of Sociology,* No. 72, (March 1967), pp. 469–478.

[15]Raymond W. Mack, "Ecological Patterns in an Industrial Shop," *Social Forces,* (May 1954), pp. 351–356.

known as "The Harbor." Thus, two communities developed side-by-side which were spatially and culturally distinct. Membership was determined solely by ethnicity but reinforced by ecology. This same pattern carried over into relationships in the work place, where segregation also continued. Italians typically worked in light repair work, while Swedes carried out the heavy repair work on railroad cars. The two groups worked on different sides of the yard and worked in different specializations within the railroad-car building industry. A similar pattern was also evident in Gans' *Urban Villagers* (1962), an Italian community in Boston which was voluntarily segregated from the rest of the community.[16] The style of life in this setting resembled that of a small rural village with respect to its isolation, provinciality, and ethnocentricity.

Segregation of Occupational Groups

The fact that people in different occupations tend to have different incomes, educations, and life-styles prompts them to choose housing in certain areas. The result of this is a segregation of occupational groups within certain geographical areas. Because of the tendency of certain ethnic groups to be concentrated within certain occupations, there is often a blending of ethnic and occupational segregation, to a degree which can only be analyzed through multivariate statistical techniques. For example, in the 1950's when the young professionals began to live in the suburbs, Whyte (1956) characterized this group as "organization men."[17] The suburban house, with its accompanying suburban life-style, became the necessary status symbol for the young highly educated professional, on his way up on the ladder of success within the rapidly expanding American corporate world. Since the 1950's, a variety of different types of suburbs have developed, varying from "white-collar suburbs" to "blue-collar suburbs" and even including a large number of black areas in the outlying and suburban areas.

Some of the "new towns," such as Reston in the Washington, D.C. area, have become the preserve of upwardly mobile blacks who work for industry and government.[18] In these developments, a kind of new life-style has emerged, with a sprinkling of the older elements of black ghetto sub-culture, along with the newer bureaucratic trends. It also should be remembered that many of the new housing developments built after World War II, such as Levittown, New Jersey, emerged primarily because of the availability of low down-payments and low interest mortgages (made available through VHA and FHA).[19] Levittown attracted a wider-than-average range of families having different occupations and educations. Thus, although the tendency of new mass-produced housing developments to have dwellings which

---

[16]Herbert J. Gans, *The Urban Villagers* (New York: The Free Press, 1962).
[17]William H. Whyte, Jr. *The Organization Man* (New York: Simon and Schuster, 1956).
[18]Carlos C. Campbell, *New Towns* (Reston, Virginia: Reston Publishing Co., 1976).
[19]Herbert J. Gans, *The Levittowners* (New York: Random House, 1967), pp. 22–43.

resemble "tiny little boxes looking all the same," suggests homogeneity of income, ethnicity and, life-style, the homogeneity of the subculture is often more apparent than real.

That residential segregation of occupational groups exists is borne out by a study of twenty-two counties in the New York metropolitan area conducted by Hoover and Vernon (1959). They employed an index of residential specialization to monitor the degree to which different occupational groups differed from the distribution of occupational groups in the overall area.[20] The metropolitan area was divided into four rings differing in transportation accessibility to Manhattan. The index identified whether a given occupational group was under-represented or over-represented in any ring. Hoover and Vernon found that the housing of upper white-collar occupations (professionals and managers) was disproportionately concentrated in the third ring (the suburban commuting zone), located about twenty to thirty miles from Manhattan, although within the high-rent areas of Manhattan, a second clustering of high-income professionals was also found. In contrast, the lower white-collar groups (clerks and sales personnel) were disproportionately located in the second ring, in the boroughs of Brooklyn and Queens and the one New Jersey county that borders on Manhattan. These areas, predominantly apartment houses and attached single-dwelling units, are all served by subway and elevated trains. Blue-collar workers, on the other hand, were over-represented in the fourth or outermost ring. This heterogeneous area was somewhat beyond the regular commuting range and was made up of industrial communities, various suburbs and resort areas. Within this last ring, blue-collar workers were segregated. Craftsmen and skilled workers lived in suburban areas, but semi-skilled workers and laborers tended to live nearer the industrial area. Service workers such as domestics, barbers, elevator operators and janitors were most heavily over-represented in the innermost ring, Manhattan itself.

A more recent large-scale study of occupational segregation is reported by Vanneman in a 1977 article.[21] Examining the occupational concentration in 78 census tracts of the Peoria, Illinois metropolitan area, Vanneman found a geographic clustering of various workers, depending upon their position within the social strata. Occupational segregation revealed "working- and middle-class clusters." These residential clusters are shown in Figure 12.1. The reader can see that even within the major clusters (working-class and middle-class), a pattern of occupational segregation is evident. Managers, engineers, and doctors tend to live in different neighborhoods than less prestigious and lower-paid groups. Within the working class, technicians typically reside in different neighborhoods than carpenters and skilled construction workers.

[20]Edgar Hoover and Raymond Vernon, *Anatomy of a Metropolis* (Cambridge, Mass.: Harvard University Press, 1959).

[21]Reeve Vanneman, "The Occupational Composition of American Classes," *American Journal of Sociology,* 82:4 (January 1977), pp. 783–807.

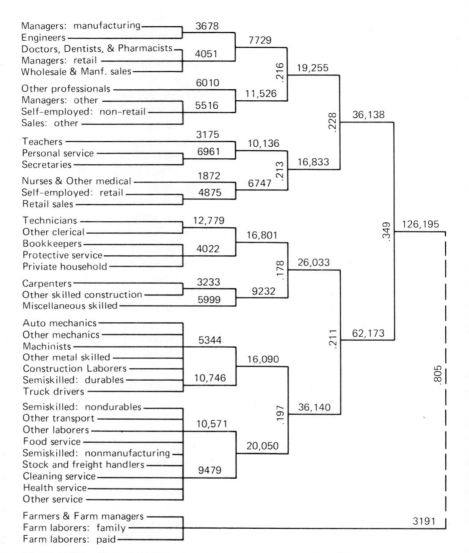

Figure 12.1 Clustering by residential integration: Peoria SMSA. Horizontal figures indicate the number of people in each cluster; vertical figures indicate the segregation coefficient between the two clusters. The farm-nonfarm cluster was computed for the entire SMSA. All the remaining clustering was computed only for the urbanized portion of the SMSA. This explains why the total for the nonfarm cluster is larger than the sum of the totals for the working- and middle-class clusters. *Adapted from "The Occupational Composition of American Classes," by Reeve Vanneman, American Journal of Sociology, Volume 82, No. 4, January (1977), p. 800.*

Residential Segregation Indices

There are a number of methods for determining the pattern and extent of residential segregation. The most frequently used method was developed by Karl and Alma Taeuber (1965).[22] In an analysis of segregation of American cities for the years of 1940, 1959 and 1960, the Taeubers developed a measure known as the "index of dissimilarity." It provides an index number which represents the proportion of nonwhites would have to have changed the area in which they lived in order to create a racial balance like that of the larger area. For example, for a larger area in which twenty percent of the population is black, the index would be zero if two of every ten households in the sub-area in question were black. Similarly, the area which is being categorized would have an index of one hundred if no households in that area were black. In essence, the index has a range of zero to one hundred, with zero representing no segregation as compared to the overall area and one hundred representing total segregation when compared to the overall ethnic percentages of the area.

For the largest 237 cities in the United States, the index of dissimilarity was 75 in the year 1970. In other words, for the typical American city, 75 percent of the nonwhites, would have to have changed the area in which they lived in order to produce a totally unsegregated pattern. Among the 237 largest cities in the United States, Fort Lauderdale had the highest segregation (an index of dissimilarity of 98); in contrast Eugene, Oregon had the lowest (with an index of 27). Throughout the United States, it was found that nine out of ten of the cities had indices of dissimilarity of over fifty, meaning that half of the black households would have to move in order for complete desegregation to occur. In sum, the index clearly points out that American blacks are highly segregated, probably to an extent beyond any other ethnic or racial group.

The cities of the North and West are less segregated when compared to southern cities.[23] The South generally has the highest indices (over 90). The data also show, however, that there were slight decreases in the extent of desegregation between 1960 and 1970 throughout most of the United States. While these figures suggest trends for overall regions of the United States, they do not point out some divergencies among individual cities. For instance, El Paso had a lower segregation index than either Detroit or Portland, Maine. The suburbs of Little Rock, Arkansas, had a lower index than Las Vegas's suburbs. The Taeubers' figures show that between 1940 and 1950, the overall trend in the United States was toward greater segregation, but for the subsequent period (1950–1960), there was a decline in segregation. In an earlier study done by Lieberson (1963), figures for ten major

---

[22]Karl E. Tauber and Alma F. Tauber, *Negroes in Cities: Residential Segregation and Neighborhood Change* (Chicago: Aldine, 1965).
[23]Van Valey, Roof, and Wilcox, *Trends,* pp. 831–835.

273

Table 12.1 *Region and Trends in Segregation for SMSAs: 1960 and 1970 (Source: Thomas L. Van Valey, Wade C. Roof, and Jerome E. Wilcox, "Trends in Residential Segregation: 1960î970,"* American Journal of Sociology, *Vol. 82, No. 4, January, 1977, p. 839.)*

Region	N	1970 Index	1960 Index	Average Difference	% Change
South Atlantic	22	71.2	71.0	+0.2	0.3
East South Central	10	73.3	72.7	+0.6	0.8
West South Central	22	75.3	76.3	−1.0	−1.3
South	54	73.3	73.5	−0.2	÷0.3
Mountain	6	71.6	79.7	−8.1	−10.2
Pacific	13	71.3	75.8	−4.5	−5.9
West	19	71.4	77.0	−5.6	−7.3
West North Central	9	79.3	78.9	+0.4	0.5
East North Central	31	79.8	79.3	+0.4	0.5
North Central	40	79.7	79.3	+0.4	0.5
Middle Atlantic	16	75.2	74.8	+0.4	0.5
New England	8	72.3	69.3	+3.0	4.3
Northeast	24	74.2	73.0	+1.2	1.6
Total	137	75.1	75.6	−0.5	−0.7

cities in the central and northeastern regions of the United States revealed decreasing segregation both in terms of race and national origin.[24]

The latest (1977) analysis of black segregation employing the Taeuber index of dissimilarity indicates a general decline in the average level of segregation within metropolitan areas between 1960 and 1970.[25] Van Valey found that the census tracts of American metropolitan areas registered almost a six percent decline in segregation within this ten-year time span. The decline in segregation was greatest in the western states (7.3%), but the northeastern states actually increased slightly in segregation (1.6%). Most of the nationwide changes, however, mark reductions in segregation in the smaller metropolitan areas and growing areas. In essence, the very areas which have the largest minority populations continued to show increases in the level of segregation during the most recent period (see Table 12.1).

In general, while useful in determining the overall extent of desegregation,

[24]Stanley Lieberson, *Ethnic Patterns in American Cities* (Glencoe, Illinois: The Free Press, 1955).

segregation indices by themselves provide only a broad indicator of the extent of assimilation into American life. Although providing demographic trends, the indices give little insight into the causes and consequences of segregation patterns, either in terms of race, national origin, income, education, or other demographic characteristics.

Ecological Process and Segregation

One study, conducted by Charles Tilly (1965) in Wilmington, Delaware, monitored the changes in black population of that city between 1940 and 1960.[26] It was shown that the black movement into outlying areas usually proceeded over the years along certain transportation arteries in predictable directions. Specific suburban areas became very popular for upwardly mobile blacks. During the 1950's, the term *block-busting* became popularized. Simply stated, once an area was open to a single black family, a kind of panic often set in, particularly in blue-collar areas. A large number of "For Sale" signs would go up at one time. Some realtors bought up properties at deflated rates from whites who were fleeing to other areas and sold them at inflated rates to blacks who wanted to move into areas which were opening up. Again, while the availability of FHA and VHA housing has had some impact, particularly in opening up new suburban developments, the pattern prevails; blacks move into areas in clusters which subsequently become labeled as "black" areas. In the chapter on housing we have discussed some of the notions of tipping points with respect to racial invasion. There are no data at this time that indicate there is a change in the pattern uncovered by Tilly.

Segregation of Mexican-Americans

According to census figures, in 1970 there were about four and a half million persons of Mexican descent in the United States, and there were over nine million persons of Spanish heritage (including Puerto Ricans, Cubans, and South Americans). Overall, Mexican-Americans make up about three percent of the population of the United States. Concentrated in the Southwest and California, Mexicans have now begun to migrate to northern cities, particularly Chicago.

Spanish-speaking people may be classified into three groups representing when they came to the United States and where they came from. *Spanish-Americans* are descended from the early residents of New Mexico and California; they lived there before the areas became states or territories. The second group is the *Mexican-Americans,* people who migrated from Mexico since the Mexican revolutions of the early twentieth century and still have strong cultural affiliations and ties with

---

[25]Van Valey, *et al., Trends,* pp. 831–823.
[26]Charles Tilly, Barry Kay, and Wagner Jackson, *Race and Residence in Wilmington, Delaware* (New York: Teachers College Press, 1965).

Mexico. The third group, *Mexicans,* are the most recent arrivals and differ culturally from the "Anglo" community.

Mexican-Americans are over-represented in low-paying, low-skilled jobs. In
Texas and California, Mexican-Americans make up a high percentage of the agricultural labor force. They have been the center of a controversy regarding the
unionization of farm laborers. Generally, the Spanish-speaking population is
slightly less poverty-stricken than blacks; Mexican-Americans have a lower average
income than Cuban-Americans. Many of the latter left Cuba after the revolution.
These skilled expatriates have the highest incomes of Spanish-speaking people. The
1970 census reveals that about one-quarter of persons of Spanish heritage are below
the poverty level. In 1970, less than one-half percent of all Mexican-Americans had
annual incomes of over twenty-five thousand dollars, a figure which is less than half
that of all U.S. households.

Mexican-Americans have been less militant than American blacks. This pattern is related to the fact that even for recent migrants (who are over-represented in
low-income jobs, poor housing and social agency populations) the overall quality of
life in the United States is vastly superior to that of the poverty-stricken areas from
which many Mexicans have migrated. Family income in American cities adjacent to
border cities like Juarez and Tiajuana is two or three times higher. This situation is
compounded by the fact hat many persons of Mexican ancestry are illegal immigrants to the United States and therefore do not wish to draw attention to themselves. The United States Immigration Service estimates the number of illegal
Mexican immigrants entering the United States at about a quarter of a million a
year. The unofficial estimates, however, placed a number of *mojados* or "wet-
backs" as high as one million.[27]

In sum, the degree of segregation and acculturation of Mexican-Americans
appears to be directly related to the time period in which the particular segment of
the population migrated to the United States. Recent migrants have found assimilation more difficult. The relative accessibility of Mexico makes it possible for many
Mexicans to pass back and forth over the border as employment opportunities
become available on either side. The border has also meant closer ties to the parent
Mexican culture, thereby delaying or negating the kind of assimilation often experienced by European immigrants.[28]

Japanese-Americans

In contrast to the assimilation of Mexican-Americans of recent arrival is that of
Japanese-Americans. It has been well-documented that the Japanese-Americans
living in the West Coast (California) suffered tremendously as a result of policies
directed toward them during World War II. Thirty years have pased since the

[27]Palen, *Urban World,* p. 228.
[28]*Ibid.,* pp. 229–230.

time of the war-time internment camps. Collectively, Japanese-Americans have now risen above this obstacle and have become one of the most successful minority groups in the United States. In terms of earnings, education, and leadership in the community, the Japanese have been even more successful than native-born whites.[29]

In short, Japanese-Americans have been extremely successful in assimilating the values and life-styles which Americans hold most highly. They follow the American success ideal almost to a greater extent than the white Anglo-Saxon Protestant.

Japanese-American immigration first occurred on a large scale during the 1890's. In the year 1900, slightly over thirty thousand Japanese migrated to the United States, with the largest number arriving between 1901 and 1907. In 1924, however, an Immigration Act limited the number of arrivals to 385 per year. By 1970, there was a total of 591,000 Japanese-Americans, 217,000 of whom lived in Hawaii.[30]

Generally, the massive migrations during the early 1900's were perceived as threatening by organized labor. This first generation of Japanese immigrants (known as the Issei) was viewed as taking the jobs of workers living on the west coast. This fear was manifest in a panic in California known as the "Yellow Peril." One result of the crisis was that the United States and Japan agreed to limit the number of immigrants. California also adopted land laws which denied non-citizens the right to own agricultural land or to lease it for more than three years at a time. The result was that many Japanese-American farmers did not have the right to own land. But rather than give up the land, they assigned the deeds to their children (known as the Nisei). The Supreme Court upheld these California laws which forbade aliens the same rights as native-born Americans. The Immigration Act of 1924 excluded all aliens who were ineligible for citizenship, resulting in a virtual cessation of a Japanese migration to the United States.

With the bombing of Pearl Harbor on December 7, 1941, marking the American entry into World War II, anti-Japanese sentiment in the United States (particularly in California) rose to a crescendo. Japanese-Americans were often viewed as spies or fifth columnists. In February, 1942, President Franklin D. Roosevelt, by executive order, established interment camps for persons who posed a national security threat. All persons of Japanese ancestry were evacuated from the three western coastal states and parts of Arizona to these camps. The forced internment included children and those having as little as one-eighth Japanese ancestry. Two-thirds of those ordered to the camps were United States citizens. More than 110,000 Japanese were placed in the camps during this period.[31] As a result, the interned Japanese-Americans suffered a financial loss of over 400 million dollars due to abandoned

[29]William Petersen, "Success Story: Japanese-American Style," *The New York Times Magazine*, January 9, 1966.
[30]Palen, *Urban World*, p. 234.

businesses and property. The United States eventually compensated these claims at a rate of five or ten cents to the dollar.

Following the war, many Japanese chose to move to the East where opportunities were better than the West. Resentment was still harbored in the West. Since that time, the third generation of Japanese-Americans (the Sansei) have become successful in achieving both wealth and status. Generally, Japanese have moved into the professions, such as engineering and business administration, as well as other positions of trust in the community. While many Japanese-Americans on the west coast still live in ethnic communities, most have lost knowledge of the Japanese language and many of the old customs. In addition, assimilation has occurred through marriages with persons of non-Japanese ancestry. In a short time, the Japanese-American community has assimilated the values of the total American culture and appears to be moving toward intermarriage and complete absorption into the general American society.

The Chinese-Americans

During the latter part of the nineteenth century, a large number of Chinese migrated to the United States to work as laborers in lumbering, railroad construction, and mining. They provided a ready source of cheap labor for the expansion of American industry, particularly in the western part of the United States. This migration started primarily on the west coast, but over the years the Chinese have moved into other cities throughout the United States, particularly in the larger metropolitan areas. During the frontier era in the West, some of the Chinese men performed what might be called "women's work," particularly that of cooking, washing, and domestic service.[32] In this way, the stereotypic Chinese laundry service got its start. Lee indicates that most of the Chinatowns in the smaller cities have now either declined or disappeared. Chinese, like other ethnic groups, increasingly are concentrating in the great metropolitan areas like Chicago, New York, and San Francisco.

Presently, Chinatowns still provide a series of services which are necessary in large metropolitan areas. But Chinese restaurants and laundry services can only compete with other such services where there is a large enough demand, usually within a large metropolitan area. Chinatowns, as distinct from outlying Chinese enterprises, such as restaurants, offer principally tourist attractions of foods, goods, services, Oriental art work, and crafts. In some metropolitan areas such as San Francisco, Chinatown represents a real community with a social organization and style of life which is self-contained yet dependent on the larger community. San Francisco's Chinatown, however, appears to be undergoing a state of transition. In the 1940 census, 70% of San Francisco's Chinese population lived in Chinatown; by

---

[31]*Ibid.*, p. 236.

[32]Rose Hum Lee, "The Decline of Chinatowns in the United States," *American Journal of Sociology*, 54, March (1949), pp. 422–432.

San Francisco's Chinatown, the gateway to the West's biggest Chinese settlement is guarded by temple dogs and roofed with green, glazed tiles surmounted by ocher dragons. *San Francisco Convention & Visitors Bureau.*

1950, this proportion had declined to 40%. New York's Chinatown presents a similar pattern; in 1940, it contained half of the Chinese living in New York City, whereas in 1950 contained only a third.[33]

The Jewish-Americans

American Jews have suffered the consequences of being a religious minority group far more than Catholics in the United States. Not only are Jews a smaller population numerically, but the history of the Jewish people in the United States reveals the impact of prejudices and discriminatory practices to a greater extent than those experienced by other minority groups. Jewish solidarity as a minority has also been tightened as the result of the horrors of Nazism, culminating in the murder of millions of Jews in concentration camps during World War II. Jews have been the most successful of all religious minorities in assimilating into the American educational and occupational system, where they, to an even greater extent than the

[33]*Statistical Abstract on the United States,* 1962, p. 29.

Japanese-Americans, occupy positions of great responsibility and prestige in industry, government, education, arts, literature, and music, as well as the local business community. American Jews to a greater extent than almost any other minority have faced the dilemma of assimilation versus pluralism. Some merge into the American culture, losing much of their cultural identity; others preserve certain elements of ethnic identity, at the same time taking on the cultural characteristics of the larger American society. Unlike many minority groups, the leadership of the Jewish religious community has been able to adopt more deliberate stance, where choices and future policies are open rather than closed. The factor of intermarriage with members of other religious groups has not been as great as it has for Protestants or Catholics. Jews have not been faced with substantial numbers of the community out-marrying into other religious groups. Will Herberg in his book *Protestant-Catholic-Jew* suggests that second-generation Jews go through a period of frantic assimilation, during which they wish to eliminate all vestiges of their Jewish identity.[34] The next generation, however, attempts to return to its ethnic and religious roots, in an effort to re-establish ties with its forefathers. During the early 1900's, large numbers of Jews lived in Jewish neighborhoods in the larger cities throughout the United States. Presently, over two-thirds have moved to the suburbs.[35] This trend has been accompanied by an increase in inter-ethnic contacts in schools and in jobs, the growth of friendship patterns between Jews and Gentiles, an increase in the rate of intermarriage, and the shift away from the Jewish Orthodoxy toward Conservative and Reformed congregations.[36]

Simpson and Yinger conclude, however:

> In the face of these trends, paradoxically, there are clear signs of continuing strong group identity and even a revival among Jews. In the last twenty years, an increasing proportion of Jewish families have joined and participated in the programs of synagogues. Between 1900 and 1958, the number of Jewish children enrolled in schools for religious instruction increased from 45,000 . . . to over 55,000. . . . In suburbs where Jews may be a small minority, they tend to come together, not only around their institutions but in informal friendship circles. There are many interreligious friendships, but best friends are usually Jewish. And evening leisure-time activities particularly are likely to be shared within the ethnic group. This is not necessarily the result of conscious choice, but is the consequence of a search of a relaxed setting for the pursuit of shared interests.[37]

In sum, despite the rapid acculturation of the Jews into American culture, and their increasing involvement in most phases of American life, most Jews continue to think of themselves as members of an ethnic community.

The American Jews are important in the study of urban sociology because the majority are predominately urban. Their dilemma—of assimilation versus plu-

---

[34]Will Herberg, *Protestant-Catholic-Jew* (Garden City, New York: Doubleday, 1955).
[35]Simpson and Yinger, *Racial Minorities,* p. 231.
[36]Judith R. Kramer and Seymour Leventman, *Children of the Gilded Ghetto* (New Haven, Conn.: Yale University Press, 1961).
[37]Simpson and Yinger, *Racial Minorities,* p. 231.

ralism—is similar to that with which most minority groups will eventually have to come to grips.

Urban Ethnic Problems

"The most conspicuous fact of life in the city is racial division," says Edward C. Banfield in *The Unheavenly City Revisited*. "A hundred times a day, there are confrontations between black and white, and almost everyday an explosion turns some part of the city into a battleground. The residential suburbs are mostly white—often "lily white"; the central cities, especially their older, more deteriorated parts, and above all their slums, are predominantly or entirely black. Many observers see little reason to hope for improvement. The city, they say, has always exploited, humiliated, and degraded its immigrant groups. But whereas all the others eventually have been able to escape their oppressors by joining them, the black, marked as he is by skin color, can never do so. For him, in this view, the city is degradation without hope."[38]

"The dark ghettos," says Kenneth B. Clark, "are social, political, educational, and, above all, economic colonies. There inhabitants are subject peoples, victims of the greed, cruelty, insensitivity, guilt, and fear of their masters."[39] But Banfield's basic claim is that the main disadvantage suffered by blacks is similar to that of other minorities during their first several generations in the United States, specifically, the fact that they are the most recent, most unskilled, and thus relatively the lowest-income migrants to come to cities from rural areas. Most of the variables, however, which explain this low-income level, according to Banfield, are not due to race, but rather to differences in family background, socialization, education, occupational prestige, and number of siblings.[40]

In fact, Banfield continues, "Much of what appears (especially to blacks) as race prejudice is really *class* prejudice or, at any rate class antipathy. Similarly, much of what appears especially to whites as 'black' behavior is really lower-class behavior."[41]

Banfield identifies lower-class behavior characteristic of American blacks as "present oriented."[42] Describing this present orientation, Banfield continues:

> At the present-oriented end of the scale, the lower-class individual lives from moment to moment. If he has any awareness of a future, it is of something fixed, fated, beyond his control; things happen *to* him, he does not *make* them happen. Impulse governs his behavior, either because he can not discipline himself to sacrifice a present for a future satisfaction or because he has no sense of the future. He is therefore

[38]Edward C. Banfield, *The Unheavenly City Revisited* (Boston: Little, Brown, and Co., 1974), p. 87.

[39]Kenneth B. Clark, *Dark Ghetto* (New York: Harper and Row, 1965), p. 11.

[40]Banfield, *Unheavenly City,* pp. 81–82.

[41]*Ibid.,* p. 87.

[42]*Ibid.,* p. 61.

radically improvident; whatever he can not use immediately he considers valueless. His bodily needs (especially for sex) and his tastes for "action" take precedence over everything else—and certainly over any work routine. He works only as he must to stay alive, and drifts from one unskilled job to another, taking no interest in his work. . . . The lower-class individual has a feeble, attenuated sense of self; he suffers from feeling self-contempt and inadequacy, and is often apathetic or dejected. . . . The lower-class household is usually female-based (although the women who head it are used to having a succession of mates who contribute intermittently to its support or take little or no part in rearing the children). In managing the children, the mother (or aunt or grandmother) is characteristically impulsive; once children are past babyhood, they are likely to be neglected or abused, and at best they never know what to expect next. . . . The "stress on masculinity," action, risk-taking conquests, fighting, and "smartness" makes lower-class life extremely violent.[43]

It is, according to Banfield, these "lower-class" characteristics which give rise to much of the pathology of the lower class black community, *e.g.*, the high rates of unemployment, crime, illegitimacy, and mental illness. But other writers have stressed problems of the lower-class black community which are brought about by race as opposed to class. Some of the points are summarized by Christopher Jencks in his famous work on the effect of family and schooling in America.[44] Commenting on the low occupational status of blacks, traced to race, Jencks concludes:

Many people assumed in 1962, and some still assume today, that blacks were concentrated in low-status occupations primarily because they were victims of a "vicious circle of poverty." According to this theory, blacks had low-status parents, and therefore had less than equal opportunities. This meant that they ended up in low-status jobs themselves. But this does not seem to explain much of the difference between the blacks' and whites' occupations. . . .

Many people also assume that blacks get lower-status jobs because they are short on cognitive skills measured by standardized tests. Like low-status parents, however, low test scores explained only a small fraction of the status gap. Whites with IQ scores of 85 are likely to end up with occupations 12 points below the white mean. Blacks with similar scores end up 24 points below the white mean—or did in 1962. At most, then, cognitive differences accounted for half the occupational gap between blacks and whites at that time.[45]

Thus, tracing Banfield's argument, it is not the effect of race, but rather that of class, which is then translated into occupational status and earnings. In contrast, according to Jencks' analysis, which covers the period up to 1962, Banfield's argument does not hold. There are external factors which affected the ability or capacity of Blacks to achieve occupational equality. These factors seem to be embedded in a pattern of institutionalized status and roles in a closed labor market which have been characterized as institutional racism.

[43]*Ibid.*, pp. 61–63.

[44]Christopher Jencks, Marshall Smith, Henry Acland, Mary Jo Bane, David Cohen, Herbert Gintis, Barbara Heyns, and Stephan Michelson, *Inequality* (New York: Basic Books, 1972).

[45]*Ibid.*, pp. 190–191.

The Great School Busing Controversy

In 1966, the United States Department of Health, Education and Welfare released a report entitled *The Equality of Educational Opportunity*. It was prepared by James S. Coleman, sociologist at Johns Hopkins University, with the help of a large staff of social scientists. Coleman and his group concluded at that time:

> The great majority of American children attend schools that are largely segregated—that is, where almost all of their fellow-students are of the same racial background as they are. Among minority groups, Negroes are by far the most segregated. Taking all groups, however, white children are most segregated. Almost 80% of all white pupils in first grade and in twelfth grade attend schools that are 90 to 100% white. And 97% at grade one and 99% at grade twelve, attend schools that are 50% or more white.
>
> For Negro pupils, segregation is more nearly complete in the South (as it is for whites also); that is, it is extensive in all other regions where the Negro population is concentrated: the urban North, Midwest and West. . . .
>
> In its desegregation decision of 1954, the Supreme Court held that separate schools for Negro and white children are inherently unequal. This survey finds that, when measured by that yardstick, American education remains largely unequal in most regions of the county, including all those where Negroes form any significant proportion of the population.[46]

Coleman and his group also found:

> There is direct evidence that school factors are more important in affecting the achievement of minority-group students among Negroes; this appears especially so in the South. This leads to the notion of differential sensitivity to school variations with the lowest achieving minority group showing highest sensitivity.[47]

Coleman concluded:

> The higher achievements of all racial and ethnic groups in schools with greater proportions of white students is largely, perhaps wholly, related to effects associated with the student body's educational backgrounds and aspirations. This means that the apparent beneficial effect of a student body with a high proportion of white students comes not from racial composition per se, but from the better educational background and higher educational aspirations that are, on the average, found among white students.
>
> Taking all these results together, one implication stands out above all: the schools bring little influence to bear on a child's achievements that is independent of his background and general social context; and this very lack of an independent effect means that the inequalities imposed on children by their home, neighborhood, and peer environment are carried along to become the inequalities with which they confront adult life at the end of school. For equality of educational opportunity through the schools must imply a strong effect of schools that is independent of the child's immediate social environment, and that strong independent effect is not present in American schools.[48]

[46]James S. Coleman, *et al.*, *Equality of Educational Opportunity*, (Washington, D.C.: United States Government Printing Office, 1966).
[47]*Ibid.*, p. 297.
[48]*Ibid.*, p. 325.

The variable of family background to which Coleman alluded was based upon measurement of the environment of the child's background. This includes the community in which the child and mother grew up, the parents' education, the structural integrity of the home, and size of the family. Also measured with regard to variance in educational achievement tests were items in the home, such as telephone, record player, refrigerator, automobile, vacuum cleaner, etc., whether there was reading material in the home, the parents' interest in the child, interest regarding education, and the parents' educational desires.[49]

The Coleman Report concluded that the child's family background, including the attributes cited above, accounts for most of his success or lack of success in school Children from disadvantaged minority groups appear to benefit slightly (in terms of variance explained in educational achievement scores) from attending schools which contain a high proportion of middle-class white children having high educational performance and having aspirations for higher levels of education.

Brown vs. the Board of Education

In a civil suit brought against a number of school boards, the Supreme Court decided in 1954 that dual school systems must be disestablished. The Court concluded:

> That in the field of public education, the doctrine of "separate but equal" has no place. Separate educational facilities are inherently unequal, therefore we hold that the plaintiffs and others simiarly situated for whom the actions have been brought are, by reason of the segregation complained of, deprived of the equal protection of the laws guaranteed by the Fourteenth Amendment. This disposition makes unnecessary a discussion whether such segregation also violates the due process clause of the Fourteenth Amendment.[50]

In two subsequent cases, *Swann vs. Charlotte-Mecklinburg* and *Keyes vs. Denver School District No. 1,* the court strengthened and clarified the precedents established by the *Brown* case and also found that the neighborhood school concept, where it promoted deliberate racial segregation, was unacceptable and unconstitutional. The impact of these decisions for many school districts throughout the United States has been that large numbers of children must be bused from their neighborhoods of residence to schools some distance away, in order to establish quotas which reflect the general racial characteristics of the overall area in which the school district is based.

The debate has continued regarding the efficacy in terms of educational policy. Controversy centers around whether the *Brown vs. Board of Education* decision, which declared that separate schools were inherently unequal, was accurate with

---

[49]*Ibid.*, p. 298.

[50]349 U.S. 294 (1955), (May 31, 1955) in Nicolaus Mills, ed., *The Great School Bus Controversy* (New York: Teachers College Press, 1973), p. 51.

respect to the social science evidence which has been collected to date. David Armour, in an article called "The Evidence on Busing" (1972) has reviewed the results of busing with respect to its impact on achievement scores. Armour concludes:

> To these questions of symbolic and long-term benefits of reduced school integration, the existing studies provide no answer. What they do show is that, over the period of over two or three years, busing does *not* lead to significant measureable gains in student achievement of interracial harmony (although it does lead to the channelling of black students to better colleges). The available evidence thus indicates that busing is *not* an effective policy instrument for raising the achievement of black students or for increasing interracial harmony. On the other hand, the existing studies do not rule out the possibility that in the longer run or in other respects, busing may indeed prove to have substantial positive consequences.
>
> The available evidence on busing, then, seems to lead to two clear policy conclusions. One is that massive mandatory busing for purposes of improving student and interracial harmony is not effective and should not be adopted at this time. The other is that voluntary integration programs . . . should be continued and possibly encouraged by substantial federal and state grants.[51]

Many sociologists, however, suggest that Armor presents a distorted and incomplete view of the topic of busing.[52] They maintain that Armor's review of busing was incomplete, and that blacks attending integrated schools have indeed shown gains in educational performance as measured by achievement tests, all of which may be traced to the results of busing.

In general, the trend toward busing, whether for achieving racial balance, or for other purposes, continues to grow. In 1919, less than 2% of American school pupils were transported; by 1969, this figure had grown to 43%.[53] Nicolaus Mills suggests that much of the rhetoric on busing is indeed a composite of five myths. First, busing goes against tradition; it represents a break with past approaches to improving education. Based on Mills' examination of the history of busing in the United States the direct opposite is true. Second, busing is the exception; the neighborhood school is the most desirable.[54] (Mills discounts this theory.) Third, the decision to bus has, until recently not been guided by social beliefs or principles.[55] This notion is also rejected by Mills. Fourth is "Riding on the school bus is bad for children."[56] No evidence supports this contention, says Mills. Fifth, busing is invariably a financial burden on the community.[57] Mills also rejects this contention.

---

[51]David J. Armour, "The Evidence on Busing," *The Public Interest,* 28, Summer, (1972), pp. 125–126.

[52]Thomas F. Pettigrew, *et al.,* "Busing: A Review of the Evidence," *The Public Interest,* 30, Winter, (1973), pp. 90–126.

[53]Mills, *School Bus,* p. 8.

[54]*Ibid.,* p. 10.

[55]*Ibid.,* p. 11.

[56]*Ibid.,* p. 12.

[57]*Ibid.,* p. 12.

The Great White Flight

Nathan Glazer, reviewing the history of the school bus controversy (1972), comments on the flight of white families to avoid segregation:

> Again and again reading the briefs and the transcripts and the analyses, one finds the words "escape" and "flee." The whites must not escape, they must not flee. Constitutional law often moves through strange and circuitous patterns, but perhaps the strangest yet has been the one whereby beginning with the effort to expand freedom—no Negro child shall be excluded from any public school because of his race—the law has ended up with as drastic a restriction of freedom as we have seen in this country in recent years. No child of any race or group, may "escape" or "flee" the experience of integration. No school district may facilitate such an escape. Nor may it even (in the Detroit decision) fail to take action to close the loopholes permitting anyone to escape.[58]

Following the same logic, James Coleman has recently reviewed the evidence with respect to white flight to avoid integrated schools or busing. In a paper which has attracted a great deal of attention, he concludes that busing has indeed spurred such a flight.

> Perhaps a broader conclusion about policy may be stated from these results. The extreme strong reactions of individual whites moving their children out of large districts engaged in massive and rapid desegregation suggests that in the long run the policies that have been pursued will defeat the purpose of increasing overall contact among races in schools. It is clear that for this purpose to be achieved there should have been far greater attention to the reactions of whites with the economic means to move. That the instrument through which most desegregation was accomplished—the courts—must be blind to such consideration. Other branches of government can initiate policies such as desegregation in ways that excite fewer fears among middle-class parents and thus generate less counteraction. Thus, a major policy implication of this analysis is that, in an area such as school desegregation which has important consequences for individuals and in which individuals retain control of some actions that can in the end defeat the policy, the courts are probably the worst instrument of social policy.[59]

Coleman in this paper suggests that those school districts which underwent massive desegregation between 1967 and 1971 suffered a large exodus of whites, which he considers a direct result of the desegregation policies enforced by the courts.

The great school bus controversy continues. Whether desegregation of schools via busing is actually bringing about a reversal of the inequalities cited in the *Brown vs. Board of Education* case remains doubtful. As this chapter is being written in 1977, the school bus issue continues to be clouded in political rhetoric. In 1976, federal courts in Detroit have ruled that even suburban areas must "cross-bus" white students into cities while blacks are brought in the opposite direction, in order to desegregate the schools in the larger area.

[58]Nathan Glazer, "Is Busing Necessary?" *Commentary,* March, (1972). In Mills, *School Bus,* p. 203.

[59]James Coleman, *et al.,* "Recent Trends in School Integration," (Washington, D.C.: The Urban Institute, 1975), pp. 21–22.

Although inequalities do exist in the schools, and the fact that these inequalities are often associated with the racial balance of the schools is undeniable, busing has not remedied these inequalities. Differences in school characteristics are strongly related to residential segregation patterns. Probably, until the residential communities become less segregated, and until a fuller integration in overall American life is achieved, these interracial differences in achievement scores and resulting inequalities will persist. Whether the normal pattern of assimilation and accompanying changes in public policy will remedy this situation in a short time, or whether it will take many decades to resolve, will be the subject of study of social scientists over the coming years.[60]

Policies for the Future

Occupational Inequality

The low occupational levels of some minorities, particularly blacks, is typically traced to lower levels of education and training. Coupled with this factor is the urban labor market itself, with its underlying occupational structure which is gradually becoming dominated by jobs which require technical skills. In contrast, the old pattern of service jobs and unskilled labor predominated in the early 1900's. Increased opportunities for job training and education for minority groups will help to remedy some of the inequities in this situation, as will a general increase in national productivity. Too, as blacks and other minority groups become involved with small business ownership (black capitalism) they, like other minority groups, will probably come to be represented in the same proportion as other ethnics in the American population in these occupations.

Manpower policy is closely connected to a number of other issues such as minimum wages, and the creation or support of certain jobs by the government sector. Urban economists and sociologists will be involved in future planning. With more jobs in the government sector, this will have a long term impact on future generations with respect to their occupational patterns and overall life-styles. Probably even more important will be the impact upon families in areas which have not been previously considered in developing manpower policies, such as mental health and divorce.

Housing

The issue of housing, as it affects urban minority groups, has been discussed in a previous chapter. The key to the solution of this problem, or at least the reduction of

---

[60]For more recent critiques of the "white flight" hypothesis, see Christine Rossel, "School Desegregation and White Flight," *Political Science Quarterly,* 90:4, Winter, (1975–76); also Thomas Pettigrew and Robert Green, "The Legitimizing of Racial Segregation?" *Urban Education,* 10:4,

its severity, is a determination of what the city itself should be like in the future (as compared to the suburbs and other areas). Federal policy continues to have the effect of subsidizing public housing in urban core areas; as a result, the concentration of poor minority families in the inner city continues to increase. If, in the future, federal policy emphasizes the dispersion of public housing units into outlying metropolitan areas, the concentration of poverty-stricken minority groups in the cities and the effects of ghetto living will be somewhat dissipated.

The current cost of housing is also a factor in housing urban minorities, particularly with new housing in the suburbs now averaging over forty thousand dollars per unit. Obviously, alternatives to current construction techniques and financing of housing must be explored. lower cost housing, too, must be subsidized through federal programs. New technologies, such as modular housing, mobile homes and preservation of older housing, must be investigated before engaging in a massive attempt to construct four bedroom, two-and-a-half bath houses for the entire American population.

Schools

The studies which we have examined suggest that the quality of schools varies considerably between inner city areas with a preponderance of minority population and the outlying suburban areas. The current school busing controversy will not be easily resolved. Irrespective of the direction which the solution to the school busing takes, the provision of higher quality education, including curriculum, teachers, and buildings, must be emphasized. The public school is such a basic institution in American life that the busing controversy must not be allowed to detract from the gradual evolution of better schools, using the most up-to-date methods possible. The schools must be incorporated into the overall fabric of the community, whether it be as a metropolitan area school or a community school (neighborhood school). The sociologist must be a visionary in this evolving process.

Overall Social Life

The degree of segregation which still exists in American cities cannot be described simply as cultural pluralism. While some of the inequities in education and jobs are being remedied by federal statutes and court decisions, the overall separateness of some ethnic groups with respect to their geographical isolation and restrictive lifestyles makes it difficult to create policies which allow for equal opportunity in the major institutions which all Americans share (schools, jobs, public accommodations, etc.). Probably the key to this dilemma is the capacity of choice. If equal opportunity is available to choose housing, or schools, or to participate in labor force, all ethnic groups will profit.

Conclusion

The issues faced by the urban sociologist in studying minorities range from residential segregation to police-community relations. In the United States, the factors of social class and ethnicity have often been difficult to separate conceptually. The sociologist will continue to dissect what looks to most to be simple, but which appears, upon close examination, to be otherwise. In doing so, hopefully, he will raise further questions which lead to wiser policy decisions.

part 4

Urban Policy and Planning

chapter 13

Social Science and Public Policy

The question of how social science should relate to public policy comes up often within the area of urban sociology. Most of us now live in urban areas and have mixed feelings about the quality of life we experience there. The problems of the cities are constantly in the news. And yet urban sociology, as such, has not had a consistent applied orientation. Urban sociologists have been concerned with understanding the city more than with trying to cope with its problems, until quite recently. The practical problems of the city have been left to public administrators or city planners. With the problems of the cities more pressing and the character of urban life more problematic, however, urban sociologists are joining in the effort to relate their findings to public policy issues. This trend has accelerated with the increasing emphasis the federal government has been placing upon applied research since the 1960's.

It is appropriate, therefore, for us to examine the broader issues of science and public policy in a text on urban sociology. In order to do this, we find it helpful to begin with a major turning point in the science–public policy relationship that happens to be outside the social sciences. This transformation came about in physics as a result of the push to develop the atomic bomb—the Manhattan Project. Prior to 1939, few physicists would have expected that their specialty would become enmeshed in the machinations of nations and the very survival of the planet. Since detonation of the first atomic bomb in 1945, however, the hands on the clock of the *Journal of Atomic Physicists* have warned of impending disaster and called all physicists to assume their share of responsibility in averting this disaster.[1]

The second example of the intricacies of the relationship between science and

---

[1]The name of this journal has been changed to the *Bulletin of Atomic Scientists*.

public policy comes from utilization of social science research in the formulation of the majority opinion of the Warren Court in the controversial *Brown* decision of 1954. In the legal abolishment of "separate but equal" schools, social science research played an important, but not necessarily decisive, role. The subsequent attempt to implement the decision in public policy has shown more clearly both the strengths and the weaknesses of the research that influenced that decision.

Our third example will be taken from the much studied effort at eliminating poverty that produced the Economic Opportunity Act of 1964. This war on poverty sought to apply dramatic social science concepts to the root of poverty and to promote community organization through an agency that would monitor the results of the intervention and advance the state of our knowledge.

The chapter concludes with an attempt to look at social science in a different way. By recognizing the strengths and weaknesses of distinctive styles of research, it is possible to better relate them to the peculiar needs of the policy process. After Warren Bennis, we would encourage the researcher to make use of the "inside track" and the information acquired as a result of being a member of the society. We end on the optimistic note that it is possible to integrate the special knowledge of the expert into the public policy process without either destroying his expertise or rendering the democratic process obsolete. Such an integration requires a major cultural revolution, the main parameters of which are only now becoming clear.

Scientists and Social Responsibility

The scientific community today is deeply divided over the extent to which the scientist, as scientist, should assume responsibility for the social consequences of his research. Historically, the most dominant image portrays the scientific approach as "value-free." The scientist as a private citizen has the same rights as any other citizen in a democracy to participate in the formulation of public policy, but his scientific approach is essentially above opinion and debate and concerned only with the discovery of facts about the world in which we live.

The lay image of the dedicated scientist at work in his laboratory vacillates between respect for a man of learning who somehow contributes to an increasingly higher standard of living and fear of a Frankenstein making use of his special knowledge for inhumane purposes.

Because most science demands a great deal of effort and cultivates a particular approach to the world, which is only partially captured in the image of the laboratory scientist, and because politics demands different skills and an equal dedication of time, most scientists are not active politically. Max Weber fostered the view of the value-free scientist in the social sciences. He was convinced that the values of the professor had no place in the classroom. He also wanted to establish the image of neutrality in order to gain access to the study of the Prussian State. He was personally quite involved in the politics of his day, but he did not see this as a part of

The Hexahedron. Can social scientists invent viable environments for the twenty-first century?

his scientific role. On the other hand, he clearly saw science as a vocation, and was a major advocate of an intuitive methodology he called *Verstehen*.

The common way of coping with the political values of scientists has been to assume that they should have nothing to do with the scientific role. To the extent that the scientist's personal values affect his work, his work is distorted. In an effort to prevent the emergence of a scientific autocracy, the information of scientific experts has characteristically been put into the political process through the consulting role. Citizens, politicians, decision-makers can call upon the scientific expert for information about the city and its myriad problems, but the expert cannot and should not decide the policy. Some representative body of persons is assigned this responsibility. This distinction is well made in the city planning office. In almost all cases, this office employs the scientific expert in a number of fields in the formulation of a plan or the development of a policy statement on some aspect of urban development, most commonly land use and its associated issues. But the city planner has no political power. The mayor and the board of aldermen or the city manager is perfectly free to accept or reject his proposals.

Lessons from Alamagordo

The image of science as a value-free method of discovering true facts about the world, and the scientist as a neutral observer of events persists into the present. Since the dawn of the atomic age in 1945, however, it has increasingly come under attack. The involvement of scientists in the politics of the atomic age began at least in 1939. In that year, Albert Einstein, who had recently emigrated from Hitler's Germany, wrote a letter to Franklin D. Roosevelt. Einstein stated that he had reason to believe that it was not only theoretically possible to split the atom, but, more critically, that the Germans were already well on the way to developing the technology to do it. This was the reason, he claimed, for their building a deuterium, or heavy water, plant in Norway. He concluded that the United States must embark on a massive effort to beat the Germans in this race if the free world were to have a chance against the German onslaught.

Notice that it is difficult to distinguish the scientific from the political roles in all of this. The theoretical knowledge informed the political convictions. Einstein was one this. The theoretical knowledge informed the political convictions. Einstein was one of the few people in the world who could have interpreted what the Germans were up to at the time and who also had reason to believe that they would be successful. After all, no one had ever built an atomic bomb before. His advocacy of what turned out to be the Manhattan Project follows directly from his scientific understanding of what was happening. Because of his distinguished position in the scientific community and his spreading fame throughout the world, he was, furthermore, one of the few persons who might have had a chance to influence the president of the United States. Roosevelt was convinced, and shortly afterwards the Manhattan Project began. It was one of the first massive team efforts by a group of scientists and technicians from several disciplines and can be said to mark the emergence of "big science" in the United States. The national interest and the process of scientific research were so fatefully linked in this project that the character of the scientific community, particularly that portion committed to atomic physics, and its relationship to the political process, were forever changed. The transformation did not come about easily or without cost.

The symbol of the conflict this effort in politicized science induced in many scientists is found in the biographies of Robert Oppenheimer, who was called upon to direct the project. Oppenheimer was torn by the moral issues he saw in releasing the power of the atom. He rebelled at the secrecy imposed upon the project. In other wars, scientists from hostile countries had conversed more or less freely about their research, but too much was at stake in this venture. Scientists became nationalized "for the duration," and strict secrecy was imposed upon their research. Ironically, Oppenheimer was later denied the security clearance necessary to participate directly in atomic research because he was known to have Communist friends. He could not officially have access to his own work.

When the first bomb was scheduled to be detonated on the salt flats of Alamagordo, New Mexico, no one knew for certain whether or not such a blast would start a chain reaction that would destroy the world. Oppenheimer had become increasingly anxious about the prospects and privately expressed his concerns, a point which contributed to the suspicion that he was a Communist spy. The involvement of scientists in public policy increased after the bomb became a reality.

Large numbers of scientists were opposed to its deployment as a strategic weapon. When President Truman ordered the bombing of Hiroshima and Nagasaki in 1945, he did so with full knowledge of the growing opposition within the scientific community.

The Bulletin of Atomic Scientists was born out of the anguish experienced by many scientists who saw in the flames of these Japanese cities the terrible misuse of their labors. They felt responsible and frustrated and sometimes enraged at the abuse. No one but the atomic physicists who contributed to the development of the bomb could have experienced the depth of anguish reflected in the articles of this journal. To make matters worse, scientists of equal stature held conflicting views about what to do now. This conflict is perhaps most dramatically represented in the continuing battles between Edward Teller, known as the "father of the hydrogen bomb," and Linus Pauling, who defiantly refuses to work on the further development of atomic energy because of his convictions that, in the long run, the costs will be much higher than the benefits.

With the advent of big science and the atomic age, the involvement of scientists in the political process has increased enormously, although there are many ways in which scientists have chosen to assume some degree of responsibility for the consequences of their research. The debate continues as to whether this assumption of responsibility is a legitimate aspect of their scientific role. More and more of what is called science is dependent upon government for funding, and more and more of government is dependent upon science for information.

One dramatic assumption of social responsibility is represented by Barry Commoner's approach in the Committee for the Dissemination of Nuclear Information, which he helped to found.[2] This group was largely responsible for alerting the government (and the Atomic Energy Commission) to the hazards of nuclear fall-out, particularly strontium 90. This danger was convincingly demonstrated by research conducted on baby teeth collected from children all over the nation. The findings proved that a dramatic build-up of this destructive isotope was occurring. The committee saw its major role as one of educating both the public and their representatives about this and other dangers associated with the development of atomic energy. It never assumed a direct role in the political process. In contrast to the C.D.N.I. approach, the group headed by Linus Pauling openly lobbies in Washington for its cause. It attempts to directly influence legislation that will reduce the likelihood of atomic destruction.

The concern over the consequences of atomic fall-out has been a major factor in the development of the science of ecology and the study of natural systems. In the debates and lawsuits over land use and energy development, the public has become aware of the fact that not only do expert scientists disagree on how research should be used in the formulation of public policy, but they disagree, often violently, over the interpretation of research findings. Scientists, however they might like to see

---

[2]Barry Commoner, *Science and Survival* (New York: Viking Press, 1963).

themselves, are seen as advocates for their particular position in the public debate.[3] It is not possible to argue that facts alone will resolve the debate and settle the policy issues once and for all. The facts do not speak for themselves, even to the knowledgeable. The politician and the lawyer often delight in the disagreement of scientific experts and often deliberately select experts with known opinions on critical issues to support their private causes. Edward Teller has become a favorite of the Defense Department because of his advocacy of the hydrogen bomb.

Linus Pauling often speaks for the Friends of the Earth and other conservation groups. Scientific knowledge has become so critical to the formulation of public policy in our time that various means of supplying the president and the congress with reliable information have been tried and different roles have been assumed by scientists in the effort. Some scientists see the matter as so critical that they are giving up their seientific careers and running for office. Thus, it is increasingly difficult to distinguish the scientific from the political role as events push more and more federal funds into applied research in which government has a direct interest in the outcome.[4] For good or for ill, the nature of the scientific enterprise has been radically changed for many scientists who cannot sit back any longer and watch how other people dispose of the knowledge and technology they have generated.

Lessons from the Brown Decision

Social science first became dramatically involved in the public policy process in 1954, when the research of psychologists and sociologists on the effects of racial discrimination persuaded the majority of the Warren Court to abolish the doctrine of "separate but equal" schools that had been established in *Plessey vs. Ferguson* in 1896.

Embodied in the Court's ruling was the notion that not only would the physical plant of the schools be unequal if the races were separated, but also the "opportunity nets" available to whites would be much greater than those available to blacks. A considerable portion of the value of the educational process derives from the informal friendships and associations cultivated while in school. White students, all other things held equal, tend to know more influential people, and hence have greater access to jobs and privileges. So, too, segregation of the races, coupled with discrimination against blacks, has been shown to have detrimental effects on blacks, ranging from negative self-images to increased instances of mental retardation. The environment within which blacks were raised was singled out again and again as the cause of their relatively poor showing in school and in the job market. The social

---

[3]An interesting study of the role of advocacy within the scientific community itself is found in Ian Mitroff, "Norms and Counter-Norms in a Select Group of Apollo Moon Scientists: A Case Study of the Ambivalence of Scientists," *American Sociological Review* (Aug. 1974), pp. 579–595.

[4]A well documented study of the effect of the source of funding on scientific enquiry can be found in Roger C. Kohn, *The Social Shaping of Science* (Westport, Conn.: Greenwood Publishing Corporation, 1971).

science data tended to come down hard on environmental, as opposed to racial, factors in explaining the so-called pathologies of blacks. Drawing upon this data to bolster its view of the injustice of the separate school systems, the Court became a major instrument in the redress of grievances long held by blacks.

However, it seems reasonable to assume that the Supreme Court can be considered an agent of change only under the following circumstances: (1) the court is "packed" with a majority of justices favorable to the change; (2) a majority of the population is willing, or becomes willing, to accept the change; and (3) the political context is such that the Court's capacity to assure the realization of other major policies to which it is committed is not jeopardized. If this is true, then the extent to which social science data, as such, can be considered responsible for change must be limited. Realistically, the Court drew upon the data to support its case. The majority of the justices, for whatever reason, favored the abolition of *Plessey vs. Ferguson*. But the public was not with the Court on this issue. In spite of the fact that the idea of integrated schools is ideologically compatible with our notions of equality, many people were, and remain, opposed to integration in practice.

Therefore, in assessment of the effect the *Brown* decision has had upon public education, it becomes necessary to distinguish a number of levels upon which change can be considered to have taken place. The simple calculation that by 1970, 16 years after the *Brown* decision, only 23 percent of all black students attend integrated schools, and the observation that school districts are even now being torn apart by busing to achieve integration reflects only a part of the transformation. The precedent the Court established influences other courts' decisions and, no doubt, gave impetus to the civil rights movement in the late fifties and early sixties. The Montgomery bus strike that brought the Southern Christian Leadership Conference into the national news occurred in 1958. Martin Luther King was deeply impressed by the precedents of the law and spoke of the value of the 1954 decision to blacks. Southern integration seems to have proceeded more steadily than reform in the North, in spite of the more obvious forms of discrimination that existed in the South. The very ambivalence of the North on the question of true equality between the races has proven to be one of the factors retarding change in the North.

Since the *Brown* decision and the research that supported the majority opinion, much more research has been conducted on the effects of public school education on blacks. Findings are often contradictory. A majority of studies favor the notion, for example, that so-called objective IQ tests unfairly discriminate against blacks, because they are subculturally biased. Research has shown that, under certain conditions, the expectations of the teacher have a greater effect upon student accomplishment than ability as measured by these tests. The famous Coleman Report concluded that dollars didn't seem to make the difference one might expect between educational success in the inner city schools, which are heavily black, and the suburban schools, which are heavily white.[4] Jencks concludes in his *Inequality* that the schools are not as much to blame as the family and its background in accounting for the success or failure of the black students.[5] And so it goes.

There are findings that will support almost any political opinion at present, although the bulk of the evidence supports the notion that separate school systems should be abolished. Busing may not be the way to do this. Indeed, considering the situation in Boston and many other cities since Little Rock, some very high costs have been incurred through use of this method. One of the more apparent results is the continued exodus of whites from the inner city school systems. At present there is little research to guide us toward alternative courses of action. Although there is no consensus, there is greater agreement in the research effort that defines the problem in terms of the adverse effects of discrimination than there is research that will point the way toward a more just solution.

Lessons of the Economic Opportunity Act of 1964

Finally we come to a case in which social science research was, rightly or wrongly, directly utilized in the engineering of a major federal program to combat poverty. After the extensive criticism of the social welfare institutions in social science literature, a new agency was conceived that would bring new resources and new insights directly to bear on the problem of poverty, rather than utilizing existing welfare agencies and enlisting the support of City Hall. Moynihan contends that the ideas behind the Act arose on the college campus, were hostile from the start to the political process, and were implemented by persons who, for the most part, chose to ignore the intent of Congress in formulating the Act. This is particularly true in the case of the interpretation of the phrase "maximum feasible participation."

In Moynihan's view, the phrase "maximum feasible participation" retained four distinct meanings to various elements involved in the formulation and administration of the Community Action Program, the Title II portion of the Economic Opportunity Act designed to organize the community around the more effective resolutions of the problems of the poor. To the Ford Foundation, whose "gray areas" program was a major source of information about how community action programs had worked in select cities before formulation of the Act, it meant essentially organizing the power structure. To Cloward and Ohlin, whose work on delinquency in Mobilization for Youth in New York provided much of the theoretical underpinning of the venture, it meant expanding the power structure. (MFY had an executive board of 26 persons, derived from its full board of 67 representing a variety of interests in the community.) To persons influenced by Saul Alinsky's Industrial Areas Foundation, which included the first director of O.E.O. and many of his staff, it meant confronting the power structure. To persons in the Kennedy Administration's Juvenile Program, it meant assisting the power structure after the

[5]James Coleman, *et al.*, *Equality of Educational Opportunity* (Washington D.C.: United States Government Printing Office, 1966).

fashion of Sargent Shriver's Peace Corps. The Bureau of the Budget, for example, supported the venture primarily because it promised greater evaluation of how funds were spent than most governmental programs, and B.O.B. had been pressing for greater accountability. All of these meanings co-existed during the drafting of the legislation and persisted into the administration of the program. It was soon evident that the various components of the program were working at cross-purposes without even knowing it.[6]

Moynihan's greatest accusation against the program, however, is his contention that the government did not know what it was doing and would not confess to its ignorance. The social science theory upon which the program was based, while held by some reputable social scientists, was by no means adequately supported by research. And yet it was being advanced as an adequate explanation of the causes of poverty. The essence of the official understanding, Marris and Rhein contend, was that poverty is caused by the poverty cycle and bureaucratic indifference.[7] Both of these were conceived of as essentially institutional failings which had the effect of reducing opportunities available to the poor. This explanation owed much to Cloward and Ohlin's understanding of juvenile delinquency, in which the delinquent was seen as basically ascribing to the values of the larger society, while at the same time, he was denied the means to achieve them. Thus he reacted to frustration in delinquent ways. The poor were conceived of as living the way they do because of limited access to the mainstream of American society. There is some uncertainty here, however.

For example, Moynihan himself had produced a furor when an administrative memo which he intended to circulate only amongst some two hundred persons in the executive branch was released by the Government Printing Office to the general public as a booklet entitled *The Negro Family: The Case for National Action.*[8] While it is true that Moynihan does state that the problem of unemployment is a major cause of the problems of the black family, the focus of the report is on the "tangle of pathology" that constitutes the life-style of at least one-third of poor black families. The female-headed family was correlated with all sorts of pathologies, ranging from increased rates of illegitimacy, juvenile delinquency, and crime, to increased rates of mental illness. Great stress was placed upon the fact that, while only about a third of all poor black families were headed by females at any one time, over half of all black children live in such a family at least part of their lives. The argument advanced was that the socialization of children in such families was not only inadequate by middle-class standards, but was a significant cause in the perpetuation of poverty. Children from such families had a greater tendency to

---

[6]Christopher Jencks, *Inequality: A Reassessment of the Effects of Family and Schooling in America* (New York: Basic Books, 1972).

[7]Daniel P. Moynihan, *Maximum Feasible Misunderstanding: Community Action in the War on Poverty* (New York: The Free Press, 1969).

[8]Peter Marris and Martin Rhein, *Dilemmas of Social Reform* (New York: Atherton Press, 1967).

remain in poverty than children raised in other types of families, or so the argument went.

For many, the policy implications of such a view of poverty were clear. It was necessary to break the poverty cycle through cultural enrichment programs that exposed the children to a better way of life and gave the parents, particularly the mothers, more skills with which to manage their households and raise their children. Some advocated the removal of the children from their homes for extended periods of time so that they could more effectively socialize into the larger society. Fortunately, these plans were never realized. Almost parenthetically it was acknowledged that jobs for both men and women were necessary, but the focus tended here to be on job training programs rather than "make-work" efforts to create new jobs.

In the case of "community action," it became increasingly clear to some of those who managed the program that what the poor needed was power. They needed to be directly involved in the planning and administration of programs designed to reduce poverty and improve the character of their neighborhoods. In practice, community action came to mean increasingly confronting the power structure. Since the poor knew better than the experts "what ailed them," since they aspired to the same high standards of living as everyone else, and since the normal political channels tended to ignore their plight through introverted concentration on agency survival, the poor must be mobilized to fight their own political battles. They must fight City Hall if they are ever going to change the basic conditions of their life and increase their opportunity to live the good life.

Moynihan takes great glee in chiding the middle-class mind set for its presumption that it understands the problems of the poor better than anyone else. He finds it ironic that academically trained white women can assert that they understand what it means for a black man to fight for his masculinity. He delights in pointing out that Alinsky himself, the idol of many in the program, called C.A.P. "political pornography." Alinsky believed C.A.P. could not face up to the fundamental contradiction involved in expecting the federal government to fund elements of society that were intent upon its radical transformation. The animal must defend itself, and when it did, the academician often cried "foul." The political naïveté of the master planners was enormous, in Moynihan's view.

Marris and Rhein take a more hospitable view in contending that while the program made many political blunders, it did contribute something new to the political scene, an agency intent upon advocating the cause of the poor.[9] Its major problem, they contend, was that it could not achieve a sufficient degree of single-mindedness in its advocacy and, in fact, attempted to advocate too many divergent causes. Of course, this agency has now been disbanded, and we are still debating the extent to which it was effective in reducing poverty. Its demise was hastened through the combined efforts of two quite traditional elements of our political

---

[9]Daniel P. Moynihan, *The Negro Family: The Case For National Action* (Washington, D.C.: United States Government Printing Office, 1965). See also the account in Lee Rainwater and William L. Yancey, *The Moynihan Report and the Politics of Controversy* (Cambridge: M.I.T. Press, 1967).

system. The mayors refused to allow federal funds, over which they had no control, to be spent in their cities in order to foment agitation for reform. They led the fight outside of Washington. The Bureau of the Budget put the quietus on the program from within the administration by withholding funds for C.A.P. until it was satisfied that there was greater accountability through the established political channels.

The extent to which social science was, in fact, used in the establishment of this program and in its administration continues to be debated. One thing is clear: if the objective of the program was the elimination of poverty, it has only been very partially successful.

Styles of Research and Policy Needs

From the above examples, it should be clear that science has assumed a political role in our time. It is really no longer a question if it should, but rather of how it should do so.[10] There are a number of ways in which scientific experts can be involved in the policy process. Each of them has its own peculiar costs and benefits. The least realistic and most costly of these is the continued attempt to define science as a value-free enterprise in which personal or political values should not intervene, even if in point of fact they always do. This approach is the most costly because it disguises values that do in fact dominate the considerations of scientists and thus prevents them from being critically analyzed.

On the other hand, the blind advocacy of one's personal or political values under the guise of scientific authoritativeness is not particularly effective either. This was the charge Moynihan leveled against the social scientists who backed the legislation that produced O.E.O. It was not that they were advocating, but rather that they encouraged the view that what they were advocating had greater supporting evidence behind it than it in fact did. They were not honest about the risk involved in such a policy.

If science is anything from the point of view of the policy-maker, it is only one way by which uncertainty can be reduced. At one time, it was thought by some that science would do away with all matters of uncertainty and debate by discovery of true facts about the world in which we live, but no longer.[11] It is one means by which this uncertainty may be reduced, but never eliminated. It can also be, as the case of the atom bomb illustrates, a means by which uncertainty can be increased. It has become popular for scientists to point out that, while some matters become clarified, others become more complex. Science opens up more questions than it answers, in this view.

[10]Marris and Rhein, *Dilemmas*.

[11]A short version of how sociology should be linked to social policy is found in Morris Janowitz, *Sociological Models and Social Policy* (New York: General Learnings Press, 1971). See also John Friedman and Barclay Hudson, "Knowledge and Action: A Guide to Planning Theory," *American Institute of Planners Journal* (Jan. 1974), pp. 2-15.

Nevertheless, in the crude and common atmosphere of everyday life, we assume that a world that is verified by means of scientific analysis is less uncertain than one that is not and that, given a particular policy alternative, it ought to be possible to reduce the uncertainty of its being accomplished through use of the scientific expert. But in what way might this be so? In order to talk about this matter in any other than the commonly developed models of how science can be related to the policy process, it is necessary to look a bit closer than we have done up to now.

Let us begin with the essential question: how do we know that something is not possible? Or, more practically, how can we have reasonable confidence that what we are proposing in terms of a program to eliminate poverty will be possible? The pragmatist would argue that we will not know what is possible until we try it out. But we are not certain that it will not work even after we have tried it and failed. To come back to our example of poverty, what we seem to have learned from it is that the program did not work as the planners had intended. Nevertheless, Marris and Rhein contended that it initiated a new structural approach to poverty, even if this approach has since been abandoned.

Moynihan gives a hesitant "yes" to his own rhetorical question about the existence of a social science with a body of information to which men of widely different political persuasions would give assent. He also contends that the proper role of social science is in the evaluation of what has been accomplished by a particular public policy, not to be directly involved in the definition of new programs. Therefore, he would argue, the job of social science is to tell the policymaker what happened as a result of his war on poverty. Presumably he should not tell the policy maker to wage, or not to wage, the war in the first place. This sounds simple at first blush and reasonable in light of the conservative nature of science as science; it has better hindsight than foresight, in spite of all the ballyhoo about prediction. But assessment of whatever has happened is bound up in the assessment of what to do next.

Having concluded that the war on poverty reduced the incidence of poverty by such and such a percent, with the likely costs to the taxpayer of so many dollars, the rational policy-maker would assess the desirability of continuing the program. He would consider a new set of priorities and resources in order to attempt to reduce poverty even further. As long as we can maintain the illusion of a policy-maker acting, a social scientist evaluating the effect of the action, and the two remaining distinct in role and in influence, science becomes solely allocated to an assessment of what is and policy to what ought to be. This is the traditional model, and it is totally unreal. It is a very poor guide to the interrelationships that do exist, and an even poorer guide to accounting for what ought to be. You cannot derive the ought from the is. Positivists have picnicked on this rock ever since.

Styles of Social Science Methodology

The impossibility of deriving the "ought" from the "is" is peculiar to the positivist tradition within the social sciences, which takes it as axiomatic that facts can be empirically verifiable and values cannot be. From the perspective of styles of research, this approach chooses arbitrarily to place its greatest confidence in the empirically verifiable and has fostered "the scientific method" as the major means by which this verification is supposed to take place. There are other styles.

The Scientists.   Persons choosing this style of research are inclined to call themselves "scientists." They seek to perfect instruments (ranging from statistical techniques to scales and observational techniques) that will eliminate observer bias from the gathering of data. The assumption is that the facts once adequately separated from value biases, will speak for themselves. In sociology such scientists are inclined to favor precision of measurement over adequacy of observation, but they rarely acknowledge this distinction, since their intention is to increase the perfection of various measurement techniques with the ultimate goal of better solutions to urban problems. The hope is that urban problems can be solved in much the same way as a mathematician can solve a complex mathematical problem. The scientists thus concentrate their efforts upon increasing the objectivity of their research and the verifiability of their information. They have the greatest confidence that this approach will more likely yield reliable data about their world.

On the other hand, it is clear that this style of research is only one of many. In American sociology, it has been a dominant style until the present, but at all times other styles are observable. These other styles rely on quite different approaches to research.

The Generalists.   The *generalists* concentrate upon developing a logically consistent model of social reality. Talcott Parsons is a prime example of this approach in his work on social, psychological, and cultural systems. The generalists believe that they know what they know about the world around them to the extent that this information fits into their logically constructed model of reality. Action theorists, systems analysts, computer simulators, theorists of the middle range, and to some extent symbolic interactionists tend to find this approach rewarding. What is sacrificed is the rich diversity of human experience in the attempt to make a general statement about it.

Thus, in the case of family studies, the nuclear family, as conceived of in structural functional theory, is a social institution that, by definition, is the elemental building block of the social structure. It functions everywhere to provide economic cooperation or a division of labor between the spouses which contributes to the greater survival capacity of the conjugal pair, the reproduction of children, and their education into society, thereby replacing members lost through death, desertion, etc. Finally, it is the major means of regulating sexual behavior so that this explosive human energy will not destroy the fabric of society. If the husband, wife, and children that comprise the membership of this nuclear family did not, to some degree, fulfill these functions, the society would soon fall apart.

What is overlooked in such a quest for universals is the obvious observation that all societies have institutionalized one or more alternatives to the nuclear family. Historically speaking, the nuclear family, when it has been functional, has not been the building block of the social structure, but rather has been an unstable equilibrium between more basic structures: the extended family and the various dyads that comprise it, especially the mother-child dyad. Moynihan assumes that the nuclear family is the building block of the social structure when he proposes his family policy and when he calls attention to the female-headed black family as a "case for national action." Within his view of the world, he is, of course, quite correct, but his view of the world is quite limited and his generalities hide the functional alternatives.

The Realists.   The *realists* are a group of social scientists who are most concerned about the adequacy of their data. They are concerned to reflect the rich variety of experience found in human societies, and they are consequently reluctant to make general statements about human behavior and social organization. The techniques preferred by this style of research are likely to include participant observation, ethno-methodological and naturalistic observation techniques and, to some degree, phenomenology. Here it must be noted that the latter two, particularly the ethno-methodologists, are quite interested in making general statements about human behavior based on detailed observation of what most of us take for granted about our worlds (and, therefore, are most controlled by). However, the desire to get beneath the surface of things has produced, in practice, a wealth of material about the particulars of human situations and little as yet that seems generalizable.

The concern for adequacy seeks to fit the methodology of research to a model of man that assumes that human experience is somehow richer than animal existence and, therefore, requires special consideration of phenomena which are otherwise anathema to scientists, such as meaning and value. These persons are not particularly concerned to call themselves scientists.

The Utilitarians.   Finally, there are growing numbers of persons who call themselves scientists but who place greatest confidence in knowing what they know when the information can be shown to be useful. These we can call the *utilitarians*. Their motto is, of course, "If it works, it's true." Usefulness is pragmatically determined and is not assumed. It must work well enough for the purposes at hand. If these persons are consultants to businesses or governments, what they propose must work well enough so that business makes a profit or government realizes its objectives. So long as this occurs in the short run, there is little concern with the long-run consequence. Indeed, there is the tendency to argue that, should something be so wrong that it brings about long-run disastrous results, we will be able to make adjustments when we get there. In political science, these persons are inclined to call themselves *incrementalists*.

The point is that these, and possibly other, styles of research are evident in the community of social scientists. They do not presuppose a single scientific method. They do assume quite different things about their worlds and the ways in which one should go about studying them. They all tend to assume a common metaphysic to some degree, wherein the underlying reality they are studying is ever more adequately approximated by their models of it. This is truest for the generalists and least true for the realists, who are becoming more inclined to talk about diverse realities. In similar fashion, the matter of value is least important to the scientists and most important to the realists and the utilitarians, but for quite different reasons. The utilitarians presuppose the accomplishment of value-ladened objectives as partially verifying their knowledge. The realists contend that fact and value cannot be separated and must be taken jointly into consideration in the quest for adequacy of explanation.

Policy Relevant Research

While each style discussed above has something to offer the policy-maker, none seem ideal as currently practiced. In order to better relate social science to public policy, the matter must be approached in a radically different way. This approach can only be sketched in this chapter, but any description must begin with the observation that the social scientist stands in a different relation to the objects of his investigation than the natural scientist. As a person who has been socialized into a society, often the very society he is attempting to investigate, the social scientist has what Warren Bennis has called "an inside track."[12] He knows about his society in his bones, because he was in part created by it. The tacit knowledge of one's own society is much richer than one's tacit knowledge of an atom.[13]

Traditionally social science has tried to ignore or minimize the effect of this kind of knowledge. Anthropologists struggled against ethnocentricism and sociologists against subjective biases, both of which directed attention to the limitations of generalizing from one's personal experience. Lay persons have become aware of this issue in the continuing discussions of stereotyping, the retention of a generalization about a group of people in spite of evidence that contradicts it. But in the reaction against stereotypes, there has been an abandonment of the willingness to explicitly take into account the information about a way of life that one has acquired by virtue of living that life. Some reflection should convince us that this knowledge is much richer and more reliable for many of our encounters than that small portion of our information about the world which we have been able to state in logically relatable hypotheses and expose to empirical verification.[14]

The major trouble with this information is that we do not understand well enough the conditions under which it is likely to hold true. From this perspective, social science research can be seen as an attempt to make explicit the limitations of our personal understandings about the world by confronting us with situations that are different from our own. It is evident taht sociology does indeed provide a service by simply describing the life styles of persons who live differently than we do—and

---

[12]A central axis of the sociological debate over fact and value is found in David Frisby, "The Popper-Adorno Controversy: A Methodological Dispute in German Sociology," *Philosophy of Social Science* 2 (1972), pp. 105–119.

[13]Warren Bennis, *Changing Organizations* (New York: McGraw-Hill, 1966).

[14]Michael Polanyi, *Personal Knowledge: Toward a Post Critical Philosophy* (Chicago: University of Chicago Press, 1958).

therefore, cannot be intuitively comprehended as well as we might comprehend those who life in a fashion similar to our own.

From this "inside-out" perspective, social theorizing becomes the activity of discovering oneself in the context of ne's community and heritage by virtue of common allegiances to a similarly defined reality. What is problematic is not the reality, but the conditions under which it is constructed. This reduces in practice to a study of the conditions under which various types of communities were established and an attempt to understand the value (costs/benefits) of the life styles of these communities given these conditions.

This reformulation of the social science venture calls into question the historically accepted distinction between fact and value. The empirically verifiable "facts" of the *social* worlds of these communities have significance—indeed are only selected for investigation in the first place—because they are given significance by a particular community. The power of these social worlds to define their own separate realities is most dramatically illustrated in the case of those eastern mystics who do indeed walk on coals. The ability of these persons to perform these feats has been verified by western scientists who have measured the heat of the coals and have assured themselves that there is no hidden protection for the feet. It seems that the mind of these mystics, in the context of their culture, is able to prevent the foot from being burned by coals that would sear any normal western person's foot to the bone. Strangely enough, when these persons become converted to another way of life, they lose the capacity to walk on coals.

Information about what is real in the world is always gathered in a value context about what is significant or desirable. Scientific methods do not control this condition of the human experience by ignoring it. It is not possible to completely control the "value" component of information by an attempt to become aware of one's values, although this is a helpful exercise in itself. The problem of the irreducible reality behind socially constructed worlds is not resolved by this approach, which continually asks to what extent the physical world is a social construct.[17] These issues are not solved; they are ignored. The focus of this "inside-out" approach to social science forces the social scientist to examine other aspects of his world, specifically those pertaining to the social construction of reality and the formation of human communities with visions of the future and adequate means of coping with the present. The priorities of these diverse human communities and their visions of what is possible and desirable are thereby, given much greater

---

[15]Anselm Strauss and Barner Glazer go part way in linking personal data to public policy in "Discovery of Substantive Theory: A Basic Strategy Underlying Qualitative Research," *American Behavioral Scientist* (Feb. 1965). See also their *The Discovery of Grounded Theory: Strategies for Qualitative Research* (Chicago: Aldine Publishing Company, 1967).

[16]Alan F. Blum, "Theorizing" in *Understanding Everyday Life,* Jack D. Douglas, ed., (Chicago: Aldine Publishing Company, 1970).

[17]Joseph Chilton Pearce, *The Crack in the Cosmic Egg: Challenging Constructs of Mind and Reality* (New York: Pocket Books, 1973), Ch. 6.

weight in the scientific enterprise thus conceived. For the individual, it becomes important to ask "Why do we want to conceive of the world in this way and act as though this particular vision of the world were the correct one?" Whereas the comparable traditional question has been, "Is this vision of reality the true, or a truer, one?" For the policy-maker, it becomes important to know the likely consequences of a particular policy or a particular community through personalized channels of communication that allow as much of the context of the issues to emerge as possible.[18]

A New Vision of Planning

Given the above reformulation of the social science venture, and accepting some definition of democracy as a desirable political structure within which planning ought to occur, it becomes possible to conceive of planning in a quite different way. Following John Friedman and Amitai Etzioni, the focus of this redefinition is first of all on the relationship of the planner to the policy process.[19] He becomes more central, but at the apparent cost of his expertise. At least, he cannot hide behind his expertise.

Friedman has a radical vision of a learning society, in which perhaps forty percent of the population would be directly involved in the day-to-day process of societal guidance. They would do this through a cellular society resembling Jefferson's Republic of Wards, in which small groups of people representing distinct and functional communities would coordinate their work with other cells through representatives who might be called planners or guidance specialists. These persons would be in direct contact with their cells or subcommunities and in direct contact with those who make decisions about public policy. Without this direct and personal channel, tacit information about the problems of the cells and shared conceptions of desirable futures could not adequately be transferred.

The policy-makers and planners are not conceived of as experts who by any acquirable skill can attain the competence to formulate the problems of society. The definition of social issues must involve all those living in a learning society through the personalized channels of their representatives. Policy decisions are made on behalf of others only in the sense that legislation reflected the efforts of a few in behalf of the many.[20]

This vision is to be distinguished from our commonly held ideal of representative democracy, not only in the personalized channels through which information is transferred, but primarily in the assumption that there can be no expert (as we have

[18]Peter Berger and Thomas Luckman, *The Social Construction of Reality* (Garden City, N.Y.: Doubleday, 1966).

[19]John Friedman, *Retracking America* (Garden city, New York: Doubleday, 1973). Etzioni, *The Active Society* (New York: The Free Press, 1968), pp. 94–131.

[20]See Chapter 8 on the city as community.

tended to define him in the past). Since social reality is a social construct, social issues are and must be defined by persons who are confronting them daily within the contexts of their particular communities or cells. This definition of a social issue need not be considered final for the purposes of policy for the entire society, but it must be taken directly into account in the formulation of that policy. The insights of experts would not be ignored in this learning society, since it is obvious that some of us are more skilled than others in specific aspects of coping with our world, but the expert input can never have pre-eminence over the lay definition.

This is a utopian world. It seems unlikely that we would establish such a mode of societal guidance, given our present concerns. Most of us would not prefer to participate in "dirty politics," even if we could find the time to do so. Most of us still believe that there are a few experts who can define the problems for us. We want to trust them to act in our interests somehow. Most experts still feel that only they really understand the nature of our problems (in spite of their poor track record in solving them). Our schools do not adequately assist most of us to think for ourselves. A virtual cultural revolution would have to occur for the learning society to be realized in practice.

The very least that would have to happen is that our romance with "the scientific method" would have to end. The primacy of scientific knowledge over other forms of knowledge would have to be denied. We need to see that the tunnel-vision of scientific investigation, however useful it might be in the analysis of increasingly narrowly defined problems, is totally inadequate as the guide to policy-making, or, for that matter, the evaluation of policy impacts. Once the world-view of any society is fragmented by analysis of this narrow sort, it is not to be put back together again. Like the biologists attempting to study the cell through its dissection, we don't even know what we have lost in our attempt to understand.

To the extent that urban problems are seen as issues that require continual coping and guidance rather than resolution, to this extent we will be assisted in making the transition to a learning society.

To the extent that we reaffirm the value of a democracy in which no one is acknowledged as wise enough to govern another without his consent and a truly informed electorate is thought desirable, to this extent we will be assisted in the transition to a learning society.

To the extent that we recognize that the process of governing is as important as the product of government, and to the extent that the rush of events in our times will permit us the luxury of reshuffling our basic ideals, to this extent we will be assisted in making the transition to a learning society.

To the extent that we attempt to calculate the human costs of our solutions in assessing the efficiency of our current mode of governance, going beyond narrow economic assessments of costs and benefits, to this extent we will progress toward a learning society.

To the extent that we will tolerate a redistribution of advantages both economic and political (money and power) to approach a greater realization of this nation as a nation of average persons, to this extent we will be assisted in becoming a learning society.

No society on earth has gone very far down this path. Perhaps the most accomplished group of people in this regard are the 90,000 or so who live in Israel's kibbutzim. In this limited context, a small group in a tiny nation, gathered around ideological commitments to equality and electing to be primarily an agricultural economy within their own communities, something approaching a learning society has been in existence for over sixty years and is presently raising its third generation. Whether a complex industrial nation such as ours can go even as far as they have remains to be seen. Perhaps the intractable problems of our cities will move us toward consideration of such a radical alternative. Perhaps not.

Conclusion

Since 1939, science has become intertwined with public policy in a number of ways. Big science is increasingly dependent upon federal funds for its very survival. Governments depend upon scientists for theirs. Scientists are increasingly called upon to provide information about the character of our everyday problems, some of which become ever more complex and ever more incomprehensible to the average citizen.

The most common way of including the information of the scientist in the public process is to consider that the scientist is a consultant who is called upon to give information or sketch alternative scenarios for coping, but is not given the power to make policy. This is ideally to be entrusted to some body of persons who represent the public. Another basic way of getting scientific information into the policy process has been to contend that the scientist, like any other citizen, has the right, and indeed the obligation, to argue his case in the public arena. He does so not as a scientist, but as a citizen. This distinction is difficult to make in practice, especially under pressure of complex ecological issues in which reputable scientists take sides and disagree on both the nature of the problem and its resolution.

Social scientists can no longer afford to ignore or try to eliminate the tacit knowledge they have by virtue of the fact that they have been socialized into a society and know how it works from the inside out. This "inside track" needs to be considered in the context of others' inside information and the intersubjectively verifiable information, or public knowledge, that is the domain of traditional science. To focus upon how it is that groups of people construct their own special version of reality is to increase understanding of how communities are formed, their priorities for the future, and the things they consider problematic.

Transactive planning, as suggested by John Friedman, is a vision of planning that would attempt to involve a large minority of the society directly in the societal guidance process. By establishing personalized channels of communication between representatives and citizenry, and by involving as many as possible in the planning process, the definition of social problems within the ambit of public policy will be greatly enriched. The planner cannot under any circumstances assume that his knowledge or expertise is adequate information upon which to base policy, nor can he simply accept the preferences from an uneducated population. In a learning society, even those who are not directly involved in societal guidance will be expected to be sufficiently informed on public policy matters and the problems of their communities so that they can give informed definitions of both problems and desirable policy alternatives to those who must decide.

This vision of a learning society goes a great deal beyond what we have been able to realize in our society. It assumes the necessity of extensive citizen participation, not only because such participation is democratic, but also because the guidance process requires such citizen input. The planner cannot do his job without it. Until events press us into reassessing our current values, such a process seems too expensive, too inefficient and, therefore, quite unrealistic. It will require a cultural revolution in order to establish the primacy of the reflexive planning approach. Such a revolution may never take place. On the other hand, the increasing recognition that we cannot solve our urban problems after the fashion of an engineer or mathematician may force us into such a reconsideration of priorities. Only time will tell.

chapter 14

Urban Political Process and Social Planning

Introduction

The crisis mentality of our times often inclines us to look at our urban areas and their problems in short-term, superficial ways. Issues such as poverty, public transportation, race relations, taxation, and the problems of the public schools come to the attention of most of us through the mass media. They quickly become defined as "crises" by one authority or another, and we begin to clamor for a solution, or at least a way out. We want someone to solve our crises painlessly, if possible, through public programs or private initiatives that we can all agree upon. More often than not we are given "solutions" in legislation that reflect moral indignation, rather than reasoned analysis. Nevertheless, upon passage of legislation and the promise of public officials to do something about the matter, we typically consider the problem solved because the shouting has died down.

Whether we choose to use crisis terminology to describe what is happening to our cities or not, there is a strong concern to do something to improve them. While almost no one favors doing nothing, there is a great disagreement over what should be done. John Friedman, therefore, looks at the situation in a somewhat different way. He calls the problems of our cities a "crisis of knowing and valuing."[1] As he sees it, the problems of urban societies are as much problems of purpose and values as of inadequate resources or under-utilized technologies. What do we want our cities to become? How do we go about determining what we want? Who, in the last analysis, are "we"?

*In this chapter we are particularly indebted to our colleague, Dr. Daniel Rich, for his comments and contributions.
[1]John Friedman, *Retracking America* (Garden City, N.Y.: Doubleday, 1973), pp. 85–115.

313

Philadelphia's City Hall is one of America's largest and one of its most notable municipal government buildings. The Tower, rising more than 547 feet above street level, is surmounted by a heroic-sized statue of William Penn, founder of the city and the state of Pennsylvania. The statue, by Alexander Milne Calder, is the largest sculpture on top of any building in the world.

The Two Faces of American Cities

For some, the city has symbolized the good life. Urbanization is seen as concurrent with the improvement of human welfare and, our cities and ourselves are better off than they have ever been. For others, the city is a symbol of deprivation, blight, and insecurity, a testimonial to human indifference and failure. Such disparate views continue to exist side by side, often with equal credibility, precisely because our cities themselves are bifurcated, if not schizophrenic, in character. They manifest the extremes of American society, and no simple summation of pluses and minuses can accurately portray their contradictory conditions. As Ira Sharkansky has suggested, the dualism of American cities is their most dominant characteristic.

> The cities present two sides of America. Their attractive side includes productive manufacturing, innovative service industries, striking architecture, and experimental programs on the frontiers of social policy. Their unattractive side features slum housing,

grinding poverty, widespread crime and attendant social programs that seem unable to cope with the people's needs and occasional disorders that threaten the political fabric.[2]

It is in the cities that human interdependence is most extensive, yet it is in the cities that social and economic distances are often greatest and institutional fragmentation most acute. It is in the cities that concentrations of wealth abound; yet it is in the cities where poverty is most manifest and where governments seem unable even to support themselves. Historically the city has been the source of democratic principles; yet the modern city challenges the viability of all forms of government. The existence of cities has been justified by the function they serve in expanding the boundaries of human choice and opportunity; yet all around there is evidence which leads us to question not only the viability of cities, but the extent to which purposive human choice is possible.

The dualism of American cities leads us to equivocate about the existence of an urban crisis. Yet such an equivocation does not mean that the problems of the cities, any more than their virtues, can be easily overlooked or dismissed. The problems are apparent whether or not we choose to define such problems as constituting a crisis.

In some cities the problems faced are more acute than in others. The older cities such as New York, Philadelphia, St. Louis, and Chicago seem to be plagued with problems more than newer cities such as Houston, San Diego, or Seattle. Industrial cities seem more beset by difficulties than governmental centers or trading centers. Yet, despite such variation, the pattern of urban unease is rather similar for most cities: an exodus of middle-income families to the suburbs, an increase in the concentration of the poor and of urban minorities, a loss of retail markets, a declining skilled labor market, a deteriorating tax base, traffic congestion, the spread of slums and urban blight, a loss of industrial and commercial institutions, an increase in the cost of public services, a decrease in the ability of government to pay for such services, a fragmentation of political and governmental authority, and a diffusion of public responsibility.

The pattern is well known and needs little elaboration; such a pattern serves as the backdrop for the day-to-day problems with which we are most familiar. Thus, for example, the patterns described above have contributed to the predicament of the city of New York, whose expenditures for public services continue to increase while its sources of revenues deteriorate. It is now faced with a series of alternatives which seem equally unappealing. Local banks will not support the city's municipal bonds, a necessary source of revenue, unless city expenditures are curtailed. Reduction of expenditures, however, will result in a decline in the quality of public services delivered, which will further encourage individuals and institutions to leave the city and further erode the city's revenue base.

In St. Louis, the electorate has consistently voted against school revenue bonds, contributing to a decline in the quality of public education, which in turn,

[2]Ira Sharkansky, "Two Faces of the American City" (1955), p. 71.

helps to encourage the middle-class exodus to the suburbs and increases the concentration of the poor and minorities in the city. As a result, the economic infrastructure of the city continues to decline, and support for public education becomes less and less available.

These problems seem to require concerted public action, but the problems themselves have contributed to the diffusion of political authority. As the problems of the cities worsen, the exodus to surrounding regions increases, contributing to a general pattern of metropolitan decentralization and political fragmentation. It is estimated that by the year 2000, there will be 31,600 non-school governmental units in our metropolitan areas. In the New York area, there are over 1,400 political geographic jurisdictions, units too small to solve their own problems, yet unable and unwilling to participate in a consistent way in regional solutions. Such patterns suggest that the viability of governance in our cities is at stake. Political scientists and sociologists have been preoccupied with determining who governs the city, but the pattern of problems in our cities would lead us to question whether or not there is governance at all. The city has all but lost its political and governmental integrity.

In the midst of governmental decentralization, the growth and development of our cities proceeds haphazardly. A promising plan in one area is offset by a disaster in planning or lack of planning in another area. Urban sprawl continues and it contributes not only to a decline in the aesthetics of the urban region but complicates transportation, communications, and coordination. Expressways built to relieve downtown congestion often further exacerbate the problem. Some advocate actions to accommodate the need for automobile transportation, while others deliberately ignore the automobile in the hope of driving it from the city.

In the face of these problems, our resources for coping may seem meager. The catalogue of public and private programs that passes before us in the morning newspaper often appears to be a litany of failure, a documentation of our inability to make cities work as we desire. Government programs often epitomize bureaucratic inefficiency and impersonality. Not infrequently, such programs themselves become added to the list of city problems. Public welfare programs have been attacked by individuals along the entire spectrum of ideological outlooks. Critics differ in their proposed solutions, but the programs continue in much the same manner year after year and public attention is often diverted from the problems of deprivation to the problems of the programs intended to resolve deprivation.

Our experience with private initiatives has been no more encouraging. Periodically, business leaders in many communities have committed themselves to grandiose schemes for urban redevelopment. Almost without exception, such schemes are rationalized as being in the public interest and almost without exception, the principal beneficiary is the business community itself. The programs have generally emphasized development spectaculars to revitalize the central business district, with little attention to the impact of such development on other groups in the city. The results manifest the schizophrenic character of our cities. There arises a downtown oasis, complete with glass and steel monuments linked to the surrounding area by impressive expressways. These enable businessmen to make the daily trek from the suburbs and return in the evening largely oblivious to the slums and blight which surrounds the oasis, to the dislocations of people, and to the social antagonism generated by such development.

More cynical observers have suggested that it is precisely the pursuit of private profit that has exacerbated crisis and can hardly solve it. Indeed, the private sector often has been held responsible for the failures of cities—for the seemingly unplanned and capricious patterns of growth and decay. "What the private market could do well, American cities have done well; what the private market did badly, or neglected, our cities have been unable to overcome."[3] With such an assessment in mind, we frequently have turned again to the public sector, hoping to overcome the perceived limitations of the market place. Predictably this has resulted in a further proliferation of government programs contributing to the weight of urban bureaucracy and stimulating greater pessimism about prospects for resolving our problems. Regardless of our ability to effectively govern, behind the two faces of our cities is a struggle for power.

The Nature of Community Power

Sociologists are prone to study normative integration; economists study utilitarian integration; and political scientists study coercive integration. Power, expressed most dramatically in the ability to take life, lies at the base of every constitution. Power has been variously defined, but within the Weberian tradition, it essentially means the ability to impose one's will on another in spite of the other's resistance. When power is studied in the field, a major focus is on the decision-making process, either directly, in an attempt to determine who makes the policy decisions in a community, or indirectly, insofar as it is possible to describe those who have the reputation of being decision-makers.

No one seriously contends that cities change solely in response to political decisions. This is a much too simple view of their transformation and development. Urbanization seems much less a product of intentional governmental policy in the United States than it does in Europe, particularly the socialist countries there. Further, all intentional change attempted through public policy is now widely acknowledged to bring with it unintended consequences that make it difficult to predict likely policy outcomes and, therefore, to rationally plan over long time frames. But it is also evident that policy does affect the growth of cities, however rational or irrational it may be thought to be. And since it is an element over which we seem to have some control, it deserves our attention and perfection. C. Wright Mills wrote:

> Power has to do with whatever decisions men make about the arrangements under which they live, and about the events which make up the history of their times. Events that are

[3]*Loc. cit.*

beyond human decision do happen; social arrangements do change without benefit of explicit decision. But in so far as such decisions are made, the problem of who is involved in making them is the basic problem of power. In so far as they could be made and are not, the problems becomes—who fails to make them?[4]

The question of who makes the decisions tends to be answered in one of two basic ways. The elitists, of which Mills is one of the best representatives, contend that there is a single power elite, a small group of persons who at the national level determine basic policy in their interest. In this view, politics is a fracus at the middle level of power and the politician is the major power broker. The masses have virtually no say in the policy that affects their lives. In contrast to this position, the pluralists contend that there are many powerful groups which tend to become involved in the policy process when their interests are threatened. Pluralists tend to stress the importance of voluntary associations and interest groups as means by which large numbers of persons become indirectly involved in the making of public policy. Clearly the elitist model runs counter to democratic ideals, while the pluralists seem to court these ideals at least superficially. It is quite possible to conceive of non-democratic pluralist societies, however. Indeed, Theodore Lowie contends that what he calls "interest group liberalism" is a fundamentally destructive form of participation in the political process, because it readily leads to the weakening of popular government.

The Power Elite

C. Wright Mills coined the term *power elite* to describe the coalition of interests— "the high military, the corporation executives, the political directorate"—which has emerged in America since World War II. Mills understood that this elite of a few thousand families did not involve itself in every issue of the day, but stood together on issues of "war and peace, boom or bust." The interest of these three groups coalesced, in Mills's view, around American foreign policy, where they are the principle actors in the political drama and are heavily affected by our military posture. On the home front, their interest is not so much in how our resources will be distributed—they receive the lion's share in any event as members of the top one percent of the nation's wealthy. In domestic policy, they are much more interested in the size of the pie—the nature and strength of economic growth. Their investments in this area are also overlapping.

It is not necessary to assume an intentional conspiracy on the part of the power elite in order for Mills's interpretation of the power structure to hold. He assumes that persons who are members of the power elite are naturally drawn together by the converging interest in the big issues of our day and that they see these issues from a distinctively limited perspective which favors their own best interests as they per-

[4]C. Wright Mills, "Structure of Power in America" in Irving Louis Horowitz, ed., *People, Power and Politics* (New York: Basic Books, 1968).

ceive them. They are not so much malicious as unresponsive to broader interests. Mills also did not assume that the power elite could make things come out the way they wanted them to, even in the major areas of their interests. They more often seem like staggering giants wielding mighty clubs wreaking havoc on their environment. They have power, but they may well not use it rationally or even effectively in their own best interests. If anyone can realize interests through the political process, the member of the power elite comes closest to being able to realize his. In any event, Mills was absolutely certain that "The issues that now shape man's fate are neither raised nor decided by any public at large."[5]

In Mill's view, middle America, where the drama of politics is carried out, is far down the power pyramid from the power elite. Most of politics, in his view, is concerned with how to get a piece of the pie, not making decisions about how large the pie shall be. Labor unions react, they do not lead. Politicians trade patronage for votes. The new middle class, less than 20 percent of the labor force, exists to manage the organizations of the upper classes.

While the power elite was coalescing at the apex of the political pyramid, the public at large was opting out of the process. It was becoming a mass rather than a public. Mills contended that the preservation of a public requires: (1) a civil service that is firmly linked with the world of knowledge and sensibility, skilled staff, independent of corporate interest; (2) nationally responsible parties that openly debate and clarify the issues confronting the nation and the world; (3) an intelligentsia inside as well as outside the universities, who carry on the big discourse of the western world and whose work is relevant to and influential among partisans, movements, and publics; and (4) free association among families, communities, and publics.[6]

In Mills' view, mass communications place more and more individuals on the receiving end of information without an opportunity or desire to react publicly to it. Their opinions, therefore, are being formed for them while they passively acquiesce. Many more Americans receive opinions than give them. The voluntary associations and interest groups into which the average citizen is lead, do not, in fact, reflect his interests, because they have been infiltrated by government and corporate officials who sway the opinions of their less influential fellows. Too many public officials are beholden to others for their jobs, as Watergate so tragically impressed upon us.

Floyd Hunter's study of Atlanta, Georgia, remains the classic documentation of a power elite model on the local community level.[7] Hunter's methodology has given his approach the title of "reputational," because he sought out persons reputed to be powerful, rather than observing persons in the decision-making process exercising their power. The principal question Hunter asked of a group of forty

[5]C. Wright Mills, *The Power Elite* (New York: Oxford Books, 1959).
[6]*Ibid.*, Ch. 14.
[7]Floyd Hunter, *Community Power Structure* (Chapel Hill, N.C.: University of North Carolina Press, 1952).

persons reputed by a panel of informants to be powerful in the Atlanta area was "If a project were before the community that required decision by a group of leaders—leaders that nearly everyone would accept—which ten on this list of forty would you choose?" This approach yielded twelve names sufficiently often to convince Hunter that they were, indeed, the power elite. They were men from the private sector rather than the public.

In the more traditional way of studying power—by assuming that the occupants of office were powerful—these persons would not have been covered at all. But only four in the original forty influentials in Hunter's list were office holders. Hunter concluded:

> . . . the dominant factor in political life is the personnel of economic interests. It is true that there is no formal tie between the economic interests and the government, but the structure of policy-determining committees and their tie-in with the other powerful institutions and organizations of the community make government subservient to the interests of these combined groups. The government departments and their personnel are acutely aware of the power of key individuals and combinations of citizens' groups in the policy-making realm, and they are loath to act before consulting and "clearing" with these interests.[8]

Many criticisms have been levelled against the reputational approach. The most basic is the accusation that the methodology itself determines the outcome of finding a power elite. If you go around asking who are the top leaders here, you slant the response with the assumption that there is only one set of top leaders. Second, it is not power, but the reputation of power that is being measured. Third, there is no room for a reasonable assumption that power may vary from one political domain to another. Thus office holders might be more powerful determining how funds get allocated in the maintenance of a city, while private citizens may exercise more power over the tax base. Fourth, why stop at only 40 reputedly powerful, why not study the top 100 or 1,000?[9]

Pluralist Models

Robert Dahl's approach to the study of community power yielded quite different results. His study of New Haven, Connecticut, entitled "Who Governs," concluded that a plurality of leaders are to be found in a community. Dahl approached the study of community power by determining a number of "key issues" and then identifying people who seem to be involved in policy relating to these issues. Dahl identified three basic issues: school decisions, urban renewal, and political nominations. He found that different leaders were identified with each issue. Only the mayor bridged all three issues. Dahl concluded that "in New Haven, economic and

[8]*Ibid.*, pp. 100–101.

[9]Robert L. Lineberry and Ira Sharkansky, *Urban Politics and Public Policy* (New York: Harper and Row, 1971), pp. 152–153.

social notables add relatively little influence on government decisions.''[10] In his study, public officials tended to be the major power brokers.

Critics of the decisional approach find the same shortcoming in Dahl's as in Hunter's methodology—people were asked to specify who made the decisions rather than actually observing the decisions being made. Second, there is a clear arbitrariness in the selection of issues. Why not some other more salient ones, using a different criteria? The ones selected, in fact, tended to favor the involvement of office holders, as all were political decisions in the classical sense.

John Walton reviewed the major community power studies and concluded, ''the disciplinary background of the investigator tends to determine the method of investigation he will adopt, which, in turn, tends to determine the image of the power structure that results from the investigation.''[11] Political scientists favor pluralists models; sociologists favor elitist models.

Neo-Elitism

The study of community power has been further complicated by the introduction of a distinctive perspective which takes the researcher's attention away from decision-making to non-decisions and the mobilization of bias. Peter Bachrach and Morton Baratz identified the ''two faces of power'' in their study of the War on Poverty.[12] They point out that what the decisionalists call ''key issues'' may, in fact, be rather trivial issues that do not really threaten the basic distribution of resources or disturb the established power structure. Because those in power have the capacity to establish the public agenda and define what is an issue in the first place, it is unlikely that they will allow issues to be raised that go against the elite's perceived best interest. The accumulated advantages of wealth and private property, the assumption of equal opportunity and equal treatment before the law, are all overlooked by the investigator eager to discover ''key issues.'' In short ''values and biases that are built into the political system . . . and the dominant values and the political myths, rituals, and institutions which tend to favor the vested interests of one or more groups, relative to others''[13] are ignored by the decisionalists.

A major debate thus rages amongst the analysts of community power. The debate is centered intellectually around the pluralist-elitist controversy, but more practically focused on the issue of the true significance of the formal political process. Elitists are inclined to minimize the power of office holders in favor of the economically powerful private citizens whose class interests are often portrayed as

[10]Robert Dahl, *Who Governs? Democracy and Power in an American City* (New Haven: Yale University Press, 1961).
[11]John Wolton, ''Discipline, Method and Community Power: A Note on the Sociology of Knowledge,'' *American Sociological Review* 31 (Oct. 1966), p. 688.
[12]Peter Bachrach and Morton Baratz, *Power and Poverty* (New York: Oxford University Press, 1970).
[13]*Ibid.*, p. 11.

the nation's interests ("What's good for General Motors is good for the nation.") Pluralists find it possible to extend the policy domain to include not only relatively more powerful office holders, but also various interest groups that make their wills known in the policy process through lobbying, block voting, etc. It is possible to combine both views under a power elite model if we remember that Mills was quite clear about the stage upon which his elite operated, issues of national war and peace, boom or bust. While these issues must be operationalized in order to be tested, it is compatible with the Millsian view to subsume a pluralist model under his elite and to allow the pluralist to rant and rage at the middle level, which to Mills is the level on which politics does indeed operate in a pluralist fashion. A clarification of what issues specifically call for elite attention, or to take the non-decision approach, which values are inherently supportive of the elite and therefore do not require their conscious intervention, would be needed in order to make this model fit a given urban context.

Metropolitan Government

As we suggested in the introduction to this chapter, the reality of urban politics is characterized by fragmentation, inefficiency, crisis management, and general concern over whether or not our urban areas are governable at all. The state and federal governments have also taken up various aspects of city government in an attempt to set things right. Nevertheless, the cities, especially the old cities, continue in the red, deteriorating physically almost as rapidly as they are being renewed. Urbanization in the United States has indeed been a largely unplanned "private enterprise."

The local response to the rush of population to the urban areas has been a proliferation of governmental units and programs, ostensibly to better meet the needs of citizens clamoring for services. But fragmentation has resulted in greater inefficiency especially in those areas where regional or subregional problems prevail (air pollution, water, power, etc.). The general conclusion now being reached is that

> The present system of local government fails to answer the needs of a clearly metropolitan society. Fragmented and overlapping government in metropolitan areas: 1. aggravates the mismatch between resources and social needs, 2. makes the solution of metropolitan social problems more difficult and 3. inhibits efficient administration of services.[14]

The attempt to reorganize metropolitan governments in order to make them more effective agents of public policy has met with great resistance from suburban populations, which currently benefit from federal policy and funding because of their greater population growth. The courts attempt to re-apportion the vote on a one

[14]Social Science Panel, National Research Council, "Toward an Understanding of Metropolitan America" (San Francisco: Canfield Press, 1975), p. 105.

The ultramodern city hall in Toronto, Ontario. The $30 million building, designed by Finnish architect Viljo Revell, was opened in 1964 and is now a major attraction with visitors. *(Canadian Government Office of Tourism Photo.)*

person-one vote basis has increased the handicap of the cities, which are losing population. Thus while many major metropolitan reorganization schemes have been proposed since the end of World War II, only ten have been adopted by referendum, and all of these were in metropolitan areas with populations of less than one million.[15] The failure of such reorganization efforts has led to the attempt to establish special tax and service districts. These have found more general approval because they focus upon redress of a specific grievance without disruption of the vested interests of general purpose jurisdictions.

Councils of government (COG) have also been set up in metropolitan areas in the attempt to establish voluntary cooperation between jurisdictions in the confrontation of common problems. However, there is no evidence to date that COG's have solved or effectively coped with a single major metropolitan problem.[16] There is no evidence that they are likely to take on the function of a metropolitan government.

One of the most successful attempts to cope with the provision of services was developed in Lakewood in Los Angeles County. The essence of the Lakewood Plan

[15]*Ibid.*, p. 115.
[16]*Ibid.*, p. 120.

involves the contract with an already established service district to provide the services needed. Thus Lakewood contracted with Los Angeles to have all of its municipal services provided by that city. The tendency to enter into such agreement is directly correlated with size—the larger the size of the community, the greater the inclination to enter into service contract agreements. Hawley found that 63 percent of the 2,375 municipalities responding to a questionnaire had entered into formal or informal agreements with other public or private units for the supply of services.[17]

Hawley analyzes the problem of urban localism in terms of the diverse impact of the urban environment on the different economic strata. In line with the more optimistic view advanced by Banfield, it seems reasonable to conclude that for most upper- aand middle-class persons, who rely on urban government only for basic housekeeping, protective services, and education, things were looking up through the sixties.[18] But today even these classes are becoming disenchanted with the fear of crime in the streets, congestion and pollution. The burden to date on urban services, however, is born disproportionately by the lower-middle class. The silent majority increasingly resents its hard-earned dollars going to support supposed indolents and the undeserving poor. Finally, the lowest income group, who must look to government for gratification of their most elementary wants (basic subsistence, housing, education, and a viable social environment) find government most lacking.

Some critics talk of the beneficial effects of decentralization and revenue sharing as the major means of making government more responsive to the needs of all its citizens. But Janowitz concludes that "the problem of local groups as well as that of the outside community derives less from a concentration of power than from lack of an articulated system for making decisions at all."[19] As the city and metropolitan governments fail, the states and federal government will have to assume increasing responsibility.

Public Policy and Social Well Being

Private Initiative and Public Policy

While there is strong sentiment in America to let the market take care of as many of our problems as possible under the guise of private initiative and free enterprise, there is an even stronger inclination to rely on government to solve our problems as a last resort through public policy. It is not uncommon to find the rhetoric of free enterprise issuing forth from corporate executives who turn right around and lobby for government subsidies for their firms. In the case of school desegregation, the

---

[17]*Ibid.*, p. 122.

[18]Raymond Vernon, *The Myth and Reality of Our Urban Problems* (Cambridge: Harvard University Press, 1964), p. 32.

[19]Martin Janowitz, "Converging Perspectives in Community Political Analysis," in M. Janowitz, ed., *Community Political Systems* (Glencoe, Ill.: The Free Press, 1961), p. 61.

"little man" who has relied on government to protect his interests declares that, "You can't legislate morality," which everyone in America knows is a private matter indeed. The interplay between seeking solutions through public policy and fostering private initiative is complex. In large measure, this is so because the historically cherished distinction between the public and private spheres is becoming increasingly untenable in policy matters.

Our inclinations to seek public solutions to urban problems have often resulted from a perceived need for greater accountability of the institutions which guide the development of our cities. There is good reason for our suspicions that private institutions are resistant to public accountability and respond to an economic calculus of value, despite their professed commitments to a general social welfare. At the same time, however, we have often discovered that, while public institutions are accountable in principle, in practice they are often remarkably impervious to accountability. As a result, recent surveys suggest a growing public cynicism of public and private institutions alike. Large private institutions often influence their communities as decisively as public governments, and government agencies often manifest undue responsiveness to quite narrow private interests. In such a context, the dilemmas of the cities are not likely to be resolved simply by transferring responsibilities from the private to the public sector or vice versa. In both areas the problems of accountability and responsiveness remain; in both areas the potential to change the character of our way of life remains great.

The Crises of Knowing and Valuing

To whom, then, and for what purposes should our major public and private institutions be accountable? While most legislation in our society is rationalized by saying that it is being formulated, "in the public interest," most observers would see it as the product of much narrower interests. In practice the values, interests, and prejudices of the upper classes seem to have dominated the formulation of policy. It is the life-style of these classes that is being protected by the law and, for the most part, social well-being has meant their well-being. Anatole France observed long ago that, "The law in its majesty forbids the rich and the poor alike to beg on the streets and sleep under the bridges of Paris." In our own tradition, Hamilton argued persuasively in *The Federalist Papers* that the way to insure a government's stability was to entrust its administration to the hands of the wealthy, for they had much to loose if it fell. But, in so far as policy is formulated and administered by upper-class persons in their own interests, they do not see how the law can be seen by large numbers of persons as unjust, or that government can be called indifferent, or that there should be much of a question about public interest.

When the poor and other minority groups are taken into consideration, however, the notion of a just government acting in the public interest becomes less unassailable. The interests of the poor and the interests of the propertied are common only in a very abstract sense. We do not entrust domestic policy to a single government agency as a concession to this continuing conflict. Both rich and poor cry out for justice, but what is meant by "just" differs. A policy design to insure full employment seems to be in the interests of the able-bodied unemployed person who wants to work and cannot find a job. But to guarantee him a job runs counter to the perceived interests of the labor unions who have their own favored techniques for insuring job security, and it infuriates the business leaders who prefer to hire and fire as the needs of their industries dictate.

There can be no value-free solutions to the problems of the cities, and there is little consensus as to what values in urban society should be maximized. There exists no simple formula or social science recipe for engineering a "good" city. Government of the people, by the people and for the people is more properly to be seen as a compelling vision of what ought to be, rather than what is. We can suggest some of the parameters of the process by which it may come into being, but it has not yet arrived, in the opinion of many. We are deeply unsure of the value of this vision and lacking in the precise knowledge of how to realize it in practice. This is a considerable part of what we referred to earlier as the *crises of knowing and valuing*.

The crises of knowing and valuing are often manifested in the average citizen's feelings of insufficiency to understand, much less suggest, solutions to the problems of the cities. As a consequence, we are often tempted to appeal to expertise and to entrust decision making to professionals and politicians in hopes that they will discover the appropriate technique or organizational plan to resolve our dilemmas. Such deference to expertise, while perhaps comforting, is unrealistic, if not deceptive. Technical skill can be successfully mobilized when goals are clearly defined and accepted and where there exists an agency capable of overall management and coordination. Our techniques for planning and organization are not well suited to an environment in which goals remain ambiguous and contradictory, and where there exists no central hierarchy for implementation.

Technological solutions are not value-free. Our deference to expertise may well constitute an invitation to experts to substitute their own values for those of clients or constituents. Some of the problems which seem most susceptible to solution through the application of technical skill, like water pollution and transportation, are high on the agenda of the people who live in the suburbs, but low on the agenda of the city poor, black or white. This means, of course, that the very act of focusing on such problems represents a commitment to certain values and a determination of whose values will have priority. In addition, as we become more familiar with problems that appear to be technical in nature, their underlying political characteristics become more apparent. Decisions on such matters as automobile emission control, highway location, water quality, etc., tend ultimately to be resolved through political considerations. There is no domestic agency capable of overall coordination of technical efforts. Indeed, fragmentation of authority is one of the major problems of our cities. Moreover, it is unlikely that Americans would grant overall power to any single agency in domestic affairs as they have done in foreign affairs. All of these problems make the expectation of simple technical solutions to the problems of the city appear to be naive.

The issue is not whether expertise is needed, but how it is to be used. Dependence on technical skill can become a means by which we abdicate our collective responsibilities as citizens for the guidance of public policy. An example is the controversy over the fluoridation of water supplies. In some communities, decisions on whether or not to fluoridate the water were made by local government officials and technical advisors; in other communities, the decision was submitted to referendum. In almost every case the decisions made by public officials and technicians approved fluoridation; in almost every case, referendums decided against fluoridation. Subsequent analysis indicated that negative decisions on referendums resulted from a general feeling among the citizens of these communities that they were not capable to judge the merits and faults of fluoridation; that the decision was a technical one requiring expertise which they did not possess. While most technical experts favored fluoridation, a few opposed it, and the general populations of these communities felt unable to resolve the conflict among the experts. As a result, many voted against the referendum as the most non-commital and least risky choice. As subsequent interviews indicated, most community residents wanted the decision to be made by public officials and technical advisors who possessed the required expertise. The negative referendums, thus, represented the population's determination to "choose not to choose." As such, they represent an act of default to expertise, a virtual abdication of democratic responsibilities. In this context, expertise is depended upon to pre-empt the decision of the citizen, rather than to inform the citizens in making such a decision. This need not be the case. In any case, the crises of knowing and valuing cannot be adequately managed without the input of all segments of our society. The overarching issues remain: to what extent are we as a people committed to our vision of democracy, and by what practical means can we go about realizing it in a nation of 200 million persons?

Elements of Societal Guidance in a Democracy

We can begin by affirming what may seem to some as a truism, namely that the overarching objective of societal guidance in a democracy ought to be social well-being.[20] The objective of specific legislation may meet the interests of some portion of the population more than others. This is inevitable, given the complexity of our society and the issues with which it must deal. In the formulation, however, of all policy, the narrow interests must not be allowed to obscure the common interests. This must mean at least that we unambiguously affirm our pluralist society in principle, as well as in practice.

[20]Albert Hunter, "The Loss of Community: An Empirical Test Through Replication," *American Sociological Review* 40 (Oct. 1975), pp. 537–553.

Social well-being in a complex pluralistic society must mean that many flowers have the right to bloom; no life-style, no interests should be excluded from the policy process, either in terms of making some input into the formulation of policy or in terms of reaping benefits from that process. There ought not to be any powerless groups before the law in either its execution or its formulation. To the extent that such groups do exist, social well-being is reduced.

Since the concrete aspects of social well-being differ from group to group in significant ways, it becomes all the more important that the policy and planning processes reflect the life-styles and interests of the diverse groups involved. Guarantee of access to the planning and policy processes is an easy thing to conceptualize, but an extremely difficult one to realize in practice. One practical matter that derives from this orientation, however, is that the process of planning and the mode of decision-making must be at least as important in the eyes of the planners and policy makers as the end-products of their activities. In this frame of reference, it is impossible for experts alone to adequately plan policy, much less implement it.

Another minimum component of well being must be relative freedom from the accumulated disadvantages of deprivation. The overarching policy objective in this regard should be to realize in practice what we proclaim in our ideology, that we are indeed a nation of average men as far as access to economic resources is concerned. Having a job is the major, if elementary, means by which persons are recognized as having social status in a community. This is not simply a matter of economics, it goes much beyond the ability or inability to purchase items in the market. A job means that one is minimally acceptable as a member of our society. The only way one retains a degree of social acceptability without a job is to be considered disabled or handicapped, in such a way as to prevent one from being able to work or by being too young or too old to work. Nevertheless, even these persons generally have less status in our society, hence less well-being than those who are considered "productive" by virtue of having a job. As utopian as a guaranteed job may seem to some of us at the present time, it is a critical component of our feeling of well-being, as millions of Americans who are currently unemployed but able and willing to work can testify. The job guarantees minimum access to the status systems as well as the market.

The specific details of well-being that particular individuals or groups develop as a matter of their own unique life-style must be regulated only in so far as these life-styles threaten to hearm others or unduely infringe upon the rights of others. We have always assumed this basic tenet of our democracy, but have a very difficult time realizing it in practice, because we have defined "harm" too broadly. Some people think differently, speak out against things we hold dear, and live by values we find repugnant. They threaten us, and we are forever tempted to suppress these deviants by whatever means we find available. Failing this, we are tempted to simply exclude them from having any significant influence upon public policy, as we have historically done in the case of the poor.

Developing the cultural civility that can reduce suppression of a different

life-styles threaten to harm others or unduly infringe upon the rights of others. We it is an extremely important policy objective to realize at this present time.

New Towns and Intentional Communities

It seems reasonably to assume that metropolitan governments are increasingly less able to cope with the problems of government and the provision of the basics for a good life. A number of alternatives are being attempted on the microlevel to restore the viable human community by means of the intentional construction of communities. "New Towns" are the most dramatic national effort, involving millions of dollars and enormous commitment of human and physical resources. At a much less dramatic level, however, some urban neighborhoods are resisting the disintegration that seems characteristic of their surroundings and are intentionally changing their own environment.

A recently documented example of this is provided by Albert Hunter and his study of Rochester, New York.[21] Over twenty-five years ago this neighborhood was studied by Foley to predict its deterioration. Hunter has taken Foley's three indices of community, use of local facilities, neighboring, and sense of community and documented the extent to which the fears of the original investigator have not been borne out. This residential neighborhood near the University of Rochester has not, in fact, suffered a loss of a sense of community. Its residents continue to think highly of their neighborhood and have attempted to improve its character. There has been no reduction in the amount of neighboring, even though the neighborhood has become racially integrated. The only indicator that registered a loss over the twenty-five year period was the use of local facilities. Many residents prefer to do their banking and shopping outside of the neighborhood.

Hunter concludes that the predicted loss of community did not occur, because the people in this neighborhood intentionally sought it out and have tried to restore its viability. Homes are a bargain, they are large and well-built. Families with several children attached to the university find it convenient. Furthermore, Hunter found, persons in this neighborhood typically rejected the stereotypic suburban image and were consciously seeking an urban alternative. They were also seeking a stable racially integrated neighborhood. A few of the families were particularly attracted to a stable integrated neighborhood because they were themselves racially mixed.

Their local community organization, the 19th Ward Association, was formed in 1960 as a community response to two pressing problems: noise and air pollution from the county airport, and "block busting" by local realtors. Two standing committees within this organization attempted to cope with these issues more or less successfully. The Association also has social events that attract local politicians and

[21]*Ibid.*, p. 550.

provide civic entertainment for the neighborhood. Hunter prefers to characterize his neighborhood, the 19th Ward, as a group of people who have attempted to live a community existence based on a rather limited set of "transcendent values" which run counter to the dominant urban trends. Unlike communes, which have made much more radical intentional departures from the conventional path, the 19th Ward has attempted to realize its limited set of values, while at the same time pursuing careers, raising families, and in general participating in the American way of life. Nineteenth Warders are not living in a utopian community, they are, following Manheim's distinction, living in an ideological community.

> ...Though it differs in form and content from the "utopian community" with its total commitment, the more limited "ideological community" as a partial counter force may prove to be more prevalent and persistent in the effort to ward off a loss of community.[22]

New Towns

While intentional communities may attempt to resuscitate deteriorating urban neighborhoods, another more radical trend is under way in the construction of total communities or "New Towns." In the 1960's, there was much more federal commitment to this venture. The Nixon Administration took a generally cold view of the whole matter, and the recession of the 1970's further contributes to the uncertainty of the venture. During the 1960's, there was much talk about building 1,000 or more new towns in America, but there are only about 30 under current development and about 30 more in the planning stage.[23] We will examine only three characteristic types in the following section.

Reston. While Americans have built New Towns in other decades, Reston is the first of the new breed. Conceived in the 1960's by private developer Robert E. Simon, Reston currently houses some 30,000 persons on its 7,000 acre site near Washington, D.C. in Fairfax County, Virginia.[24] It is the first New Town to succeed financially. The intent of the developers and the residents was to provide a rich and personal environment for a heterogeneous urban population. Reston thus provides housing for 1,000 federally assisted families. It also is home for some 2,000 blacks.

The Town invites citizen participation. Its three village councils affect the quality of village life and encourage neighboring within village areas. Cluster groups manage an even smaller section of Reston. A number of community organizations recruit volunteer help. Restonites participate in local government to a considerably greater extent than their neighbors in Fairfax County. However, Reston is not an incorporated area and comes under the governance of Fairfax County. The failure of the county council to understand some of the objectives of the new town

---

[22]Carlos Campbell, *New Towns: Another Way to Live* (Reston, Va.: Reston Publishing Company, Inc., 1976), p. 20.

[23]*Loc. cit.*

[24]*Ibid.*, p. 72.

has created difficulties in the past, but increasingly there is an emerging agreement on major issues. The major shortcoming at the county level at present is the failure of the county to keep pace with Reston growth and development in the provision of schools, social services, community facilities, water and sewer facilities, and road construction.

The Reston Community Association is an independent organization "to promote Reston's growth as a New Town within the framework of county government, and to help foster a community spirit." It has a volunteer staff and responds to issues on an ad hoc basis. It has, however, been effective in keeping the spirit of the Master Plan and insuring that newcomers understand the concept of Reston.

> The concept is essentially an entirely different life-style that requires a high degree of participation in management and decision-making relating to a variety of maintenance, social and recreational activities within each area defined as a cluster.[25]

Not everyone takes to the concept well, as illustrated by the following comment from a newcomer.

> It didn't take long to find out what it was about. We were burdened with several layers of government which we felt were not necessary. We lived among 37 attached houses which was called a cluster. The cluster association bought the street and made it private. They also planted trees in our yard and didn't tell us anything about it. We didn't want the trees. There was a terrible imposition into our life.[26]

The three levels of governance within Reston according to Carlos Campbell are: 1. the Reston Home Owners Association, "a nonprofit corporation created to operate and maintain parks, parking areas, open spaces, paths and other facilities;" 2. the Reston Community Association; and 3. the cluster association. With these opportunities, it is no wonder that some feel liberated and some oppressed by such excess.

Cedar-Riverside.   Cedar-Riverside is one of the newer New Towns. It has been dubbed a "New Town in town" because it is an attempt to revive part of the downtown of Minneapolis-St. Paul, Minnesota. It is a planned 340-acre community that currently houses about 4,000 persons and expects to expand over the next twenty years to a population of some 30,000 residents. Current residents are heavily Scandinavian in origin and retain a sense of the old country in their festivals which greatly contribute to the community's old world charm in a new world context.

Cedar-Riverside is expected to have five neighborhoods, each with a child care and health clinic to accommodate the needs of all income groups. Minorities are encouraged to locate in the town and are given special incentives in finance, employment, and construction contracts. Black contractors have contributed significantly to its construction.

At present, this development is largely privately financed and managed. It is too small to have the complex government of Reston, but has begun to develop a

[25]*Ibid.*, p. 41.
[26]A basic model of societal guidance is found in Amitai Etzioni, *The Active Society* (New York: The Free Press, 1968), Ch. 5.

community spirit, out of which some viable community organizations should begin to emerge. Its most important resources to date include its location in the Twin Cities, which have long favored conservation and housing programs and the talent of the many persons devoted to its success. If Cedar-Riverside fails to revitalize the downtown of the fifteenth largest American city, many persons doubt that it will be possible to do so.

Soul City. While some attention is given to lower-income families in the New Towns, a fair observation would have to be made that they do nothing for the very poor. Soul City is an exception. At present it is much more of a dream than a reality, but the challenge it faces is worthy of some description. Under the able leadership of Floyd McKissick, a former civil rights leader, Soul City is situated on 5,000 acres of farmland in one of the nation's poorest counties. Warren County, North Carolina has a per capita income of $1,638, compared with the national average of $3,119. It is 60 percent black. It lacks most of the services obtainable in urban areas, such as water and sewage. McKissick is faced with the enormous task of attracting industry to the New Town's industrial park, Soultech I. He envisions that it will eventually consist of 40,000 square feet of manufacturing and processing space and 12,000 feet of office space, and will provide the basic employment opportunity for the city's residents. If Soul City cannot meet the needs of low-income black Americans, it is doubtful if any new town venture can.

Conclusion

America has become an urban society, but the process of urbanization has made the governance of our cities very difficult. There are too many people too quickly. Governmental response to exponentially developing needs is inadequate. An imbalance between need for services and a shrinking tax base resulting from white exodus has made many wonder, is it possible to govern our great metropolises? The cities thus present two sides of the American dream. On the one hand, their culture, architecture, and ethnic diversity suggest the richness of the full human drama and the possibility of its superb orchestration. On the other, the slums, deteriorating public services, and political fragmentation suggest the decay of a civilization. It is by no means clear which tendency will win out.

Those who have studied our cities in terms of the political power structures within them draw different conclusions on the nature of the power structure, depending upon their disciplinary backgrounds. Sociologists such as C. Wright Mills and Floyd Hunter tend to see the power of the city vested in a power elite whose interests are well-preserved in the ethos of privatism and personal achievement. Looking for those who have a reputation for power in a community, they tend to discover a small number of men at the top. In contrast, pluralists, who are mainly political scientists, focus on decision-making in regard to key issues and conclude that there are many centers of power in our metropolitan areas. It is tempting to combine the two approaches under an essentially elitist model, with the dynamics of pluralism operating at the middle level of city politics on relatively "safe" issues.

From the perspective of city planning, the crisis of our cities is seen not so much as a problem of resource and technology, but rather as one of knowing and valuing. We do not understand some of the complex issues we face well enough. Furthermore we lack consensus about what we want to do about them. We have no widely shared vision of what our cities ought to be and, therefore, we lack the policy to attempt to achieve those objectives. Advocates of this view contend that what is needed is not only expert information and skills, but citizen participation in the definition of a dream and a viable set of objectives. Transactive planning is the name John Freidman attaches to a process he deems necessary in order to achieve a truly learning society able to cope with its urban problems.

While the cities turn in trouble, some have attempted to totally rebuild communities in the form of New Towns. The New Town movement is currently undergoing a recession and may never achieve the fanciful objectives set forth in the early 1960's, but what is clear is that radically different kinds of urban experiences are available in New Towns for the middle and upper classes. As yet, none of them have met the needs of the poor. Soul City may be the first to succeed in providing low-income families with new housing in a totally new and freeing environment. If so, the vision of the new towns will have indeed been fulfilled.

chapter 15

World Urbanization

Sociologists generally study urbanization from both a demographic and cultural framework. In its traditional sense, urbanization usually refers to the concentration of population in cities and surrounding areas. More recently, however, social scientists have become concerned with the behavioral aspects of urbanization and all that this implies. This cultural transformation has been referred to as *urbanism,* or when studying developing countries, as *modernization*. It is the former usage (demographic) which is the focus of this chapter. The growth of urban population and the phenomena associated with this process, particularly in developing countries, provides a starting point for the study of urban problems, and a forum for development of worldwide population policy.

In this chapter we focus upon two major questions: First, what are the worldwide trends with respect to urbanization, particularly as these relate to the "demographic transition?" Second, what are the specific trends with respect to urbanization in the various areas of the world?

The answers to these questions inevitably lead to questions of population policy and other issues of planning and development. The recent growth of cities and urbanized areas throughout the world provides a basis for testing some of the sociological theories which have been discussed elsewhere and in this book.

The Demographic Transition

The current population of the world is approximately four billion people.[1] In recent years the world's population has grown annually by approximately two

[1]United Nations, *Demographic Yearbook* (New York: 1974).

Copenhagen, Denmark. In November, 1962 wheeled traffic was banned from the first shopping street of Copenhagen "Stroget" to the great enjoyment of Copenhageners. The more than half a mile long popular street is the longest pedestrian street in Europe. Shopowners feared that trade would drop, but found that in three years business rose by thirty percent. *(Royal Danish Ministry for Foreign Affairs.)*

percent. For this trend to persist, the number of births must exceed the deaths for most areas of the world. Currently, worldwide, there are thirty-three births for every thirteen deaths during a typical year.[2] Western countries (Europe and North America), while still having more births than deaths, have a more even ratio than less urbanized parts of the world such as Africa and Latin America.

Modern population theory is generally traced to the work of Thomas Malthus (1798).[3] Malthus believed essentially that the human population of the earth would grow at a geometric rate, whereas the food supply would grow at an arithmetic or linear rate. In support of his theory, Malthus enumerated a number of "checks" which limit the population. These checks were of two types: First, "positive" or natural factors such as hunger, disease, war, and vice which limited population growth. Vice was used in a rather puritanical sense. For example, Malthus regarded

[2]*Ibid.,* p. 105.
[3]Thomas R. Malthus, *An Essay on Population* (New York: E. P. Dutton, 1914).

the use of contraception as unnatural; thus vices, according to Malthus, permitted people to escape consequences of their immoral behavior. Second, Malthus also recognized certain "preventive" checks which act to reduce the birth rate, *i.e.,* deferred marriage and celibacy.

While some of the trends which Malthus envisioned were indeed valid in the short run, a series of new technological developments influenced the scenario. Birth control came into wide use in certain areas of the world. But more important, large families which were common in rural areas, became less functional and less common in an urban world. As the world became more urbanized, people were able to defer marriage and avoid the adverse consequences of premature pregnancies. On the other side of Malthus's equation (positive checks), the food supply in fact increased geometrically (rather than arithmetically) by the development of domesticated animals, hybrid crops, mechanized farming, high-yield fertilizers, crop rotation, and modern means of storage and preservation of foods.

Moreover, the mortality rate was reduced substantially with the advent of the germ theory of disease, the development of immunizations and the whole revolution of medical care which occurred in the nineteenth and twentieth centuries. With the understanding of what caused disease, certain widespread illnesses such as bubonic plague, cholera, typhoid, polio and diphtheria were all but eliminated in many areas of the world. Despite these advances in technology, which increased the food supply and reduced the birth rate, the problem of a world population which challenges the resources which are available throughout the world persists. Generally, when analyzing population growth patterns in different societies, social scientists employ demographic transition theory.

Demographic Transition Theory

Within the last three centuries the world's population increased approximately six-fold. Carr-Saunders has estimated that the world's population was half a billion persons in 1650.[4] By 1850, the population had more than doubled. In the next century—1850–1950—the population again more than doubled. Table 15.1 shows world population growth projected (estimated) to the year 2010.

Demographers have attempted to identify different stages of growth and development in various areas of the world. The progression is known as *demographic transition.* According to demographic transition theory, beginning in the middle of the seventeenth century, Europe's population passed through three stages: (1) a period of rapid population growth, which was brought about primarily by a decline in the death rate; (2) a decline in growth, while the death rate remained stable and the birth rate declined; (3) a change in age structure, as a larger number of people lived longer and a tendency developed toward a very low rate of growth in population (or even a decline).

[4]A. M. Carr-Saunders, *World Population* (Oxford: Clarendon Press, 1936), p. 42.

Table 15.1 *Estimated Population of the World and the Number of Years Required for It to Double (Source: Harold F. Dorn "World Population Growth," in Philip M. Hauser (ed.),* The Population Dilemma *(Englewood Cliffs, N.J., 1963), p. 10.*

Year (A.D.)	Population (billions)	Number of years to Double
1	0.25 (?)	1650 (?)
1650	0.50	200
1850	1.1	80
1930	2.0	45
1975	4.0	35
2010	8.0	?

Prior to World War II, western Europe had a fairly stable or incipiently declining population, and appeared to be in stage three. The United States was not far behind in this cycle. The population forecast for the United States during the 1950's was for a relatively stable population. However, the "baby boom" after the end of World War II marked a dramatic increase in the population growth and showed that these estimates, based upon a literal interpretation of demographic transition theory, were inaccurate. Following this "baby boom," in the 1960's, the population growth slowed, due to a very low birth rate, causing some demographers to believe that the post-war era was simply a catching-up period, and that transition theory would prevail in the long run. That is to say, the war merely caused people to postpone having children, causing a temporary surge in births. Thus, although the demographic transition theory may hold as a long-term trend, it is not extremely accurate in predicting short-term fluctuations in population.

Another demographer, Thompson, groups the nations of the world into four broad categories, according to the principles of the demographic transition theory which emphasize an area's control over birth rates and mortality rates.[5]

Group one countries have achieved a great deal of control over both birth and death rates. Countries in this group include most western European countries, Japan, United States, and Canada. Because of this capacity to control births and deaths, Thompson maintains that these nations will continue to have very low rates of natural increase. These group one countries include about one-fifth of the world's people.

Group two areas manifest a declining mortality rate, but their birth rates remain relatively high and have only recently begun to show signs of a decline. In fact, their moderate rate of population increase may continue over a long period of time. Included in group two are the countries of southern and eastern Europe, the

[5]Warren S. Thompson, *Population Problems* (New York: McGraw-Hill, 1953).

Soviet Union, Quebec, North Africa, Argentina, and Uruguay. These areas, like those of group one, contain about a fifth of the world population. Depending upon many factors, including technology and cultural values, the movement from group two into group one may require many years or may be done quickly, as happened in Japan when a national population policy was instituted.

Group three countries include most of the underdeveloped or newly developing countries: most of Asia, Latin America and black Africa. These areas have very high, but somewhat variable, death rates and consistently high birth rates. The death rates in these areas are effected primarily by famines and epidemics which periodically wipe out large numbers of people. In other words, the population trends and age structure in group three countries are regulated by Malthus's positive checks (famine, war, and disease). Usually the first check which is impacted by modern medical technology is the death rate. The infant mortality rate is curtailed by modern immunization and prenatal care. In group three areas, although there is a decrease in the death rate brought about by these technological advances, the birth rate still remains high. It is these areas, which contain about three-fifths of the world's population, which account for most of the rapid (2 percent) annual increase shown in the world population.

Group four countries are those which maintain low (but fluctuating) birth rates and low death rates. These countries have passed into an era of economic development and urbanization wherein the advantages of technology and education have resulted in a conscious control over both mortality and fertility. Examples of areas in this stage of demographic transition would include England, Wales, and some areas of North America. In certain cases, group four areas may actually undergo a decline in population as the result of a slight excess of deaths over birth. This latter phenomenon is sometimes referred to as a stage of "incipient decline." Very few areas of the earth have yet reached this stage of demographic transition. (See Figure 15.1)

The major problem with demographic transition theory is that it is really not a theory, but rather represents an abstraction or description of trends. It is entirely possible that an area may be able to skip a stage, or remain in one of the earlier stages. Thus, although the "theory" implies a transition as reflected in history, what the future may hold for the world is not predicted by this scheme.

The Measurement of Urban Trends

In most nations of the world, censuses are conducted infrequently. As a result, demographers make use of estimation basedon population projections. Kingsley Davis provides population estimates for three points in time (1950, 1960, 1970).[6] The data from 1970, however, are principally an extrapolation of the trends from the previous two points. From this time series, it is possible for demographers to make

[6]Kingsley Davis, *World Urbanization, 1950–1970, vol. I: Basic Data for Cities, Countries, and Regions (1969), Vol. II: Analysis of Trends, Relationships, and Development* (Berkeley, California: Institute of International Studies, 1972).

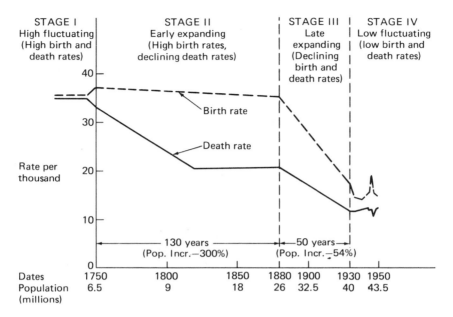

| STAGE I
High fluctuating
(High birth and
death rates) | STAGE II
Early expanding
(High birth rates,
declining death rates) | STAGE III
Late
expanding
(Declining
birth and
death rates) | STAGE IV
Low fluctuating
(low birth and
death rates) |

Figure 15.1

projections far into the future, but it must be remembered that these projections will hold only if the same conditions of growth or decline in previous years persist into the future. Thus, if any major shift in births, deaths, or migration occurs, such as those brought about by a war, famine, use of birth control, or advances in nutrition, the projections will be inaccurate.

Usually in measuring urban population trends, three types of measurements are employed. The first is a measure of the rate of growth of an individual city or urban area. If a city's population increased from 10,000 to 20,000 between 1960 and 1970, the rate of growth, expressed as a percentage, would be 100 percent. The size of the city, of course, has an effect on the rate of growth which is possible and probable. Smaller areas can register high rates of growth with a relatively small increase in population. Secondly, demographers study the overall increase (or decrease) in the population of an area. Between 1950 and 1975, the population of the United States grew by over 50 million people—an increase of about 33 percent. During the same period, however, the urban population of the United States grew at a considerably greater rate. The third type of measure employed by demographers is the rate of urbanization. For example, in 1960, the urban population of Australia was 77 percent of the total; by 1970, this percentage had increased to 84 percent.[7] Most countries have employed an arbitrary dividing line between urban and rural

[7]*Ibid.*, Vol. I, Table a.

based upon a minimum population of 2,000 or 5,000 inhabitants. This concept, of course, does not specify land area, but merely the number of people living within an area. In the United States, the Bureau of the Census classifies all towns and cities with a population of 2,500 or more as urban. In the urban sociology literature, when a reference is made to cities or great cities, this usually means a place with a population of 100,000 persons or more.

Urban vs. Rural Growth

Countries differ in their degrees of urban growth, based mainly on the stage of demographic transition which they are undergoing. For instance, Japan has undergone a pronounced period of urban growth between 1950 and 1970 and an extremely sharp decline in rural population.[8] Much of this growth is closely tied to the development of Japanese industry, following recovery from defeat in World War II. In contrast is the United Kingdom, where the rate of growth for urban areas is only slightly higher than the total population increase for the nation.[9] Rural population in the United Kingdom also appears to have reached a phase of stability. In most developing countries, the urban growth rate is approximately twice that of non-urban areas. This trend is true with one major exception. In India, the growth of the urban areas has been somewhat lower than the nation-wide trend. It must be remembered, however, that it is the absolute numbers in which we are interested. Despite a fairly moderate percentage of growth, India's cities increased by more than 40 million persons during a period of twenty years. During the same period, rural population increased by about 150 million. This rapid population growth, both urban and rural, presents a serious problem with respect to management of resources in India.

The Concept of Urban Primacy

When urbanization begins to effect a developing area, it usually begins in two or three major cities which exceed all others in size, influence and prestige. In many developing countries, the difference in *primacy* between the largest city and the next largest city is so great that it effects the degree of urbanization for the entire country. For instance, Lima, Peru has over thirteen times more population than the next largest city in that country. This in itself tells us something about the state of urbanization in Peru. In contrast, the city of Rotterdam, Netherlands is approximately the same size as the next largest city, Amsterdam.

The *primacy ratio,* then, is obtained by dividing the population of an area's largest city by that of its second largest city. A ratio of five, for instance, suggests that the largest city is five times as large as the second largest. Among industrial countries there is considerable variation among primacy ratios. An example of this

---

[8]*Ibid.,* Vol. I, Table a.
[9]*Ibid., Op. cit.*

Table 15.2 *Primacy Ratios of Cities, 1970 (Source: Calculated from Kingsley Davis,* World Urbanization, *1950–1970, vol. I (1969), Table E.*

Lima	13.1	Istanbul	2.1
Buenos Aires	11.5	New York	1.7
Manila	11.6	Moscow	1.7
Budapest	10.5	Rome	1.6
Santiago	8.6	Calcutta	1.5
Copenhagen	7.7	Johannesburg	1.3
Vienna	7.4	Sydney	1.2
Paris	7.1	São Paulo	1.2
Teheran	6.5	Rotterdam	1.0
Havana	6.0	Belgrade	1.0

is shown in Table 15.2. Countries vary considerably in primacy. The United States shows a low ratio, with New York only 1.7 times larger than the next largest city (Los Angeles). In contrast, Buenos Aires is many times larger than the next largest city in Argentina, having a primacy ratio of 11.5.

Employing a single city as a primacy indicator has its limitations for showing the overall degree of urbanization in an area. Davis has developed what he calls a four-city index.[10] In this technique, the index is developed by comparing the population of the next three largest cities. Using this system, an index of four for an area means that the largest city is four times larger than the combined population of the next three in population. For highly urbanized countries, such as western European countries, this index is more sensitive in capturing the concept of primacy than the single city counterpart. For instance, Copenhagen is about eight times larger than the second largest city in Denmark, (a primacy ratio of 8) but a four-city index (which combines the next three cities) gives it an index of 3.5. When Davis's four-city index is computed for developing countries areas like Peru and the Philippines, we find very high indices, while China and Nigeria have quite low indices. In sum, the primacy concept shows what part of a nation's population is living in its largest cities. If the index is high, this suggests a distinctive urban-rural dichotomy, which is most characteristic of developing countries. If the index is low, this indicates that urbanization is more firmly entrenched in the area and that the lifestyle and economy have distinctively urban characteristics.

In most nations the primate city is also the political capital. In an age of international politics, the fact that a city is a capital usually spurs urban growth. For example, although Washington, D.C., is not the primate city of the United States, the overall metropolitan area experienced rapid urban growth ever since the era of international politics (post-World War II). Primate cities also attract businesses, national and international organizations, and mass media which reflect the position of the city within the nation's communications network.

[10]*Ibid.,* Vol. I, pp. 242–246.

Johannesburg, the primate city of South Africa.

High primacy within a country may also inhibit economic and social development of some areas because of the dominance of one city or series of cities. In Latin
America and Asia, the primate metropolis may attract a huge number of migrants
from primitive rural areas, simply because the city is well known. Also, primate
cities usually attract more than their share of national investments and tax monies.
They may also monopolize valuable human resources such as artists, writers, and
highly skilled professionals who are drawn to the larger cities because of the standard of living and the style of life. The United Nations focused upon this problem in
a report issued in 1968:

> As long as the few large centers continue to attract a disproportionate share of the
> existing industry or commercial activity, professional people and modernizing institu-
> tions, the gap between metropolis and the remaining institutions of the nation will
> widen, for there will be proportionately fewer industrial jobs, educational opportunities,
> or chances to learn new skills in the outlying areas. There will be proportionately fewer
> doctors and administrators, lawyers, teachers and so on able to handle the service and
> organizational apparatus of the small cities of the rural regions.[11]

World Population Trends

The population of the earth has grown more than sixfold during the last 300 years
(see Table 15.3). During this period, the greatest growth has been registered in

[11]United Nations, Department of Economic and Social Affairs, *Urbanization, Development,
Policies and Planning* (New York: 1968), p. 85.

Table 15.3 *Estimates of World Population by Regions, 1650–1960 (Source: United Nations, The Determinants and Consequences of Population Trends, 1953. Larry K. Y. Ng (ed.), The Population Crisis Bloomington, Ind., 1965), p. 34.)*

Estimated population in millions

Source of estimates and date	World	Africa	Northern America*	Latin America†	Asia (excl. USSR)‡	Europe and Asiatic USSR‡	Oceania	Area of European Settlement§
Willcox:								
1650	470	100	1	7	257	103	2	113
1750	694	100	1	10	437	144	2	157
1800	919	100	6	23	595	193	2	224
1850	1,091	100	26	33	656	274	2	335
1900	1,571	141	81	63	857	423	6	573
Carr-Saunders:								
1650	545	100	1	12	327	103	2	118
1750	728	95	1	11	475	144	2	158
1800	906	90	6	19	597	192	2	219
1850	1,171	95	26	33	741	274	2	335
1900	1,608	120	81	63	915	423	6	573
United Nations								
1920	1,810	140	117	91	966	487	9	704
1930	2,013	155	135	109	1,072	532	10	786
1940	2,246	172	146	131	1,212	573	11	861
1950	2,495	200	167	163	1,376	576	13	919
1960	2,972	244	200	207	1,665	641	16	1064

*United States, Canada, Alaska, St. Pierre and Miquelon.

†Central and South America and Carribean Islands.

‡Estimates for Asia and Europe in Willcox's and Carr-Sanders' series have been adjusted so as to include the population of the Asiatic USSR with that of Europe.

§Includes northern America, Latin America, Eurpoe and the Asiatic USSR and Oceania.

Table 15.4 *Population, rate of increase, birth and death rates, surface area and density for the world, macro regions and regions: selected years (Source:* United Nations, *Demographic Yearbook, 1975, p. 139. (New York: 1977))*

Macro regions and regions	Estimates of mid-year population					
	1950	*1955*	*1960*	*1965*	*1970*	*1974*
WORLD TOTAL	2 501	2 722	2 986	3 288	3 610	3 890
AFRICA	219	243	273	309	352	391
Western Africa	65	72	80	90	102	113
Eastern Africa	62	69	77	88	100	111
Northern Africa..........................	52	58	66	74	86	96
Middle Africa 26		29	32	36	40	44
Southern Africa..........................	14	16	18	21	24	27
AMERICA[2]	330	370	415	461	509	550
NORTHERN AMERICA[2]	166	182	199	214	226	235
LATIN AMERICA	164	188	216	247	283	315
Tropical South America	86	100	116	134	155	174
Middle America (mainland)	36	42	49	567	67	76
Temperate South America	25	28	31	33	36	38
Caribbean	17	18	20	22	25	27
ASIA[3,4]	1 368	1 492	1 644	1 824	2 027	2 206
EAST ASIA[3]	675	729	788	854	926	989
China	558	605	654	710	772	825
Japan	84	90	94	99	104	109
Other East Asia..........................	33	34	39	45	50	55
SOUTH ASIA[4]	693	763	856	970	1 101	1 218
Middle South Asia	475	520	581	656	742	817
Eastern South Asia	173	192	217	248	283	315
Western South Asia	44	51	58	67	77	86
EUROPE[3,4]	392	408	425	445	459	470
Western Europe	122	128	135	143	148	152
Southern Europe	109	113	118	123	128	131
Eastern Europe	89	93	97	100	103	105
Northern Europe	72	74	76	79	80	82
OCEANIA[2]	12.6	14.1	15.8	17.5	19.3	20.9
Australia and New Zealand	10.1	11.4	12.7	14.0	15.4	16.6
Melanesia	1.8	2.0	2.2	2.5	2.8	3.1
Polynesia and Micronesia	0.7	0.8	0.9	1.0	1.2	1.3
USSR..	180	196	214	231	243	252

[1]Population per square kilometre of surface area. Figures are merely the quotients of population divided by sufrace area and are not to be considered as either reflecting density in the urban sense or as indicating the supporting power of a territory's land and resources.

344

	Annual rate of population increase		Birth rate	Death rate	Surface area	Density₁
1975	*1965–75*	*1970–75*	*1965–75*	*1965–75*	*1975*	*1975*
3 967	1.9	1.9	32	13	135 830	29
401	2.7	2.6	47	20	30 319	13
115	2,5	2.6	49	24	6 142	19
114	2.7	2.7	48	21	6 338	18
98	2.8	2.7	44	16	8 525	11
45	2.4	2.3	45	23	6 613	7
28	2.9	2.7	43	16	2 701	10
561	2.0	2.0	28	9	42 082	13
237	1.0	0.9	17	9	21 515	11
324	2.7	2.7	38	9	20 566	16
180	3.0	2.9	39	10	14 106	13
79	3.2	3.2	43	9	2 496	32
39	1.5	1.4	24	9	3 726	10
27	1.9	1.9	35	9	238	113
2 256	2.1	2.1	35	14	27 580	82
1 006	1.6	1.7	27	10	11 756	86
839	1.7	1.7	28	10	9 597	87
111	1.2	1.3	18	7	372	298
56	2.2	2.2	31	9	1 786	31
1 250	2.6	2.5	42	17	15 825	79
837	2.5	2.4	42	19	6 785	123
324	2.7	2.7	43	15	4 498	72
88	2.8	2.8	42	15	4 542	19
473	0.6	0.6	16	10	4 937	96
153	0.6	0.6	15	10	995	154
132	0.7	0.9	19	9	1 315	100
106	0.6	0.6	16	10	990	107
82	0.4	0.4	16	11	1 636	50
21.3	2.0	2.0	23	10	8 510	3
16.8	1.9	1.8	19	9	7 956	2
3.1	2.4	2.4	42	18	524	6
1.3	2.6	2.6	33	6	30	43
255	1.0	1.0	18	8	22 402	11

²Hawaii, a state of the United States of America, is included in Northern America rather than Oceania.
³Excluding the USSR, shown separately.
⁴The European portion of Turkey is included with South Asia rather than Europe.

345

North America, the area which has also experienced the greatest increase in urbanization. North America grew by a factor of 80 in the same 300-year period. Within the same time span, Africa experienced the lowest rate of growth of all the major areas of the world, increasing by only a factor of two.

In this section, we examine several areas of the earth in terms of urban development during the last several hundred years. Current population estimates, birth rates, and death rates for the various regions may be found in Table 15.4.

Urbanization in Central and South America

Extensive consideration was given in chapter II to the prehistoric cities in Latin America. These cities, which developed independently from the great cities in the Fertile Crescent of the Middle East, provided a small urban core for the very large continent. The next major urbanization occurred during the Conquest of the 1500's and 1600's, when the Spanish developed their colonial cities principally as administrative centers and military outposts. The city was employed as a base from which the surrounding mining and agricultural areas could be dominated and from which materials could be exported to the mother country. The actual administration took place from Spain. A deliberate policy prevented the cities from becoming commercial or trade centers, as later occurred in the United States and Canada. These cities, however, have persisted to the present time (unlike some of the prehistoric cities) and today comprise many of the largest cities in Latin America. Growth during the sixteenth and seventeenth centuries was limited to some extent by the Spanish Council of the Indies. The Council had two major goals: (1) to make the colonies into producers of gold, silver, and precious stones; and (2) to limit their consumption of manufactured goods to those produced in Spain, shipped in Spanish ships from Spanish ports, and destined for a few fortified seaports, principally Vera Cruz, Cartagena, and Callao.[12]

Generally, Latin American cities were deliberately laid out around a central plaza, similar to cities in Spain, surrounded by ceremonial buildings such as cathedrals and governmental offices. Streets were developed in a rectangular pattern; houses were typically enclosed by walls which provided a great deal of privacy to the inhabitants. Typically the upper class lived nearest the center of the city, whereas people with less important jobs and lower status lived toward the outside, in the European pattern. In contrast to the larger cities, frontier settlements were thought of as having low status and were of little interest to those who held important governmental posts. Farming was relegated to the Indian natives.

Today, three centuries later, the central areas of the older cities have maintained their dominance, although the advent of the automobile has caused some suburbanization. Older streets and roads, however, were not originally laid out with

---

[12]T. Lynn Smith, "The Changing Functions of Latin America," *The Americas,* Vol. 25 (July, 1968), p. 74.

the thought of thousands of vehicles circulating daily. Air and noise pollution have caused considerable discomfort for those remaining in some central locations. Thus, many of the older cities of Latin America suffer from the problems of congestion and pollution, much like the older European cities of Madrid and Paris.

Urban Growth.   In 1950, 30 percent of the population of Latin America lived in places of twenty thousand or more; by 1960, this figure had expanded to 50 percent, and to 57 percent by 1975.[13] Within a period of about twenty years, some areas of Latin America have changed completely from an agricultural orientation to a metropolitan complex. The United Nations has indicated that in 1970 the degree of urbanization in South America was 54 percent as compared to the worldwide figure of 53 percent.[14] Although Latin American cities show a high annual growth rate of 4.5 percent, the primate cities register the highest rate of all. Mexico City, for instance, grew in population from one million in 1930 to six million in 1975. Although this urbanization has not yet affected some of the most remote parts of Latin America, some countries like Uruguay, which has 80 percent of its population living in cities, as well as Venezuela and Cuba, represent the most urbanized places in the world.

Most of the urban growth in Latin America has occurred because of two trends: a large natural increase and a migration from rural areas. In terms of demographic transition theory, many Latin American countries are in stage two, where the death rates have decreased because of modern health programs, *i.e.,* sanitation, prenatal care, and vaccination. But the birth rates remain very high. The second factor, migration, contributes substantially to the growth of primate cities and accounts for more than half of the growth of some cities in Brazil and Venezuela.[15] With the rapid advent of industrialized agriculture, large numbers of unskilled farm laborers are no longer in demand. Thus, rural dwellers are forced to leave the land and the tradition which they have known for generations and to seek employment in cities. Unfortunately the level of technological development is insufficient to generate enough jobs to accommodate the influx of rural, unskilled laborers.

The rapid growth of urban population has caused major problems in maintaining a pattern of orderly growth in urban areas. This crisis has been manifest in planning and zoning, and even more in critical problems of providing necessary services such as education, health, police, and fire protection for the burgeoning urban populations. Massive numbers of rural migrants have located in squatter settlements, which ring all the great cities of South America. In most squatter settlements, people live in makeshift housing, fashioned from whatever materials are available. There are no sewer systems; transportation to and from the cities is extremely expensive. In Caracas, the capital of Venezuela, over a third of the people live in squatter settlements. The prospects of massive public housing programs to accommodate these new residents seem remote at this time. The other

---

[13]Carmen A. Miro, "The Population of Latin America," *Demography*, Vol. I, 1964, pp. 21–24.
[14]J. John Palen, *The Urban World*, (New York: McGraw-Hill, 1975), pp. 342–343.
[15]*Ibid.*, pp. 344–345.

alternative, moving people back to rural areas, seems an even more unacceptable policy alternative.

Urbanization in Africa

The population of Africa in 1974 was estimated to be 391 million.[6] The annual growth rate was 2.7 percent, which is considerably above the annual world growth rate of 1.9 percent. If this rate of growth continues, Africa will more than double its population by the year 2000. Africa, like Latin America, is a stage two area in terms of demographic transition. Death rates are falling, but the birth rate remains quite high. Until the birth rate declines (which is unlikely to occur within the next decade), the high rate of natural increase in Africa will continue. Because of the effect of a high birth rate on the economies of the newly emerging African countries, policies will probably evolve within the next few years which attempt to cope with this problem. Although economic growth receives the highest priority, the fact that substantial resources will have to be diverted to dependent urban populations suggests that policies will soon be developed which will attempt to curb the high birth rates.

African Cities. The most urbanized areas of Africa are found in the north, bordering the Mediterranean, and in South Africa in the areas originally colonized by the British. Areas in the middle of Africa vary considerably in the degree of urbanization. Generally, the countries bordering the Mediterranean have between 20 and 40 percent of their population in cities of twenty thousand or more, whereas west and central Africa have only 15 percent of their population in such cities. East Africa (bordering the Indian Ocean) is the least urbanized area of the continent. Only Zambia has more than 10 percent of its population in cities. The Republic of South Africa is the most urbanized and industrialized area, having approximately 45 percent of its population in urban places. In contrast, the country of Burundi, which has less than 2.2 percent of its population living in urban areas, is the least urbanized area of the continent.[17]

Many of the north African cities were founded during the prehistoric era. For instance, Alexandria was founded in 332 B.C. North Africa was dominated at that time by the Roman Empire, as were most areas surrounding the Mediterranean. In the sixteenth century, Europeans began to colonize the sub-Saharan area, beginning with the Portuguese who founded the first European settlements. However, these first attempts at colonization failed, and until the late nineteenth century very little was done to colonize Africa. It was only within the last one hundred years that the western European countries of Britain, France, Germany, Belgium, and Portugal began to colonize Africa on a large scale. Many of the major cities of Africa were founded during the colonial era: Accra, Ghana (1876); Brazzaville, Congo (1883);

---

[16]United Nations, *Demographic Yearbook,* 1974.
[17]Palen, *Urban World,* p. 345.

Leopoldville, Belgium (Kinshasa, Zaire) (1886); Nairobi, Kenya (1899); and Johannesburg, South Africa (1886). Most of these cities remained fairly small until after World War II. Africa still remains the least urbanized continent of the world. It was only after the African independence movement that many of its countries began to experience substantial urban growth.

In Africa, like Latin America, squatter slums on the outskirts are characteristic of most of the larger cities. In some parts of Africa, these are called *Bidonvilles* (tin can cities). Bidonvilles manifest the same problems of housing, sanitation, schooling, and welfare which typify their Latin American counterparts.

During Africa's colonial era, laborers were forcefully recruited from rural tribes to work in areas where manpower was required. This pattern was common in mining, agriculture, and construction. Workers were not pushed off the land; rather, people were pulled off to work in some of the colonial ventures. Today, laborers are still recruited by paying fees to tribal chiefs for sending laborers to work on corporate plantations. Indentured labor, too, is still common. Because of the influx of people into large cities, foreigners are often limited or forcefully deported by revolutionary governments. This is true of Ghana, the Ivory Coast, and Zaire. In the 1960's, some African countries even appropriated properties of people of Asian origin and expelled them from the land. This practice was particularly evident in Uganda, where in 1972, all property belonging to Asians was seized, and all Asians were forced to leave the country. Most Indians have now left Africa.[18] The current major controversy in Africa centers around Rhodesia and South Africa, where black nationals are in a state of rebellion against the whites who dominate the government and maintain a system of *apartheid*. Blacks in these areas are rebelling against the economic and political domination. During 1976, over two hundred blacks were killed in a rebellion which has caused work stoppages protesting the exploitation of this group.

Urbanization in Asia

From the standpoint of size of land mass, Asia is the largest area on the earth. Asia, too, has many ancient cities and a tradition of urbanism which, like that of the middle East, traces its origins to the pre-Christian area. In juxtaposition with the ancient cities of China are some of the newly developing areas like Korea, Vietnam and the new Soviet cities of the arctic region.

It is very difficult to gain accurate estimates of the Chinese population. The United Nations Demographic Yearbook of 1974 estimates that China alone has a population of 989 million and that all of Asia has a population of two billion two hundred and six million, with an annual growth rate of 2.1 percent. This is slightly below the world's average of 1.9 percent.[19]

[18]*Ibid.*, pp. 355–381.
[19]United Nations, *Demographic Yearbook,* 1974.

The Soviet Union.   The Soviet Union not only has many cities of over a hundred thousand population, but also has some of the world's larger cities, including Moscow, Leningrad, and Stalingrad. Since the revolution of the 1920's, the U.S.S.R. has undergone rapid industrialization and urbanization and with this, increasing migration to metropolitan centers. The Soviet government has attempted to control the rate of growth by ''assigning'' workers to outlying areas and giving incentives for living in areas that cause some hardship, such as Siberia.

In 1970, the Soviet Union had over two hundred cities with a population of 100,000 or more, and ten with populations of over a million. The largest by far was Moscow, which had a population of seven million, followed by Leningrad, which had slightly under four million. Overall, the Soviet Union is one of five countries with a very large number of cities. Other countries in this category include: Japan, India, and the Peoples' Republic of China. In 1920, at the beginning of the Russian revolution, Russia had roughly 15 percent of its population or twenty-one million people living in cities. In comparison, fifty years later, one hundred and thirty-four million persons were counted as residents of cities. The urban population comprised 56 percent of the total population of the country. Thus, while Russia's total population doubled in fifty years, its urban population increased by a factor of six. Between 1960 and 1970, while the total population grew by 16 percent, the growth rate of urban areas was 36 percent. An actual decline in population occurred in the rural areas. About half of the increase in urban population occurred because of immigration and the rest because of natural increase. The current level of urbanization in the Soviet Union is similar to that of the United States in 1940, just prior to World War II.[20]

India.   In 1974, the population of India was estimated to be approximately five hundred and eighty-six million.[21] In four short years, India's population is estimated to have grown by over forty million. Because of the size of the population of India, its 2.1 percent annual increase results in massive increments added to the population each year.

A few Indian cities were founded by foreigners; Bombay and Calcutta, founded by the British, are the best known of these. The ecology of these cities presents a contrast to older areas established before colonization. The English colonizers even built a new city immediately adjacent to an old one; New Delhi was erected next to Delhi. Central to most Indian cities is a market place surrounded by small shops selling a variety of specialized personal and household items. Street merchants sell jewelry, furniture, and clothing. Nearby are little hotels, small manufacturing plants, some residences, and professional offices. In effect, the central business districts of Indian cities are not nearly as highly specialized as those of Western cities. Unlike the Western pattern, government functions have a tendency to be dispersed throughout the city, rather than concentrated in the central area. In

[20]Noel P. Gist and Sylvia F. Fava, *Urban Society* (New York: Thomas Y. Crowell, 1974), pp. 124–125.
[21]United Nations, *Demographic Yearbook,* 1974.

The busiest section of Tokyo at the present is the Marunouchi-Ginza area located to the east of the vast Imperial Palace Grounds.

fact, most activities and land usages are not concentrated in particular locations as is common in Western cities. Areas which are populated by Indians are usually over-crowded, whereas the neighborhoods occupied by Europeans are fairly quiet areas, containing large houses separated by large plots of land.

In Indian cities, the most poverty-stricken residents live in areas around the perimeter rather than in the innermost areas, as is true in America. Like Latin America and Africa, Indian cities frequently have squatter settlements, or *bustees,* as they are called. The slums of Indian metropolises are infamous for their squalor. Large numbers of people sleep on the streets; sewage and water supplies are often nonexistent. Like Latin American cities, Indian cities are constantly burdened by an unending stream of migrants from the country. Most come to the city in search of work, but the unskilled migrant who finds a job is rare. In general, the urban labor markets are unable to accommodate the massive number of untrained laborers. It is estimated that the city of Calcutta alone contains seven million people who live at a level of poverty which is probably the worst in the world. Among the seven million are at least three hundred thousand persons who live their entire lives on the streets, without even the simple amenities of a squatter community.

The prognosis for urban Indian remains poor, in spite of some of the reform policies instituted during the emergency of 1975, many of which still remain in effect during 1976. Industrial underdevelopment and overfertility in India remain a key problem. It is ironic that India has now conquered many age-old problems, such as the plagues and famines, which persisted for thousands of years, but the problems which still remain, such as high birth rate, a highly uneducated population, and problems of governance, appear insurmountable, even when compared to the urban problems of Latin America and Africa.[22]

The Republic of China.   The last population census of China was conducted in 1953 and resulted in a total count of five hundred and ninety million people. China's 1974 population is estimated by the United Nations to be approximately eight hundred and twenty-five million. This figure represents an increase of over fifty million people from the 1971 estimate of seven hundred and seventy-two million. China's annual rate of growth (1.7 percent) is considerably above that of the United States (0.9 percent), but is below the world average of 1.9 percent.[23] Virtually all projections indicate that China will have a population of well over one billion persons by the year 2000. Most of the nation's population is concentrated in two areas, the south and the east.

Manufacturing and industry in China developed primarily under the influence of Western powers around treaty ports. In the 1800's, some of the cities in the Manchu dynasty were totally dominated by foreigners who lived in separate sections of the city and were policed by European troops. At the present time, approximately one out of every five Chinese, approximately two hundred million, live in cities. Shanghai is now the largest city in the world.

In 1949, the Peoples' Republic of China was established, and the old regime was exiled to Taiwan (Formosa). Since then, millions of Chinese have migrated from rural areas to cities. The government, through a deliberate policy, has attempted to reverse this trend by forcibly relocating skilled people to rural areas, with the goal of spurring economic development in the hinterland. During the 1960's, a "Cultural Revolution" was waged, wherein unemployed "youth labor-battalions" and those guilty of certain political crimes were shipped in massive numbers to rural areas. Some of these people later drifted back to cities. The government policy of relocating urbanites possessing certain skills into the countryside continues, however.

Unlike India, China has been quite successful in dealing effectively with unemployed urban populations. It has been possible to stimulate employment in China because of the strong centralized government, which has an administrative structure which makes it feasible to carry out massive manpower policies based on relocation. Palen points out, "In 1963, following the economic crisis, brought on by the failure of the "great leap campaign," the Chinese government decided to stabilize the urban population at one hundred and ten million, considered a manageable figure. In order to do this, it was decided to "rusticate," or return to the countryside, urban school graduates; this would lessen the pressure on the urban economy and help promote agriculture and indigenous industry in rural areas. Today the combination

[22]Palen, *Urban World,* pp. 396–400.
[23]United Nations, *Demographic Yearbook,* 1974.
[24]Palen, *Urban World,* pp. 401–402.

of extreme pressure and ideological conviction results in many urban-educated youths ''volunteering'' for permanent resettlement in the countryside. ''Volunteers'' include all graduates of urban secondary schools and universities who have not been accepted in an educational institution at the next higher level or who have not been assigned to a post in urban industry or service units.[25] Because of this policy, it is estimated that within two years, between ten and fifteen million youths ''volunteered'' to migrate to rural villages. Overall, the effect of this policy is that the educated elite of China are increasingly being transferred from cities to rural areas where their skills are most needed.

In the 1970's, China re-opened to Westerners. While travel is still severely restricted, reports coming from Western journalists and others traveling in China suggest that extremes of both wealth and poverty have apparently been limited, but the average person lives at a standard which is optimal, given the current economic resources of China. Reports indicate that the cities of China are well managed, clean, free of crime, and still provide many of the cultural amenities which China has offered throughout its history. Many of the old patterns of drug abuse, prostitution, and gambling are gone. China, of all the larger countries which can be characterized in demographic transition theory as undergoing stage two, seems to be furthest along in solving many of the problems associated with urbanization and industrialization.

Over-Urbanization of the World

The concept of over-urbanization suggests that there are too many people living in cities. The idea has several other connotations. First, there are too many people living in urban regions, considering the requirements of urban labor market and economy. The skills of many people now living in the largest urban areas might be better utilized if some migrated to less urbanized areas where their skills are needed more. Second, there are too many people living in urban areas, given the service systems available in these areas. Service gaps are most accute in the areas of housing, health and social services, and education. Third, there are too many people in urban areas, given the social and psychological needs of individuals. This is not unlike Wirth's concept, that the size, density, and heterogeneity of urban places often leads to an atomization of social ties, to anonymity and other urban alienations. Thus, in economic terms, areas may be over-urbanized if their labor market does not provide enough jobs or expand rapidly enough to provide jobs and incomes for newly arriving households. These problems, coupled with the declining supply of certain natural resources, such as crude oil and metals, may compound the problems already faced by urban areas.

Of course, many of the problems associated with over-urbanization might be

[25]*Ibid.*, p. 403.

reduced or eliminated, if the world were to move toward a state of zero population growth or to an era of population decline. The available resources would then be sufficient to raise the standard of living for all the nations of the earth. This, of course, is a long term and probably unrealistic answer to many of the problems of over-urbanization. The problems of inadequate service systems and of urban alienation will remain, despite improvements in urban labor markets and even relocation to rural areas. No doubt the fact that urban dwellers in underdeveloped and modernizing countries are becoming aware of the improved standards of living attainable through modern technology will also have an impact on the style of life for the world as a whole.

In the future, urban sociologists will study not only the world population patterns, the patterns of urban primacy, and the patterns of growth in developing countries, but will also focus on many of the traditional urban problems which have already been encountered or experienced in the industrialized countries of the Western world. As countries undergo urbanization, they will experience increases in crime, alienation, unemployment, educational problems, and most of the problems which have already been faced by urbanized countries. But the vision of the "good life" within the American culture may appear considerably different, when compared to the individual and cultural goals of other societies. The suburban home with four bedrooms, two and one-half bathrooms and two television sets, festooned with a boat and camper in the driveway, may not be the epitome of the good life, as seen by the Japanese, the Africans, or the people of the oil-rich Middle East countries, even if the resources are present to support patterns of conspicuous consumption.

Urban life-styles, even in the Western countries, differ considerably. The Eastern urbanite is still not accustomed to commuting an hour each way by car to work. He takes for granted the city and its virtues and faults. Contrast him to the resident of Los Angeles, where a car is necessary to go to the neighborhood grocery store for a loaf of bread. Should a world-wide urban culture ever develop, it will probably be as a result of the communications media, which have so strongly affected Europeans and Americans, particularly those in the working and middle classes. Given adequate resources, the media may ultimately mold all the urban peoples of the world into a common life-style.

Conclusion

In this chapter we have surveyed the trend toward urbanization throughout the world. We have examined theories of population growth, beginning with Malthus and ending with demographic transition theory.

Our survey suggests that the pressures brought about by urbanization are only beginning in many areas. Although some of the problems are related to the traditional social pathologies of cities—*e.g.*, crime, mental illness, and alienation—more fundamental problems in developing countries are related to the incapacity of urban regions to provide jobs and services to expanding populations. Indeed, the future of cities everywhere will depend upon man's ability to achieve more efficiency in the utilization of human and physical resources.

Index

357